The Economics of Inequality, Poverty, and Discrimination in the 21st Century

Contents

Chapter 1

Introduction and Guide to the Readings

Robert S. Rycroft

WHAT THIS BOOK IS ABOUT ... AND WHAT IT IS NOT ABOUT

In the fall of 2011, the Occupy Wall Street movement began gathering in New York City.[1] Although the movement's goals were and remain to this day a bit fuzzy, clearly a major motivating factor was the high level of income and wealth inequality in the United States, one of the world's most affluent societies, and a fear that pathways to upward mobility were being closed off. Protests similar in nature spread to over 80 countries including such comparably affluent societies as Australia, Belgium, Canada, Denmark, France, Germany, Ireland, Israel, Italy, New Zealand, Norway, South Korea, Switzerland, and the United Kingdom (Wikipedia 2012b). Regardless of what ultimately becomes of the movement, the moral of this piece of street theater undoubtedly is that even in these relatively prosperous societies there is a great deal of discomfort about whether abundance is being shared fairly. I think this book appears at the right time. One of the problems of the Occupy movement wherever it has sprouted is that it has tended to be long on emotion and short on facts. This book is a collection of chapters by leading scholars, people who have devoted their careers to studying these issues, on the current state of thinking about many of the most important aspects of inequality, poverty, and discrimination.

The clear emphasis of this project is on the United States, with some attention paid to similarly prosperous and free societies. There is little attention paid to most of the rest of the world, those countries often thought of as part of the less developed world. By the World Bank's commonly used poverty indicator of $1.25 per day, over 20 percent of the world's population (about 1.4 billion people) are poor (World Bank Development Indicators 2008). By that same standard, probably not a single American nor resident of any other similarly prosperous country is poor. In fact, the poorest American is probably better off than over two-thirds of the world's population (Milanovic 2011, 117). The field of development economics is not being addressed in this book. While there are certainly commonalities in inequality, poverty, and discrimination problems across all types of societies, the differences in the types of issues that need to be addressed are too great. Experts in inequality, poverty, and discrimination problems in the affluent world are seldom experts about the less developed world, and vice versa. The resulting book would consist of way too many volumes. There is one chapter by development economists addressing development issues as a point of comparison.

CONTROVERSY AND POINT OF VIEW

It goes without saying that inequality, poverty, and discrimination issues are controversial. These issues touch on personal material well-being and justice. The nature and extent of the problems and what to do about them are all contested. And the contest can be explosive. The Occupy Wall Street movement has not simply politely addressed the rest of society. There have been demonstrations, destruction of property, violent police-demonstrator confrontations, and arrests. The chapters here do not go that far. Each is a professional treatment of the issue. There is no shouting and name-calling. But different points of view will be evident. No attempt was made to recruit authors with the same or similar points of view.

A useful distinction economists make is between positive and normative economics (Friedman 1953, 1970). Positive economics is the economics of what is. It is the economics of how the economy actually works. For example, how will an increase in inequality influence intergenerational mobility, what impact will raising the minimum wage have on teenage employment, how will restrictions on low-skill immigration influence the income of highly skilled native workers, and so on? Positive economics is the scientific, objective part of economics. Economists are experts in positive economics because economists know the models and methodologies needed to find the answers to positive questions. This does not imply that determining the answers is an easy thing to do. It is a very hard thing to do, but economists are better at it than anyone else. Normative economics is the economics of what should be. It is economists advocating for or against particular policies. For example, should we take steps to reduce inequality, should we raise the minimum wage, should we restrict low-skill immigration, and so on? Good normative economics rests on good positive economics, but it goes further because it brings in the personal values (or point of view) of the economist. Any policy has winners and losers. If we reduce inequality, we may get greater intergenerational mobility, but reducing inequality will probably require public programs funded by new taxes on someone. A higher minimum wage may be beneficial to teenagers who retain their jobs and to older, more skilled employees who now have less to fear from unskilled competition, but it may not work so well for the teenagers who lose their jobs and employers. Greater unskilled immigration may be great for the unskilled immigrants, native skilled workers, and employers. It may not be so great for native unskilled workers who see their wages dropping and job opportunities drying up. To advocate for or against any of these policies means weighing the benefits to the winners versus the costs to the losers. Normative economics is an inherently subjective part of economics, but it is a part of economics that economists cannot claim to be experts at because the personal values of economists are not necessarily superior to the personal values of anyone else.

To distinguish between whether a statement represents positive or normative economics, all we have to ask is whether the statement can, in principle, be proven to be true or false. Consider statements A and B:

A: Raising the minimum wage reduces teenage employment.
B: We should raise the minimum wage.

Statement A is positive economics. In principle we can employ research tools that would allow us to definitively answer this question.

Again, it is not an easy task. Statement B is normative economics. Whether we should raise the minimum wage depends on the answers to a whole host of positive questions with our personal values thrown into the mix. There is no right or wrong answer to the question. Other disciplines have the same positive-normative distinction, although they may not call it that nor be as explicit about it as economists are.

The chapters presented in this book, by economists, sociologists, philosophers, and lawyers, represent both positive and normative treatments of the issues at hand. Most of the chapters are mostly positive. Some of the chapters are explicitly normative, but all of them have some normative aspect thrown in. With 44 authors of the 31 chapters, there are 44 sets of personal values on display. I suppose that means that just about every reader will find something they agree with and something they cannot stand. My hope is that every author will be given a fair hearing.

PLAN FOR THE BOOK

The chapters in the book can usefully be grouped into five categories:

1. *Measurement*: The first three chapters take on measurement issues. **Steven Pressman** in **"Cross-National Comparisons of Poverty and Income Inequality"** analyzes data from the Luxembourg Income Study, a project initiated in 1983. The goal of the project was to collect income and household data from many countries using comparable definitions so that cross-national comparisons can be made. Pressman presents the most recent data on poverty rates and income inequality from a sample of 36 countries, and offers hypotheses about what explains the differences. It is interesting to note that in sharp contrast to the beliefs of many who consider the United States to be a particularly prosperous and equal society, in comparison with countries at a similar level of development, the United States ranks quite low in terms of income equality and high in terms of percentage of the population poor.

   Edward N. Wolff in **"The Distribution of Wealth in the United States at the Start of the 21st Century"** looks at recent data from the United States on household net worth. He finds that while household net worth continued its long-term rise during the first decade of the 21st century, much of the increase was due to rising home prices and associated with a major increase in household debt. While the distribution of household wealth became much more unequal during the 1980s, the subsequent years have shown little change. Wolff also compares household net worth by race, ethnicity, and age.

William Levernier's chapter on **"The Geography of Poverty in the United States"** addresses an oft-overlooked aspect of poverty, namely, its spatial distribution in the United States. He looks at variations in poverty rates across states, regions, counties, metropolitan and nonmetropolitan regions, city and suburb, and neighborhood. He next discusses explanations for why there are persistent poverty regions in the United States and suggests policies to reduce the geographical variation in poverty rates.

2. *Inequality and Mobility*: Measures of the degree of income (or other measures of economic status) inequality at a particular point in time can be thought of as a "snapshot" of society. What would be more useful to us is a movie. We would like to be able to follow individuals over long periods of time and see what happens to their income. A society in which people with low incomes at one point in time can rise up the income distribution ladder later in their life or in which their children can do so is a very different society than one in which the poor and their children are relegated to be poor throughout their lives. Largely as the result of the availability of large longitudinal databases from many countries, economists and others have started to reveal the processes at work in different societies.

Isabel V. Sawhill in **"Do We Face a Permanently Divided Society?"** notes the high and increasing level of income inequality in the United States, and finds that while there is substantial economic mobility in the United States both intragenerationally (over an individual's career) and intergenerationally (between parents and children), the extent of mobility has not increased in recent decades, making the rise in annual income inequality especially problematic. With the evidence (admittedly tentative at this point) pointing to lower mobility in highly unequal societies, she fears the United States is heading in the direction of becoming a permanently divided society. In line with the oft-expressed attitudes of Americans, she calls for greater spending on programs that will increase opportunity, not simply redistribute income.

Miles Corak in **"Inequality from Generation to Generation: The United States in Comparison"** argues that "that there is a disconnect between the way Americans see themselves and the way the economy and society actually function." The evidence we have is that mobility in the United States is not particularly high compared to many similar countries around the world. He develops a simple model explaining how economic inequality can slow down the rate of mobility and points out what government policy can achieve. He then uses it to explain why Canada, probably the country most similar to the United States, is both more equal and more mobile than the United States.

3. *Institutions and Choices*: A useful distinction is between the proximate cause of some phenomenon and the fundamental cause (Rycroft 2009, 232–37). The proximate cause is the "nearest" cause. For example, let the phenomenon of interest be low wages, and we know low wages are directly caused by limited skills. That makes limited skills the proximate cause of low wages. But we know limited skills do not just happen. Limited skills are the result of a whole chain of events. To get to the fundamental cause, you need to trace back along the chain of causation. What caused limited skills? Perhaps it was poor education. But what caused poor education? Perhaps it was the person's family lacking the means to reside in a school district with good schools. When you can trace back no further you have reached the fundamental cause. Symbolically, if we let low wages be D, limited skills be C, poor education be B, and limited family means be A, then our chain of causation runs A→B→C→D. In this chain, C is the proximate cause of D, but A is the fundamental cause. (Note that this is just an example to illustrate the terms. In no way is it a complete analysis of low wages.)

   The proximate cause of poverty is of interest, but knowing that gives us little guide to policy. Changing the proximate cause of poverty is of little benefit if we cannot change the fundamental cause. Ultimately, there are two competing explanations of the fundamental cause of poverty: people and institutions. The "problem is people" argument is that people might have low IQ, lack a work ethic, have bad morals, and so on. There are two "the problem is institutions" arguments. One would place major blame on well-intended but misguided government policies: the minimum wage, occupational regulations, disincentives for work, saving and investment built into tax and transfer programs, and many more. The other would place major blame on corporate power and its capture of government and the creation of a whole set of institutions that work to the advantage of the wealthy and the detriment of the poor.

The next two chapters look at why poverty exists in the richest nations on earth, and why there is such an enormous gap between the developed world and the rest of humanity. In "**The Causes of Poverty and Inequality in the United States: Toward a Broader View**," **Kristin Marsh** rejects "the problem is people" view and develops a model of poverty and inequality in highly affluent societies along the lines of the second "the problem is institutions" approach mentioned previously. For an example of the first type of "the problem is institutions" model, see Williams (1984).

As explained earlier, poverty in the United States and other developed economies contrasts sharply with poverty in the rest of the world. Development economists **Shawn Humphrey** and **Christine Exley** in "**Why Is So Much of the World Poor?**" provide a succinct review of the development economics literature that attempts to explain the persistence of such huge income gaps between the minority of the world in the developed societies and the majority of the world in the less developed societies.

4. *Demographic Groups and Discrimination*: While no one is immune to the possibility that they might end up poor, the troubling fact is that poverty is much more likely to be found in some demographic groups than others. That raises the specter of discrimination. The first seven chapters in this part review the current status and future prospects for groups that have often been identified as victims of unfair treatment by society.

Thomas N. Maloney and **Ethan Doetsch** in "**What Explains Black-White Economic Inequality in the United States in the Early 21st Century?: The Effects of Skills, Discriminatory Legacies, and Ongoing Discrimination**" review the progress that African Americans have made as they moved from slavery toward full and equal participation in American society and what barriers remain to be surmounted.

Joyce P. Jacobsen in "**Closing the Gender Gap: What Would It Take?**" discusses various measures of differences between men and women in terms of well-being. While it is true that women continue to have less access to and control over what is most important, namely, productive resources, comparison along other dimensions of well-being paints a more mixed picture. For example, men do not live as long as women, and are more likely to be victims of violent crime or be incarcerated. She then asks what it would take to close the remaining gender gap.

An often-overlooked demographic group in discussions of poverty and inequality in the United States is Native Americans. In **"From Dependency to Self-Determination: Native Americans and Economic Development in the 21st Century,"** Sarah Dewees and **Raymond Foxworth** point out that Native Americans are not simply another demographic group operating under the constraints imposed by American society. Rather, on the reservation they can be thought of as members of native nations coexisting uneasily with the behemoth United States of America. Their understanding of the issues is that federal government policy for centuries has blocked Native people from developing the way they would have chosen. In recent years the federal government has granted greater autonomy to the tribes, and so a path to greater prosperity appears to be revealing itself.

The largest minority group in the United States is Hispanics. **Pia Orrenius** and **Madeline Zavodny** in **"Trends in Poverty and Inequality among Hispanics"** look at the economic status of Hispanics, provide explanations for the gaps, and speculate on what the future holds.

Asian Americans have often been called the "model minority." As **Arthur Sakamoto** and **ChangHwan Kim** show in **"The Economic Characteristics of Asian Americans in the 21st Century,"** the term "Asian American" actually refers to many groups whose economic characteristics vary widely. Although discrimination and evidence of bigotry toward Asian Americans still take place, overall they conclude that "the economic statistics on the typically favorable characteristics of this minority group suggest that relatively successful racial integration into mainstream society may be a more accurate description of contemporary Asian Americans in general."

Arguably, the minority group most in the news these days, although the news has little to do with economics, is gays and lesbians. They are highly visible on television shows and in the movies, and the battles for same-sex marriage and the ending of "don't ask, don't tell" by the U.S. military have made them a fixture on the evening news and in newspapers. As **Michael E. Martell** explains in **"Are Gays and Lesbians 'Mainstream' with Respect** to Economic Success?," a common misperception is that gays and lesbians are an especially prosperous group. What he shows is that economically gays and lesbians are actually a little bit below average in society. He suggests some policy actions that could work to close the gaps that exist.

Mary Ellen Benedict and **John Hoag** in "**Pension Policy and Income Inequality in the 21st Century**" review the economic status of the elderly in the United States and show the impact of pension policy on the well-being of the elderly.

The last two chapters in this part review the issue of discrimination at a more general level. **Matt Parrett** in "**What We Know about Discriminatory Differentials in Labor Market Outcomes**" explains in an accessible manner the methodologies economists use to identify and measure the extent of discrimination, and also what we have learned from these studies.

The environment that surrounds us both while growing up and as adults has been recognized as having important consequences for our economic well-being. Among the concerns are whether where we reside inhibits us from having access to good jobs, how the quality of the housing we live in influences our health, whether our neighbors are good role models for our children, and whether we are safe from violence in our neighborhoods. The policy issue is access to good housing and neighborhoods. The extent of "**Housing Discrimination and Residential Segregation**" in the United States is reviewed by **Haydar Kurban**.

5. *Policy*: What can be done about inequality, poverty, and discrimination? The chapters in this part review the current thinking on a wide variety of policy initiatives. A traditional policy prescription, at least on the part of noneconomists, has been to increase the minimum wage. If people are poor, force their employer to pay higher wages—financed out of profits. And there are no trade-offs that have to be taken into account. There is at least a bit of highly publicized academic research that could be viewed as supportive of this (Card and Krueger 1995). Mainstream economists would caution that while the policy would raise the wages of many low-paid workers, the inevitable trade-off is reduced job, training, and fringe-benefit opportunities and worsened working conditions affecting mainly the people the policy was intended to help. **David Neumark** reviews recent empirical work in "**Do Minimum Wages Help Fight Poverty?**" After carefully studying

what is a complex and sometimes ambiguous literature, he concludes that the conventional wisdom of the mainstream model is largely supported by the evidence and that minimum wage laws do very little to reduce poverty.

Two of the most hotly contested contemporary policy issues are globalization and the related topic of immigration. **Keith Gunnar Bentele** and **Lane Kenworthy** in "**Globalization and Earnings Inequality in the United States**" review the recent evidence on the impact of globalization on inequality. They allow that globalization could very well increase inequality, but the evidence is not yet crystal-clear in that regard.

The controversy associated with immigration is not just economic in nature. There are national security and cultural identity issues as well. In the context of the United States, the main concern is the impact of immigration on inequality. Since the bulk of the immigrants (legal and otherwise) are low-skill, the mainstream economic model would predict a reduction in low-skill worker wages as the result of an increase in labor supply, and an increase in high-skill worker wages as the result of an increase in their productivity from being able to work with more complementary low-skill workers. There is some evidence to support this view (Borjas 1999). Canada represents an interesting contrast. Their laws provide greater encouragement to high-skill immigrants. **Laura J. Templeton** and **Sylvia Fuller** in "**Immigration and Inequality: Why Do High-Skilled Immigrants Fare Poorly in Canada?**" find that high-skilled immigrants are not faring all that well and provide an explanation why.

Education policy can never be far from any discussion of inequality and poverty. **David T. Burkam** in "**Educational Inequality and Children: The Preschool and Early School Years**" reviews the literature on inequalities affecting children during the preschool and early school years. He finds clear evidence of what he calls the Matthew effect—the children of richer families arrive at school ahead of the children of poorer families, are beneficiaries of superior educational resources, and widen the gap throughout the rest of their time in school. This is especially problematic since the older a child is, the more difficult it is to compensate for educational shortcomings (Carneiro and Heckman 2003, 128–48).

A "new" idea that has actually been around for a long time is school choice. As opposed to the standard approach used by public schools all around the country of assigning students to "neighborhood" schools (with the rich being able to opt out for private schools), school choice is a term representing a variety of ways to give all parents the right and wherewithal to send their children to the school of their choice. **Patrick J. Wolf** and **Anna M. Jacob** review the evidence in **"School Choice"** and reach the conclusion that several flavors of school choice policies are successful in reducing educational inequities.

Family issues are the subject of the next three chapters. In **"The Link between Nonmarital Births and Poverty,"** **Laura Argys** and **Susan Averett** try to untangle the vexing problem of nonmarital births. The nonmarital birth rate increased during much of the latter half of the 20th century. There was a brief respite in the 1990s, but the increase has subsequently resumed in the first decade of the 21st century. They review what is actually a fairly complex literature on the effect of nonmarital births on the mother, father, and child. Since the daughters of poorer families are more likely to give birth out of wedlock than the daughters of richer families, the nonmarital birth epidemic in the United States is a contributing factor to the cycle of poverty.

A major policy initiative during the Clinton administration was the welfare reform act of 1996. The passage of 15 years has given us a good opportunity to evaluate the effect of the act. **David C. Ribar** and **Carolyn M. Wolff** in **"What Happened to Cash Assistance for Needy Families?"** find that the act has a mix of positive and negative outcomes. The major beneficial effects have been a reduction in the number of single-parent households in poverty and an increase in the employment of single mothers. The main negative effect has been a reduction in the overall level of resources available to many poor families.

A frequently overlooked part of the social safety net is the child welfare system. This system provides protection and support for children who are victims of abuse or neglect. The system is federally supported but state-run. As **Mary Eschelbach Hansen** reports in **"Inequalities across States in a Federally Funded System: The Case of Child Welfare Subsidies,"** this structure means that the resources available to children differ significantly and arbitrarily by their state of residence. Since poor support for children often leads to adult dependency, she advocates for policy changes to equalize resources across the states.

A major domestic policy accomplishment of the Obama administration has been the enactment of health care reform legislation that will extend affordable health insurance to millions of Americans. **Lynn Paringer** in **"The Impact of Health Care Reform on Vulnerable Populations"** analyzes the expected impact of the legislation on the poor, the near-poor, young adults, the near-elderly, and immigrants. She finds that the "expansions in coverage should lead to improved access to health care and, hopefully, to improved health status among some of the most vulnerable population groups."

Another traditional view is that labor unions are an essential institution to promote fairness in the labor market and equity in the distribution of income. However, in the United States and throughout much of the developed world, labor unions have been on the wane, at least in the private sector. **Richard B. Freeman** and **Kelsey Hilbrich** speculate about the future of the labor movement in the United States in **"Do Labor Unions Have a Future in the United States?"** What could spark a revival of labor? Currently, there is nothing on the horizon, but that was true just prior to labor's greatest spurt of organizing in the 1930s. The depth of the current "Great Recession," the lack of esteem for business leaders, and a series of antiunion moves by state politicians may just be the spur labor needs.

The next two chapters look specifically at policies to reduce discrimination. **Kimberley Kinsley**, a lawyer, in **"Employment Discrimination Law"** clarifies the current state of the tangled web of federal antidiscrimination laws, enforcement agency policies, and judicial rulings. In **"Affirmative Action: Pro and Con,"** **Barbara R. Bergmann** explains what affirmative action means and argues for continued reliance on it for the foreseeable future.

For literally centuries, a society's customs, institutions, and laws regarding inheritance of wealth have been a flashpoint in the argument over what constitutes a fair society. **Sally Wallace** in **"The Role of the Estate and Gift Taxes in Income Redistribution"** reviews what economists know about the impact of estate and gift taxes on revenue collected, charitable contributions, savings and wealth accumulation, and the types of gifts and bequests given and their impact on recipients. Contrary to popular opinion, there are no simple answers here. But she is able to conclude that estate and gift taxes likely have some small impact on reducing income and wealth inequality.

The final two chapters are much more speculative than the previous policy chapters. **Yeva Nersisyan** and **L. Randall Wray** in **"Universal Job Guarantee Program: Toward True Full Employment"** argue the efficacy of a program that makes the government the employer of last resort for all unemployed workers. **Karl Widerquist** in **"Is Universal Basic Income Still Worth Talking About?"** goes even further, making the case for a guaranteed annual income unrelated to any expected work effort on the part of recipients.

I wish to thank all of the authors who gave so generously of their scarce time to contribute chapters to this book. While horror stories abound of the prickly relationship between editor and authors, that was not the case here. Chapters were delivered promptly and feedback was accepted graciously. It was a joy to work with this group. I wish to thank Brian Romer, senior acquisitions editor for business and economics for ABC-CLIO-Greenwood-Praeger, for encouraging me to take on this project and guiding me through it. I owe a debt of gratitude to Tim Owens of the Division of Teaching and Learning Technologies at the University of Mary Washington for getting the graphics in proper shape. The biggest problem I had was with Mother Nature. The production of this book was affected by an earthquake, hurricane, and freak snowstorm. But everyone pulled through and the result is these two volumes. Learn and enjoy.

NOTE

1. Despite all the publicity Occupy Wall Street has garnered, the movement probably did not have American origins (Wikipedia 2012a).

BIBLIOGRAPHY

Borjas, George J. 1999. *Heaven's Door: Immigration Policy and the American Economy.* Princeton, NJ: Princeton University Press.

Card, David E. and Alan B. Krueger. 1995. *Myth and Measurement: The New Economics of the Minimum Wage.* Princeton, NJ: Princeton University Press.

Carneiro, Pedro and James J. Heckman. 2003. "Human Capital Policy." In *Inequality in America: What Role for Human Capital Policies?*, ed. James J. Heckman and Alan Krueger, 77–239. Cambridge, MA: MIT Press.

Friedman, Milton. 1953, 1970. "The Methodology of Positive Economics," *Essays in Positive Economics.* Chicago: University of Chicago Press.

Milanovic, Branko. 2011. *The Haves and the Have-Nots: A Brief and Idiosyncratic History of Global Inequality.* New York: Basic Books.

Rycroft, Robert S. 2009. *The Economics of Inequality, Discrimination, Poverty, and Mobility.* Armonk, NY: M.E. Sharpe.
Wikipedia: The Free Encyclopedia. 2012a. http://en.wikipedia.org/wiki/Occupy _wall_street (accessed February 23, 2012).
Wikipedia: The Free Encyclopedia. 2012b. http://en.wikipedia.org/wiki/Occupy _movement#Protests (accessed February 29, 2012).
Williams, Walter E. 1984. *The State against Blacks.* New York: McGraw-Hill.

Part I

Measurement

Chapter 2

Cross-National Comparisons of Poverty and Income Inequality

Steven Pressman

It is only human to make comparisons. People compare themselves to others. Who is better looking? Who makes more money? Nations also get compared. Where do people live the longest? Which country has the best business climate and the highest living standard?

THE LUXEMBOURG INCOME STUDY

Before the Luxembourg Income Study (LIS), studies of poverty and inequality usually focused on just one country. Attempts to actually compare nations and draw lessons from these cross-national comparisons faced numerous obstacles. There were national differences in how much income was unreported and in how this problem was corrected; countries dealt with sampling errors in different ways; and there were different ways raw data got manipulated to reflect the demographic composition of the entire nation.

Another problem is that data come from national surveys, and different nations can define key terms in different ways. For example, measures of household income could differ from country to country. The United States counts only money income, ignoring in-kind benefits such as food stamps and housing vouchers. Other nations might include the monetary value of these benefits as part of family income. Likewise, the definition of a family could differ from nation to nation. For example, do you have to be legally married to be a family? How do you count same-sex marriages?

As a result of all these differences, cross-national comparisons of poverty and income inequality could seem more like comparing apples and oranges than similar notions of poverty or inequality.

The LIS was created in April 1983 to circumvent these problems as much as possible. Its goal is to employ common definitions of key income variables and household concepts, ensuring that all variables are measured according to uniform standards across countries. The LIS also makes consistent decisions about various statistical issues. As a result, researchers can be confident that data have been harmonized as much as possible, and their cross-national analyses are as comparable as possible.

By the summer of 2011, 36 countries were part of the LIS. Datasets are organized into several "waves," each separated by around five years. Wave #1 contains datasets from the early 1980s. The most recent data, Wave #6, covers the mid-2000s. Historical data going back to the late 1960s and 1970s exist for a few countries. Wave #7 data (covering the late 2000s) began to come online toward the end of 2011.

LIS data for each country at each point in time contain extensive detail regarding income sources and socio-demographic information.[1] Income data include information on wages, property income, lottery winnings, in-kind benefits, alimony and child support, and numerous government cash transfers. There is also information on several different tax payments. Demographic information is available on the education level of the household head and spouse, the industries where they are employed, their occupations, the age of all household members, their immigration status, and their ethnicity.

As intended, the LIS has been used extensively to measure poverty and income inequality across nations. In what follows we first look at the extent of poverty across nations; then we examine various measures of income distribution.

CROSS-NATIONAL DIFFERENCES IN POVERTY

How to measure poverty has been a vexing problem for over half a century. A first issue concerns the unit of account. Should we focus on individuals or on households? Most scholars look at households, believing that income will be shared equally among all household members. This means that if one person is poor in a family, everyone in the family is poor. While this may not hold when family members are not married (e.g., siblings living together), such cases are relatively rare. Some scholars have gone further and argued that this assumption may not be true of married couples, and that many women are poor because their husband refuses to share income with them (Folbre 1986). Most studies, however, assume that income gets shared equally by all household members.

A second issue involves how to deal with households of different sizes. This is known in the academic literature as the problem of equivalence scales. To take a simple example of this problem, an annual income of $24,000 can support a single individual in the United States reasonably well. In 2009, it would have provided more than twice a poverty-level income. But for a family of five, $24,000 provides each person with just $4,800 on average. This cannot support the same lifestyle as $24,000 for a single individual; in fact, a family of five in the United States would have been counted as poor with this income in 2009.

One way of dealing with household size differences is to treat the income needs of all household members equally and look at per capita household income. We made this adjustment in the previous paragraph when we divided income by household size, and compared the income of a single individual making $24,000 with the average income of $4,800 for a family of five. This solution, however, ignores economies of scale in living arrangements. Two people can live more cheaply together than separately and will have a higher standard of living than two single individuals with the same combined income. There is only one place to rent and heat, only one cable TV bill, and just one set of pots and pans will be needed for cooking. Groceries are also cheaper to buy in bulk. In brief, we need some middle ground between focusing on per capita income, assuming no economies of scale in living arrangements, and assuming that household size does not matter at all for household living standards.

There are several possible solutions to this problem. One set of equivalence scales was developed by the Organisation for Economic Co-operation and Development (OECD) (1982). Recognizing different needs for children and adults, the OECD recommended that the income needs of additional adults in a household be counted as 0.7 of the first adult and the income needs of all children be counted as 0.5 of the first adult. This means a household with two adults must have 1.7 times the income of a single individual to have the same living standard, and a family with two adults and two children must have income 2.7 times that of a single adult. Consequently, a single individual making $24,000 has the same standard of living as a married couple making $40,800 and the same standard of living as a family of four whose income is $64,800.

A revised set of OECD adjustments treats the income needs of additional adults and children older than 14 as 0.5 of the needs of the household head and the income needs of each child 14 and younger as 0.3 of the needs of the household head (see Atkinson, Rainwater, and Smeeding 1995). According to these revised adjustments, a single individual making $24,000 has the same standard of living as a married couple making $36,000 and a family of four (containing two young children) with an income of $50,400.

A second approach makes adjustments for household size regardless of whether the additional household members are adults or children. The LIS follows this approach and suggests dividing household income by the square root of the number of household members to get an equivalent standard of living. In concrete terms, this means that a household with four members will need twice the income as one with two members, and implies that the cost of each additional child is lower than the cost of the previous child. A single adult making $20,000 would have the same living standard as two adults (or one adult and one child) with an income of $28,000. These households would also have equivalent incomes to a three-member household with an income of $34,000 and a family of four with an annual income of $40,000.

The bad news is that there is no agreement on the best equivalence scales to use. My own preference is the original OECD scales because it tracks the Orshansky poverty lines (more on this shortly) the closest. The good news is that the actual choice of equivalence scales does not matter at a practical level. Results are highly correlated for different equivalent scales; they are very similar with regard to the rankings of countries in terms of poverty and inequality (Buhmann et al. 1988). Of course, the actual numbers will vary. But we can be confident that if a country has relatively high poverty rates using one equivalence scale, it will also have relatively high poverty rates on other equivalence scales.

A third measurement issue concerns whether poverty should be defined in absolute or in relative terms. Should we identify some minimum necessary income, which everywhere and for all times counts as the dividing line between being poor or not poor? Or, should we measure poverty in terms of what is necessary to live in particular country at a particular time?

The United States uses an absolute poverty measure developed in the early 1960s by Mollie Orshansky (1969) of the Social Security Administration. She was given this task because President Johnson was about to declare a war on poverty and wanted to be able to measure his progress in this endeavor. Using Department of Agriculture data on the minimum amount of food requirements, Orshansky calculated the cost of a subsistence food budget for families of different sizes. Then she looked at government surveys (from the 1950s) of household expenditures, which found that families spent around one-third of their income on food. Orshansky multiplied the cost of a minimum food budget for each family type by three to arrive at their poverty threshold. The U.S. poverty rate is the percentage of households that fall below their poverty threshold. Every year poverty thresholds get increased based upon the annual rise in consumer prices. Thus they represent a constant real standard of living. The poverty rate is the fraction of households that cannot obtain this standard of living with their income; being poor involves not having enough income to purchase some minimum set of necessities during the year.

The Orshansky poverty measure has been criticized on several grounds. Harrell Rodgers (2000) points out that Orshansky's minimum food requirements were designed for short-term emergency situations and could not meet the nutritional needs of a family for an entire year. Since these food budgets were 80 percent of what was necessary to provide a nutritional diet for the entire year, Rodgers argues that U.S. poverty thresholds are 80 percent too low. Harold Watts (1986) criticizes Orshansky for ignoring taxes. In the early 1960s the poor paid no income taxes and virtually no Social Security taxes. However, after Social Security taxes rose sharply in the 1970s and 1980s, poor families faced a considerable tax burden. This lowered their disposable income and made it harder for them to buy basic necessities.

Steven Pressman and Robert Scott (2009) argue that poverty computations ignore the impact of interest payments from past consumer debt, much of which was incurred to survive during years with little income. The Orshansky poverty thresholds were created at a time (the early 1960s) when most poor and middle-class households lacked access to credit. This is no longer true. Today many poor and middle-income households rely on borrowing to get them through difficult economic times (such as medical expenses, divorce, and unemploy-ment), and they pay extremely high interest rates on that debt. This reduces the money available to purchase goods and services. Millions of households have income levels above their poverty threshold, but still cannot purchase the goods and services needed to survive during the year.

The most frequent criticism of the Orshansky methodology, how-ever, has been that it is an absolute measure of poverty. Since people are social animals, the minimal standard must vary from time to time and from place to place. Private baths, telephones, and television sets were not necessities in the 1920s, but are necessary today. Likewise, child care was not a necessity in the 1950s. But as more and more fam-ilies have two earners, or just one adult, child care has become an important family expenditure.

For this reason, the European Commission measures poverty in rel-ative terms. Households are considered poor if their income (adjusted for household size) falls below 50 percent of the median adjusted income of the country for the year. Others have suggested using 40 per-cent or 60 percent of median income (adjusted for household size) as the appropriate poverty threshold.

As we saw with equivalence scales, there is good news and bad news regarding poverty lines. The bad news is that there exists consid-erable debate about the best way to draw poverty lines. The good news is that the debate has few practical consequences. Different cutoff points change the poverty numbers (a 60% cutoff leads to more poor people), but neither time trends in one country nor cross-national rankings are affected much by decisions about where to actually draw the boundary line between poor and nonpoor households.

Once we decide how to adjust household income based upon house-hold size and how to set poverty thresholds for different households, it becomes a simple matter to calculate the percentage of households that are poor and the percentage of poor people in any nation at any point in time.

Table 2.1 presents poverty data for 17 developed nations. The figures come from (June 2011) LIS summary statistics on poverty and income distribution. They use LIS conventions regarding equivalence scales and poverty; poor households are those whose adjusted income falls below 50 percent of median adjusted household income.

The figures shown are the latest available for each nation. National figures generally do not vary much from year to year. Countries with

Table 2.1
Cross-National Poverty Rates, Developed Nations

Country	All Persons	Children	Elderly
Australia (2003)	12.2%	14.0%	22.3%
Austria (2004)	7.1%	7.0%	9.4%
Belgium (2000)	8.1%	7.2%	15.4%
Canada (2004)	13.0%	16.8%	6.3%
Denmark (2004)	5.6%	3.9%	8.5%
Finland (2004)	6.5%	3.7%	10.1%
France (2005)	8.4%	9.7%	7.8%
Germany (2004)	8.5%	10.7%	8.6%
Ireland (2004)	13.2%	15.8%	23.8%
Italy (2004)	12.1%	18.4%	11.2%
Luxembourg (2004)	8.8%	13.3%	4.5%
Netherlands (2004)	6.3%	9.1%	2.4%
Norway (2004)	7.1%	4.9%	8.5%
Sweden (2005)	5.6%	5.0%	6.6%
Switzerland (2004)	8.0%	9.2%	15.2%
United Kingdom (2004)	11.6%	14.0%	16.3%
United States (2004)	17.3%	21.2%	24.6%

Source: LIS database, key figures, as of June 2011.
Note: Poverty rates based on 50 percent of adjusted household income.

low poverty rates in one year tend to have low poverty rates in other years. Most of the action occurs across countries, where there is considerable variation in poverty rates from one country to another country. Some nations have very low poverty rates year after year; in others, the poverty is considerably higher and tends to remain high over time.

Looking at the first data column, poverty rates roughly fall into three clusters. First, in many nations the national poverty rate falls below 9 percent. In this group are the Nordic countries, plus several Western European nations (Austria, Belgium, France, Germany, Luxembourg, the Netherlands, and Switzerland). Denmark and Sweden, with poverty rates of 5.6 percent, share the distinction of having the lowest poverty rates in the developed world.

Next come several countries with aggregate poverty rates of around 12 percent. This group includes Italy and most Anglo-Saxon countries (Australia, Canada, Ireland, the UK). At the bottom, in a group by itself, is the United States, with an aggregate poverty rate of 17.3 percent.

Table 2.2
Cross-National Poverty Rates, Other Nations

Country	All Persons	Children	Elderly
Brazil (2006)	20.5%	31.1%	3.7%
Columbia (2004)	21.1%	26.7%	22.3%
Czech Republic (2004)	5.8%	10.3%	2.2%
Estonia (2004)	12.6%	15.4%	13.0%
Greece (2004)	12.5%	13.2%	19.7%
Guatemala (2006)	25.9%	30.5%	29.1%
Hungary (2005)	7.4%	9.9%	4.0%
Israel (2005)	19.2%	25.3%	21.7%
Mexico (2004)	18.4%	22.2%	27.3%
Peru (2004)	27.2%	33.6%	32.2%
Poland (2004)	11.5%	17.2%	3.4%
Romania (1997)	8.1%	10.0%	10.4%
Russia (2000)	18.7%	22.1%	13.7%
Slovak Republic (1996)	7.0%	9.8%	N.A.
Slovenia (2004)	7.1%	5.5%	15.4%
South Korea (2006)	14.0%	10.4%	41.4%
Spain (2004)	14.1%	17.2%	23.4%
Taiwan (2005)	9.5%	7.7%	28.7%
Uruguay	16.7%	26.4%	6.9%

Source: LIS database, key figures, as of June 2010.
Note: Poverty rates are all based on 50 percent of adjusted household income.

Table 2.2 examines cross-national poverty rates for 19 other nations. These countries are considerably more diverse than those in Table 2.1. They include the transitional economies of Eastern Europe, Israel, several Latin American nations, a few Asian nations (South Korea and Taiwan), as well as a few European countries (Greece and Spain).

Given this diversity, it is hardly surprising to see a greater spread of national poverty rates. And given the lower levels of income and economic development in these countries, poverty rates are substantially higher in this set of countries.

Like for Table 2.1, we can divide the countries of Table 2.2 into three groups. A few nations, all former Communist countries (the Czech Republic, Hungary, Romania, the Slovak Republic, Slovenia), have very low poverty rates—under 8 percent. With a recent history of income equality, as well as a set of institutions and expectations that the government would assist low-income households, these institutional factors continue to play a role in these countries, even after transitioning to more market-based economies. They show up in the national figures on poverty.

There is a second and broad group of nations with poverty rates in the 10 to 15 percent range. This includes some former Communist countries (Estonia and Poland), one Asian nation (South Korea), plus a few Western nations (Greece and Spain).

Finally, several nations have very high poverty rates—around or exceeding 20 percent. Many Latin American countries (Brazil, Colombia, Guatemala, Mexico, Peru) as well as Israel and Russia fall into this cluster.

Many commentators have expressed particular concern about child poverty. Besides children having no control over their economic fate, child poverty has many negative long-term consequences for children. It hinders the educational and intellectual development of the child, leads to health problems, and slows the social and psychological development of the child. Holzer et al. (2007) estimate that childhood poverty costs $500 billion per year, or nearly 4 percent of U.S. GDP. It does this through lowering productivity (and hence income), increasing crime rates, and raising health expenditures. Each of these factors contributes around one-third of the overall loss.

The second data column in Table 2.1 shows that, for most developed nations, aggregate poverty rates and child poverty rates are quite similar, although child poverty tends to be a bit higher. Countries with low aggregate poverty rates also have low child poverty rates, and countries with high aggregate poverty rates also tend to have high child poverty rates. There are a few notable exceptions to this, including Canada, Luxembourg, and the United States, where child poverty is 3 to 5 percentage points greater than aggregate poverty, and Italy, where child poverty rates are more than 6 percentage points higher than the aggregate rate. At the other extreme, Denmark, Finland, and Norway have child poverty rates 2 to 3 percentage points lower than aggregate poverty. A large part of the reason for this is the many generous programs that aid families with children in these countries (Rainwater and Smeeding 2003).

In Table 2.2 we see even greater divergence between child poverty rates and aggregate poverty. Many countries in this table have child poverty rates exceeding the national poverty rate by 4 percentage points or more. In a couple of cases, the difference is around 10 percentage points

(Brazil, Uruguay). Only in South Korea is the child poverty rate substantially below the average rate for all households in the nation.

Finally, many scholars have been concerned with poverty experienced by the elderly (those 65 and older). A large percentage of the elderly are vulnerable economically and unable to work. Their standard of living depends on both the wealth they accumulated during their working years and the generosity of national retirement programs. For those making relatively little during their working years, saving money for retirement is usually difficult. The elderly also run the risk of living too long and using up all their accumulated savings. For this reason, one main force affecting elderly poverty rates across nations is the generosity of national retirement programs, especially the fraction of income they replace for those whose earnings were relatively low.

For developed nations, as Table 2.1 shows, poverty rates for the elderly generally follow the pattern of aggregate poverty across nations. Like child poverty rates, they tend to be a bit higher than the national average. Among the major exceptions here are Australia, Belgium, and Switzerland, which have much higher (7 to 10 percentage points) poverty rates for the elderly. Finland (with a very low aggregate poverty rate) and the UK (with a moderate aggregate poverty rate) also have higher elderly poverty rates. In a few cases (Canada, Luxembourg, the Netherlands) elderly poverty is substantially below aggregate poverty rates, while elderly poverty in Italy is slightly below the national average.

For our other set of nations, poverty rates for the elderly follow a very different pattern than overall poverty and child poverty, and there are a few surprising results. Brazil and Uruguay have elderly poverty rates in the single digits, although these countries have much higher aggregate poverty rates. Also, in one transitional economy (Poland) elderly poverty rates are substantially below the aggregate figures, and in several countries (the Czech Republic, Hungary, Peru, Russia) they are 2 to 5 percentage points lower. These results stem from several factors. Like developed countries, most transitional economies have rather generous retirement programs for the elderly. A more important factor is demographic—the large number of extended families in these countries. When elderly individuals live with their children, rather than living on their own, their income depends on the income of their children rather than the generosity of government retirement programs. Since we assume that all households share income, the elderly are assumed to do very well because they continue to live with their children.

Finally, at the other end of the spectrum, elderly poverty in several nations is substantially above the aggregate figures (Korea, Mexico, Slovenia, Spain, Taiwan). In some cases, it is two or three times the nation's aggregate poverty rate. For example, while Taiwan has a national poverty rate below 10 percent, the poverty rate for elderly households is nearly 30 percent.

CROSS-NATIONAL DIFFERENCES IN INCOME INEQUALITY

Like poverty, income inequality is of great concern for a number of reasons. Empirical research has established that countries with greater income inequality experience a broad array of social problems, even after controlling for income levels. They have higher crime rates, lower life expectancy, less charitable giving, higher rates of teen pregnancy, worse school performance, greater incidence of obesity, and reduced social mobility.

Epidemiologists Richard Wilkinson and Kate Pickett (2010) identify several causal mechanisms responsible for this. Inequality causes stress. Stress floods our bodies with the hormone cortisol. This hinders memory and problem solving; poor school performance is one consequence of this. Cortisol also affects judgment, contributing to greater teen pregnancies and drug use among the poor, as well as higher crime rates. When produced continuously, it leads to problems with one's immune system, cardiovascular system, and glucose metabolism. As a result, life expectancy is adversely affected. In addition, hormones are secreted during times of stress that cause people to crave comfort foods that are fatty and sugary. The result is an obesity epidemic, along with all the health problems that stem from obesity. People are also likely to crave drugs and alcohol to help relieve this stress.

As with attempts at measuring poverty, there is considerable controversy about how to best measure income inequality. Scholars have failed to agree upon a single best measure, mainly because income distribution is a complex notion involving many households at different parts of the distribution. They tend to look at several different measures to gauge the extent of income inequality in a country at a particular point in time. Three of the most popular measures of income inequality are the Gini coefficient, the ratio of income received by the household at the 90th percentile (the top 10% of all income earners) to the income received by the household sitting at the 10th percentile (the bottom 10%), and the ratio of income received by the household

Figure 2.1
The Lorenz Curve and the Gini Coefficient.

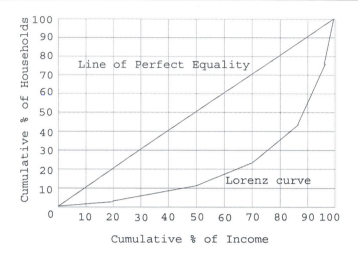

Cumulative % of Income

at the 90th percentile to the median household income, or the household at exactly the 50th percentile. Each measure has its own strengths and weaknesses.

The Gini coefficient is probably the most frequently used inequality measure. It comes from two relationships—the Lorenz curve and the line of perfect equality. To understand these, think about rank ordering every household from the poorest to the richest. As we move along the x-axis in Figure 2.1, we move from the poorest household to the richest household. The percentages tell us the ranking of each household along this continuum. On the y-axis we cumulate, or add up, the percentage of total income received by households as we move from the poorest household to the richest.

The line of perfect equality shows what would happen if everyone received exactly the same income. The 5 percent poorest households get 5 percent of total income, the 20 percent poorest get 20 percent of total income, etc. At the other extreme, perfect inequality occurs when one household gets all the income. As we cumulate incomes, the percentage is zero as we move along the horizontal axis, until we reach the richest household. At that point we go to the top of the figure, as they receive 100 percent of national income.

The Lorenz Curve shows the actual distribution of income in the country—the proportion of total income going to the poorest 5 percent of the population, the poorest 20 percent, etc. The Gini coefficient measures (somewhat counterintuitively) where the actual income distribution falls within the range between perfect income equality (0), where everyone receives exactly the same income, and perfect income inequality (1), where one household gets all the income. Formally, it is calculated by taking the area between the Lorenz Curve and the line of perfect equality, and then dividing this by the area of the entire right triangle.

Two main criticisms have been lodged against the Gini coefficient as a measure of income inequality. First, there is a technical issue. The Gini coefficient is particularly sensitive to changes in the densest part of the income distribution (usually the middle part of the distribution). Changes in distribution over time, therefore, will not be captured well by the Gini coefficient if the biggest changes occur at the high or low ends of the income distribution, which do not get sufficiently weighted in the Gini coefficient, or when the densest part of the distribution changes over time. For similar reasons, the Gini coefficients of two different countries may not reflect differences in the entire income distribution.

Another problem with the Gini coefficient is that the numbers themselves are difficult to understand intuitively. What exactly does 0.252 (the Gini for Finland) mean? How much has income inequality in Finland increased between 1987 and 2004 as a result of the Gini coefficient increasing from 0.209 to 0.252? And how much more unequal is the United States, with a Gini coefficient of 0.372 than Finland?

The ratio of the income received by the household at the 90th percentile compared to the income received by the household at the 10th percentile provides one of the simplest measures of inequality. In contrast to the Gini coefficient, which is sensitive to the middle of the distribution, this measure eliminates the middle portion of the distribution entirely, and estimates the gap between those with high incomes and those with low incomes. This measure, too, has some limitations. First, as noted earlier, it ignores the entire middle part of the income distribution. Second, this measure also ignores what is happening to the very rich, or those at the top 1 percent. According to Thomas Piketty and Emmanuel Saez (2006), this is where most of the action has occurred recently, especially in the United States. Since the 1980s, but particularly since the 2000s, multimillionaires have gotten much richer at the expense of everyone else. The 90:10 ratio fails to capture this important fact.

The 90:50 ratio is similar to the 90:10 ratio, except that it compares the household at the 90th percentile with the household in the middle or having the median income. It shows how the wealthy are doing relative to average, middle-income households. This measure also has limitations. It says nothing about how the bottom or poorest part of the population is doing relative to other groups; and like the 90:10 ratio, this measure also ignores the very rich.

Despite such problems, these three are among the best measures of income inequality that we have; they provide a good sense of how some households are doing relative to others. Lacking better alternatives, we must use them, while fully acknowledging their limitations. It is also important to look at several different measures and try to discern consistency in the stories that they tell.

The first data column in Table 2.3 provides Gini coefficients for 17 developed countries. As with our poverty data, nations fall into several clusters. First, possessing the greatest income equality are several nations with Gini coefficients of around 0.250 (or even less)— Denmark, Finland, Norway, and Sweden. These are pretty much the same countries with low poverty rates, which is only to be expected since greater income inequality generally means fewer poor people. Second, several continental European nations (Austria, Belgium, France, Germany, Luxembourg, the Netherlands, and Switzerland) have Gini coefficients close to 0.280. These are generally the developed nations with moderate national poverty rates. Finally, a few nations have Gini coefficients that exceed 0.3, mainly Italy and all the Anglo-Saxon countries. In addition to having the highest poverty rate in the developed world, the United States has the highest Gini coefficient, at 0.372.

The 90:10 and 90:50 ratios tell a somewhat similar story about income inequality. Here too we can organize countries into different clusters. Several countries (Denmark, the Netherlands, Norway, Sweden) have 90:10 ratios under 3. Most nations have ratios between 3 and 4. Italy and the Anglo-Saxon countries have the greatest income inequality on this measure, with 90:10 ratios greater than 4. By far the country with the highest 90:10 ratio is the United States; its ratio of 5.68 indicates that wealthy U.S. households have 5.68 times the income of the poorest U.S. households, or that the richest make a great deal, the poor make very little, or both.

What is true of the 90:10 ratio is likewise true of the 90:50 ratio. Its numeric values are smaller because of the larger denominator (median income rather than the income of the household at the 10th percentile).

Table 2.3
Cross-National Inequality Measures, Developed Nations

Country	Gini Coefficient	90/10 Percentile Rank	90/50 Percentile Rank	Percent Middle Class
Australia (2003)	0.312	4.24	1.98	40.3%
Austria (2004)	0.269	3.25	1.79	54.6%
Belgium (2000)	0.279	3.30	1.74	55.0%
Canada (2004)	0.318	4.38	1.96	46.2%
Denmark (2004)	0.228	2.78	1.56	62.9%
Finland (2004)	0.252	3.04	1.68	55.8%
France (2005)	0.278	3.45	1.88	51.3%
Germany (2004)	0.278	3.45	1.82	52.1%
Ireland (2004)	0.312	4.12	1.91	42.9%
Italy (2004)	0.338	4.41	2.01	46.8%
Luxembourg (2004)	0.268	3.47	1.83	54.0%
Netherlands (2004)	0.263	2.97	1.72	58.5%
Norway (2004)	0.256	2.87	1.60	59.7%
Sweden (2005)	0.237	2.82	1.63	61.1%
Switzerland (2004)	0.268	3.28	1.76	50.7%
United Kingdom (2004)	0.345	4.46	2.14	45.0%
United States (2004)	0.372	5.68	2.13	38.6%

Source: LIS database, key figures, as of June 2011, except for percent middle class, which comes from author calculations.
Note: Percent middle class is the percentage of households with adjusted gross income that falls between 75 percent and 150 percent of median adjusted gross income.

The Nordic countries have the most equal 90:50 ratios, with values around 1.6. Other European nations have values around 1.8, and the Anglo-Saxon nations (and Italy) have values of 2 and greater. On this measure the United States does not have the highest value or most unequal income distribution by far, indicating that median U.S. households do much better than low-income households from a comparative international perspective—a result that is consistent with the cross-national poverty data we examined earlier.

Table 2.4 repeats the process for our other set of nations. Focusing on the Gini coefficient in the first data column, we first note the higher values and greater inequality compared to the nations in Table 2.3. In the developed world, many countries (a large majority) had Ginis of less than 0.3. For these nations, only five countries fit into this category,

Table 2.4
Cross-National Inequality Measures, Other Nations

Country	Gini Coefficient	90/10 Percentile Rank	90/50 Percentile Rank	Percent Middle Class
Brazil (2006)	0.486	9.61	3.28	33.5%
Columbia (2004)	0.508	11.24	3.39	28.9%
Czech Republic (2004)	0.267	3.20	1.84	63.0%
Estonia (2004)	0.340	4.67	2.16	46.7%
Greece (2004)	0.329	4.43	2.04	46.2%
Guatemala (2006)	0.507	12.65	3.39	26.7%
Hungary (2005)	0.289	3.31	1.87	58.8%
Israel (2005)	0.370	5.99	2.26	36.0%
Mexico (2004)	0.458	8.49	2.98	33.8%
Peru (2004)	0.507	15.38	3.34	27.0%
Poland (2004)	0.320	4.17	1.97	49.2%
Romania (1997)	0.277	3.38	1.80	55.9%
Russia (2000)	0.434	8.37	2.76	39.6%
Slovak Republic (1996)	0.241	2.88	1.62	65.5%
Slovenia (2004)	0.242	3.13	1.72	58.8%
South Korea (2006)	0.311	4.51	1.90	45.0%
Spain (2004)	0.315	4.50	1.92	44.2%
Taiwan (2005)	0.305	3.96	2.02	46.8%
Uruguay	0.428	7.07	2.86	35.5%

Source: LIS database, key figures, as of June 2011, except for percent middle class, which comes from author's calculations.
Note: Percent middle class is the percentage of households with adjusted grossincome that falls between 75 percent and 150 percent of median adjusted gross income.

all of them former Communist nations (the Czech Republic, Hungary, Romania, the Slovak Republic, and Slovenia). Another seven countries have Ginis of greater than 0.4, while three Latin American countries (Colombia, Guatemala, and Peru) have Gini coefficients that exceed 0.5. The Gini coefficients for these last two groups exceed the U.S. Gini coefficient, which was by far the largest Gini in Table 2.1.

What is true of the Gini coefficient is likewise true of the 90:10 and 90:50 ratios. While values for the 90:10 ratio tend to range between 3 and 4 for developed nations, in Table 2.4 only a few countries have such low 90:10 ratios (the same five former Communist countries with Gini coefficients below 0.5). Consistent with their high poverty rates, a number of these countries have very high values for the 90:10 ratio. Many countries have 90:10 ratios of between 5 and 9, while several have values exceeding 9.5 (Brazil, Colombia, Guatemala, Peru). The range spreads from a bit under 3 (the Slovak Republic) to an astounding 15.38 (Peru).

The 90:50 percentile ratios in Table 2.4 look more like developed-country data, with a large number of countries having values between 1.5 and 2. In addition to the five former Communist countries, Greece, Poland, Slovakia, and Taiwan all fall into this range. Nonetheless, many Latin American nations have 90:50 ratios that exceed 3 (Brazil, Colombia, Guatemala, Peru) while both Mexico and Uruguay are not much below 3. As with Table 2.2, the substantially smaller figures here show that, in many countries, those at the bottom of the income distribution receive little income relative to everyone else.

Finally, there has recently been concern with the size of the middle class in different nations (see Pressman 2007). There are a number of reasons for this. A large middle class may be necessary for democracy because social unrest increases when incomes and people become polarized. Robert Barro (1999) provides support for this view, showing that countries are more likely to be democratic when more national income goes to middle-class households.

There are also psychological reasons why a large middle class is important. Attaining a middle-class living standard comes with feelings of success and personal accomplishment. Psychological optimism likely will lead to economic optimism, resulting in more consumption, more investment, and more rapid economic growth. Moreover, with more money going to the middle class, this should lead to greater consumption and more growth, since the poor have too little and the wealthy have too much money to spend.

Issues surrounding how to measure the size of the middle class are as controversial as how to measure poverty. There is a general consensus that middle-class households are those with incomes somewhat close to the median household income, although some claim that other characteristics (such as a certain level of education and/or having a certain amount of savings) are also necessary conditions for being middle class. Nonetheless, the main point of contention is where to draw the boundary lines separating middle-class incomes from high-income and low-income levels. Two frequently used ranges are 75 to 125 percent and 75 to 150 percent of median household income (adjusted for household size). Public opinion surveys find that most households consider themselves middle class and put their own income within the range that they use to define the middle class (Pew Research Center 2008). This indicates that the latter range is preferable since it better reflects what people regard as middle-class income levels. It also has the advantage of putting more than one-third of all households into the middle class in every developed country, something that intuitively makes sense. Unfortunately, LIS summary statistics do not include information on the size of the middle class in different nations. However, it is easy to perform such computations using LIS. These calculations rely on my preferences for adjusting household income based on household size (see earlier discussion). I have also followed my predilection for including transitory income (such as lottery winnings and capital gains) as part of household income.[2]

The results closely parallel our earlier results on income inequality and point to the consistency of the many different measures of income inequality. Countries with income distributed fairly equally according to other measures of inequality also have a large middle class. And countries whose income is distributed unequally according to our other measures tend to have a small middle class.

Nordic countries have the largest percentage of middle-class households, close to 60 percent. For continental Europe, 50 to 55 percent of all households are middle class. Anglo-Saxon nations tend to have smaller middle classes, comprising only 40 percent of households. Consistent with the other measures of income inequality, the United States also does the worst here. Just 38.6 percent of U.S. households are middle class according to our definition and computation.

Table 2.4 reports figures on the size of the middle class in our other countries. As with our other data on inequality, the range here is greater than the range for countries listed in Table 2.3. Our results, again, follow the pattern of other inequality measures. Countries that have low Gini coefficients and low 90:10 and 90:50 ratios also tend to have a large middle class. Similarly, countries with high Gini coefficients and high 90:10 and 90:50 ratios tend to have a small middle class. In the former Communist nations (with the minor exception of Poland at 49.2%) more than half of all households are middle class. At the other extreme, in Latin America and Israel only around one-third of households are classified as middle class. The other nations listed in Table 2.4 fall in between these two extremes, with around 40 percent of households in the middle class.

SUMMARY AND CONCLUSIONS

Measuring poverty and inequality is important in its own right. It focuses attention on how nations are doing over time and it lets us compare one nation to another nation. But there is a more important reason for making such measurements. Data are necessary to analyze why poverty and inequality are higher in one nation than another nation, and help us identify policies to reduce poverty and increase the size of the national middle class. Studies using the LIS have come to a number of fairly firm conclusions regarding the international differences we have examined.

First, income distribution and poverty rates are quite similar in most nations before government tax and spending policies. Thus, national differences in poverty and income inequality mainly result from government policies. For example, countries with generous policies of child allowances and paid parental leave have lower poverty rates for children. The United States, which has neither program, and does little to help families with children, has the highest poverty rate for children in the developed world by far. Likewise, countries with generous retirement programs have lower elderly poverty than countries with meager retirement benefits.

Political scientists have taken this analysis one step further and focused on political factors that contribute to more generous social programs. They have concluded that, where there are many political veto points, little legislation seems to get passed that helps either the middle class or the bottom of the income distribution. For example, bicameral legislatures, filibusters, and the possibility of having a head of state from a different party than the party controlling the legislature all can keep legislation from being passed. To this we can add the cost of elections in the United States, which makes politicians of both political parties dependent on the wealthy for their employment. Consequently, it is less likely that legislation to benefit the vast majority of the nation will be enacted (Hacker and Pierson 2010).

Economic conditions also contribute to our basic results on poverty and inequality. Greater economic growth and lower unemployment rates tend to reduce income inequality and also lower the national poverty rate. In addition, economic conditions can affect the generosity of various government programs. During the 1990s, Sweden experienced a severe economic contraction, with unemployment exceeding 9 percent for most of the decade. Although having one of the most generous safety net systems in the world, they were forced to cut back on many programs due to the severe economic conditions. The result was an increase in poverty and inequality. However, when the Swedish economy rebounded in the 2000s, they reinstituted many of their social programs, leading to greater income equality.

Much work remains to be done. We need better measures of poverty and inequality. The causes of national differences in poverty and income inequality require further study. And last, but not least, we need to focus more on developing effective policies to reduce poverty and inequality. It is here that cross-national comparisons are most important. They tell us what has been effective in other countries and what might be able to be adopted elsewhere in the world.

NOTES

1. For more on the LIS, see the LIS home page at http://www.lisdatacenter.org.
2. As with other decisions, such as equivalence scales and where to draw the poverty line, this decision matters very little when it comes to overall results.

BIBLIOGRAPHY

Atkinson, Anthony, Lee Rainwater and Timothy Smeeding. 1995. *Income Distribution in OECD Countries: Evidence from the Luxembourg Income Study*. Paris: OECD.

Barro, Robert. 1999. "Determinants of Democracy," *Journal of Political Economy*, 107, pp. S158–S183.

Buhmann, Brigitte, Lee Rainwater, Gunther Schmaus and Timothy Smeeding. 1988. "Equivalence Scales, Well-Being, Inequality, and Poverty: International Comparisons across Ten Countries Using the Luxembourg Income Study (LIS) Database," *Review of Income and Wealth*, 34, 115–40.

Folbre, Nancy. 1986. "Hearts and Spades: Paradigms of Household Economics," *World Development*, 14, pp. 245–55.

Hacker, Jacob and Paul Pierson. 2010. *Winner-Take-All Politics: How Washington Made the Rich Richer—and Turned Its Back on the Middle Class*. New York: Simon & Schuster.

Holzer, Harry, Diana Schanzenbach, Greg Duncan and Jens Ludwig. 2007. *The Economic Costs of Poverty in the United States: Subsequent Effects of Children Growing Up in Poverty*. Washington, DC: Center for American Progress.

Organisation for Economic Co-operation and Development. 1982. *The OECD List of Social Indicators*. Paris: OECD.

Orshansky, Mollie. 1969. "How Poverty Is Measured," *Monthly Labor Review*, 92, pp. 37–41.

Pew Research Center. 2008. *Inside the Middle Class: Bad Times Hit the Good Life*. Washington, DC: Pew Research Center.

Piketty, Thomas and Emmanuel Saez. 2006. "The Evolution of Top Incomes: A Historical and International Perspective," *American Economic Review*, 92, pp. 200–205.

Pressman, Steven. 2007. "The Decline of the Middle Class: An International Perspective," *Journal of Economic Issues*, 41, pp. 181–200.

Pressman, Steven and Robert Scott. 2009. "Consumer Debt and the Measurement of Poverty and Inequality in the US," *Review of Social Economy*, 67, pp. 127–46.

Rainwater, Lee and Timothy Smeeding. 2003. *Poor Kids in a Rich Country: America's Children in Comparative Perspective*. New York: Russell Sage.

Rodgers, Harrell. 2000. *American Poverty in a New Era of Reform*. Armonk, NY: M.E. Sharpe.

Watts, Harold. 1986. "Have Our Measures of Poverty Become Poorer?," *Focus*, 9, pp. 18–23.

Wilkinson, Richard and Kate Pickett. 2010. *The Spirit Level*. New York: Bloomsbury Press.

Chapter 3

The Distribution of Wealth in the United States at the Start of the 21st Century

Edward N. Wolff

INTRODUCTION

The 1990s witnessed some remarkable events. The stock market boomed. On the basis of the Standard & Poor (S&P) 500 index, stock prices surged 171 percent between 1989 and 2001. Stock ownership spread, and by 2001 (as we shall see later) over half of U.S. households owned stock either directly or indirectly. Real wages, after stagnating for many years, finally grew in the late 1990s. According to BLS figures, real mean hourly earnings gained 8.3 percent between 1995 and 2001.[1]

However, 2001 saw a recession (albeit a short one). Moreover, the stock market peaked in 2000 and dropped steeply from 2000 to 2003 but recovered in 2004, so that between 2001 and 2004 the S&P 500 was down by "only" 12 percent in real terms. Real wages rose very slowly from 2001 to 2004, with the BLS real mean hourly earnings up by only 1.5 percent, and median household income down in real terms

Portions of this chapter have been adapted from Edward N. Wolff, Levy Economics Institute Working Papers 589 (2010), 502 (2007), and 407 (2004). Available online at http://www.levyinstitute.org/publications/?doctype=13. Used courtesy of the Levy Economics Institute.

by 1.5 percent. On the other hand, housing prices rose steeply. The median sales price of existing one-family homes rose by 18 percent in real terms nationwide.[2]

From 2004 to 2007, the stock market rebounded. The S&P 500 rose 19 percent in real terms. Over the period from 2001 to 2007, the S&P 500 was up 6 percent in real terms. Real wage remained stagnant but median household income in real terms showed some growth, rising by 3.2 percent. From 2001 to 2007 it gained 1.6 percent. From 2004 to 2007 housing prices stagnated, and over the years 2001 to 2007 real housing prices gained 19 percent.

I find here that median net worth demonstrated robust growth over the years from 1983 to 2007. In fact, the growth rate of median wealth accelerated from the 1980s to the 1990s and into the 2001–7 period. However, the gains of the 2001–7 period were based largely on rising home prices financed by increasing mortgage debt. Household wealth inequality increased sharply between 1983 and 1989 but showed almost no change from 1989 to 2007.

Despite the buoyant economy over the 1980s and 1990s, overall indebtedness continued to rise among American families and then skyrocketed in the early and mid-2000s. Among the middle class, the debt-income ratio reached its highest level in 24 years. The high level of indebtedness made the middle class particularly vulnerable to the collapse of the housing market at the end of the decade of the 2000s. There was also a noticeable expansion of stock ownership from 1989 to 2001, but this was followed by a mild contraction between 2001 and 2007.

The ratio of mean wealth between African American and white families was very low in 1983, at 0.19, and barely budged over the years 1983 to 2007. However, Hispanics did show some relative gains over the 2001 to 2007 period. Younger households (under the age of 55) saw their relative wealth position deteriorate over the years 1983 to 2007.

I begin in the next section with a discussion of the measurement of household wealth and a description of the data sources used in this chapter. The third section presents results on median and average wealth holdings, the fourth on the concentration of household wealth, and the fifth on the composition of household wealth. The sixth section investigates changes in wealth holdings by race and ethnicity; and the seventh reports on changes in the age-wealth profile. The eighth section provides details on stock ownership. A summary of results and concluding remarks are provided in the final section.

DATA SOURCES AND METHODS

Most studies use income as the metric of family well-being. However, wealth is also an indicator of well-being. Though certain forms of income are derived from wealth, such as interest from savings accounts and dividends from stocks, income and wealth are by no means identical. Many kinds of income, such as wages and salaries, are not derived from household wealth, and many forms of wealth, such as owner-occupied housing, produce no corresponding income flow.

Moreover, family wealth by itself is also a source of well-being, independent of the direct financial income it provides. There are three reasons. First, some assets such as owner-occupied housing provide services directly to their owner. Such assets can substitute for money income in satisfying economic needs. Second, wealth is a source of consumption, independent of the direct money income it provides. Many assets can be converted directly into cash and thus provide for immediate consumption needs. Third, the availability of financial assets can provide liquidity to a family in times of economic stress (such as occasioned by unemployment, sickness, or family breakup). In this sense, wealth is a source of economic security for the family. In these ways wealth holdings provide another dimension to household welfare over and above income flows.

The data sources used here are the 1983, 1989, 2001, and 2007 Survey of Consumer Finances conducted by the Federal Reserve Board. Each survey consists of a core representative sample combined with a high-income supplement.

I use the standard definition of wealth (or net worth), which is defined as the value of all marketable assets less the current value of debts. Total assets are defined as the sum of: (1) homes, (2) other real estate, (3) liquid assets, (4) financial securities, (5) pension plans like 401(k) plans, (6) corporate stock, (7) unincorporated business equity, and (8) trust funds.[3] Total liabilities are the sum of: (1) mortgage debt and (2) consumer and other debt.

MEDIAN WEALTH ROSE BRISKLY DURING THE 2000s

Table 3.1 documents a robust growth in wealth during the 1990s. After rising by 7 percent between 1983 and 1989, median wealth was 16 percent greater in 2001 than in 1989. Median wealth grew slightly faster between 1989 and 2001 than between 1983 and 1989. Between 2001 and 2007, median wealth grew even faster, by 19 percent overall, because of rising home prices.

Table 3.1
Mean and Median Wealth and Income, 1983–2007 (In Thousands,
2007 Dollars)

	1983	1989	2001	2007
A. Net Worth				
1. Median	69.5	74.3	86.1	102.5
2. Mean	270.4	309.8	445.1	536.1
B. Income (CPS)[a]				
1. Median	43.5	48.3	49.4	50.2
2. Mean	52.9	61.1	68.1	67.6
C. Net Worth Shares				
1. Top 1%	33.8	37.4	33.4	34.6
2. Top 5%	56.1	58.9	59.2	61.8
3. Top 20%	81.3	83.5	84.4	85.0
4. 4th 20%	12.6	12.3	11.3	10.9
5. Middle 20%	5.2	4.8	3.9	4.0
6. Bottom 40%	0.9	−0.7	0.3	0.2
7. Gini coefficient	0.799	0.832	0.826	0.834
D. Income Shares (SCF)				
1. Top 1%	12.8	16.6	20.0	21.3
2. Top 5%	26.1	30.0	35.2	37.2
3. Top 20%	51.9	55.6	58.6	61.4
4. 4th 20%	21.6	20.6	19.0	17.8
5. Middle 20%	14.2	13.2	12.3	11.1
6. Bottom 40%	12.3	10.7	10.1	9.6
7. Gini coefficient	0.480	0.521	0.562	0.574

[a]Source for household income data: U.S. Census of the Bureau, Current Populations Surveys, available at http:/www.census.gov/hhes/www/income/data/historical/household/index.html.
Source: Own computations from the 1983, 1989, 2001, and 2007 SCF. Wealth figures are deflated using the CPI-U.

Mean net worth also showed a sharp increase from 1983 to 1989 of 15 percent and then, buoyed largely by rising stock prices, another surge of 44 percent to 2001. There was an additional rise of 20 percent in 2007. Overall, its 2007 value was almost double its value in 1983. Mean wealth grew quite a bit faster between 1989 and 2001 than from 1983 to 1989. There was then a slight increase in wealth growth from 2001 to 2007. This modest acceleration was due largely to the rapid increase in housing prices in real terms over the six years counterbalanced by the reduced growth in stock prices and to the fact that housing comprised

28 percent and stocks made up 25 percent of total assets in 2001. Another point of note is that mean wealth grew about twice as fast as the median between 1983 and 2007, indicating widening inequality of wealth over these years.

Median household income (based on the Current Population Survey), after gaining 11 percent between 1983 and 1989, grew by only 2.3 percent (in total) from 1989 to 2001 and by another 1.6 percent between 2001 and 2007, for a net change of 16 percent from 1983 to 2007. In contrast, mean income rose by 16 percent from 1983 to 1989, by another 12 percent from 1989 to 2001, then fell by 0.8 percent from 2001 to 2007, for a total change of 28 percent from 1983 to 2007. Between 1983 and 2007, mean income grew about twice as fast as median income.

In sum, while household income virtually stagnated for the average American household over the 1990s and 2000s, median net worth grew strongly. In the 2000s, in particular, mean and median income changed very little while mean and median net worth showed robust gains.

WEALTH INEQUALITY SHOWS LITTLE CHANGE OVER THE EARLY AND MID-2000s

The figures in Table 3.1 also show that wealth inequality, after rising steeply between 1983 and 1989, remained virtually unchanged from 1989 to 2007. The share of wealth held by the top 1 percent rose by 3.6 percentage points from 1983 to 1989, and the Gini coefficient (an index that ranges from zero to one where zero indicates the least and one the greatest level of inequality) increased from 0.80 to 0.83. Between 1989 and 2007, the share of the top percentile actually declined, from 37.4 to 34.6 percent, though this was more than compensated for by an increase in the share of the next four percentiles. Altogether, the share of the top 5 percent increased from 58.9 percent in 1989 to 61.8 percent in 2007, and the share of the top quintile rose from 83.5 to 85.0 percent. The share of the fourth and middle quintiles each declined by about a percentage point from 1989 to 2007, while that of the bottom 40 percent increased by almost 1 percentage point. Overall, the Gini coefficient was virtually unchanged—0.832 in 1989 and 0.834 in 2007.

The top 1 percent of families (as ranked by income on the basis of the Survey of Consumer Finances data) earned 21 percent of total household income in 2006 and the top 20 percent accounted for 61 percent—large figures but lower than the corresponding wealth shares.[4] The time trend of income inequality also contrasts with that of net worth. Income inequality increased sharply between 1982 and 1988, with the Gini coefficient rising from 0.48 to 0.52 and the share of the top 1 percent from 12.8 to 16.6 percent. There was again a pronounced increase in income inequality between 1988 and 2000, with the share of the top 1 percent rising from 16.6 to 20.0 percent, that of the top quintile from 55.6 to 58.6 percent, and the Gini coefficient from 0.52 to 0.56.

The years 2000 to 2006 saw a slight abatement in the rise of income inequality. Over these years, the Gini coefficient for income rose from 0.56 to 0.57, the share of the top 1 percent from 20.0 to 21.3 percent, and that of the top quintile from 15.2 to 15.9 percent. All in all, the 2000s witnessed a moderate increase in income inequality but little change in wealth inequality.

HOUSEHOLD DEBT EXPLODES

In 2007, homes were the most important household asset in the breakdown shown in Table 3.2, accounting for 33 percent of total assets. However, home equity (the value of the house minus any outstanding mortgage) amounted to only 21 percent of total assets. Real estate, other than owner-occupied housing, comprised 11 percent, and business equity another 20 percent.

Liquid assets (bank deposits, money market funds, CDs, and life insurance) made up 7 percent and pension accounts 12 percent. Financial securities, corporate stock, and trust equity collectively accounted for 16 percent. Debt as a proportion of gross assets was 15 percent, and the debt-equity ratio (the ratio of debt to net worth) was 0.18.

There were some notable changes in the composition of household wealth over time. The first is the steep rise in the share of gross housing wealth in total assets, which jumped from 30 percent in 1983 to 33 percent in 2007. There were two factors behind this. The first was the rise in the home ownership rate, which climbed from 63 percent in 1983 to 69 percent in 2007. The second was the sharp rise in housing prices, noted earlier. The rise in housing prices by itself would have caused the share of housing in total assets to rise by 5.3 percentage points, compared to the actual increase of 4.6 percentage points.

A second and related trend is that home equity fell off from 24 percent of gross assets in 1983 to 21 percent in 2007. The difference between the two series (gross versus net housing values as a share of total assets) is attributable to the changing magnitude of mortgage debt on home

Table 3.2

Composition of Household Wealth by Wealth Class, 1983 and 2007 (Percentage of Gross Assets)

Component	All Households		Top 1 Percent		Next 19 Percent		Middle Three Quintiles	
	1983	2007	1983	2007	1983	2007	1983	2007
Principal residence	30.1	32.8	8.1	10.2	29.1	31.8	61.6	65.1
Liquid assets (bank deposits, money market funds, and cash surrender value of life insurance)	17.4	6.6	8.5	4.5	21.4	7.3	21.4	7.8
Pension accounts	1.5	12.1	0.9	5.8	2.0	15.9	1.2	12.9
Corporate stock, financial securities, mutual funds, and personal trusts	15.9	15.5	29.5	25.2	13.0	15.0	3.1	3.6
Unincorporated business equity other real estate	33.8	31.3	52.0	52.3	32.8	28.5	11.4	9.3
Miscellaneous assets	1.3	1.7	1.0	2.0	1.6	1.6	1.3	1.3
Total assets	100.0	100.0	100.0	100.0	100.0	100.0	100.0	100.0
Memo:								
Debt/equity ratio	15.1	18.1	5.9	2.8	10.9	12.1	37.4	61.1
Debt/income ratio	68.4	118.7	86.8	39.4	72.8	109.8	66.9	156.7
All stocks/total assets[a]	11.3	16.8	21.2	21.4	9.1	18.6	2.4	7.0

Note: Own computations from the 1983 and 2007 SCF.

[a]Includes direct ownership of stock shares and indirect ownership through mutual funds, trusts, and IRAs, Keogh plans, 401(k) plans, and other retirement accounts.

owners' property, which increased from 21 percent in 1983 to 35 percent in 2007.

Third, overall indebtedness climbed, with the debt-equity ratio rising from 15 percent in 1983 to 18 percent in 2007 and the ratio of debt to total income from 68 percent in 1983 to 119 percent in 2007. If mortgage debt is excluded, then the ratio of other debt to total assets actually fell off from 6.8 percent in 1983 to 3.9 percent in 2007. One implication is that over the 1990s and 2000s families used tax-sheltered mortgages and home equity loans rather than consumer and credit card loans to finance consumption.

A fourth development was the pronounced growth of defined contribution pension accounts, which rose from 1.5 percent of total assets in 1983 to 12 percent in 2007. This increase largely offset the decline in the share of liquid assets in total assets, from 17 percent in 1983 to 7 percent in 2007, so that it is reasonable to conclude that households substituted tax-deferred pension contributions for taxable savings deposits.

Fifth, if we include the value of stocks indirectly owned through mutual funds, trusts, IRAs, 401(k) plans, and other retirement accounts, then the value of total stocks owned as a share of total assets more than doubled from 11 percent in 1983 to 25 percent in 2001 but then tumbled to 17 percent in 2007. The rise during the 1990s reflected the bull market in corporate equities as well as increased stock ownership, while the decline in the 2000s was a result of the relatively small rise in the stock market over this period as well as a drop in stock ownership (see Table 3.5 later under the heading Stock Ownership First Rises Then Falls). The change in stock prices by itself would have caused the share of total stocks in assets to fall by 4 percentage points between 2001 and 2007, compared to the actual decline of 8 percentage points. Most of the decline in the share of stocks in total assets was due to sales of stocks and withdrawals from stock funds.

Portfolio Composition by Wealth Class

There are marked class differences in how middle-class families and the rich invest their wealth. As shown in Table 3.2, the richest 1 percent of households invested over three-quarters of their savings in investment assets (investment real estate, businesses, corporate stock, and financial securities) in 2007. Housing accounted for only 10 percent of their wealth, liquid assets another 5 percent, and pension accounts another 6 percent. Their ratio of debt to net worth was only 3 percent and their ratio of debt to income was 39 percent. Among the next richest 19 percent, housing comprised 32 percent of their total assets, liquid assets another 7 percent, and pension assets 16 percent, while 44 percent of their assets took the form of investment assets. Debt amounted to 12 percent of their net worth and 110 percent of their income.

In contrast, almost two-thirds of the wealth of the middle three wealth quintiles of households was invested in their own home in 2007. However, home equity amounted to only 35 percent of total assets, a reflection of their large mortgage debt. Another 21 percent went into monetary savings of one form or another and pension accounts. Together housing, liquid assets, and pension assets accounted for 86 percent of the total assets of the middle class. The rest went into investment assets. The ratio of debt to net worth was 61 percent, substantially higher than for the richest 20 percent, and their ratio of debt to income was 157 percent, also much higher than the top quintile. Finally, their mortgage debt amounted to almost half the value of their principal residences.

The rather staggering debt level of the middle class in 2007 raises the question of whether this is a recent phenomenon or whether it has been going on for some time. As shown in Table 3.2, there was remarkable stability in the composition of wealth by wealth class between 1983 and 2007. The most notable exception is a substitution of pension assets for liquid assets—a transition that occurred for all three wealth classes. The debt-equity ratio actually fell for the top 1 percent from 1983 and 2007, as did the debt-income ratio. The debt-income ratio increased slightly for the next 19 percent, while the debt-income ratio rose sharply, from 73 to 110 percent.

Among the middle three wealth quintiles, there was a sharp rise in the debt-equity ratio from 37 percent in 1983 to 61 percent in 2007. The rise was much steeper than for the other wealth groups. The debt-to-income ratio skyrocketed over this period, more than doubling. Much of the increase happened between 2001 and 2007. Moreover, the increase was much steeper than for the other wealth classes. In fact, in 1983, the debt-to-income ratio was about the same for middle class as for all households, but by 2007 the ratio was much larger.

THE RACIAL DIVIDE REMAINS LARGELY UNCHANGED OVER TIME

Striking differences are found in the wealth holdings of different racial and ethnic groups. In Table 3.3, households are divided into three groups: (1) non-Hispanic whites, (2) non-Hispanic African

Table 3.3

Household Income and Wealth by Race and Ethnicity, 1983 and 2007 (In Thousands, 2007 Dollars)

Year	Means					Medians				
	Whites	Blacks	Hispanics	Black/ White Ratio	Hisp./ White Ratio	Whites	Blacks	Hispanics	Black/ White Ratio	Hisp./ White Ratio
A. Income										
1982	64.8	34.9	39.2	0.54	0.60	45.6	25.4	30.2	0.56	0.66
2006	92.3	44.6	46.4	0.48	0.50	50.0	30.0	35.0	0.60	0.70
B. Net Worth										
1983	316.0	59.5	51.4	0.19	0.16	91.0	6.1	3.5	0.07	0.04
2007	652.1	122.7	170.4	0.19	0.26	143.6	9.3	9.1	0.06	0.06
C. Home Ownership Rate (in Percent)										
1983	68.1	44.3	32.6	0.65	0.48					
2007	74.8	48.6	49.2	0.65	0.66					

Source: Own computations from the 1983 and 2007 SCF.

Note: Households are divided into four racial/ethnic groups: (1) non-Hispanic whites ("whites" for short); (2) non-Hispanic African-Americans ("blacks" for short); (3) Hispanics; and (4) American Indians, Asians, and others.

Americans, and (3) Hispanics.[5] In 2007, while the ratio of mean incomes between (non-Hispanic) white and (non-Hispanic) black households was an already low 0.48 and the ratio of median incomes was 0.60, the ratios of mean and median wealth holdings were even lower, at 0.19 and 0.06, respectively. The home ownership rate for black households was 49 percent in 2007, a little less than two-thirds the rate among whites.

Between 1982 and 2006, while the average real income of white households increased by 42 percent and the median by 10 percent, the former rose by only 28 percent for black households but the latter by 18 percent. As a result, the ratio of mean income slipped from 0.54 in 1982 to 0.48 in 2006, while the ratio of median income rose from 0.56 to 0.60.

Between 1983 and 2007, average net worth (in 2007 dollars) doubled for white and black households, so that the net worth ratio remained unchanged. In the case of median wealth, growth was similar for white and black households (a little over half) and the ratio was, correspondingly, similar in the two years. The home ownership rate of black households grew from 44 to 49 percent between 1983 and 2007 while that for white households advanced from 68 to 75 percent, so that the home ownership rate *ratio* was almost identical in the two years.

The picture is somewhat different for Hispanics. The ratio of mean income between Hispanics and non-Hispanic whites in 2007 was 0.50, almost the same as that between African American and white households. However, the ratio of median income was 0.70, higher than the ratio between black and white households. The ratio of mean net worth was 0.26 compared to that of 0.19 between blacks and whites. However, the ratio of medians was 0.06, almost identical to that between blacks and whites. The Hispanic home ownership rate was 49 percent, also almost identical to that of non-Hispanic black households.

Developments among Hispanic households over the period from 1983 to 2007 were mixed. Mean household income for Hispanics grew by 18 percent and median household income by 16 percent, so that while the ratio of mean income between Hispanics and non-Hispanic whites slid from 60 to 50 percent, that of median income advanced from 66 to 70 percent.

Between 1983 and 2007, mean wealth increased by a factor of 3.3 among Hispanic households, so that the mean net worth ratio between Hispanics and non-Hispanic whites advanced from 0.16 to 0.26. On the other hand, from 1983 to 2007 median wealth among Hispanics remained extremely low and largely unchanged, so that the ratio of median wealth stayed virtually the same. The home ownership rate among Hispanic households climbed from 33 to 49 percent between 1983 and 2007, so that the ratio of home ownership rates between Hispanics and non-Hispanic whites advanced from 0.48 to 0.66.

Despite some progress from 2001 to 2007, the respective wealth gaps between blacks and whites and between Hispanics and non-Hispanic whites were still much greater than the corresponding income gaps in 2007. While mean income ratios were of the order of 50 percent, mean wealth ratios were of the order of 20 to 25 percent. While blacks and Hispanics were left out of the wealth surge of the years 1989 to 2001 because of relatively low stock ownership, they actually benefited from this (and the relatively high share of houses in their portfolio) in the 2001–7 period.

THE RELATIVE WEALTH OF YOUNGER HOUSEHOLDS DETERIORATES OVER TIME

As shown in Table 3.4, the cross-sectional age-wealth profiles of 1983 and 2007 generally follow the predicted hump-shaped pattern of the life-cycle model (see, for example, Modigliani and Brumberg 1954). Mean wealth increases with age up through age 65 or so and then falls off. Home ownership rates also have a similar profile, though the fall-off after the peak age is much more attenuated than for the wealth numbers. In 2007, the wealth of elderly households (age 65 and over) averaged 75 percent higher than the non-elderly and their home ownership rate was 21 percentage points higher.

Despite the apparent similarity in the profiles, there have been notable shifts in the relative wealth holdings of age groups between 1983 and 2007. The relative wealth of the youngest age group, under 35 years of age, diminished from 21 percent of the overall mean in 1983 to only 17 percent in 2007. The mean net worth of the next youngest age group, 35–44, relative to the overall mean tumbled from 0.71 in 1983 to 0.58 in 2007. The relative wealth of the next youngest age group, 45–54, also declined rather steadily over time, from 1.53 in 1983 to 1.19 in 2007. In contrast, the relative wealth of age group 55–64 and of age group 65–74 was about the same in 2007 as in 1983. The wealth of the oldest age group, age 75 and over, advanced from a ratio of 1.05 in 1983 to 1.16 in 2007. In sum, there was a clear deterioration of the wealth of younger households (under age 55) from 1983 to 2007.

Changes in home ownership rates tend to mirror these trends. While the overall ownership rate increased by 5.2 percentage points

Table 3.4
Age-Wealth Profiles and Home Ownership Rates by Age, 1983 and 2007

Age	1983	2007
A. Mean Net Worth (Ratio to Overall Mean)		
Overall	1.00	1.00
Under 35	0.21	0.17
35–44	0.71	0.58
45–54	1.53	1.19
55–64	1.67	1.69
65–74	1.93	1.86
75 and over	1.05	1.16
B. Home Ownership Rate (in Percent)		
Overall	63.4	68.6
Under 35	38.7	40.8
35–44	68.4	66.1
45–54	78.2	77.3
55–64	77.0	80.9
65–74	78.3	85.5
75 and over	69.4	77.0

Source: Own computations from the 1983 and 2007 SCF.

from 63.4 to 68.6 percent between 1983 and 2007, the share of house-holds in the youngest age group owning their own home increased by only 2.1 percentage points. The home ownership rate of households between 35 and 44 years of age actually fell by 2.3 percentage points, and that of the age group 45 to 54 years of age declined by 0.9 percentage points. Big gains in home ownership were recorded by the older age groups: 3.9 percentage points for age group 55–64, 7.1 percentage points for age group 65–74, and 7.6 percentage points for the oldest age group. By 2007, home ownership rates rose monotonically with age up to age group 65–74 and then dropped for the oldest age group. The statistics also point to a relative shifting of home ownership away from younger toward older households between 1983 and 2007.

STOCK OWNERSHIP FIRST RISES AND THEN FALLS

Table 3.5 reports on overall stock ownership trends from 1989 to 2007.[6] The years 1989 to 2001 saw a substantial increase in stock owner-ship. The share of households with direct ownership of stock climbed from 13 percent in 1989 to 21 percent in 2001, while the share with

Table 3.5
Stock Ownership, 1989, 2001, and 2007 (Percentage of Households Holding Stocks)

Stock Type	1989	2001	2007
Direct stock holdings only	13.1	21.3	17.9
Indirect stock holdings only	23.5	47.7	44.4
1. Through mutual funds	5.9	16.7	10.6
2. Through pension accounts	19.5	41.4	40.2
3. Through trust funds	1.6	5.1	4.1
All stock holdings[a]			
1. Any holdings	31.7	51.9	49.1
2. Stock worth $5,000 or more[b]	22.6	40.1	34.6
3. Stock worth $10,000 or more[b]	18.5	35.1	29.6
4. Stock worth $25,000 or more[b]	10.5	27.1	22.1
Memo:			
Direct plus indirect stocks as a percentage of total assets	10.2	24.5	16.8

[a]Includes direct ownership of stock shares and indirect ownership through mutual funds, trusts, and IRAs, Keogh plans, 401(k) plans, and other retirement accounts.
[b]1995 dollars.
Source: Own computations from the 1983, 1989, 2001, and 2007 SCF.

some stock owned either outright or indirectly through mutual funds, trusts, or various pension accounts surged from 32 to 52 percent. Much of the increase was fueled by the growth in pension accounts like IRAs, Keogh plans, and 401(k) plans. Between 1989 and 2001, the share of households owning stock through a pension account more than doubled, accounting for the bulk of the overall increase in stock ownership. Indirect ownership of stocks through mutual funds also greatly expanded over the 1989–2001 period, from 6 to 17 percent, as did indirect ownership through trust funds, from 1.6 to 5.1 percent. All told, the share of households with indirect ownership of stocks doubled, from 24 percent in 1989 to 48 percent in 2001.

In contrast, the next six years, 2001–7, saw a retrenchment in stock ownership. This trend probably reflected the sharp drop in the stock market from 2000 to 2001, its rather anemic recovery through 2004, and its modest rebound from 2004 to 2007. Direct stock ownership slipped from 21 percent in 2001 to 18 percent in 2007, and indirect stock ownership fell by 3.3 percentage points. This decrease was largely due to a sharp decline in stock ownership through mutual funds (down by 6 percentage points). Stock ownership through pension accounts was down by 1.2 percentage points from 2001 to 2007.

By 2007 the share of households who owned stock directly or indirectly dipped below half, down to 49 percent and down from its peak of 52 percent in 2001. Moreover, many of these families had only a minor stake in the stock market in 2007, with only 35 percent with total stock holdings worth $5,000 (in 1995 dollars) or more, down from 40 percent in 2001; only 30 percent owned $10,000 or more of stock, down from 35 percent in 2001; and only 22 percent owned $25,000 or more of stocks, down from 27 percent six years earlier.

Direct plus indirect ownership of stocks as a share of total household assets more than doubled from 10 percent in 1989 to 25 percent in 2001. This increase reflected in large measure the surge in stock prices over these years. However, between 2001 and 2007, the share plummeted to 17 percent. This change is a result not only of the relative stagnation of the stock market over these years but also of the withdrawal of many families from the stock market.

The distribution of total stocks owned by vehicle of ownership also shows very marked time trends. Direct stock holdings as a share of total stock holdings fell from 54 percent in 1989 to 37 percent in 2007. In contrast, stock held in mutual funds rose from 9 percent in 1983 to 21 percent in 2007. The share held in pension first increased from 24 percent in 1989 to 34 percent in 2001 but then fell off to 31 percent in 2007. The trend from 2001 to 2007 seems to reflect a substitution of stock holdings in mutual funds for those in pension plans as investors looked for safer retirement accounts. Likewise the share of the total value of pension plans held as stock more than doubled between 1989 and 2001, from 33 to 66 percent, and then plummeted to 44 percent in 2007. The sharp tail-off in stock ownership in pension plans after 2001 largely reflected the lethargic performance of the stock market over this period and the search for more secure investments among plan holders.

Stock ownership is also highly skewed by wealth and income class. As shown in Table 3.6, 93 percent of the top 1 percent owned stock either directly or indirectly in 2007, compared to 48 percent of the middle quintile and 16 percent of the poorest 20 percent. While 88 percent of the very rich also reported stocks worth $10,000 or more, only 22 percent of the middle quintile and 2 percent of the bottom quintile did so. The top 1 percent of households owned 38 percent of all stocks, the top 5 percent 69 percent, the top 10 percent 81 percent, and the top quintile over 90 percent.

Table 3.6
Concentration of Stock Ownership by Wealth and Income Class, 2007

	Percentage of Households Owning			Percentage of Stock Owned	
	Stock Worth More Than				
	Zero	$4,999	$9,999	Shares	Cumulative
A. Wealth Class					
Top 1 percent	92.6	89.1	88.4	38.3	38.3
Next 4 percent	92.2	90.7	89.5	30.8	69.1
Next 5 percent	86.8	85.0	81.4	12.1	81.2
Next 10 percent	82.1	77.1	71.2	9.9	91.1
Second quintile	65.4	54.3	47.1	6.4	97.5
Third quintile	47.7	28.9	22.1	1.9	99.4
Fourth quintile	30.3	12.3	8.7	0.5	99.9
Bottom quintile	16.3	3.5	2.0	0.1	100.0
All	49.1	36.3	31.6	100.0	
B. Income Level					
$250,000 or more	95.4	93.4	91.3	53.7	53.7
$100,000–$249,999	84.5	71.0	63.7	21.5	75.2
$75,000–$99,999	71.1	55.6	49.6	9.0	84.3
$50,000–$74,999	58.1	40.7	34.9	7.7	92.0
$25,000–$49,999	39.3	23.6	19.0	5.7	97.7
$15,000–$24,999	23.1	15.7	11.9	1.1	98.8
Under $15,000	11.2	5.0	4.3	1.2	100.0
All	49.1	36.3	31.8	100.0	

Note: Includes direct ownership of stock shares and indirect ownership through mutual funds, trusts, and IRAs, Keogh plans, 401(k) plans, and other retirement accounts. All figures are in 2007 dollars.

Stock ownership also tails off by income class. Whereas 94 percent of households in income class $250,000 or more owned stock in 2007, 39 percent of the middle class (incomes between $25,000 and $50,000), 23 percent of the lower middle class (incomes between $15,000 and $25,000), and only 11 percent of poor households (income under $15,000) reported stock ownership. The comparable ownership figures for stock holdings of $10,000 or more are 91 percent for the top income class, 19 percent for the middle class, 12 percent for the lower middle class, and 4 percent for the poor. Moreover, 84 percent of all stocks were owned by households earning $75,000 or more (the top 30%) and 92 percent by those earning $50,000 or more in terms of income. One result of the stock market bust of the early 2000s was a withdrawal of middle-class families from the stock market.

Thus, substantial stock holdings have still not penetrated much beyond the reach of the rich and the upper middle class. The big winners from the stock market boom of the late 1990s (as well as the big losers in the early 2000s) were these groups, while the middle class and the poor did not see sizable benefits from the bull market (or losses when the stock market tanked in 2000–2002). It is also apparent which groups were most exposed to the 2007–9 stock market crash.

SUMMARY AND CONCLUDING COMMENTS

Median net worth showed robust gains over the years from 1983 to 2007. In fact, the growth rate of median accelerated from the 1980s to the 1990s and into the 2001–7 period. However, the gains of the 2001–7 period were based largely on rising home prices financed by increasing mortgage debt. Household wealth inequality showed a sharp increase from 1983 to 1989 but little change from 1989 to 2007.

The biggest story of the past three decades is that despite the buoyant economy of the 1980s and 1990s, overall indebtedness continued to rise among American families and then shot up in the 2000s. Among the middle class, in particular, the debt-income ratio reached its highest level in 24 years. Mortgage debt on middle-class home owners' property exploded from 29 percent in 1983 to 47 percent in 2007. The high level of mortgage indebtedness made the middle class particularly vulnerable to the collapse of the housing market at the end of the decade of the 2000s.

Another notable development was the large increase in the value of homes as a share of total assets from 2001 to 2007 and corresponding fall in the share of stocks. These two changes largely mirrored relative price movements over the period. Pension accounts as a share of total assets also fell off a bit from 2001 to 2007. Net equity in owner-occupied housing as a share of total assets fell from 24 percent in 1983 to 21 percent in 2007, reflecting rising mortgage debt on home owners' property, which grew from 21 to 35 percent.

Evidence of the middle-class squeeze is that for the middle three wealth quintiles, there was a huge increase in the debt-income ratio from 100 to 157 percent from 2001 to 2007 and an almost doubling of the debt-equity ratio from 32 to 61 percent. Moreover, total stocks as a share of total assets fell off from 13 to 7 percent. The debt-equity ratio was also much higher among the middle 60 percent of households in 2007, at 0.61, than among the top 1 percent (0.028) or the next 19 percent (0.121).

The mean wealth of African Americans was only 19 percent that of white families in 1983, and that ratio barely budged over the years from 1983 to 2007. The black home ownership rate did climb from 44 percent in 1983 to 49 percent in 2007, but their home ownership rate relative to white households was the same in 2007 as in 1983. The mean wealth of Hispanic households was also very low compared to non-Hispanic whites in 1983, a ratio of 0.16, but Hispanics did show gains relative to non-Hispanic whites, particularly over the years 2001 to 2007, and the ratio advanced to 0.26. The home ownership rate among Hispanic households also ascended from a meager 33 percent in 1983 to 49 percent in 2007, the same level as African Americans, and the ratio of home ownership rates between Hispanics and non-Hispanic whites advanced from 48 percent in 1983 to 66 percent in 2007.

Young households (under the age of 55) saw their relative wealth position deteriorate over the years 1983 to 2007. This development made young households particularly exposed to the joint collapse of the stock and housing markets at the end of the decade of the 2000s.

NOTES

1.   These figures are based on the Bureau of Labor Statistics hourly wage series. The source is Table B-47 of *Economic Report of the President, 2009*, available at http://www.gpoaccess.gov/eop/tables09.html. The source for all the data in this section is the *Economic Report of the President, 2009* unless otherwise indicated.

2.   The source is Table 935of the *2009 Statistical Abstract*, U.S. Bureau of the Census, available at http://www.census.gov/compendia/statab/.

3.   However, I exclude automobiles, which are included in the Federal Reserve Board definition of total assets, in order to be consistent with the national accounts, where purchases of vehicles are counted as expenditures, not savings.

4.   It should be noted that the income in each survey year (say 2007) is for the preceding year (2006 in this case).

5.   The residual group, American Indians and Asians, is excluded here because of its small sample size.

6.   The 1983 data do not permit an estimation of indirect stock ownership, so I exclude 1983 from the table.

BIBLIOGRAPHY

Modigliani, Franco, and Richard Brumberg. 1954. "Utility Analysis and the Consumption Function: An Interpretation of Cross-Section Data." In *Post-Keynesian Economics*, edited by K. Kurihara. New Brunswick, NJ: Rutgers University Press.

U.S. Council of Economic Advisers. 2009. *Economic Report of the President, 2009*. Washington, DC: U.S. Government Printing Office.

Chapter 4

The Geography of Poverty in the United States

William Levernier

Poverty rates within the United States vary significantly from one area to another. They are generally higher in rural areas than in urban areas (Lichter and Johnson 2006; Levernier 2003; Levernier, Partridge, and Rickman 2000) and, within metropolitan areas, are generally higher in the central cities than in the suburbs (Cushing and Zheng 2000; Levernier, Partridge, and Rickman 2000). Within an urban area, poverty rates of neighborhoods tend to be higher when the poverty rates of surrounding neighborhoods are high (Sampson and Morenoff 2006). Among rural counties, those located near metropolitan areas generally have lower poverty rates than those that are distant from metropolitan areas (Partridge and Rickman 2008), and those located adjacent to counties with relatively high poverty rates generally have higher poverty rates than those located adjacent to counties with relatively low poverty rates (Partridge and Rickman 2007). States and counties in the American South generally have relatively high poverty rates, while those in the Northeast generally have relatively low poverty rates. In short, there is tremendous geographic variation in poverty rates across the United States.

An especially problematic type of poverty is persistent poverty, which is defined to be a poverty rate of at least 20 percent for either three, four, or five consecutive decennial Census years, depending on the specific definition that is used. As with poverty rates at a particular point in time, persistent poverty also exhibits tremendous geographic variation. Persistent-poverty counties tend to be rural and are highly concentrated in four regions of the United States: the Southern Black Belt and Mississippi Delta; the Appalachian, Ozark, and Ouachita mountains of the Southern Highlands; the American Indian reservations of the Southwest and Northern Plains; and the Rio Grande Valley of the American Southwest (Beale 1996; Miller and Weber 2004; Nord 1997). Because of the long-term nature of this type of poverty, reducing it to an acceptable level is more difficult for policy makers and other poverty fighters than reducing the poverty rate in an area that is experiencing a high short-term poverty rate that is caused by a one-time economic disturbance in the area.

GEOGRAPHIC POVERTY PATTERNS FROM THE 2009 U.S. POVERTY ESTIMATES

The official poverty rate in the United States indicates the percentage of persons whose incomes are below a poverty threshold that is established by the federal government. The threshold for a particular family depends on whether or not the householder is under the age of 65, the size of the family, and the number of children in the family who are under 18 years of age. If a family's income is below the threshold for its age-size composition, all members of the family are considered to be in poverty.

The most reliable and most accurate measures of poverty rates in the United States are computed once every 10 years in the decennial Census. For the intervening years, the U.S. Census Bureau conducts estimates of poverty rates and reports them in their Small Area Income and Poverty Estimates (http://www.census.gov/did/www/saipe/). The 2009 estimates, for states and counties, are summarized in Table 4.1 and Table 4.2. In Table 4.3, poverty rates of counties located in metropolitan areas and those located outside of metropolitan areas are compared. The tables indicate the existence of a strong geographic pattern in poverty rates at both the state and county level, and also reveal large differences between metropolitan and nonmetropolitan counties.

Table 4.1 reports the 2009 estimated poverty rates, by state, from the lowest rate to the highest. The District of Columbia is treated as a state in the table. It also indicates in which Census Region a state is located. Census Regions are groupings of states that subdivide the United States into four regions—Northeast, Midwest, South, and West. The 2009 estimated poverty rate for the United States as a whole was 14.3 percent.

Table 4.1
Poverty Rates, by State: 2009

State	Poverty Rate	Census Region
New Hampshire	8.6	Northeast
Alaska	9.1	West
Maryland	9.2	South
Connecticut	9.3	Northeast
New Jersey	9.4	Northeast
Wyoming	10.2	West
Massachusetts	10.3	Northeast
Hawaii	10.4	West
Virginia	10.6	South
Minnesota	10.9	Midwest
Delaware	11.2	South
Vermont	11.5	Northeast
North Dakota	11.7	Midwest
Utah	11.7	West
Iowa	11.8	Midwest
Rhode Island	12.0	Northeast
Nebraska	12.2	Midwest
Washington	12.3	West
Nevada	12.4	West
Wisconsin	12.4	Midwest
Pennsylvania	12.5	Northeast
Colorado	12.6	West
Maine	12.6	Northeast
Kansas	13.2	Midwest
Illinois	13.3	Midwest
California	14.2	West
New York	14.2	Northeast
South Dakota	14.2	Midwest
Oregon	14.3	West

(*continued*)

Table 4.1 (Continued)

State	Poverty Rate	Census Region
United States	14.3	**U.S.**
Idaho	14.4	West
Indiana	14.4	Midwest
Missouri	14.6	Midwest
Florida	15.0	South
Montana	15.0	West
Ohio	15.1	Midwest
Michigan	16.1	Midwest
Oklahoma	16.1	South
North Carolina	16.2	South
Arizona	16.5	West
Georgia	16.6	South
South Carolina	17.1	South
Texas	17.1	South
Tennessee	17.2	South
Alabama	17.5	South
District of Columbia	17.6	South
Louisiana	17.6	South
West Virginia	17.8	South
New Mexico	18.2	West
Kentucky	18.4	South
Arkansas	18.5	South
Mississippi	21.8	South

Data Source: U.S. Census Bureau, Small Area Estimates Branch, Table 1: 2009 Poverty and Median Income Estimates–Counties, http:/www.census.gov/did/www/saipe/data/.

There is substantial geographic variation in the state poverty rates. The rates range from a low of 8.6 percent in New Hampshire to a high of 21.8 percent in Mississippi. At the low end of the poverty distribution, five states have a poverty rate lower than 10 percent—Alaska, Connecticut, New Hampshire, New Jersey, and Maryland. At the high end of the distribution, 11 states have a poverty rate higher than 17 percent—Alabama, Arkansas, District of Columbia, Kentucky, Louisiana, Mississippi, New Mexico, South Carolina, Tennessee, Texas, and West Virginia. Each of the high-poverty states, except New Mexico, is located in the South Census Region.

There is also substantial variation in the state-level poverty rates across Census Regions. The average state poverty rate is 11.2 percent for the 9 states in the Northeast, 13.2 percent for the 13 states in the West, 13.3 percent for the 12 states in the Midwest, and 16.2 percent for the 17 states in the South. Comparing each state's poverty rate to the U.S. poverty rate, 29 states have a rate less than or equal to that of the United States while 22 states have a rate greater than the United States. Of the 29 states that have a lower rate than the United States, 9 are in the Northeast, 9 are in the West, 8 are in the Midwest, and 3 are in the South. Of the 22 states that have a higher rate, 4 are in the West, 4 are in the Midwest, and 14 are in the South. These geographic poverty patterns indicate that a state in the Northeast, West, or Midwest Census Regions is more likely to have a poverty rate that is below the U.S. poverty rate than above the U.S. poverty rate. Conversely, a state in the South Census Region is more likely to have a poverty rate that is above the national rate than below the national rate.

Table 4.2 summarizes the poverty status of the nation's 3,142 counties and independent cities. In Alaska, counties and independent cities are replaced by designations called Boroughs and Census Areas. In the remainder of this analysis, independent cities, boroughs, and Census Areas are treated as counties. There are 217 counties and independent cities in the Northeast, 447 in the West, 1,055 in the Midwest, and 1,423 in the South. The poverty rates range from a high of 62.0 percent in Ziebach County, South Dakota, to a low of 3.1 percent in Los Alamos, New Mexico. The three highest poverty rate counties in the nation are the only counties to have a poverty rate that exceeds 50 percent. Two of these counties, Ziebach County and Shannon

Table 4.2

Percentage of Counties in Each Poverty Rate Class, by Census Region: 2009

Poverty Rate	Midwest	Northeast	South	West
20% or more	9.7	2.3	40.3	15.2
15–19.9%	24.2	19.8	33.6	31.1
10–14.9%	48.0	50.2	19.6	37.1
Less than 10%	18.2	27.6	6.5	16.5
Total	100.0	100.0	100.0	100.0

Data Source: U.S. Census Bureau, Small Area Estimates Branch, Table 1: 2009 Poverty and Median Income Estimates—Counties, http:/www.census.gov/did/www/saipe/data/.

County, South Dakota, are located on Native American Indian reservations. Ziebach County is on the Cheyenne River Indian Reservation and Shannon County, with a poverty rate of 51.6 percent, is on the Pine Ridge Indian Reservation.

Some strong geographic patterns also emerge from Table 4.2. First, the South has a substantially higher percentage of counties with a poverty rate of at least 20 percent than the other three regions. In the South, approximately 40 percent of the counties have a poverty rate of at least 20 percent. The next highest region is the West with 15.2 percent of its counties having a poverty rate of at least 20 percent, followed by the Midwest, at 9.7 percent, and the Northeast, at 2.3 percent. Second, the Northeast has a substantially higher percentage of counties with a poverty rate of less than 10 percent than the other regions. In the Northeast, 27.6 percent of the counties have a poverty rate of less than 10 percent. The next highest region is the Midwest with 18.2 percent of its counties having a poverty rate of less than 10 percent, followed by the West, at 16.5 percent, and the South, at 6.5 percent. It is apparent that a county in the Northeast is much more likely to have a very low poverty rate than a county in another region of the county. A county in the South, conversely, is much more likely to have a very high poverty rate than a county in another region.

Table 4.3 examines the poverty status of the nation's counties according to whether or not they are a metropolitan or nonmetropolitan county. Metropolitan areas in the United States are designated by the Office of Management and Budget and are called Metropolitan Statistical Areas (MSAs). MSAs consist of one or more counties or

Table 4.3

Percentage of Counties in Each Poverty Rate Class, by MSA Status: 2009

Poverty Rate	MSA Counties	Non MSA Counties
20% or more	12.0	30.1
15–19.9%	27.6	29.9
10–14.9%	36.2	32.4
Less than 10%	24.1	7.5
Total	100.0	100.0
More than 30%	.55	5.09
Average Poverty Rate (%)	13.9	17.5

Data Source: U.S. Census Bureau, Small Area Estimates Branch, Table 1: 2009 Poverty and Median Income Estimates—Counties, http:/www.census.gov/did/www/saipe/data/.

independent cities that "have at least one urbanized area of 50,000 or more population, plus adjacent territory that has a high degree of social and economic integration with the core as measured by commuting ties" (Office of Management and Budget, 2). There are currently 366 MSAs containing 1,097 counties and independent cities. Metropolitan areas vary greatly in their 2009 estimated population, ranging from approximately 19 million people in the New York–Northern New Jersey-Long Island, NY-NJ-PA MSA to approximately 55,000 people in the Carson City, NV MSA (U.S. Census Bureau).

A large discrepancy between the poverty rates of counties contained in MSAs and those not contained in MSAs is revealed in Table 4.3. Counties located in metropolitan areas generally have lower poverty rates than nonmetropolitan counties, as revealed by their average poverty rates. The average poverty rate of metropolitan counties is 13.9 percent while that of nonmetropolitan counties is 17.5 percent. In terms of poverty classes, about 30 percent of the nonmetropolitan counties have a poverty rate of at least 20 percent, compared to only 12 percent of the metropolitan counties. A nonmetropolitan county is therefore about two and a half times more likely than a metropolitan county to have a poverty rate in excess of 20 percent. At the other extreme, about 24 percent of the metropolitan counties have a poverty rate of less than 10 percent, compared to only 7.5 percent of the non-metropolitan counties. A metropolitan county is therefore about three times more likely than a nonmetropolitan county to have a poverty rate of less than 10 percent. An even starker picture of nonmetropolitan counties emerges when we consider those counties that have a poverty rate that exceeds 30 percent. Slightly more than one-half of 1 percent of the metropolitan counties have a poverty rate at this level, compared to 5.1 percent of the nonmetropolitan counties. A nonmetropolitan county is therefore approximately nine times more likely than a metropolitan county to have a poverty rate that exceeds 30 percent. Clearly, a metropolitan county is much more likely to have a low poverty rate than a nonmetropolitan county and is much less likely to have a high poverty rate.

FACTORS AFFECTING THE GEOGRAPHIC VARIATION IN POVERTY RATES

The discussion so far indicates that there is tremendous geographic variation in poverty rates across the United States. Much of the variation in poverty rates among different areas of the United States can be attributed to differences in the characteristics among the areas, however, rather than to differences in the location of the areas, per se. Some areas possess characteristics that promote low poverty rates while others possess characteristics that promote high poverty rates. Prior research on this issue indicates that the characteristics of an area that most influence its poverty rate can be classified into four broad categories: (1) the demographic characteristics of the area's population, (2) the economic characteristics of the area, (3) the educational attainment attributes of the area's population, and (4) the locational characteristics of the area.

The demographic characteristics include such factors as the percentage of the population that is elderly or young, the percentage of the population that is African American or minority, the percentage of the population that is foreign-born, and the percentage of the population that moved to the area from another location. The economic characteristics of an area include such factors as the labor force participation rate, the percentage of the adult population that is employed, the percentage of employed workers that work in manufacturing or other goods-producing industries, employment growth, and the percentage of an area's income that is attributable to government transfer programs. The educational attributes of an area include such factors as the percentage of the adult population that are high school dropouts or the percentage of the adult population that graduated from college. The locational characteristics include such factors as whether the area is in an MSA, whether the area is located adjacent to an MSA if it is not in an MSA, or whether the area is adjacent to high-poverty areas (Levernier, Partridge, and Rickman 2000; Partridge and Rickman 2007; Levernier 2003; Levernier and White 1998).

An understanding of which factors most strongly contribute to high poverty rates and how these factors vary across geographic space helps explain the geographic variation in poverty rates and allows policy makers and other poverty fighters to identify which areas possess the characteristics that are commonly associated with high poverty rates and which areas possess the characteristics that are commonly associated with low poverty rates. It further helps policy makers to devise effective strategies that reduce high poverty rates by identifying the characteristics of high-poverty areas that they should focus on changing.

Models to predict the poverty rate of a particular type of area, usually a county or state, have been widely employed by economists and other social scientists seeking to explain the variation in poverty rates across areas of the United States. Levernier, Partridge, and Rickman (2000) developed a model to predict family poverty rates across U.S. counties using data from the 1990 decennial Census. They report that the family poverty rates are highest for nonmetropolitan counties, followed by central-city counties and suburban counties. They also report that there are major differences in the characteristics of the different types of counties. Some of the major differences are that the population of nonmetropolitan counties is much smaller than the population of metropolitan counties; the labor force participation rate for both males and females is much lower in nonmetropolitan counties than in metropolitan counties; the employment growth is lower in nonmetropolitan counties than in metropolitan counties; the nonmetropolitan counties have a lower share of their adult population that graduated from college than metropolitan counties; the metropolitan counties have a lower share of their population that is retirement age than nonmetropolitan counties; and the population of nonmetropolitan counties is less mobile in terms of their ability to move to a different county than the population of metropolitan counties. Partridge and Rickman (2008), using data from the 2000 decennial Census, further report that the average poverty rate of adjacent counties 10 years earlier is much higher for nonmetropolitan counties than for metropolitan counties; the employment growth in the early 1990s is higher in metropolitan counties than in nonmetropolitan counties; the percentage of the population that is foreign immigrants is higher for metropolitan counties than for nonmetropolitan counties; and the population of metropolitan counties has a higher level of educational attainment than the population of nonmetropolitan counties.

In a related study, Levernier (2003) examines differences in poverty rates between metropolitan and nonmetropolitan counties in the American South, again using data from the 1990 decennial Census. He, too, reports that poverty rates are substantially higher for nonmetropolitan counties than for metropolitan counties and determines that there are substantial differences in the characteristics of metropolitan and nonmetropolitan counties. Some of the major differences are that the percentage of the population that is retirement age is lower in metropolitan counties than in nonmetropolitan counties; the percentage of the population that immigrated to the United States from another nation is larger in metropolitan counties than in nonmetropolitan counties; the population of nonmetropolitan counties is less mobile than the population of metropolitan counties; the proportion of the adult population that are high school dropouts is much higher in nonmetropolitan counties than in metropolitan counties; the labor force participation rate for both males and females is much higher in metropolitan counties than in nonmetropolitan counties; and the percentage of the adult population that is employed is larger in metropolitan counties than in nonmetropolitan counties. Levernier and White (1998), in a study that compares poverty rates in counties located in Georgia's Black Belt region to Georgia counties located outside the Black Belt region, find that the racial composition of the population differs between counties inside the Black Belt and those outside the Black Belt; the percentage of families that are female headed is higher in the Black Belt counties than in those outside the Black Belt; and the percentage of the adult population that is employed is lower in counties inside the Black Belt than in those outside the Black Belt.

Not surprisingly, these differences in characteristics across areas contribute strongly to the geographic variation in poverty rates across the United States. Typically, the differences account for virtually all of the variation in poverty rates among areas. Levernier, Partridge, and Rickman (2000), in their study that compares family poverty rates in metropolitan counties to nonmetropolitan counties, report that the average poverty rate of metropolitan counties is 5.38 percentage points lower than that of nonmetropolitan counties. They also report that the average poverty rate of suburban counties in metropolitan areas is 6.46 percentage points lower than that of nonmetropolitan counties, and the average poverty rate of counties that contain the central city of a metropolitan area is 3.93 percentage points lower than that of nonmetropolitan counties. They find, however, that if all types of counties had the same characteristics, the average poverty rate of suburban counties would be only 2.2 percentage points lower than that of nonmetropolitan counties and that the average poverty rate of central city counties would be only 2.8 percentage points lower.

In related studies, Levernier and White (1998), in their study of poverty in Georgia's Black Belt region, report that the average family poverty rate of counties located inside the Black Belt is 3.31 percentage points higher than that of counties located outside the Black Belt. They find, however, that if counties inside the Black Belt had the same characteristics as counties outside the Black Belt, the average poverty rate of counties inside the Black Belt would be about 1.48 percentage points *lower* than that of counties outside the Black Belt. Levernier (2003), in his analysis of poverty in counties in the American South, reports that the average family poverty rate of metropolitan counties is 7.21 percentage points lower than that of nonmetropolitan counties. He finds, however, that if the two groups of counties had the same characteristics, the average poverty rate of metropolitan counties would be less than 1 percentage point lower than that of nonmetropolitan counties.

These findings indicate that it is differences in the characteristics of areas and not their location that brings about geographic differences in poverty rates. Areas with high poverty rates tend to have more of the characteristics that promote poverty and less of the characteristics that reduce poverty than areas with low poverty rates. The findings suggest that policies to reduce the geographic variation in poverty should be directed at reducing the geographic variation in the characteristics that affect poverty rates.

GEOGRAPHIC POVERTY IN A LARGE AMERICAN CITY: THE CASE OF CHICAGO

While the discussion so far has focused on examining poverty patterns using states or counties as the unit of observation, poverty can also be examined using a single urban area as the unit of observation. Sampson and Morenoff (2006) examine the persistence of poverty in urban Chicago neighborhoods during the 1970 to 1990 period. The key question they seek to answer is "whether and to what extent does the geographic concentration of poverty become increasingly entrenched in certain urban neighborhoods" (Sampson and Morenoff 2006, 176). One of their major findings is that there is substantial poverty rate variation among Chicago's neighborhoods and that "once a neighborhood passes a certain threshold of poverty or racial composition, any further change is likely to be in the direction of it becoming increasingly poor and black" (Sampson and Morenoff 2006, 176).

In their study they divide Chicago into 343 neighborhoods. The neighborhoods are constructed from 847 Census tracts, which are small, relatively permanent statistical subdivisions of a county. They find that neighborhoods that were poor in 1970 generally continued to be poor in 1990, and also find that there was dramatic growth in neighborhood poverty between 1970 and 1990. Another issue that is considered is the extent to which neighborhoods move from one poverty class to another over time. To examine this issue each neighborhood is assigned to one of six poverty rate classes—0 to 4.9 percent, 5 to 9.9 percent, 10 to 19.9 percent, 20 to 29.9 percent, 30 to 39.9 percent, and 40 percent or more—for each Census year, and the number of neighborhood movements between poverty classes from one Census year to the next is measured. They find that overall "neighborhoods tended to either stay in the same poverty category or to move to a higher poverty category," and that the neighborhoods that were relatively poor in 1970 were generally the ones that experience the largest increases in their poverty rate over the 1970 to 1990 period (Sampson and Morenoff 2006, 182). The change in a neighborhood's poverty rate is also affected by its racial composition, with poor black neighborhoods being the most likely to experience increasing poverty (Sampson and Morenoff 2006, 183).

The issue of spatial dependence, the extent to which the change in a neighborhood's poverty rate is affected by the change in the poverty rate of surrounding neighborhoods, is also considered in the study. This is a potentially important issue because if a neighborhood's poverty status is strongly affected by the poverty status of surrounding neighborhoods, the ability of a neighborhood to improve its poverty status will necessarily be limited. Specifically, if spatial dependence exists, changing the characteristics of a neighborhood without changing the characteristics of surrounding high-poverty neighborhoods will have a much smaller effect on the neighborhood's poverty status than would be the case if spatial dependence were absent. This implies, of course, that poverty-fighting policies need to be directed at groups of contiguous neighborhoods rather than at single neighborhoods. The study reveals that the change in a neighborhood's poverty rate is significantly affected by the level of its initial black population and by changes in the poverty rate of surrounding neighborhoods (Sampson and Morenoff 2006, 189). Proximity to neighborhoods that are becoming increasingly impoverished over time increases the likelihood that a neighborhood will itself become more impoverished over time.

Several important geographic-related conclusions regarding urban poverty—at least for Chicago—emerge from the study. Among them are:

1. Neighborhood poverty is persistent over time, with the initial poverty conditions determining later poverty conditions (Sampson and Morenoff 2006, 199).
2. Once a neighborhood exceeds a certain percentage black population or a certain poverty rate, future change is in the direction of

increasing racial segregation and increasing poverty (Sampson and Morenoff 2006, 199).

3. Black neighborhoods are especially likely to experience rapid increases in their poverty rate over time (Sampson and Morenoff 2006, 199).

4. Spatial proximity to change in poverty matters as much as the internal characteristics of a neighborhood, including its initial level of poverty (Sampson and Morenoff 2006, 200).

PERSISTENT-POVERTY REGIONS IN THE UNITED STATES

The issue of persistent poverty has received substantial attention from economists, geographers, and other social scientists engaged in the study of poverty in recent years. Persistent-poverty regions are areas of the United States that suffer from long-term stubbornly high poverty rates. This type of poverty is a more difficult problem for policy makers to solve than the type of poverty where an area experiences a high poverty rate for a relatively short period due to a temporary economic downturn in the area. Researchers have used varying definitions of persistent poverty. Depending on which definition is used, an area is considered to experience persistent poverty if its poverty rate has been at least 20 percent for each of the last three, four, or five decennial Census years.

Although persistent-poverty counties can be located within metropolitan areas, as stated earlier most are rural and are highly concentrated in four regions of the United States: the Southern Black Belt and Mississippi Delta; the Appalachian, Ozark, and Ouachita mountains of the Southern Highlands; the American Indian reservations of the Southwest and Northern Plains; and the Rio Grande Valley of the American Southwest (Beale 1996; Miller and Weber 2004; Nord 1997). In his examination of persistent-poverty counties during the 1960–90 period, Beale (1996) notes that only about one-eighth of the United States' persistent-poverty counties lie outside these four regions (Beale 1996, 31). In each of these four persistent-poverty regions, an overall high poverty rate for a particular demographic group is the cause of the high poverty rate for the region. In the Southern Black Belt and Mississippi Delta, it is an overall high poverty rate among the black population; in the Appalachian, Ozark, and Ouachita mountains of the Southern Highlands, it is an overall high poverty rate among the white population; in the American Indian reservations of the Southwest and Northern Plains, it is an overall high poverty rate among the Native American population; and in the Rio Grande Valley, it is an overall high poverty rate among the Hispanic population.

Miller and Weber (2004) examine how persistent poverty at the county level is affected by a county's urban status. The urban status of a county is based on the Urban Influence Codes developed by the Economic Research Service, an agency within the U.S. Department of Agriculture. The five urban status classifications used in the study are: (1) nonmetropolitan county not adjacent to a metropolitan area, (2) nonmetropolitan county adjacent to a small metropolitan area, (3) nonmetropolitan county adjacent to a large metropolitan area, (4) a county located in a small metropolitan area, and (5) a county located in a large metropolitan area. There are 382 counties in the nation that they identify as experiencing persistent poverty, using the definition of a poverty rate of at least 20 percent in five consecutive decennial Census years. A strong relationship between persistent-poverty status and urban status is revealed in the study. Ninety-five percent of persistent-poverty counties are located outside of a metropolitan area, and 16 percent of the nation's nonmetropolitan counties are persistent-poverty counties versus only 2 percent of its metropolitan counties (Miller and Weber 2004, 1). Among the nonmetropolitan counties, nonadjacent counties are the most likely to be persistent-poverty counties, followed by counties adjacent to a small metropolitan area and then by counties adjacent to a large metropolitan area. Metropolitan counties are much less likely to experience persistent poverty than nonmetropolitan counties, with counties in large metropolitan areas being less likely to experience persistent poverty than counties in small urban areas (Miller and Weber 2004, 2). Counties that are in the most remote rural places are the ones that are most likely to be persistently impoverished.

Miller and Weber (2004) also find some important urban status characteristics of the 189 counties that were persistently impoverished during the 1960 to 1990 period, but then exited their persistent-poverty status between 1990 and 2000. They note that these counties had lower poverty rates in 1990 than those that remained persistently impoverished. This suggests that it is easier for a county to exit persistent-poverty status when the county's poverty rate is relatively close to the 20 percent threshold than when its poverty rate is substantially above the threshold. They also note that metropolitan counties were more likely to exit persistent-poverty status than nonmetropolitan counties, and that nonmetropolitan adjacent counties were more likely to exit persistent-poverty status than nonmetropolitan nonadjacent counties. In short, "it seems to be that the leavers are on the fringes of the persistent poverty region. Very few of the leavers are in the center of a concentration of persistent poverty status" (Miller and Weber 2004, 5).

Persistent poverty in the Black Belt region of the southeastern United States is examined in a recent study (University of Georgia 2002). The Black Belt region is one of the nation's poorest regions as "over half of the persistently poor counties in the U.S. are in the 11 southern states known as the Black Belt" (University of Georgia 2002, 5). The sustained high poverty rate of the region is largely attributed to its lack of ability to produce goods and services:

The basic engine for creating wealth in the Southeast Region is disadvantaged when compared with other economic regions and the nation as a whole. The economy of the rural South is at risk because it lacks an able workforce and the tools with which to build wealth. This situation will continue to worsen unless and until the region gains the innate ability to produce and sustain wealth through the creation of goods and series in manufacturing, service, and/or agriculture. (University of Georgia 2002, 8)

While governmental efforts intended to reduce poverty in the region have been made in the past, they have been largely ineffective. Two possible reasons for the ineffectiveness of these efforts are offered:

1. "Much of the economic success of the South has relied on minimum-wage or low-skill jobs. As a result job growth has often not translated into income growth" (University of Georgia 2002, 10).
2. "Past policies have often left people dependent on transfer payments, resulted in intergenerational poverty, failed to support public schools and preparation of a skilled and able work force, and ignored the need for a livable wage" (University of Georgia 2002, 10–11).

POTENTIAL POLICIES TO REDUCE GEOGRAPHIC VARIATION IN POVERTY RATES AND CONCLUDING REMARKS

We have seen that poverty rates across the United States vary greatly. Poverty rates are generally higher in nonmetropolitan areas than in metropolitan areas and, within metropolitan areas, are generally higher in the central cities than in the suburbs. Within urban areas, poverty rates of neighborhoods also tend to be higher when the poverty rates of surrounding neighborhoods are relatively high and when the percentage of their population that is black is relatively high. Among rural counties, those located near metropolitan areas generally experience lower poverty rates than those that are distant from metropolitan areas. States and counties in the American South experience higher poverty rates than those in other regions of the country, while states and counties in the northeastern United States experience lower poverty rates than those in other regions.

We have also seen that a geographic pattern exists for counties that experience persistently high poverty rates. These counties tend to be rural and are concentrated in the Southern Black Belt and Mississippi Delta; in the Appalachian, Ozark, and Ouachita mountains of the Southern Highlands; in the American Indian reservations of the Southwest and Northern Great Plains; and in the Rio Grande Valley.

To effectively combat poverty in a particular area, policy makers must first identify which characteristics of the area are causing its poverty rate to be high. Once they have done this, they can devise and implement policies to adjust the characteristics in the appropriate direction. The geographic variation in poverty rates suggests that a set of "one-size-fits-all" policies designed to combat poverty probably will not be as effective as a set of policies designed specifically for a particular area. Because different high-poverty areas have different weaknesses in terms of their demographic, economic, and educational characteristics, policies designed to address these weaknesses will likely need to be area-specific. A policy that might be highly effective at reducing the poverty rate in the central county of a metropolitan area, for example, may not be as effective at reducing the poverty rate in an isolated nonmetropolitan county.

Levernier (2003) suggests five policies to combat poverty in the American South. First, policies that lower the high school dropout rate should be implemented. Such policies will likely require that local school boards and elected officials encourage students to stay in school through a reward system and, at the same time, discourage students from dropping out of school through a punishment system. Legislators in some states, for example, have either discussed or enacted laws that would prohibit a high school-age person who drops out of high school from obtaining a driver's license. Second, actions must be taken to attract jobs, especially manufacturing jobs, to impoverished areas.

Policy makers may be able to make their area more attractive to manufacturing firms through tax breaks and infrastructure (i.e., highways, water, sewage, etc.) provision. Improving the quality of the area's labor force, which could be accomplished by reducing the high school dropout rate as suggested in the first policy, is also likely to make the region more attractive to manufacturing firms that are considering locating in the region. Third, policy makers in an area should strive to increase the labor force participation rate, especially among females. This may require that policy makers reduce obstacles to females working, such as the lack of affordable child care, by providing tax credits, vouchers, or subsidies for the provision of child care. Fourth, policy makers should develop policies that encourage people who currently reside in other regions to migrate to their area. An in-flow of residents from other areas generally has the effect of reducing the poverty rate of the area to which they move. Lastly, and perhaps most importantly, policies that reduce the percentage of families that are female headed with no husband present are likely to reduce a region's poverty rate. Some prior studies have found that the effect of female-headed families on poverty rates is stronger than that of the characteristics related to the other four suggested policies, implying that a given reduction in the percentage of female-headed families will have a stronger poverty-reducing effect than an equal change in the other characteristics (see Levernier, Partridge, and Rickman 2000; Levernier 2003). Gibbs (2003) also argues that poverty-fighting policies directed toward the Southern Black Belt must encourage a higher labor force participation rate and higher levels of educational attainment, which, of course, would be accomplished if the high school dropout rate were reduced. Additionally, Whitener and Parker (2007), in suggesting policies to promote economic development in rural areas of the United States, argue that policy makers should increase investment in infrastructure, such as water/sewer facilities, highways, railroads, telecommunication facilities, and air transportation facilities (Whitener and Parker 2007, 64).

Levernier (2003) further finds, however, that some of the suggested policies herein are likely to result in a smaller reduction in the poverty rate in metropolitan counties than in nonmetropolitan counties, while others are likely to result in a larger reduction in the poverty rate in metropolitan counties. Specifically, he finds that policies that reduce the high school dropout rate or attract manufacturing jobs to an area are likely to reduce the poverty rate by a smaller amount in metropolitan counties than in nonmetropolitan counties. Conversely, policies that reduce the percentage of families that are female headed are likely to reduce the poverty rate by a larger amount in metropolitan counties than in nonmetropolitan counties.

BIBLIOGRAPHY

Beale, Calvin L. 1996. "The Ethnic Dimensions of Persistent Poverty in Rural and Small-Town Areas." In Racial/Ethnic Minorities in Rural Areas: Progress and Stagnation: 1980–1990. Economic Research Service, U.S. Department of Agriculture. 26–32. http://www.ers.usda.gov/publications/aer731/aer731b.pdf.

Cushing, Brian, and Buhong Zheng. 2000. "Re-evaluating Differences in Poverty Among Central City, Suburban, and Nonmetropolitan Areas of the US." *Applied Economics* 32: 653–60.

Gibbs, Robert M. 2003. "Reconsidering the Southern Black Belt." *The Review of Regional Studies* 33: 254–63.

Levernier, William. 2003. "An Analysis of Poverty in the American South: How Are Metropolitan Areas Different from Nonmetropolitan Areas?" *Contemporary Economic Policy* 21: 372–82.

Levernier, William, Mark D. Partridge, and Dan S. Rickman. 2000. "The Causes of Regional Variation in U.S. Poverty: A Cross-County Analysis." *Journal of Regional Science* 40: 473–97.

Levernier, William, and John B. White. 1998. "The Determination of Poverty in Georgia's Plantation Belt: Explaining the Differences in Measured Poverty Rates." *American Journal of Economics and Sociology* 57: 47–70.

Lichter, Daniel T., and Kenneth M. Johnson. 2006. "The Changing Spatial Concentration of America's Rural Poor Population." National Poverty Center Working Paper #06-33. http://www.npc.umich.edu/publications/u/working_paper06-33.pdf.

Miller, Kathleen K., and Bruce A. Weber. 2004. "How Do Persistent Poverty Dynamics and Demographics Vary across the Rural-Urban Continuum?" *Measuring Rural Diversity Policy Series* 1: 1–7.

Nord, Mark. 1997. "Overcoming Persistent Poverty—and Sinking into It: Income Trends in Persistent-Poverty and Other High-Poverty Rural Counties, 1989–94." *Rural Development Perspectives* 12: 2–10.

Office of Management and Budget, OMB Bulletin 09-01, attachment, http://www.whitehouse.gov/sites/default/files/omb/assets/omb/bulletins/fy2009/09-01.pdf.

Partridge, Mark D., and Dan S. Rickman. 2007. "Persistent Rural Poverty: Is It Simply Remoteness and Scale?" *Journal of Agricultural Economics* 29: 430–36.

Partridge, Mark D., and Dan S. Rickman. 2008. "Distance from Urban Agglomerations Economies and Rural Poverty." *Journal of Regional Science* 48: 285–310.

Sampson, Robert J., and Jeffrey D. Morenoff. 2006. "Spatial Dynamics, Social Processes, and the Persistence of Poverty in Chicago's Neighborhoods." In *Poverty Traps*, edited by Samuel Bowles, Steven Durlauf, and Karla Hoff, 176–203. New York: Russell Sage Foundation.

University of Georgia, Carl Vinson Institute of Government. 2002. "It's a Matter of Wealth: Dismantling Persistent Poverty in the Southeastern United States." http://www.poverty.uga.edu/docs/SE_Report.pdf.

U.S. Census Bureau. "Table 1. Annual Estimates of the Population of Metropolitan and Micropolitan Statistical Areas: April 1, 2000 to July 1, 2009." http://www.census.gov/popest/metro/CBSA-est2009-annual.html.

Whitener, Leslie A., and Tim Parker. 2007. "Policy Options for a Changing Rural America." *Amber Waves* 5: 58–65. Economic Research Service, U.S. Department of Agriculture. http://www.ers.usda.gov/AmberWaves/May07SpecialIssue/Features/Policy.htm.

Part II

Inequality and Mobility

Chapter 5

Do We Face a Permanently Divided Society?

Isabel V. Sawhill[1]

This chapter builds on a large literature showing that (1) attitudes in the United States are different from attitudes in other countries; (2) lifetime incomes are more equally distributed than annual incomes because people are economically mobile; (3) however, neither intragenerational nor intergenerational mobility has *increased*, suggesting that lifetime income disparities are rising along with annual income disparities; and (4) the current recession is likely to exacerbate these trends because short-term job losses have longer-term consequences, especially for individuals at the bottom of the distribution.

The chapter further argues, somewhat more tentatively, that current disparities in the United States are likely to persist or even grow in the absence of a major shift in policy because societies with large gaps between the haves and have-nots replicate those gaps in future generations. That is, the further apart the rungs of the economic ladder are, the more difficult it will be for people to climb the ladder. In short, inequality eventually affects mobility.

This argument is bolstered by the observation that the new fault lines in American society revolve around education and family structure. The children of well-educated two-parent families have a large advantage over those in less well-educated single-parent families—advantages that, as I will show, are more important than ever to the mobility process.

I conclude that opportunity-enhancing policies such as improving education and strengthening families, along with the usual calls for more progressive taxes and benefit programs, need to play a role in changing current trajectories if we wish to avoid a permanently divided society.

PERSPECTIVES ON SOCIAL WELFARE

I want to start with a discussion of social welfare to see if we are all on the same page about what this means. This discussion will be familiar to economists but not necessarily to those from other disciplines.

Economists argue that a market economy under certain simplifying if unrealistic assumptions leads to an efficient set of outcomes, meaning that no reallocation of resources could produce a higher income or general level of welfare for society as a whole. This assertion can be proved mathematically (Arrow 1951, 507–32; Debreu 1959, 90–97). The case for government intervention then rests, first, on whether there are exceptions to the simplifying assumptions, such as imperfect competition or social costs, that interfere with the efficient operation of the market, and second, on whether the distribution of income (or other goods) that one begins with is considered "fair." If the distribution of income is not fair, then some people's dollar votes in the market will get greater weight than they should. (They may also get greater weight in political markets than they should—one basis for the criticism of the Supreme Court's recent decision in *Citizens United v. Federal Election Commission*.) But fairness is subjective. It depends on what the polity judges the proper distribution of those dollar votes to be. Most people reject the idea of a completely equal distribution because they understand that it would undermine incentives to produce income. But they may also reject the free-market distribution—that is, the particular distribution that results from some combination of genetic differences, family background, luck, and rewards for effort or talent.

As discussed in more detail later, different views about how much government should intervene in the process hinge, in part, on what people believe about why economic disparities exist and how much incentives matter. Those who believe that luck or the circumstances of one's birth determine where one ends up in the distribution are likely to favor greater intervention on the grounds that these are not under the control of the individual. Those who believe that effort and talent matter more and that society needs to reward those who make good choices will have a different view.

WHY MARKETS DO NOT PRODUCE OPTIMAL DISTRIBUTIONAL OUTCOMES

To be more specific, advocates of greater social equality usually base their arguments on one of three arguments: the role of luck in the process, the social consequences of inequality, and/or their own ethical preferences.

The Role of Luck

Not everyone is born equal or begins life at the same starting line. And as John Rawls famously argued, we should be prepared to imagine what kind of society we would want to inhabit if we did not know what our own position in that society was going to be—and specifically, I would argue, our genetic endowments and the kind of family and country into which we are born and raised (Rawls 1971, 136–42). Redistributive policies in this case are designed to compensate for these initial inequalities in a way that creates a more level playing field, more equal opportunity, and more social mobility. But the goal is not necessarily greater equality of incomes per se but rather greater opportunity for all to get ahead. As we shall see, when people believe that such opportunities exist, they are much less likely to favor further redistribution.

Adverse Social Consequences

Second, we may believe that too much inequality leads to less social cohesion, poorer health, or a political system too dominated by moneyed interests (Burtless and Jencks 2003; Wilkinson and Pickett 2006). These arguments, it should be noted, are instrumental or utilitarian rather than ethical in nature. Redistributive policies in this case rest on some notion of the need to create a better-functioning society. In this chapter I want to especially address the extent to which inequality feeds on itself as the result of its effects on people's ability and desire to get ahead.

Ethical Beliefs or Preferences

Even in a society in which initial inequalities were compensated and functioned well, one might feel that the outcomes of a market system were unfair. That is, even after attempts to level the playing field (for example, by providing universal access to education and health care) and for any extremes that lead to societal dysfunction (such as by not allowing wealthy individuals or corporations to "buy" elections and distribute rewards to themselves), we may remain dissatisfied with the final distribution of income (or other goods). In democratic societies, the public can and does give voice to such preferences.

WHERE DO OUR PREFERENCES COME FROM AND WHAT DO THEY DEPEND ON?

Evolutionary biologists have shown that a sense of altruism is built into our genetic makeup. Put most simply, a species that cooperates survives. Psychologists and economists have confirmed this insight based on experimental studies or observations of behavior that show that given a choice between a large sum of money that is very unevenly divided and a smaller sum that is more evenly divided, individuals will choose the latter (Fehr and Fischbacher 2003; Camerer and Thaler 1995; Rabin 1993). Although evolutionary biology may be the bedrock upon which altruistic preferences rest, it does not explain why some societies—and some individuals within each society—have stronger preferences for equality than others.

In the United States, the Gini index for households was 0.47 in 2008 (U.S. Census Bureau). The same index was 0.31 for Europe (Eurostat). These differences in inequality reflect, in turn, the larger role of government in Europe in redistributing income and regulating product and labor markets. In an attempt to explain this difference between the United States and Europe, Alesina and his coauthor hypothesize that the variation across countries in the amount of redistribution is related to beliefs about what causes inequality (Alesina and Angeletos 2005). In the United States, people believe that where you end up depends on your own efforts and skills—that is U.S. citizens believe they live in a meritocracy. In Europe, people believe that luck, family connections, birth, and corruption are more important determinants of success. As can be seen in Figure 5.1, for example, the proportion of people in the United States who believe that "people get rewarded for their effort" (61%) is dramatically higher than the median proportion (36%) who believe this in other advanced countries. Similarly, Alesina finds that the percentage of GDP devoted to social welfare expenditures is related to beliefs about the role of luck in accounting for success. Because differences in income in the United States are believed to be related to skill and effort and because social mobility is assumed to be high, inequality

Figure 5.1

Perceptions of Mobility and Inequality in Twenty-Seven Countries, 1999.

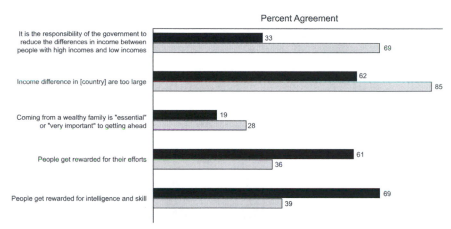

Source: Julia B. Isaacs, Isabel V. Sawhill, and Ron Haskins, *Getting Ahead or Losing Ground: Economic Mobility in America* (The Brookings Institution and The Pew Economic Mobility Project, 2008), figure 1, p. 37. Note: Brookings tabulations of data from the 1999 Social Inequality III module of the International Social Survey Program; data collected 1998–2001.

is more acceptable than in Europe and causes less unhappiness than it does in countries where the idea of meritocracy is far less prevalent (Alesina, DiTella, and MacCulloch 2004).

In another paper, Alesina digs more deeply into why preferences vary across individuals and not just across countries, focusing in this case on the United States. He finds that preferences for redistribution are greater among those who have poorer future prospects (objectively and subjectively), who believe that opportunity depends more on luck than merit, who have low current income, who have low education (holding income constant), and who are female, African American, young, and risk averse as well as more altruistic (Alesina and La Ferrara 2005).

The public in the United States has very mixed views on why some people are more successful than others. For example, a 2007 Pew study found that 62 percent of people disagree with the idea that success is largely determined by forces outside one's control, and a 2001 poll sponsored by National Public Radio, the Kaiser Family Foundation, and Harvard University's Kennedy School found that people are about evenly divided in ranking lack of personal effort or outside circumstances as the bigger cause of poverty (Pew Research Center for the

People and the Press 2007; National Public Radio, Kaiser Family Foundation, and Harvard University Kennedy School 2001). The public also clearly prefers opportunity-enhancing programs such as education and training and earmarked assistance for health care, child care, or nutrition to straight cash assistance (Haskins and Sawhill 2009, 19–31).

Other studies have noted that altruism depends, to some extent, on the ability of the donor to identify with the recipient. Put differently, altruism is selective. It depends not only on the perceived causes of someone else's misfortune (are they "deserving or undeserving") but on group ties or solidarity, which are harder to create in a large ethnically and racially diverse country such as the United States in comparison to the smaller and more homogeneous societies of Northern Europe (Haskins and Sawhill 2009, 19–22).

HOW SHOULD WE MEASURE THE CURRENT STATE OF DISTRIBUTIONAL EQUITY IN THE UNITED STATES?

This brings me to how we should assess the current distribution of income in the United States. Let me immediately admit that income is a rather narrow measure of the distribution of valuable goods in a society, but I follow the convention that it is more readily measured and more commonly used than other indicators that might be preferable on theoretical grounds (Sen 1992; Haveman 2009).

Taking income as a reasonable measure of one's economic position, the conventional approach has been to look at the distribution of income at a point in time (what I will henceforth call cross-sectional inequality) and to compare it to some earlier period of time or to benchmark it against the experience of other countries. Thus, it is commonly noted that the distribution of income in the United States has become more unequal in recent decades and that it is also more unequal than the distribution in some other advanced countries.

What this simple story about cross-sectional inequality misses is the fact that individuals change their economic position over time and that, in addition, people enter and leave the sample, with the result that we may be comparing apples to oranges. Any change in the composition of the population—for example, an influx of immigrants or a surge in the size of the elderly population or an increase in single-parent families—can affect the results. Most importantly, comments to the effect that the rich are getting richer or the poor are getting poorer suggest to the listener that we are following the same individuals or families over time and observing what has happened to their incomes when this is not at all what cross-sectional inequality is measuring. Instead, people move up and down the income ladder over time.

For this reason, it has long been recognized that incomes are more equally distributed over longer than over shorter periods of time. Consider a society in which everyone had identical incomes at each age but incomes grew with age and experience. Then, annual incomes would be very unequal but lifetime incomes would be identical (under certain simplifying assumptions about mortality, labor force participation, composition of the population, etc.). With some caveats about the effects of volatility on well-being, discussed later, the distribution of lifetime or permanent incomes seems like the right concept by which to judge the fairness of a society.

If this is the right concept, how do we measure it? Can we look at people's lifetime incomes and ask whether they are becoming more equally or unequally distributed over time? This would be possible only if we had full income histories on members of the population and also omitted from the analysis all those who are still alive—not a very interesting or appealing exercise.[2] Fortunately, there is an indirect way around this dilemma that involves combining data on short-term income inequality with data on income mobility.[3]

The important point is that the degree of inequality in a society will vary with the time period over which it is measured. If there is any earnings or income mobility over one's career or life cycle, lifetime or longer-term inequality will be less than shorter-term or annual inequality. Thus, in principle one cannot infer the state of inequality in a society without some attention to how much and what kind of mobility exists.[4]

As we will see in a subsequent section, greater income inequality (based on successive cross sections) has not been accompanied by greater mobility and may have been accompanied by less mobility. Thus, the argument that greater cross-sectional income inequality should be dismissed for this reason has to be rejected.[5]

Finally, I want to address two further complications. The first is the role of economic growth as a lubricant in the process. The second is the role of income volatility in affecting individual well-being.

In a society with no growth, one person's gains are another person's losses. Indeed, as growth (or "absolute mobility") has slowed, relative mobility has become more important. When the escalator is no longer moving, the only way to move up is to push past other people (McMurrer and Sawhill 1998; Isaacs, Sawhill, and Haskins 2008). Growth is the great lubricator of social mobility because it allows some to gain without imposing losses on others. In its absence, the losers will complain, and the political system will likely respond to those complaints. In an effort to protect the losers, the political response may then impose costs on the general population (e.g., barriers to trade). In the absence of growth, it may also be very difficult to redistribute income because such redistribution will impose absolute, not just relative, losses (e.g., in the form of tax increases and thus lower disposable incomes) on some portion of the population (Kuznets 1955; Friedman 2005).

Volatility also matters. Imagine two societies both of which had the same lifetime distribution of incomes across their populations but one of which delivered that income in a very uneven pattern. The uncertainty this created, and the need for either individual saving, borrowing, or social insurance to smooth this pattern, would then be an additional issue. Indeed, ignoring volatility seems like an especially grave omission in light of the effects of the current recession. If short-term deviations from some average level of income are of equal and offsetting value, as they would be (as a first approximation) in the context of no growth and no individual mobility, their main normative significance rests on the premise that people are risk averse. They cope with short-term swings in their incomes by saving, borrowing (dissaving), or buying insurance (or asking their government to provide it) in order to smooth their income over time. Behavioral economists have shown that people are loss averse; they do not weight a gain in income as much as a loss so volatility can indeed reduce their well-being (Tversky and Kahneman 1991). But in the real world, it is very hard to draw a line between short-term movements in income that are "bad" and those that are "good." Put differently, volatility may simply be the price of mobility. Moreover, the research on volatility has yet to determine whether it is due more to activities that are voluntarily chosen, such as a decision to retire early, or to activities that are imposed by external events, such as a recession. For both of these reasons, assessing the welfare losses associated with more volatility is difficult, and efforts to buffer people from modest shocks or those that reflect their own behavioral choices as opposed to, say, the effects of a recession or changes in employer practices can do more harm than good if carried too far.

In the next section I briefly review three bodies of empirical research that have focused respectively on cross-sectional income inequality, income mobility across generations and over the life cycle, and short-term fluctuation in income or income volatility. I will then return to the question of how cross-sectional inequality and year-to-year volatility in people's incomes affect their longer-term prospects.

INCOME INEQUALITY

Income inequality has been increasing dramatically in the United States since the late 1970s. The Gini coefficient, a measure of income dispersion across the entire distribution, has increased steadily, rising from 0.39 in 1970 to 0.47 in 2008. Another way to analyze income inequality is to look at the income shares of top earners. Thomas Piketty and Emmanuel Saez, in a seminal article on income inequality, calculate the income shares of top earners since 1913 using data from individual tax returns (Piketty and Saez 2003). After World War II, the top decile's income share stabilized at about 33 percent through the 1960s. However, since the 1970s, the top decile's income share has increased quite rapidly, rising to nearly 50 percent in 2007—a higher proportion than any year since 1917, surpassing even the peak achieved in the late 1920s (Saez 2009). The income share of the top 1 percent has fluctuated across time, but this group has experienced an especially dramatic rise in their share of income from about 9 percent in the 1960s and 1970s to over 23 percent in 2007 (see Figure 5.2).

It is not entirely clear how the current recession affects overall measures of income inequality. On the one hand, unemployment is concentrated among low-wage workers, which exacerbates inequality. However, as Saez notes, historically the top percentile's share of income has decreased during downturns, "as business profits, realized capital gains, and stock option exercises fall faster than average income." But Saez also finds that the top percentile's share of income quickly recovers after a recession in the absence of "drastic policy changes, such as financial regulation or significantly more progressive taxation" (Saez 2009). These trends at the top would, at least initially, reduce overall levels of inequality. Thus, the trends on the lower and upper ends of the income distribution seem to have competing and possibly offsetting effects on inequality in the short term. But as I will argue later, the recession is likely to have longer-term consequences that play special havoc with those experiencing job losses, a group that is concentrated at the bottom of the distribution.

Figure 5.2
Income Share of the Top 1 Percent, 1913–2007.

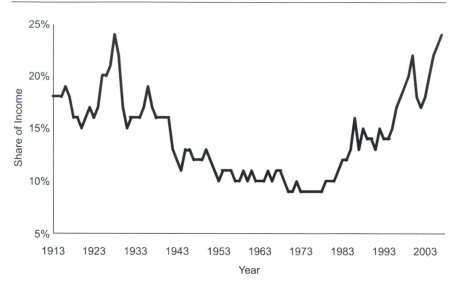

Source: Piketty and Saez, "Income Inequality in the United States, 1913–1998 (Tables and Figures Updated to 2007)," figure 2 (http:/elsa.berkeley.edu/~saez/TabFig2007.xls).
Note: Income is defined as market income (including capital gains but not government transfers).

The trends in inequality persist whether income is measured before taxes and transfers or after. According to the Congressional Budget Office, taxes and transfers reduce inequality quite substantially, and changes in government tax and transfer policy have contributed modestly to the observed trends in inequality measured on an after-tax and after-transfer basis between 1979 and 2007. A larger share of transfers now goes to the elderly for whom benefits, for the most part, are not related to income, and a larger share of taxes is collected through regressive payroll taxes rather than through progressive income taxes (Congressional Budget Office 2011; Piketty and Saez 2007).

When one incorporates the value of health insurance, which has greatly increased in value, this conclusion may have to be modified. In an interesting analysis, Burtless and Svaton (2010) show that if we counted the value of health care paid for by third parties (employers or government), income gaps between rich and poor and young and old would be reduced considerably. With a new health reform bill that will dramatically increase government subsidies for health care, their analysis takes on added meaning. As David Leonhardt (2010) of the

New York Times argued shortly after enactment of the health reform bill in March 2010, it "is the biggest attack on economic inequality since inequality began rising more than three decades ago." The bill extends Medicaid, provides subsidies to families of four making up to $88,000 a year, and pays for these extensions primarily by taxing the rich and cutting back Medicare, especially for those in private plans. A recent analysis by Burkhauser and Simon (2010) suggests that health care reform will increase the income of households in the lowest decile by over 8 percent ($797) and reduce overall income inequality by about 1 percent. This analysis does not take into account the extra taxes that will be paid by higher-income Americans, but it is a start on determining the likely effects. All told, it seems like health care reform should reduce inequality although this will not be reflected in most conventional measures.

Turning to other explanations for the trend, some of the growth in income inequality is due to changes in family composition (especially more single-parent families) and in marriage patterns (high earners marrying each other) but much is due to greater inequality in earnings (Burtless 2007).

The reasons for greater earnings inequality have been much researched, and the current consensus seems to be that most of the trend is related to skill-biased technological change (creating a big wage premium for the better educated) with such factors as unionization, minimum wages, trade, and immigration playing smaller although not insignificant roles. I have reviewed this literature elsewhere and will not repeat the details here (Haskins and Sawhill 2009).

INCOME MOBILITY

There is considerable income mobility in the United States. People move up and down the economic ladder both over the life course (intragenerationally) and across generations (intergenerationally).

One reason that incomes increase over time is because of economic growth. Normally, wages and incomes increase with productivity both during one's working career and from one generation to the next. In recent decades, economic growth has slowed and whatever prosperity we have had has been less broadly shared with the result that a rising tide is no longer any guarantee of higher incomes for most people. Between 1979 and 1999 (both business cycle peaks) real median family income increased by only 15 percent and stagnated thereafter even before the current recession began (Haskins and Sawhill 2009, 49–50). Slower and less broadly distributed growth has, in turn, focused greater attention on relative mobility—that is, the tendency for people to move up and down within the ranks or to change their position relative to others in the distribution.

While absolute mobility has slowed, the story about relative mobility is more complicated. Over the life course, a typical pattern is for individuals to have relatively low incomes when they are young and to experience rising incomes with age and years in the labor market. In addition, incomes may rise or fall as a result of an illness, a divorce, a second earner's decision to enter or leave the labor force, a business success or failure, or for other reasons. About 60 percent of all working-age families change income quintiles (a relative measure that does not include the effects of economic growth) over a 10-year period, and almost half of those in the bottom quintile at the beginning of each decade have moved into a higher quintile by the end of the decade. Moreover, these proportions have not changed much over the past five decades (see Figure 5.3 for data on the last three decades; the longer-term picture is reviewed in Haskins and Sawhill [2009, 69]). Thus, the best evidence suggests that intragenerational mobility is relatively high and unchanging. Moreover, it almost certainly reflects primarily the natural rise of earnings with age and experience.

Turning to intergenerational mobility, or the extent to which children's economic status is affected by their parents' income or socioeconomic status, we now have good data suggesting that people do move up and down the ladder but that it helps if you have the right parents. Although children born into middle-income families have a roughly equal chance of moving up or down the ladder once they become adults, those born into rich or poor families have a much higher probability of remaining rich or poor as adults. Roughly 40 percent of those born into the bottom or the top quintile of the income distribution will remain in that same quintile when they become adults (see Figure 5.4). Moreover, the United States has less intergenerational mobility than some other advanced nations, especially the Nordic countries where cross-sectional inequality is also much lower than in the United States (Haskins and Sawhill 2009, 66) (see Figure 5.5).

Studies of whether intergenerational mobility has increased or decreased in the United States in recent decades have come to quite different conclusions, with some suggesting it has decreased and some suggesting it has remained roughly constant. (No study has found an

Figure 5.3
Intragenerational Earnings Mobility.

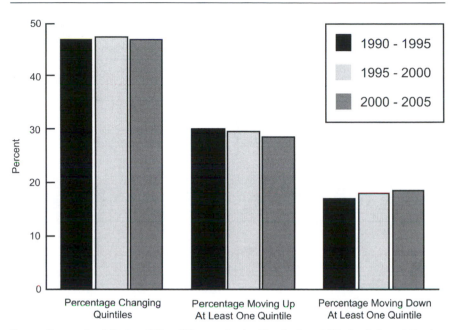

Source: Congressional Budget Office, "Changes in the Distribution of Workers' Annual Earnings between 1979 and 2009" (2009), figure 8, p. 27. The data are from the Social Security Administration's Continuous Work History Sample.

Note: The sample that CBO used consisted of people ages 25 to 54 with earnings that included wages and salaries, tips, and other forms of compensation but excluded self-employment income and deferred compensation. Earnings were adjusted for inflation using the price index for personal consumption expenditures. To examine mobility, CBO arrayed workers ages 25 to 54 by their earnings in the first year of a period and separated them into five equally sized segments (or quintiles). It did the same for workers ages 25 to 54 five years later. Workers who "changed quintiles" were in a different quintile in the later year than in the earlier year.

increase in mobility that might have compensated for the increase in cross-sectional inequality.) Our ability to measure these trends is constrained by the fact that we do not yet have data on the adult incomes of the youngest generations, who were born during the 1980s and 1990s when inequality was growing rapidly, especially at the top of the distribution (Sawhill 2008, 27–35).

It would be nice to understand why it is that one's economic prospects are strongly influenced by one's family of origin. As Bowles and Gintis have noted, the mechanisms are something of a black box, but as they and others have pointed out, education appears to be the

Figure 5.4
Family Income of Adult Children, by Parents' Family Income.

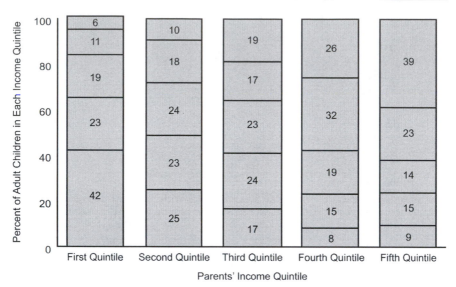

Source: Julia B. Isaacs, Isabel V. Sawhill, and Ron Haskins, *Getting Ahead or Losing Ground: Economic Mobility in America* (The Brookings Institution and The Pew Economic Mobility Project, 2008), figure 4, p. 19. *Note:* Columns may not add to 100 due to rounding. Family incomes are five-year averages from the Panel Study of Income Dynamics (PSID) for 1967–1971, when parents were 41 years old on average, and again in 1995–2002 when their adult children were 39 years old on average.

most important intervening variable linking parental status and their offspring's later success in life (Bowles, Gintis, and Groves 2005, 1–22; Hertz 2006; Harding et al. 2005, 100–144). Parents and children share genetic endowments. In addition, the family, school, and neighborhood environments of children born into more advantaged families help them get ahead in life. However, efforts to unpack this black box have not produced much consensus about the mechanisms involved or about their relative importance. At the same time, this literature raises some fundamental normative questions about how any society goes about providing more equality of opportunity. If the advantages that families provide their children (both genetically and environmentally) are key, and we are not willing as a society to interfere much in this private arena, then our ability to provide genuine opportunities for children born into less advantaged circumstances is somewhat limited (Jencks and Tach 2006; Harding et al. 2005). Access to high-quality education and health care or other community resources can help, of

Figure 5.5
Intergenerational Earnings Elasticity.

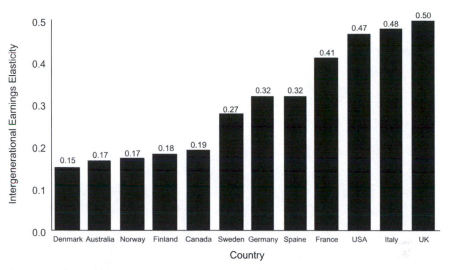

Source: Anna Cristina D'Addio, "Intergenerational Transmission of Disadvantage: Mobility or Immobility across Generations? A Review of the Evidence for OECD Countries," Working Paper No. 52 (OECD Social, Employment and Migration Working Papers, 2007).
Note: A lower level of earnings elasticity between fathers and sons equates with a higher level of intergenerational mobility. Earnings were adjusted for inflation using the price index for personal consumption expenditures. The percentage change in earnings is defined here as $((et - et-1)/((et + et-1)/2) * 100)$.

course, but may not be sufficient to move the needle very far toward greater equality of opportunity (Harding et al. 2005). In this case, some argue, the only alternative is to redistribute income or other valuable resources after the fact. One problem with this solution is that it has little political support in the United States, and is inconsistent with the public's strong belief in meritocracy.

INCOME VOLATILITY

Income mobility is normally measured over relatively long periods of time, such as a decade in the case of intragenerational mobility and an entire generation in the case of intergenerational mobility. Another body of literature has looked at very short-term fluctuations in income from year to year and found that such fluctuations have become more common than in the past. The best-known work on this topic is Jacob Hacker's and he finds that such volatility more or less doubled between 1969 and 2004 (Hacker 2008; Hacker and Jacobs 2008). Most other studies have found something similar, although the magnitude of the increase and the reasons for it have been open to debate. Karen Dynan and her colleagues (Dynan 2010) find that household income volatility increased by about one-third between the late 1960s and the middle of the current decade. Much of this volatility is driven by the fact that there are a relatively small proportion of households (e.g., 10%) that experience very large changes in their incomes (e.g., a 50% change). Some of these large changes are the result of a voluntary event (e.g., a decision to leave the labor force to start a family) and some are due to an involuntary event (e.g., loss of a job), making their normative significance somewhat unclear. In addition, a recent Congressional Budget Office analysis shows no trend in year-to-year earnings variability for either men or women since 1989 (Congressional Budget Office 2007). Whatever these income shocks are due to, they have raised questions about the adequacy of social insurance benefits such as unemployment or health insurance, parental leave policies, and the replacement of income in the case of disability or retirement. Moreover, almost all of the research cited here was done before the current recession began, and the kinds of income drops precipitated by that recession are likely to dwarf anything we have seen in recent decades.

HOW DOES AN INCREASE IN SHORT-TERM INCOME INEQUALITY AFFECT THE DISTRIBUTION OF LIFETIME INCOMES?

I next address the question of whether greater cross-sectional inequality affects the extent of mobility. Does a society with more poverty and inequality risk becoming one in which there is also less opportunity to join the middle class? When the rungs of the income ladder are further apart, does it become more difficult to climb the ladder?[6]

Hypothesis 1: Inequality in the annual distribution of income (or earnings) produces more mobility and thus less long-term inequality because people will try harder to win the prizes that success brings. In the face of more unequal rewards for performance, people will have a greater incentive to get a good education, work hard, and be successful on the job. For example, the argument is made that very high salaries for top executives may not be needed as much to incentivize those executives as to motivate those in middle management who aspire to be equally successful.

This thesis about the positive effects of inequality is by now well worn and much touted in conservative circles. Reviewing all of the empirical evidence relating to it is beyond the scope of this chapter, but I want to make at least a few comments on its current relevance. First, the effects are almost certainly nonlinear. That is, a top tax rate of 90 percent (a rate that actually existed in the United States for a period of time) has a very different effect than a top tax rate of 35 percent or even 50 percent. Second, the effects of any marginal rate may be largest when incomes are low rather than high, and some of the highest implicit marginal rates are imposed on low-income families when they lose benefits as their earned income rises. Raising taxes on high-income families but lowering them on those who might be called lower middle income could be a good mobility-enhancing strategy. For similar reasons, another good idea is policies that condition assistance on mobility-enhancing behaviors. Examples are the Earned Income Tax Credit, educational grants conditioned on school performance, and health insurance subsidies that vary with health behaviors such as exercise and diet.

Hypothesis 2: Cross-sectional income inequality produces less mobility and thus more long-term inequality because the rungs of the ladder are further apart. A high level of inequality in family incomes may make it more difficult for children from less privileged families to escape their circumstances. They experience less positive home environments and harsher parenting; they are more likely to live in troubled neighborhoods and to go to inferior schools; and they may have difficulty competing for good jobs with career paths that lead to higher earnings over time. Their more affluent peers may have all kinds of advantages, by contrast, from parents who emphasize learning and self-control at an early age to expensive universities and lucrative career contacts and knowledge of the world later in life.

More specifically, consider the current distribution of income across families with children. Not only is it less equal than in the past, it also has two other features worth noting. It is more highly correlated with education and it is more highly correlated with family structure than in an earlier era.

It is more correlated with education because the returns to education have risen sharply as the demand for skilled workers has outpaced the supply in recent decades. Thus, if we ranked today's parents by their earnings ability, we would also be ranking them, as a first approximation, by their education level. Yes, there are PhDs driving taxi cabs or operating ski lifts and there are high school dropouts who have created new computer technology, but the general tendency of earnings to rise sharply with education—and more sharply than in the past—is well documented (Goldin and Katz 2008).

On both theoretical and empirical grounds, education is widely seen as the most important mediating variable between a parent's status and a child's success. But in a world of almost universally available free public education, how do more educated parents help their children acquire more human capital? Some of the linkages are obvious. For genetic reasons, better educated parents tend to have more able children who then do better in the classroom than their less able counterparts. Their parents can also afford to live in better neighborhoods and enroll their children in better schools, send them to college, and afford the tuitions of elite schools. Many of these children do not have just one well-educated parent; they often have two. This greatly increases their family's potential income, which can be translated into actual income if the second parent works and into valuable time with children if he does not. Some of the reasons for the linkage between education and children's prospects are less obvious, harder to measure, and more controversial. But it is probably the case that the children of educated parents have been better socialized to be successful, to have different attitudes and aspirations, and to have spent time in environments where education occurs not just in but also *outside* of school (Loehlin 2005). Parental investments in the health care of their children may play a similar role with more advantaged parents having both the resources and the knowledge to respond more fully to childhood disabilities and illnesses that if left untreated can have lifelong consequences.

But if we were looking for another variable to rival education in explaining the distribution of income, it would be family structure (Haskins and Sawhill 2009). Those at one tail of the distribution are mostly less-educated single parents and those at the other tail are mostly highly educated married parents. Research by Adam Thomas and myself (2002) shows that the decline in marriage rates since the 1970s has had a very large effect on the proportion of children living in poverty even after adjusting for the obvious fact that marriage is selective of those parents with greater advantages. Indeed, what is striking is the extent to which family structure as well as education is the new dividing line between the haves and have-nots in American society. Educated women continue to have children within marriage. Less educated women have children much earlier, usually outside of marriage, and often before they have completed their schooling. As shown in Figure 5.6, the marriage gap between educated and less educated women has widened dramatically since the late 1960s. In addition, there are big differences between the two tails of the distribution

Figure 5.6a
Never-Married Mothers by Educational Attainment: 1968–2009.

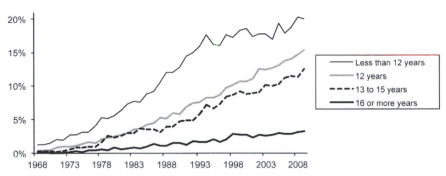

Source: Brookings tabulations of the Current Population Survey, Annual Social and Economic Supplement.

in the extent to which children are planned, the maturity of their parents at the time of their birth, and the number of siblings with whom they must compete for parental time or other resources (Sawhill, Thomas, and Monea 2010). For whatever reasons, the literature on child development shows that two parents are better than one for a variety of behavioral and cognitive outcomes (McLanahan, Donahue, and Haskins 2005).

Figure 5.6b
Mothers Not Currently Married by Educational Attainment: 1968–2009.

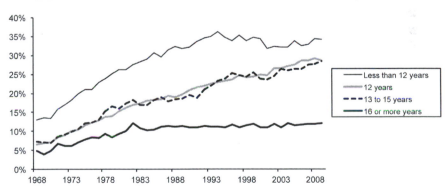

Source: Brookings tabulations of the Current Population Survey, Annual Social and Economic Supplement.
Note: The sample includes noninstitutionalized civilian women ages 16 to 64 with a child under age 18 living in their house. Never-married women are those who have never been married. Mothers who are not currently married are those who are never-married, divorced, widowed, or separated.

To summarize, we know that: (1) income is less equally distributed than it was a few decades ago, (2) it is more correlated with education, and (3) it is more correlated with family structure. Since both parental education and family structure have reasonably well-known effects on children, even if parental income per se were not correlated with children's success, we would have good reasons to believe that the particular form of income inequality we have experienced in the United States has set the stage for the greater persistence of class in the future. To be sure, it is a class structure largely based on meritocratic principles and on stable family ties rather than on the inheritance of wealth, connections, and winning life's lottery. But it does suggest the importance of dealing with the distribution of educational opportunities and with differences in family structure, not just income.

Possible conclusion: There is a U-shaped relationship between inequality and mobility. Up to a point, more inequality leads to greater mobility, but beyond some point the level of effort and skill needed to climb the ladder becomes much more difficult. My own view is that current disparities in the United States threaten the mobility that has long been heralded as a peculiarly American condition. Although there is no strong or consistent evidence that mobility has declined, some studies suggest that it has, especially among men (Mazumder 2005; Kopczuk, Saez, and Song 2010; Fields 2008; Sawhill 2008). Kopczuk, Saez, and Song (2010), in particular, show that mobility has increased for women but declined for men. But now that women are quite well integrated into the labor market and the gender wage gap has shrunk, especially for younger cohorts, the increased mobility of women that has masked declining mobility among men may fade away, exposing a society that risks getting into a vicious cycle in which inequality breeds more inequality. We can also look to studies of child development for more direct evidence that low (relative) income adversely affects such outcomes as schooling, health, and labor market success. Here, too, the evidence is somewhat mixed with some scholars (e.g., Duncan, Kalil, and Ziol-Guest 2008) finding significant adverse effects and others (e.g., Mayer 1997) finding few. What I have emphasized in this chapter is the need to look more carefully at what it is about higher-income parents that makes a difference. Is it just their income and the material resources they can provide to their children or is it attributes that are highly correlated with income, such as parental education and family structure, that make the difference (Haveman and Wolfe 1994, 246)? My guess is that it is primarily the latter.

Cross-national evidence reinforces the general view that inequality and social mobility are linked. The nations with the least inequality (e.g., the Nordic countries) also have the most intergenerational mobility. Interestingly, the OECD has come to the conclusion that inequality does interfere with social mobility, and has pointed to these cross-national findings to support their view (D'Addio 2008). At least one academic study, using cross-national data, has shown that an increase in inequality is associated with lower mobility (Andrews and Leigh 2009). Finally, Alan Krueger has used these cross-national data to argue that "it is hard to look at these figures and not be concerned that rising inequality is jeopardizing our tradition of equality of opportunity" (remarks delivered at the Center for American Progress, January 12, 2012).

HOW DOES VOLATILITY AFFECT THE DISTRIBUTION OF LIFETIME INCOMES?

This question has taken on added resonance as a result of the current recession. Imagine that the recession has minimal effects on the current earnings of those whose lifetime earnings are expected to be high but seriously depresses the current earnings of those whose lifetime earnings (before the recession) were expected to be low—if for no other reason than the fact that they are much more likely to be unemployed for a considerable period (Blank and Card 1993). Even if the earnings of the second group bounce back strongly to what those earnings would have been in the absence of the recession, they will have lower lifetime earnings (partly offset by unemployment insurance) for this reason alone. But a full bounce back is unlikely. These unemployed workers now have less experience and probably lower levels of skill than if they had been continuously employed. They may also have to adapt to the changing structure of the economy, abandoning hopes of returning to their old jobs and needing to find employment in newly growing sectors that demand a new set of skills or that require moving to a new community with all that implies in terms of uprooting families and selling a home in a difficult market. In all these cases, an earnings shock can have longer-term ramifications that cannot be easily dismissed.

Empirical evidence in favor of this thesis comes from a series of articles that have focused on the longer-term consequences of job loss, often as the result of a mass layoff. In their seminal article, Jacobson, LaLonde, and Sullivan (1993) use administrative data from

Pennsylvania for the period 1974 to 1986, and find that six years after workers separated from their firms, they experienced an earnings loss of 25 percent of their expected earnings (without displacement). More recently, Von Wachter and his coauthors (2009) employed a much broader dataset using Social Security records to analyze the effect of job displacement on long-term earnings. They find that workers who were displaced in the early 1980s experienced earnings losses of 20 percent 15 to 20 years after the displacement. These studies are based on job losses associated with mass layoffs. Stevens (1997) uses national-level, longitudinal data from the Panel Study of Income Dynamics to examine the effect of almost all involuntary job separations on earnings. She finds that subsequent job losses after the original displacement play an important role in a worker's long-term losses in earnings after displacement. "Average earnings reductions 6 or more years after a job loss are approximately 9%. If the effect of a single displacement is isolated, however, average earnings 6 or more years after a worker's most recent job loss are only 1% below their expected level" (Stevens 1997, 186).

The pernicious effects of a sluggish economy on a worker's long-term earnings are not restricted to individuals already in the labor force. Kahn (2009) uses data from the National Longitudinal Survey of Youth to investigate the impact of economic conditions at the time of college graduation on future earnings and other labor market outcomes. Her sample is comprised of individuals who graduated from college between 1979 and 1989 so that she can estimate the effect of economic conditions on those who graduated during the recession of the early 1980s as well as those who graduated before and after it. She restricts the sample to white males, as "their labor supply decisions are least sensitive to external factors such as childbearing or discrimination." Individuals whose graduations coincide with inferior economic conditions experience "persistent, negative wage effects." These individuals also tend to experience lower occupational attainment and slightly higher educational attainment and job tenure.

CONCLUSIONS AND IMPLICATIONS

I have argued that what matters most from a normative perspective is disparities in lifetime incomes, and that in the United States at least the connection between inequality and welfare (or happiness) is attenuated because of our belief in meritocracy. Because mobility rates do not seem to have changed very much (if anything, they have declined), the more widely used measure of inequality based on a cross section of annual incomes appears to be a reasonably good proxy for assessing trends (although not levels) in these disparities.

But with inequality reaching new highs not seen since the 1920s or earlier, it is worth asking if we are headed for a vicious cycle in which greater inequality tamps down mobility, producing still more inequality in the future. For this reason, it is important to understand how inequality at a point in time may affect mobility over time. I have hypothesized that this relationship may be U-shaped. Up to a certain point more inequality produces more mobility, but after some point it has a negative effect and we enter a vicious cycle. I have also argued that the new face of inequality—one that is increasingly characterized by disparities in education and family structure—has implications for children's future prospects and thus for the chances that inequality will persist into the future. That the rungs of the economic ladder are further apart than in the past is beyond dispute. But they may also be harder to climb than in the past and that is even more worrisome.

For those who agree with this view and want to do something about current disparities, I would also argue that a focus on opportunity (that is, mobility) instead of poverty and inequality may make sense for at least two reasons. First, Americans believe that they live in a meritocratic society. Although the facts are only partially consistent with this belief, it is a deeply entrenched view, and public opinion polls and attitudinal surveys show that the public is more willing to support investments in education, health, and other opportunity-enhancing programs than they are to redistribute income via taxes and transfers after the fact. Second, policies that affect parental education and family structure are likely to have larger intergenerational effects than policies that affect only income. At the same time, we should not ignore the need to shore up the economic position of the poor and near-poor as this is both easier to do and likely to have some modest effects as well, especially if whatever assistance is provided is designed to encourage education, work, and stronger families.

NOTES

1. This chapter was originally presented at Tobin Project conference on *Democracy & Markets: Understanding the Effects of America's Economic Stratification*, April 30–May 2, 2010. The author would like to thank Daniel Moskowitz for his assistance with this chapter. isawhill@brookings.edu.

2. We would also have to worry about how to handle all those who died prematurely and thus had foreshortened income histories for this reason alone.

3.   Ideally one would want to measure mobility over a lifetime as well and would thus be faced with some of the same practical problems that exist for measuring lifetime incomes. To my knowledge, no one has tried the latter strategy. And virtually everyone who studies mobility worries about the lack of data on the most recent birth cohorts.

4.   For this reason, students of inequality and mobility—e.g., A. F. Shorrocks (1978)—have suggested that a good (although indirect) measure of mobility is the ratio of one to the other. Specifically, Mobility = 1–an index of long-term inequality/an index of short-term inequality. Although widely used and useful for many purposes, Gary Fields has criticized this measure because it treats mobility that leads to greater equality the same as mobility that leads to less equality (Fields 2008).

5.   This conclusion, while widely made, may be premature. It is not just the amount of mobility that matters but also its nature or pattern. Gary Fields illustrates this well by comparing two simple scenarios, which he labels the "Gates winning" and "Gates losing" scenarios. Gates winning is represented by 1, 3 → 1, 5 in this two-period, two-person model where the first number represents the income of person 1 and the second number represents the income of person 2. Gates losing is represented by 1, 3 → 5, 1.

Note that in the Gates-winning scenario total lifetime income is 1, 8 and in the Gates-losing scenario it is 6, 4. Lifetime incomes are more equally distributed in the second scenario. Fields's point is that the mobility index is not very sensitive to this kind of reranking. Using a measure of mobility designed to capture whether changes in mobility are equalizing or disequalizing of long-term incomes, Fields (2008) finds that mobility was equalizing up until about 1980 but disequalizing after then.

6.   Mobility is commonly measured by looking at the intergenerational income elasticity (the coefficient from a regression of offspring's income on parental income). This elasticity will be smaller than the correlation between the two generations' incomes during periods when inequality is rising. If r = the correlation and B = the coefficient, then r = B (standard deviation of parental incomes/standard deviation of children's incomes).

BIBLIOGRAPHY

Acs, Gregory, Pamela Loprest, and Austin Nichols. 2009. "Risk and Recovery: Understanding Changing Risks to Family Incomes," Paper 14 (Low-Income Working Families, Urban Institute).

Alesina, Alberto and George-Marios Angeletos. 2005. "Fairness and Redistribution," *The American Economic Review* 95, no. 4, pp. 960–80.

Alesina, Alberto, Rafael Di Tella, and Robert MacCulloch. 2004. "Inequality and Happiness: Are Europeans and Americans Different?" *Journal of Public Economics* 88, pp. 2009–42.

Alesina, Alberto, and Eliana La Ferrara. 2005. "Preferences for Redistribution in the Land of Opportunities," *Journal of Public Economics* 89, pp. 897–931.

Andrews, Dan and Andrew Leigh. 2009. "More Inequality, Less Social Mobility," *Applied Economics Letters* 16, pp. 1489–92.

Arrow, Kenneth J. 1951. "An Extension of the Basic Theorems of Classical Welfare Economics," *Proceedings of the Second Berkeley Symposium on Mathematical Statistics and Probability*: pp. 507–32.

Barlevy, Gadi and Daniel Tsiddon. 2006. "Earnings Inequality and the Business Cycle," *European Economic Review* 50, no. 1, pp. 55–89.

Blank, Rebecca M. and David Card. 1993. "Poverty, Income Distribution, and Growth: Are They Still Connected?" *Brookings Papers on Economic Activity*, no. 2, pp. 285–339.

Bowles, Samuel, Herbert Gintis, and Melissa Osborne Groves. 2005. "Introduction," in *Unequal Chances: Family Background and Economic Success*, edited by Samuel Bowles, Herbert Gintis, and Melissa Osborne Groves (Princeton: Princeton University Press), pp. 1–22.

Burkhauser, Richard V. et al. 2009. "Recent Trends in Top Income Shares in the USA: Reconciling Estimates from March CPS and IRS Tax Return Data," Working Paper 15320 (National Bureau of Economic Research).

Burkhauser, Richard V. and Kosali I. Simon. 2010. "Measuring the Impact of Health Insurance on Levels and Trends in Inequality," Working Paper 15811 (National Bureau of Economic Research).

Burtless, Gary. 2007. "Globalization and Income Polarization in Rich Countries," Issues in Economic Policy 5 (Brookings).

Burtless, Gary and Christopher Jencks. 2003. "American Inequality and Its Consequences," in *Agenda for the Nation*, edited by Henry J. Aaron, James M. Lindsay, and Pietro S. Nivola (Washington, DC: Brookings Institution Press), pp. 61–108.

Burtless, Gary, and Pavel Svaton. 2010. "Health Care, Health Insurance, and the Distribution of American Incomes," *Forum for Health Economics & Policy* 13, no. 1.

Camerer, Colin and Richard H. Thaler. 1995. "Ultimatums, Dictators and Manners," *The Journal of Economic Perspectives* 9, no. 2, pp. 209–19.

Congressional Budget Office. 2007. "Trends in Earnings Variability over the Past 20 Years."

Congressional Budget Office. 2009. "Changes in the Distribution of Workers' Annual Earnings between 1979 and 2009."

Congressional Budget Office. 2011. "Trends in the Distribution of Household Income between 1979 and 2007."

D'Addio, Anna Cristina. 2007. "Intergenerational Transmission of Disadvantage: Mobility or Immobility across Generations? A Review of the Evidence for OECD Countries," Working Paper No. 52 (OECD Social, Employment and Migration Working Papers).

D'Addio, Anna Cristina. 2008. "Intergenerational Mobility: Does It Offset or Reinforce Income Inequality?," in *Growing Unequal? Income Distribution and Poverty in OECD Countries* (OECD), pp. 203–21.

Debreu, Gerard. 1959. *Theory of Value: An Axiomatic Analysis of Economic Equilibrium* (New Haven: Yale University Press).

Duncan, Greg J., Ariel Kalil, and Kathleen M. Ziol-Guest. 2008. "Economic Costs of Early Childhood Poverty," Issue Paper 4 (Washington, DC: Partnership for America's Economic Success).

Dynan, Karen. 2010. "The Income Roller Coaster: Rising Income Volatility and Its Implications," *Pathways* (Spring), pp. 3–6.

Dynan, Karen E., Douglas W. Elmendorf, and Daniel E. Sichel. 2008. "The Evolution of Household Income Volatility," (Brookings Institution and Federal Reserve Board).

Ellwood, Daniel T. and Christopher Jencks. 2004. "The Spread of Single-Parent Families in the United States since 1960," in *The Future of the Family*, edited by Daniel P. Moynihan, Timothy M. Smeeding, and Lee Rainwater (New York: Russell Sage Foundation), pp. 25–65.

Eurostat, "Inequality of Income Distribution: Gini Coefficient" (http://nui.epp .eurostat.ec.europa.eu/nui/show.do?dataset=ilc_sic2&lang=en).

Fehr, Ernst and Urs Fischbacher. 2003. "The Nature of Human Altruism," *Nature* 425, pp. 785–91.

Fields, Gary S. 2008. "Does Income Mobility Equalize Longer-Term Incomes? New Measures of an Old Concept," working paper (Cornell University, ILR Collection).

Friedman, Benjamin M. 2005. *The Moral Consequences of Economic Growth* (New York: Alfred A. Knopf).

Goldin, Claudia and Lawrence F. Katz. 2008. *The Race between Education and Technology* (Cambridge, MA: Harvard University Press).

Gosselin, Peter. 2008. *High Wire: The Precarious Financial Lives of American Families* (New York: Basic Books).

Gottschalk, Peter and Robert Moffitt. 2009. "The Rising Instability of U.S. Earnings," *Journal of Economic Perspectives* 23, no. 4, pp. 3–24.

Hacker, Jacob. 2008. *The Great Risk Shift* (New York: Oxford University Press).

Hacker, Jacob and Elisabeth Jacobs. 2008. "The Rising Instability of American Family Incomes, 1969–2004: Evidence from the Panel Study of Income Dynamics," Briefing Paper No. 213 (Economic Policy Institute).

Harding, David J. et al. 2005. "The Changing Effect of Family Background on the Incomes of American Adults," in *Unequal Chances: Family Background and Economic Success*, edited by Samuel Bowles, Herbert Gintis, and Melissa Osborne Groves (Princeton: Princeton University Press), pp. 100–144.

Haskins, Ron and Isabel Sawhill. 2009. *Creating an Opportunity Society* (Washington, DC: Brookings Institution Press).

Haveman, Robert. 2009. "What Does It Mean to Be Poor in a Rich Society?," in *Changing Poverty, Changing Policies*, edited by Maria Cancian and Sheldon Danziger (New York: Russell Sage Foundation), pp. 384–408.

Haveman, Robert and Barbara Wolfe. 1994. *Succeeding Generations: On the Effects of Investments in Children* (New York: Russell Sage Foundation).

Hertz, Tom. 2006. "Understanding Mobility in America" (Center for American Progress).

Isaacs, Julia B., Isabel V. Sawhill, and Ron Haskins. 2008. *Getting Ahead or Losing Ground: Economic Mobility in America* (The Brookings Institution and The Pew Economic Mobility Project).

Jacobson, Louis S., Robert J. LaLonde, and Daniel G. Sullivan. 1993. "Earnings Losses of Displaced Workers," *The American Economic Review* 83, no. 4, pp. 685–709.

Jencks, Christopher and Laura Tach. 2006. "Would Equal Opportunity Mean More Mobility?," in *Mobility and Inequality: Frontiers of Research in Sociology and Economics*, edited by Stephen L. Morgan, David B. Grusky, and Gary S. Fields (Stanford: Stanford University Press), pp. 23–58.

Kahn, Lisa B. 2009. "The Long-Term Labor Market Consequences of Graduating from College in a Bad Economy," working paper (Yale School of Management).

Kopczuk, Wojciech, Emmanual Saez, and Jae Song. 2010. "Earnings Inequality and Mobility in the United States: Evidence from Social Security Data since 1937," *The Quarterly Journal of Economics* 125, no. 1, pp. 91–128.

Kuznets, Simon. 1955. "Economic Growth and Income Inequality," *The American Economic Review* 45, no. 1, pp. 1–28.

Leonhardt, David. 2010. "In Health Bill, Obama Attacks Wealth Inequality," *The New York Times*, March 24, p. A1.

Loehlin, John C. 2005. "Resemblance in Personality and Attitudes between Parents and Their Children: Genetic and Environmental Contributions," in *Unequal Chances: Family Background and Economic Success*, edited by Samuel Bowles, Herbert Gintis, and Melissa Osborne Groves (Princeton: Princeton University Press), pp. 192–207.

Mayer, Susan E. 1997. *What Money Can't Buy: Family Income and Children's Life Changes* (Cambridge, MA: Harvard University Press).

Mazumder, Bhashkar. 2005. "Fortunate Sons: New Estimates of Intergenerational Mobility in the United States Using Social Security Earnings Data," *The Review of Economics and Statistics* 87, no. 2, pp. 235–55.

McLanahan, Sarah, Elisabeth Donahue, and Ron Haskins. 2005. "Introducing the Issue." *The Future of the Children* 15, no. 2, pp. 3–12.

McMurrer, Daniel P. and Isabel V. Sawhill. 1998. *Getting Ahead: Economic and Social Mobility in America* (Washington, DC: Urban Institute Press).

National Public Radio, Kaiser Family Foundation, and Harvard University Kennedy School. 2001. "Poverty in America" (http://npr.org/programs/specials/poll/poverty/summary.html).

Nichols, Austin. 2008. "Trends in Income Inequality, Volatility, and Mobility Risk" (Urban Institute).

Nichols, Austin and Seth Zimmerman. 2008. "Measuring Trends in Income Variability" (Urban Institute).

Pew Research Center for the People and the Press. 2007. "Trends in Political Values and Core Attitudes: 1987–2007" (Washington, DC).

Piketty, Thomas and Emmanuel Saez. 2003. "Income Inequality in the United States, 1913–1998," *The Quarterly Journal of Economics* 118, no. 1, pp. 1–39.

Piketty, Thomas and Emmanuel Saez. 2007. "How Progressive Is the U.S. Federal Tax System? A Historical and International Perspective," *Journal of Economic Perspectives* 21, no. 1, pp. 3–24.

Rabin, Matthew. 1993. "Incorporating Fairness into Game Theory and Economics," *The American Economic Review* 83, no. 5, pp. 1281–1302.

Rawls, John. 1971. *A Theory of Justice* (Cambridge, MA: Harvard University Press).

Saez, Emmanuel. 2009. "Striking It Richer: The Evolution of Top Incomes in the United States (Update with 2007 estimates)" (http://elsa.berkeley.edu/~saez/saez-UStopincomes-2007.pdf).

Sawhill, Isabel V. 2008. "Trends in Intergenerational Mobility," in *Getting Ahead or Losing Ground: Economic Mobility in America*, edited by Julia B. Isaacs, Isabel V. Sawhill, and Ron Haskins (The Brookings Institution and The Pew Economic Mobility Project), pp. 27–35.

Sawhill, Isabel, Adam Thomas, and Emily Monea. 2010. "An Ounce of Prevention ... Policy Prescriptions for Reducing the Prevalence of Fragile Families," *The Future of Children* 20, no. 2.

Sen, Amartya. 1992. *Inequality Reexamined* (New York: Russell Sage Foundation).

Shorrocks, A. F. 1978. "The Measurement of Mobility," *Econometrica* 46, no. 5, pp. 1013–24.

Stevens, Ann Huff. 1997. "Persistent Effects of Job Displacement: The Importance of Multiple Job Losses," *Journal of Labor Economics* 15, no. 1, pp. 165–88.

Thomas, Adam and Isabel Sawhill. 2002. "For Richer or for Poorer: Marriage as an Antipoverty Strategy," *Journal of Policy Analysis and Management* 21, no. 4.

Tversky, Amos and Daniel Kahneman. 1991. "Loss Aversion in Riskless Choice: A Reference-Dependent Model," *The Quarterly Journal of Economics* 106, no. 4, pp. 1039–61.

U.S. Census Bureau, *Historical Income Inequality Tables*, table H-4 (http://www.census.gov/hhes/www/income/histinc/ineqtoc.html).

von Wachter, Till, Jae Song, and Joyce Manchester. 2009. "Long-Term Earnings Losses Due to Mass Layoffs during the 1982 Recession: An Analysis Using U.S. Administrative Data from 1974 to 2004," working paper.

Wilkinson, Richard G. and Kate E. Pickett. 2006. "Income Inequality and Population Health: A Review and Explanation of the Evidence," *Social Science & Medicine* 62, no. 7, pp. 1768–84.

Chapter 6

Inequality from Generation to Generation: The United States in Comparison

Miles Corak

INTRODUCTION

Snapshots leave more to the imagination than movies. This is certainly the case when it comes to measuring and understanding inequality. Whether the degree of inequality in a society is "too high" or "too low" is hard to say, and therefore it is hard to imagine what the public policy implications should be. How did it arise? What will happen to it in the future? These seem to be reasonable questions to ask in trying to interpret a picture taken at a particular point in time.

Knowing the dynamics of inequality over the horizon of a working lifetime is certainly important in developing a fuller picture, but particularly important as well is a movie whose frames play out over an even longer horizon, between two generations or more. How does inequality get transmitted from parents to their children? Do low-income families raise children who grow up to be low-income adults and in turn raise the next generation of poor children? Or for that matter how likely is it that rich kids become the next generation of rich adults? Seeing a society from this perspective gives more context and helps us to understand how inequality of outcomes came about and how it will evolve.

When our focus is on changes in inequality from generation to generation, that is, when we are speaking about intergenerational mobility, we are able not only to describe how inequality is transmitted from parents to children, but just as importantly this description speaks to underlying values—like equality of opportunity—that in some sense might allow us to say that there is "too" much or "too" little inequality in society.

Indeed, "equality of opportunity," as opposed to "equality of outcomes," is a value that Americans hold dear. The idea that individual talent, energy, and motivation determine outcomes and accomplishments, as opposed to family background and status, is central to living the "American Dream." A poll conducted by the PEW Charitable Trusts in 2009 found that about three-quarters of Americans strongly held the view that the American Dream meant "being free to accomplish anything with hard work," and about 90 percent said hard work and having ambition were either essential or very important to getting ahead in life (Economic Mobility Project 2009).

But the major message of this chapter is that there is a disconnect between the way Americans see themselves and the way the economy and society actually function. Many Americans may hold the belief that hard work is what it takes to get ahead, but in actual fact the playing field is a good deal stickier than it appears. Family background, not just individual effort and hard work, is importantly related to one's position in the economic and social hierarchy. This disconnect is brought into particular relief by placing the United States in an international context. In fact, children are much more likely as adults to end up in the same place on the income and status ladder as their parents in the United States than in most other countries.

These comparisons beg the question as to why. Addressing this question is the second major message of the chapter. To understand the degree of intergenerational mobility in the United States, and the differences between Americans and others, it is important to appreciate the workings and interaction of three fundamental institutions: the family, the market, and the state. But comparisons can also be misleading. The way in which families, labor markets, and government policy determine the life chances of children is complicated, the result of a particular history, societal values, and the nature of the political process.

It might be one thing to say that the United States has significantly less intergenerational mobility than Denmark or Norway, but it is entirely another thing to suggest that these countries offer templates for the conduct of public policy that can be applied on this side of the Atlantic. There is no way to get from here to there. For this reason the third major objective of the chapter is to focus on a particularly apt comparison, that between the United States and Canada, and to illustrate how the configuration of the forces determining the transmission of inequality across generations differs in spite of the fact that both of these countries share many other things in common, particularly the importance and meaning of equality of opportunity and the role of individual hard work and motivation.

FOCUSING THE LENS: A FIRST LOOK AT MEASURING INTERGENERATIONAL MOBILITY

The measurement and description of the degree to which family background is related to the adult attainments of children has a long history in the social sciences and has been done in a number of different ways. Broad swaths of the literature in sociology deal with the degree to which children as adults have the same status among their counterparts as their parents did a generation earlier. "Status" is often measured on the basis of occupation or some related indicator of the position or degree of control an individual may have in the workplace. It is also often related to "class," and the objective in this literature is to describe the degree of mobility across distinct thresholds associated with this concept.

For some decades there has also been a focus on earnings and income as the outcomes of interest. This has naturally led to the most often used statistic in this literature, namely, the "intergenerational elasticity in earnings," which is the percentage difference in earnings in the child's generation associated with the percentage difference in the parental generation. For example, an intergenerational elasticity in earnings of 0.6 tells us that if one father makes 100 percent more than another, then the son of the high-income father will, as an adult, earn 60 percent more than the son of the relatively lower-income father.[1] An elasticity of 0.2 says this 100 percent difference between the fathers would lead to only a 20 percent difference between the sons. A lower elasticity means a society with more mobility.

The primary focus of much of this research has been on the father-son relationship because it is the least complicated and, because of the availability of data, the most convenient to obtain reliable estimates of from a large number of different countries for purposes of international comparisons.[2] Comparisons involving daughters and mothers, or a focus on relationships that also account for marital choices and not just labor market choices, have also been studied. There are also studies addressing, among others, total income, self-employment income, assets, and receipt of government transfer payments like welfare and unemployment insurance.

We should be clear from the very beginning that the use of the intergenerational elasticity of earnings is an exercise of description, and in and of itself does not offer a story about the underlying causal forces and, as such, does not lead to clear policy recommendations.

We should also be clear that this is a much more difficult statistic to measure than those associated with cross-sectional inequality, and in fact there has been a good deal of controversy about these measurement issues. This is because of the data requirements and challenges of translating theoretical concepts into practical measures.

To accurately measure the intergenerational earnings elasticity requires estimates of the lifetime earnings prospects of both parents and their children in their adulthood. Because earnings tend to rise over the life cycle but annual earnings fluctuate a great deal, good estimates of lifetime earnings require having several years of earnings data during a period in the life cycle when individuals are established in their career jobs (when they are 40 to 50 or so years of age), and these estimates must be available for both the parent and the child. As such the members of a family have to be followed and connected to each other over a period that easily spans several decades.

A good deal is at stake in getting these measurement issues right: they have been shown to matter for the ultimate statistic, and hence description of how families and labor markets work. Becker's (1988, 10) summary of the state of the literature as it existed up to about the mid-1980s implied an intergenerational elasticity of about 0.2. But this empirical literature has evolved with the availability of more accurate and more representative data. Corak (2006) suggests that the best estimate for the United States is somewhere between 0.4 and 0.6.

Figure 6.1 shows a 22-country comparison of intergenerational elasticity estimates. The estimates range from less than 0.2 in countries like Denmark, Norway, and Finland to a high of almost 0.7 in Peru. Part of the variation across the countries is due to the process of economic development, with lower-income countries generally having a higher

Figure 6.1

Comparable Estimates of the Intergenerational Elasticity between Father and Son Earnings.

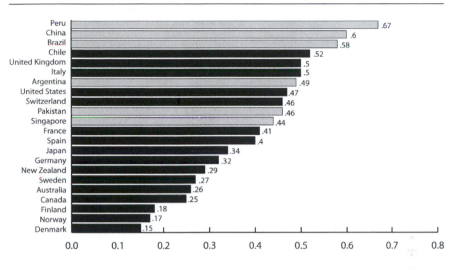

Intergenerational Earnings Elasticity

Note: Lightly shaded bars indicate countries that are not member states of the OECD, generally taken to mean lower-income countries.

proportion of inequality transmitted across the generations. And part of the reason for some of the very high estimates have to do with the exclusion of particular groups in the full participation in the labor market and society, be it some segments of the aboriginal population in Peru, and to some extent the rural population in China.

But there is more to this variation than the overall level of economic development or broad structural factors. If we restrict our attention to the rich countries, there remains considerable variation, with the United States standing out, along with Italy and the United Kingdom, as the least intergenerationally mobile. In these countries the estimate is in the neighborhood of 0.5, being two or more times as large as the most mobile countries who are characterized by estimates of about 0.2 or even a bit less.

The natural question to ask is why?

A FRAMEWORK FOR UNDERSTANDING CROSS-COUNTRY DIFFERENCES

To understand these differences we need to appreciate the possible underlying causes of generational mobility, and an important starting point is Solon (2004), who has adapted a standard perspective in the economics literature and made it appropriate for comparisons across countries. Very broadly speaking, the reasons for the differences in the intergenerational elasticity across countries have to do with the role of three fundamental institutions determining the life chances of children—the family, the labor market, and the state—and the different balance struck between their influence across countries.

Solon's model invites us to think of families differing in their capacities and resources to invest in their children, but also as facing different incentives to do so according to their socioeconomic status and the social context in their country. While some of these capacities and incentives to invest in children may be genetic or due to family history and culture, others are influenced by how families interact and interface with the labor market and public programs. It is these latter influences that are related to public policy and choices.

Parents invest in and influence the adult outcomes of children in a whole host of ways, but these investments can have particularly important implications at certain stages of a child's life. We should not therefore understate the role of families, but at the same time we need also to appreciate the context within which they live and the social supports offered to them.

The argument is often made that a particularly important window of opportunity in a child's development occurs during the early years, up to about five years of age. This meshes very much with developments in the science of early brain development. The central idea is that the stimulation infants and young children receive from their environment influences their neural development and will ultimately define the outer limits of their capabilities. Children raised in families at the high end of the socioeconomic scale are more likely to be exposed to a stimulating environment that leads to an advantageous path in life with respect to health, cognitive development, and social skills. If the brain does not receive the requisite environmental stimulation at certain critical periods, the window of opportunity closes and development fails to occur (Knudsen et al. 2006).

This so-called "neural sculpting" occurs at different times for different brain functions, but timing is important. The point is that this process establishes the "initial conditions" of a life and sets the individual down a particular pathway, a pathway in which a series of cumulative experiences may set further constraints or present further opportunities. The series of steps leading through important transitional periods in life look something like this: socioeconomic circumstances early in life (and even in the prenatal period) → birth weight and cognitive/social/emotional development → readiness to learn → language development → behavioral problems in school and educational achievement → labor market success and job characteristics → stress, mental well-being, socioeconomic status, success in family formation → parenting.

The intergenerational earnings elasticity is a summary relationship of the overall outcome of a whole series of gradients that appear at each of these steps. Parents influence child outcomes at each of these stages, but outcomes at any one stage have their roots in earlier stages and child's cumulative experience up to that point. Someone born to parents with low income faces a higher risk of less successfully transiting through these stages and of ending up in a precarious labor market situation, which in turn diminishes his or her capacity for positive parenting. This raises the odds of a generational cycle of poverty, but money is as much the result as the cause of the vicious circle.

For example, the child of a high-income, dual-earner couple (with perhaps only one other child) may well be raised in an environment with more resources that improve his or her future adult prospects than the child of a single parent with limited education. These resources are both monetary and nonmonetary. The advantaged household will certainly be able afford more things and activities for the child, but may also be more likely to spend more time with the child and offer linkages and contacts to the neighborhood and community that will both nurture and offer opportunities for growth and advancement. The support parents offer may extend well into adolescence by helping to direct their children through the labor market, offering advice and contacts as they get their first jobs and establish a foothold that will influence their career prospects. Consequently, we can expect the intergenerational elasticity to differ across countries for reasons associated with demographics, family formation, single parenthood, as well as parenting skills and time devoted to children.

As another example, an increase in the cost of human capital investment, such as in market-based provision of child care or health care, private primary schooling, or higher college tuition fees, will imply lower human capital investment. In a similar way a higher potential return to human capital will create an incentive for more investment. Solon (2004) takes the rate of return to education as an indicator of the degree of inequality in the labor market and shows that societies with labor markets characterized by more cross-sectional inequality—that is, a higher return to education—will be less generationally mobile. This is not only because a higher-income, dual-earner family with fewer children has a higher capacity to invest in the education of their children than a single-parent low-income family, but also because the incentives to do so are greater. Inequality in demographics and labor markets in the here and now will have an influence on the degree of inequality in earnings in the next generation. Consequently, we can expect the intergenerational elasticity to differ across countries for reasons associated with the costs and returns of investing in a child's human capital, the way in which the labor market works and how "good jobs" are obtained, and the income inequalities between parents.

But Solon (2004) also suggests that public policy can both accentuate and dampen the influence of labor market inequality. He shows that generational mobility is promoted by "progressive" public programs, those that are of relatively more benefit to the relatively less well-off. Two countries may spend the same fraction of their gross domestic product on education, but if this spending is directed to high-quality early childhood, primary, and secondary schooling, it is likely to be of relatively more benefit to families lower on the socioeconomic scale than if it was directed to the subsidization of tertiary education. In fact, this refers to more than just public transfers or publicly provided programs directed to children: it also includes all aspects of public actions that influence the relationship between families and the labor market. The structure of taxation and regulations is also part of the story. Hacker and Pierson (2010) focus on changes in these policies to explain the increase in cross-sectional inequality in the United States, but their analysis also has longer-term implications for intergenerational mobility.

In a rough way we can see the outcomes of these forces at work in Figure 6.2, which plots the intergenerational earnings elasticities presented in Figure 6.1 against a cross-sectional measure of inequality (the Gini coefficient). More inequality at a point in time is associated with less generational mobility. Once again, this picture is one of association. The underlying causes relate to the process of child development and the role of socioeconomic inequalities influencing it, but these forces may differ in their significance across these countries: in some early childhood development may be the decisive factor, while in others it may be limited access to quality tertiary education due to

Figure 6.2
Higher Inequality Is Associated with Lower Earnings Mobility across Generations.

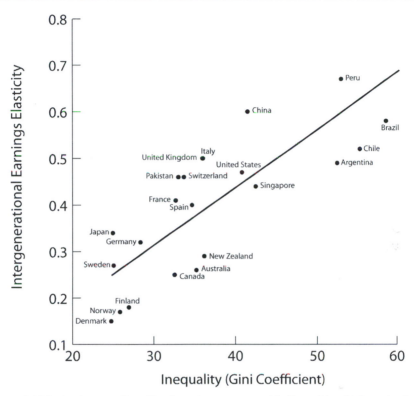

Source: Published estimates collected by the author as presented in Figure 6.1 and information from the World Bank for the Gini coefficient. Note that data points for Italy and the United Kingdom overlap.

early tracking of students during the primary years, and in others still it may be due to labor markets in which access to good jobs is determined by family contacts, discrimination, or outright nepotism.

Haskins and Sawhill (2009) offer a clear portrait of the life chances of American children as the outcome of the interaction between family background and resources, growing inequalities in the labor market, and changes in government policy. Their analysis offers the kind of detail and institutional backdrop to interpret these raw statistics. To appreciate which aspects of demography, of labor markets, and of government policy are central in determining different outcomes in a comparative framework would require an analysis with this kind of detail across many countries. This is no small challenge, but one comparison that may be both feasible and apt is that with Canada because the nature of the family and the structure of labor markets are broadly similar between these two countries.

THE UNITED STATES AND CANADA

The information in Figure 6.1 suggests that the intergenerational earnings elasticity of 0.47 in the United States is more than twice as high as the Canadian estimate of roughly 0.20, but this likely even understates the difference between the two countries. Corak (2010) suggests that the estimates calculated by Mazumder (2005a, 2005b), which are as high as 0.61, are more directly comparable to estimates of about 0.23 produced with Canadian data by Corak and Heisz (1999): both studies using administrative data on virtually the same age cohorts of men at the same period of time. This suggests that the intergenerational elasticity between father and son earnings is almost three times as high in the United States as it is in Canada.

This difference is the result of different patterns in the degree of mobility at the two extremes of the earnings distribution. In both countries there is a considerable degree of mobility among the broadly defined middle-earnings group, but both the sons of high- and low-earning fathers are more likely to grow up to be, respectively, high- and low-earning adults.

In the United States 26 percent of the sons born to fathers in the top 10 percent of the earnings distribution grow up to have earnings that place them in turn in the top 10 percent, and the majority of these sons are in at least top 30 percent of their earnings distribution, while only 3 percent fall to the bottom 10 percent. There is also stickiness in earnings at the top in Canada, but not as great: 18 percent of top-decile sons remain in the top decile, about 40 percent are in the top 30 percent, and about 8 percent fall to the bottom. Similarly, there is stickiness across the generations for sons raised by low-earning fathers, and once again more so in the United States, where 22 percent of bottom-decile sons remain in the bottom 10 percent as adults, and one-half remain in the bottom 30 percent. In Canada 16 percent remain in the bottom, while about 4 in 10 remain in the bottom 30 percent of the earnings distribution (Corak 2010, Figures 2 and 3).

In general there is somewhat more upward mobility from the bottom in Canada than in the United States, with Canadian sons born to fathers in the bottom third of the earnings distribution more likely to rise into the top half of their adult earnings distribution than their American counterparts (Corak 2010, Figure 4).

This is a particularly important difference, and in part reflects the fact that children in the bottom of the income distribution are less well-off in an absolute sense in the United States than in Canada. Greater inequality in the American earnings distribution is reflected in the monetary circumstances of children. Corak, Curtis, and Phipps (2011, Figure 4) show that if Canadian children were placed in the overall American income distribution, their family income would tend to be considered as lower middle class, being disproportionately between the second and fifth deciles. About two-thirds of Canadian children would be found above the bottom 10th of the income distribution but no higher than the middle. When American children are placed in the overall income distribution they are more likely to be at the very bottom and the very top.[3]

But this difference in monetary resources is also reflected in a host of indicators associated with nonmonetary resources, particularly with family resources and other social and community supports. In Canada children are more likely to be living with a mother who is married, and more likely to be living with both biological parents. About three-quarters of Canadian children younger than 13 live with both biological parents, while in the United States this proportion is about two-thirds. Further, in the United States mothers tend to be younger, with teenage births being more common. This is particularly so for lone mothers, where in addition to being younger and less educated they also have more children than their Canadian counterparts.

All of this implies that not just monetary resources but also nonmonetary resources—particularly those associated with the time parents spend with their children—are likely to be less enriching for the children of the disadvantaged in the United States. While it is difficult to obtain comparable information on time use, parenting style, and other nonmonetary investments parents make in their children, Corak, Curtis, and Phipps (2011) note that children in low-income and lone-parent families are less likely to be read to. This said, the proportion of low-income children read to daily, at almost 55 percent in Canada versus about one-third in the United States, is significantly different.

The care and time devoted to children also depends upon how families interface with the labor market, and the alternative care arrangements available to their children. As suggested labor markets are more polarized in the United States, and there are different patterns of labor force participation in the two countries. "Parental participation in the labour market is both cause and effect of child care arrangements. The choice or need to work means that parents must find alternative arrangements for their children; the availability of care outside of the home offers opportunities to work or to work more hours" (Corak, Curtis, and Phipps 2011, 87).

In fact, Canadian mothers have higher labor force participation rates, but parents who are in the labor market in the United States work longer hours. In the United States mothers are more likely to work full-time or not at all, with about 40 percent of children having mothers who worked 40 or more hours per week. In Canada only about one-quarter of children are in this situation, there being a greater tendency for mothers to work part-time. In the United States lone mothers are more likely to be working than married mothers, with only one-fifth not working at all compared to almost one-third of married mothers. About one-half of lone mothers work more than 40 hours per week in the United States, but in Canada only about one-quarter do so.

As suggested, labor market participation is both cause and effect of the availability of alternative child care arrangements, so these differences are mirrored in differences in care arrangements for young children. Over one-half of all children up to two years of age are cared for exclusively by their parents in Canada, compared to 4 in 10 in the United States. This difference likely reflects the very different maternity and parental leave available for working mothers of newborn children.

Parental benefits are much more generous in Canada, with mothers of newborns who had sufficient work experience being provided with the opportunity to stay home for up to 25 weeks after the birth of their child during the 1990s, and with this package of benefits, administered by the federal government through the national unemployment insurance program, being extended to one year in 2001. Maternity benefits are much more limited in the United States. Parents are entitled to 12 weeks of leave without pay if they work in a company with more than 50 people, but with there being a tax deduction for day care when it is used because of parental employment. Corak, Curtis, and Phipps

(2011) conclude their much more extensive statistical review by stating that the

> family context in which children are raised in the United States is more challenging than in Canada, raising the risks that some children will not see the full development of their capabilities. American labour markets are also more unequal raising the stakes for child outcomes, both elevating opportunities and heightening risks. Finally, public policy is less "progressive," not compensating in the same degree for family background and labour market inequality. (Corak, Curtis, and Phipps 2011, 102)

This also relates to a number of measures of human capital, including mental and physical health as well as those associated with education. Overall outcomes are on average higher in Canada, and there is less disparity.

For example, education outcomes that are measured both by the mother's assessment of the child's performance and on tests administered to the child indicate significant differences in outcomes between these two countries. Canadian four-year-olds score significantly higher on comparable tests of school readiness (the Peabody Picture Vocabulary Test). American mothers of school-age children at the bottom of the socioeconomic scale are twice as likely to report that their children are performing below the middle or near the bottom. And according to other tests of mathematics and literacy skills, young teens perform on average better in Canada than in the United States. While the schooling system does not seem to significantly narrow initial gaps, it remains unclear as to the extent to which they are amplified or what particular institutional designs at what particular stages can contribute to narrowing them.

CONCLUSION

The nature of inequality at any point in time can be better understood if we appreciate the extent to which it is related to family background, the extent to which one's starting point in life in some sense preconditions ultimate adult social and labor market outcomes.

If rich children are predestined to grow up to be rich adults, and if poor children are similarly predestined to be the next generation of those living in poverty, then inequalities of outcomes are in some sense the result of rigid structures in our society that may lead us to question the extent to which there is equality of opportunity.

On the other hand, if the same degree of inequality is associated with a fluidity of status across generations, with poor parents as likely to raise children who will be top earners as rich parents, then there is less reason to question the existence of equality of opportunity.

There is in fact a good deal of fluidity in the American earnings distribution across the generations with the children of most middle-earning parents experiencing outcomes that are not strongly associated with their parents' income levels. But even so, on average the United States stands out as being among the least generationally mobile among the rich countries, and in particular the overall degree of relative earnings mobility across the generations is almost three times greater in Canada, a country to which it might be most apt to make a comparison. This difference is due to a greater stickiness in earnings across the generations at both the top and the bottom.

At the broadest level we should understand the cross-country differences in the transmission of inequality as arising from differences in the investments these societies make in their children as well as differences in the returns to these investments. This process reflects the workings of the family, the structure of labor markets and how families interact with them, and the role of public policy. Inequality at a point in time is both the outcome and cause of the degree to which economic status is passed across the generations.

The greater the capacity of families to invest in their children, in both monetary and nonmonetary terms, the more likely children will develop the human capital to succeed in marriage and labor markets. The more equal the returns to education in the labor market, the lower the stakes and the more level the incentives to make these investments. And finally, the more progressive the public policy—that is, the more relative benefit it is to the relatively disadvantaged—the more level the playing field.

All of these factors come into play in understanding the differences in the degree of generational mobility between the United States and Canada, and for that matter between the United States and other countries.

It is unlikely that the degree of generational earnings mobility will change significantly in the United States, at least for the current generation of children growing into adulthood, without there being important changes in the circumstances of the least advantaged. These changes include demographic changes that increase the capacity of parents to invest in the early years of their children's lives—a decline in single parenthood, increases in parental education and age at first birth, and increases in both the quality and quantity of time invested in children during their preschool and early school years.

Further, the very substantial increases in earnings inequality during the past few decades, which in significant part reflect stagnation in the earnings of those in the bottom half of the earnings distribution and important increases in the share of total earnings going to those at the top, also suggests that intergenerational mobility is unlikely to increase. This will be particularly the case if labor market inequalities translate into political power that determines the extent to which progressive reforms can be made to public policy. These include increasing the quality of schooling and health care for the disadvantaged, offering more support to parents raising young children—both monetary but also in terms of parental leave that allows more time to be spent with their children—and improving access to higher levels of education.

Without changes in these underlying factors, the transmission of inequality from the current generation to the next will remain a movie that is played to the same script as that viewed by past generations.

NOTES

1. Slightly more formally, if Y represents permanent income and t is an index of generations, then the relationship between the adult outcomes of children and their family background can be represented as: $ln\ Y_{i,t} = \alpha + \beta\ ln\ Y_{i,t-1} + \epsilon_{i,t}$. In this expression the adult income (in natural logarithms) of family i's child, $lnY_{i,t}$, is made up of three components: the average income of the children of generation t (as represented by α); the deviation from this average reflecting family income ($\beta\ ln\ Y_{i,t-1}$); and all other influences not associated with parental income and including luck ($\epsilon_{i,t}$). The intergenerational elasticity in earnings is β. If this expression is converted from logarithms to dollars, it would be expressed as $Y_{i,t} = \exp(\alpha) \times \exp$ $(\beta\ ln\ Y_{i,t-1}) = \exp(\alpha) \times (Y_{i,t-1})^{\beta}$ if $\epsilon_{i,t}$ is ignored. This implies that the ratio of incomes for children from high-income (H) and low-income (L) backgrounds is $Y_{H,t}/Y_{L,t} = (Y_{H,t-1}/Y_{L,t-1})^{\beta}$, that is, the ratio of their parents' incomes raised to the β power. A clear introduction to this statistic is offered by Solon (2008), and more intuition on its nature and use is available in Corak (2004, 2006) and Mulligan (1997).

2. But clearly a single statistic cannot give a full picture of the nature of generational mobility. The elasticity refers to relative mobility through time, but it should also be recognized that a certain percentage change in earnings may mean, in absolute terms, something different across countries if the variation in the underlying earnings distributions is different. It may not take much of a change in earnings to make say a 10 percent change in one's position in countries like Norway or Denmark while at the same time taking a good deal more to make the same percentage change in the United States, where there is a good deal more dispersion in the earnings distribution. For this reason a standardized measure of intergenerational

mobility, the correlation coefficient that refers to mobility in terms of the standard deviation of the earnings distribution, is also often used. As an example see Bjorklund and Jäntti (2011), who show that among the countries they examine there is less of a difference in correlation coefficients than in elasticities.

3. It should be noted that these comparisons are based strictly upon monetary resources obtained from the labor market and do not account for the role of taxes and transfers, and particularly in-kind transfers.

BIBLIOGRAPHY

Becker, Gary S. (1988). "Family Economics and Macro Behavior." *American Economic Review*. Vol. 78, No. 1 (March), pages 1–13.

Becker, Gary S. and Nigel Tomes (1979). "An Equilibrium Theory of the Distribution of Income and Intergenerational Mobility." *Journal of Political Economy*. Vol. 87, pages 1153–89.

Becker, Gary S. and Nigel Tomes (1986). "Human Capital and the Rise and Fall of Families." *Journal of Labor Economics*. Vol. 4, pages S1–39.

Bjorklund, Anders and Markus Jäntti (2011). "Intergenerational Economic Inequality." In Wiemer Salverda, Brian Nolan, and Timothy M. Smeeding (editors). *Oxford Handbook of Economic Inequality*. Oxford: Oxford University Press.

Corak, Miles and Andrew Heisz (1999). "The Intergenerational Earnings and Income Mobility of Canadian Men: Evidence from Longitudinal Income Tax Data." *Journal of Human Resources*. Vol. 34, No. 3 (Summer), pages 504–533.

Corak, Miles (2004). "Introduction." In Miles Corak (editor). *Generational Income Mobility in North America and Europe*. Cambridge: Cambridge University Press.

Corak, Miles (2006). "Do Poor Children Become Poor Adults? Lessons for Public Policy from a Cross Country Comparison of Generational Earnings Mobility." *Research on Economic Inequality*. Vol. 13, pages 143–88.

Corak, Miles (2010). *Chasing the Same Dream, Climbing Different Ladders: Economic Mobility in the United States and Canada*. Economic Mobility Project, PEW Charitable Trusts. 25 pages. Available at http://www.pewtrusts.org/news_room_detail.aspx?id=56877.

Corak, Miles, Lori Curtis and Shelley Phipps (2011). "Economic Mobility, Family Background, and the Well-Being of Children in the United States and Canada." In Timothy Smeeding, Markus Jäntti, and Robert Erickson (editors). *Persistence, Privilege and Parenting: The Comparative Study of Intergenerational Mobility*. New York: Russell Sage Foundation. Pages 73–108.

Economic Mobility Project (2009). *Opinion Poll on Economic Mobility and the American Dream*. Washington, DC: Pew Charitable Trusts. Available at http://www.economicmobility.org/poll2009, accessed July 26, 2011.

Goldberger, Arthur S. (1989). "Economic and Mechanical Models of Intergenerational Transmission." *American Economic Review*. Vol. 79, No. 3 (June), pages 504–13.

Grawe, Nathan D. (2004). "Intergenerational Mobility for Whom? The Experience of High and Low Earning Sons in International Perspective." In Miles

Corak (editor). *Generational Income Mobility in North America and Europe.* Cambridge: Cambridge University Press.

Hacker, Jacob and Paul Pierson (2010). *Winner-Take-All Politics: How Washington Made the Rich Richer—and Turned Its Back on the Middle Class.* New York: Simon and Schuster.

Haskins, Ron and Isabel V. Sawhill (2009). *Creating an Opportunity Society.* Washington, DC: Brookings Institution Press.

Knudsen, Eric I., James J. Heckman, Judy L. Cameron, and Jack P. Shonkoff (2006). "Economic, Neurobiological, and Behavioural Perspectives on Building America's Future Workforce." *Proceedings of the National Academy of Sciences.* Vol. 103, No. 27, pages 10155–62.

Mazumder, Bhashkar (2005a). "Fortunate Sons: New Estimates of Intergenerational Mobility in the United States Using Social Security Earnings Data." *Review of Economics and Statistics.* Vol. 87, No. 2 (May), pages 235–55.

Mazumder, Bhashkar (2005b). "The Apple Falls Even Closer to the Tree than We Thought: New and Revised Estimates of the Intergenerational Inheritance of Earnings." In Samuel Bowles, Herbert Gintis, and Melissa Osborne Groves (editors). *Unequal Chances: Family Background and Economic Success.* Pages 80–99. Princeton: Princeton University Press and Russell Sage.

Mulligan, Casey B. (1997). *Parental Priorities and Economic Inequality.* Chicago: University of Chicago Press.

Solon, Gary (1992). Intergenerational Income Mobility in the United States. *American Economic Review.* Vol. 82, No. 3 (June), pages 393–408.

Solon, Gary (2004). "A Model of Intergenerational Mobility Variation over Time and Place." Pages 38–47. In Miles Corak (editor). *Generational Income Mobility in North America and Europe.* Pages 38–47. Cambridge: Cambridge University Press.

Solon, Gary (2008). "Intergenerational Income Mobility." In Steven Durlauf and Lawrence Blume (editors). *The New Palgrave Dictionary of Economics.* Second Edition. London: Palgrave Macmillan.

Zimmerman, David J. (1992). "Regression toward Mediocrity in Economic Structure." *American Economic Review.* Vol. 82, No. 3 (June), pages 409–29.

Part III

Institutions and Choices

Chapter 7

The Causes of Poverty and Inequality in the United States: Toward a Broader View

Kristin Marsh

The United States is one of the richest countries in the world. Given the potential to enhance the well-being of its population, why is there so much inequality? Why are so many struggling to make ends meet, to feed, shelter, and provide health care for their families, and to educate their children? The popular understanding is that poverty can be explained by bad individual-level choices and a lack of the correct cultural values and work ethic. But individual-level thinking explains little about society as a whole. Many who are hardworking and aspire to a good education are held back by stubborn institutional processes and structured disadvantages (MacLeod 2009). Instead, a broader perspective is helpful in an effort toward unraveling the paradox. In essence, the institutions of society matter in shaping unwarranted levels of inequality and poverty in the United States. Social policy, and rules having to do with labor relations, private ownership, and social assistance, have consequences for everyone's life chances and autonomy. Our cultural beliefs about the American Dream and individual responsibility reproduce a public dialogue that blames the poor, demonizes social assistance, and valorizes power and wealth (Kendall 2011). Any meaningful reduction in inequality and poverty will depend on recognition of structural causes and commitment to strengthening our public support system.

MAKING CHOICES: THE PROBLEM WITH INDIVIDUAL-LEVEL EXPLANATIONS

Much of our popular understanding of inequality in the United States focuses on individuals. The reasoning is that in a wealthy country, those who are poor must be making bad choices. They are opting out of opportunities that school and hard work provide. The idea is that if we understand people in poverty, then we can better help the poor—educate them to feed their children better, teach them good work habits such as cleanliness and punctuality, or teach them interview and people skills. As Brady puts it, "The conventional approach in poverty studies is to analyze only the United States and to compare the characteristics of poor people (perhaps in poor neighborhoods) to non-poor people" (Brady 2009, 5). The problem Americans confront in trying to make sense of poverty is resolving it with a long-standing belief in the American Dream and dominant ideological understanding of the United States as a meritocracy (McNamee and Miller 2009). Accordingly, we contrast our effort and solid aspirations with a lack of family values and laziness, as supposedly evidenced by single-parent households and being out of work. This sets up a racialized understanding of the poor as "other" and less than, as undeserving "underclass" (Quadagno 1994; Gans 1995).

But an individual-level understanding misses the structural logic of poverty and inequality. It misses the point of who benefits from poverty and why it is so stable in a rich society. Individual-level explanations are not enough because while some poor may be lazy, so too are some wealthy. Most people out of work and struggling have high aspirations, have a strong work ethic, are smart, and want a good education (Hayes 2004; MacLeod 2009). Consistently, research shows us how stable inequality is across generations, and how difficult it is to overcome the accident of birth. Understanding poverty and inequality requires a broader consideration of institutions and policy.

UNDERSTANDING INEQUALITY BROADLY: SOCIAL POLICY

The questions we ponder about society and the problems we observe (e.g., violent crime, pollution, unemployment, poverty) have causes beyond the personal shortcomings of those involved. A broader view provides a clue to the rules of the game—how institutions (education, the economy, the state/government, etc.) interact to shape our options and potential. It helps us think structurally, in terms of the frame of the building that is society.

We can understand that high unemployment starting in 2008 was part of an economic crisis, the deepest recession since the 1930s. In this extreme moment, we are aware that social problems are not easily explained in terms of individuals. When much of the country is struggling, we are able to see the social context and understand personal problems in social-structural terms. A broader view helps us see that, even in the best times, institutional structures and processes affect life chances and opportunities (Mills 1959/2000).

Social policy can help soften the blow of economic hardship; or it can help stabilize inequality. Government has the potential to institutionalize programs that keep us going when times are tough, shaping the distribution and redistribution of resources.[1] In this sense, poverty and inequality in the United States result from a failure of social policy because policy leads to greater or lesser poverty and greater or lesser inequality. So—which rules matter? Which institutional arrangements? Any policy that shapes the environment in which we make our work, living, educational, and business decisions impacts economic outcomes for individuals and groups. Some effects are more direct than others, but most result from one of several overlapping arenas of social organization: (1) labor relations, (2) private ownership, and (3) social assistance.

Labor Relations

In the United States, the majority earn a living through wages and salaries. The relationship between capital and labor is a core organizational relationship under advanced, late-industrial capitalism. It is also one of the most important sources of inequality and poverty (Marx and Engels 1848/1967; Wright 1985; Aronowitz 2005). In rational terms, it is in the interest of business to maximize profit and workers to maximize their wage; this logical contradiction structures conflict into the relationship between workers (who own their own labor power) and capitalists (who own and control the means of production).

Greater access to economic resources and political influence tends to advantage the interests of capital (Domhoff 2006). Workers do not hold comparable economic power; rather their strength is in numbers and in collective, coordinated action. The economic well-being and political influence of workers have therefore been furthered by union strength and activity. Countries with a strong labor climate and history (Sweden, Norway, Austria, Denmark, Belgium, and Finland) have lower unemployment, higher tax revenue, proportionally higher spending on social security and welfare, and lower income inequality (Edsall 1984; Brady 2009). Even in the United States, where labor faces a more difficult political environment, organized labor has played a key role establishing support, protection, and benefits to the poor and working classes. Without the Depression-era efforts of labor, we may not have seen public consensus in favor of large-scale federal intervention in the economy. Organized labor helped establish Social Security, Medicare and Medicaid, public education, the Occupational Safety and Health Administration (OSHA), and federal minimum wage legislation. Labor's support of the Democratic Party helped garner commitment to progressive issues such as civil rights legislation and progressive tax policy post–World War II (Edsall 1984). Overall, unions help workers gain better wages, working conditions, and employment stability. And the very fact that collective bargaining and workplace representation is a legal right is thanks to union activity: the Wagner Act and its regulatory body, the National Labor Relations Board, were early Roosevelt-era laws.

The struggle between classes manifests differently in different time periods. While the early 20th century saw outward conflict and militant workers willing to face off with employers through sit-down strikes and walkouts, the post–World War II period of U.S. power globally set up a truce between organized labor and capital—a class compromise (Przeworski 1985). Working-class wages and working conditions, even the rules of hiring and firing, were standardized and bolstered through collective bargaining agreements. Employers gained workplace peace; workers agreed not to strike. Collective bargaining provided workers job security, fair treatment, and a middle-class living. Not everyone benefited—racism and sexism persisted in union practices; corruption (though exaggerated in cultural mythology) did exist; and some conflicts required arbitration or mediation. But this period was comparatively calm, whereby workers (unionized or not) and employers had a stable relationship of mutual responsibility.

The social contract, however, started breaking down in the 1970s (Rubin 1996; Blau 1993). Manufacturing layoffs escalated and were harder to fight. By 1993, even white-collar workers were laid off in record numbers, while workers throughout the economy found themselves precariously situated. In essence, we had changed "from a social world characterized by long-term, stable relationships to one characterized by short-term, temporary relationships" (Rubin 1996, 4). But what undermined the class compromise?

A large part of the story is the increasingly visible mobility of capital and the role of technology and organizational control in capital's reinvention of its power (Edwards 1979). A competitive global economic climate and changing trade policies encouraged shifts in the way companies did business. Generally understood as a period of deindustrialization, this represented a two-pronged strategy. On the one hand, technological innovations such as computerized robotics in manufacturing decreased the labor intensity of the production process (i.e., fewer workers were needed to match or increase levels of production) (Milkman 1997). On the other hand, production took on a more visibly global character. Companies moved production from northern states with strong union climates to southern "right-to-work" states, and then farther south to export-free processing zones (Adler 2001; Bonacich et al. 1994). Overseas production meant cheaper labor, and once this global exploitation became too politically contentious, well-known companies hid behind their contracts with local factories in countries such as Thailand and Malaysia. Global production became characterized by a complicated production chain that makes it difficult for the most socially conscious consumer to tell exactly where his or her shirt or jeans were made (Snyder 2007).

Union decline has also been part of the story, factoring into both a devolution of the regulatory environment and weakened bargaining position. Union density (percentage of workers belonging to a union) was greatest in the United States following World War II (34% in 1955), coinciding with a period of economic growth and global power. Since then, union density declined steadily and precipitously to 24.1 percent by 1979, and by 2010 only 11.9 percent of workers were unionized. The trend was sharpest in the private sector, where by 2010 only 6.9 percent of workers were union members.

Deindustrialization put unionized labor on the defensive in contract negotiations, in any influence in party politics, and in their right to represent workers. When air traffic controllers went on strike in August 1981, President Reagan not only fired the strikers, he did so in a multipronged strategy that included multiple court filings, freezing of the PATCO strike fund, and a move to decertify the union. This course of events was recognized as momentous at the time, but in hindsight it symbolized the beginning of our current antilabor climate (McCartin 2011). More immediately, during spring 2011 Wisconsin governor Scott Walker championed legislation eliminating collective bargaining for public employees. Although this may prove a galvanizing political opportunity for workers nationally, it also signals a new weakness of worker rights in the legal and political climate. The only strength workers have is in their numbers, which they coordinate through political and bargaining efforts, so this challenge to union viability represents a crucial moment in labor relations.

Union decline coincided with the breaking down of the social contract. Instead of understanding the problem as one of contradiction and conflict between classes (between top executives and workers), workers are pitted against one another in a race to the bottom. Who will work for the lowest wages, under the most tenuous conditions, and for the longest hours? With an unemployment rate at 10 percent, workers are more likely to accept jobs rendering them *underemployed*, in part-time temporary positions when they would prefer permanent full-time employment, or in jobs that underutilize their skills and credentials (Aronowitz 2005; Kalleberg 2007). Or they are going back to school in their 50s to increase their human capital. Top corporate executives, on the other hand, seem to be faring better (as discussed later). This is no coincidence in an antiunion climate; top executives are able to reap better compensation packages when they head nonunionized companies (Banning and Chiles 2007).

The backlash against labor culminates a shift evident since the 1970s. But it is particularly unfortunate today, coinciding with deep recession. The conflation of antilabor politics and weak labor markets means lower- and middle-income workers bear recession without support or coalitional strength. Labor had a voice in policy debates in the New Deal era, furthering and protecting the interests of workers and lower-middle-income families, and it should have legal ground and legitimacy for such a role again.

Private Ownership

What if we turn our question around, focusing on wealth instead of poverty? The title of Denny Braun's (1991) book, *The Rich Get Richer: The Rise of Income Inequality in the United States and the World*, hints at the core problem: the poor get poorer *because* the rich get richer. The extent of inequality in society is a function of the difference between how much the wealthiest have and how much the poorest have. But Braun's point is a larger one about the parasitic relationship. Wealth accumulation is possible only when the working class is exploited, income disparities escalate unchecked, and the effect of private property is left unexamined.

Income (the flow of resources, such as from wages/salaries, interest from savings, or stock dividends) is an important economic indicator of well-being, determining how we plan and live our daily lives. Income inequality continues to worsen and has now reached historic levels, indicating disparities not seen since the late 1920s (Saez 2008). In 2009, the bottom income quintile (20%) received only 3.4 percent of the income, while the middle 20 percent received 14.6 percent, the top 20 percent received 50.3 percent (an increase from 43.3% in 1967), and the very top 5 percent received 21.7 percent of income (U.S. Census Bureau 2010). At approximately $50,000, median incomes for white households in 2006 continued to outpace incomes for blacks ($30,000) and Hispanics ($35,000). Considerable research focuses on the racial and gender income gaps by examining disparities in earnings and job opportunities and analyzing discrimination in hiring, wages, wage setting, and promotion (England 1992; Padavic and Reskin 2002; Wilson 1987, 1997; Waldinger and Lichter 2003; Jencks and Peterson 1991). Another approach is to consider the country's elite income earners, corporate executives and CEOs, in comparison with the average worker. Company executives have always done well, but a hefty 50:1 executive-to-worker compensation ratio in the 1960s has escalated (thanks to stock options and bonuses) to over 300:1 in the 21st century (Anderson et al. 2008). Ironically, the highest-rewarded CEOs are those heading firms with the most dramatic layoffs during the recent recession (Anderson et al. 2010). As with executive compensation, occupation and earnings are only part of the picture of income flows, and the higher a person is on the income ladder, the more likely that income results from profits of financial assets (wealth) in addition to wages or salaries.

Wealth tends to be much more stable and persistent over time, and it plays an important role in maintaining living standards across the labor market and other challenges through the life course (Oliver and Shapiro 1997). Household wealth, or net worth, is measured as the accumulated sum of our assets (such as home equity, savings, real estate, stocks, etc.) minus our debts (student loans, credit card debt, other loans or credit balances). Net worth provides a crucial safety net for families in the case of a loss of income; savings can be utilized in case of a medical emergency; and when adult children go out on their own, parents with funds in a bank account or with accessible equity in their homes can help by providing *transformative assets* such as college tuition or loans for the down payment on a first mortgage (Shapiro 2004).

The distribution of wealth is a more skewed form of inequality than is income. In the United States, the wealthiest 1 percent of the population own approximately 35 percent of the net worth, and the next 19 percent own about 50 percent. This leaves only 15 percent of net asset ownership for 80 percent of the population (Wolff 2010). The distribution of net financial assets is even more unequal, with the top 1 percent owning 42.7 percent of the financial resources in 2007 and the bottom 80 percent owning just 7 percent of financial assets. Wealth inequality, by either measure, has been getting worse for the last three decades (Wolff 2010).

Further, comparing median net worth by race and Hispanic origin uncovers the persistence of racial inequality in the United States. Well into the post–civil rights era, during a time when race is no longer supposed to matter in one's life chances,[2] the modest access to wealth enjoyed by many whites continues to outpace that of black and Hispanics.[3] Much of the disparity has been shaped by historically differential access to and timing of home ownership relative to shifts in housing stock and access to mortgages.[4] Racist lending practices and racial steering in real estate kept black families from taking full advantage of the housing boom of the post–World War II period, as did structured segregation in urban and suburban neighborhoods throughout the second half of the 20th century. Even after it became illegal to factor race into lending practices, differential valuations and segregation had been established (Oliver and Shapiro 1997; Massey and Denton 1993). Wealth inequality builds on itself, so that historical discrimination in jobs, housing, and lending is amplified through time (Conley 1999).

Behind the intergenerational persistence of racialized wealth inequality are assumptions that inheritance and wealth ownership are natural and meritocratic. The passing down of wealth is such a taken-for-granted part of our social fabric that the unequal distributive consequences are left unexamined. For example, although transformative assets—the benefit of gifts or loans from parents and grandparents—makes the difference in whether families can realize their aspirational goals, they attribute that success to their own hard work and good choices rather than the privilege of wealth, not quite perceiving that the difference between their success and the next family's failure is not the difference of earning it, but the luck of family birth (Shapiro 2004). So, one of the reasons inequality is stable in the United States is that we have inheritance of property ownership that is presumed as a natural right, as something one has earned. We should recognize, at least, that this is one of the ways that privilege is passed down, as is poverty. The flip side of inheritance of property, whether home ownership, starter assets, or trust funds, is that those families who do not own property do not have equal access to the same choices or share in that part of the American Dream. Inheritance is one rule that stratifies society.

Poverty Assistance

A number of government-sponsored social programs are in place with the stated purpose of assisting those in need when ties to the labor market are broken or insufficient. Poverty assistance programs include programs such as Temporary Assistance to Needy Families (TANF), the Earned Income Tax Credit (EITC), food stamps, and assistance to Women, Infants, and Children (WIC). These programs are visible and carry a burden of scrutiny for recipients. And poverty assistance in the United States contrasts with other industrialized countries that have long-established welfare states (Hacker 2002; Handler and Hasenfeld 2007). For most of our history, private charities at the local level carried the moral and actual burden of assisting those in need; it was only gradually that government began to share responsibility (Skocpol 1992).

Throughout Europe, social assistance is a right of citizenship and legitimate function of the state. In contrast, in the United States pensions and health care are employment based, and it is primarily well-off, elite workers who have the best social insurance. In addition, as discussed earlier, in the last 30 years in the United States workplace security has given way to flexible production and labor relations. While private, employment-based security is a larger portion of the welfare state in the United States, it is precarious and available on a smaller scale to a shrinking portion of the labor force. The other privatized aspect of social assistance is charitable giving through nonprofit organizations (Handler and Hasenfeld 2007). Because the vicissitudes of the economy tend to correspond with declines in charitable giving, when they need it most, these private sources of assistance dry up.

Further, our history of social assistance is one of morality and scrutinized deservedness (Skocpol 1992; Hays 2004; Handler and Hasenfeld 2007). The fear of sponsoring bad behavior undermines public support for poverty relief, so the paucity of state-funded programs in our early history reflected a social Darwinism—the idea that the poor are in herently unfit. During the early 20th century, we began to recognize that rapid industrialization, urbanization, and immigration were societal-level processes shaping hardships for groups of people. And we began implementing more local-level programs targeting women and children. Some of these were modest mothers' or widows' pensions, explicitly limited to "worthy" women who upheld strict moral codes of behavior. However, inadequate spending meant only a few families benefited—about 2.5 percent of the 3.8 million female-headed households in 1931.

The federal government's role in social assistance expanded under the Social Security Act of 1935 and in response to demands for relief. Aid to Families with Dependent Children (AFDC) (originally Aid to Children) was designed to help families who had lost a parent. By the 1960s, AFDC recipients were predominantly unmarried women with children, because most poor, single-parent families were female headed. A large program, critics claimed that welfare created a culture of dependency and disincentives for responsible adulthood. Although we had always criticized the poor, under the Reagan administration—and continuing through the Clinton years—there was a heightened rhetoric about welfare abuse. The assumption was that these "welfare moms" were milking the system, having children to increase their benefits. This racialized stereotype depicted most recipients as black, while in fact most welfare recipients are white (though a higher proportion of blacks than whites have used welfare). In addition, teen pregnancies are unintended, not planned for the benefits; and families on welfare are not larger than average. While the program was large, benefits were not. Real AFDC benefits had declined throughout the 1980s and early 1990s so that by 1993 the average monthly payment was $377.[5]

Still, the program and its recipients were vilified. Reforms occurred piecemeal until 1996 passage of the Personal Responsibility and Work Opportunity Reconciliation Act (PRWORA). Otherwise known as Welfare Reform, PRWORA replaced AFDC with Temporary Assistance for Needy Families (TANF). As the name of the act makes clear, it was concomitantly about teaching women to be responsible and getting them back in the labor market and off welfare. TANF has two major programmatic themes, work first and a two-parent family. Strict rules and bureaucratic complexity render the experience especially punitive (Hays 2004).

As a limited block grant to states, TANF further decentralized a welfare system that was already administered locally. Allowing for considerable discretion across states as to how the block grant was spent (as opposed to line-by-line funding under AFDC), TANF represents a new devolution of programmatic implementation (Winston 2002; Hays 2004). Decentralization is an effective strategy against any organizing potential on behalf of the poor. It deflects conflict onto the local level, making it harder to collectively advocate for assistance (Winston 2002). And TANF has a federally mandated lifetime limit of five years at most, while some states further limit the number of consecutive years. TANF can report a reduction in the number of welfare recipients, not because of renewed self-sufficiency for individuals, but because of sanctions and denial of support (Hays 2004).

The U.S. history of poverty assistance questions any claim that our welfare programs are intended to help the most needy or equalize distribution. To the contrary, Piven and Cloward (1993/1971) establish that poverty assistance is extended only in the face of mass protest and to ward off rebellion. In the 1930s and 1960s, poor people's movements rose up when the government ignored escalating, mass-based need. These protest movements were effective to the extent that New Deal and Great Society programs specifically targeted poverty. Piven and Cloward also show that once disruptive protest subsided, support for the poor dried up, and work-based policies were soon replaced by cash assistance, then abolished.

Vilification of the poor as undeserving is clearest in deleterious labels such as "underclass" and "welfare queen" and the media coverage that furthers these constructions (Gans 1995). Gans establishes not just that we misunderstand poverty, but that poverty and the poor are functional for society. On a social-psychological level, we feel better about ourselves when there is a group against whom we compare favorably. Economically, increased poverty results in jobs related to social services, criminal justice, and mental health. In addition, welfare recipients and the working poor keep wages low, "staffing a 'reserve army of labor'" (Gans 1995, 94; see also Piven and Cloward 1993/1971). Poverty and unemployment ensure competition for jobs, keeping the labor force anxious for any job at any price.

COMMITMENT TO CHANGE

If everything is so unequal in the United States, why not simply change the rules? Why not change labor laws, tax policy, and inheritance rules, and set up a more generous welfare system? We could, but we choose not to because the essential beliefs and values that dominate our discourse in the United States lead us to think that whatever inequality in outcomes exists must be basically fair. Our usual explanation of inequality, that of personal choice and deservedness described earlier, has roots in our cultural ideas about the American Dream, equality of opportunity, and personal responsibility. The United States, after all, was founded in opposition to the feudal stasis of nobility and birthright; we are the land of opportunity, competitive individualism, morality, and personal responsibility (Ladd 1994).

Following this basic belief in individuality and opportunity for achievement, our ideas about each of the sets of rules described earlier—labor relations, private property, and social assistance—are harder to change. In terms of labor relations, the very idea of a "right to work" state shapes an understanding of labor relations that is antiunion as if unions are antifreedom. The idea that we deserve what we earn shapes an understanding of welfare that makes those in need (and their grandchildren) look undeserving and fosters belief that those who are wealthy (and their grandchildren) have earned it.

This myth belies a reality having more to do with the accident of birth in a highly unequal—if rich—society. Nevertheless, we also believe that we are a uniquely moral society (Ladd 1994). Consensus should follow, then, that widespread poverty is no way to show off our country's sense of national pride. If the United States has too much visible poverty, too much economic suffering, and too many children at risk of hunger or homelessness, we all look bad. Domhoff (2006) reminds us to ask "Who wins?" from any social or political outcome—this question generally leads us to a more informed answer about power. So, who wins from high levels of inequality and poverty? From a shrinking middle class? From policies that espouse "trickle down" welfare for corporations and a retrenchment of social services that might sustain the neediest among us? What we resist in our ideology and in our policy practices is the understanding that in order to alleviate poverty and reduce inequality, we have to commit ourselves to reducing wealth and privilege. The United States is a wealthy country with the potential to share resources more equitably and more equally, and it is an injustice that we decide, as a society, not to do so.

NOTES

1.   Brady (2009) argues that the distinction between *distributive* and *redistributive* economic policy gives the appearance that economic distribution (who gets what and how much through the operation of business and the market) somehow precedes social assistance policy (redistribution) and is therefore unfettered by government interference. By implication, redistributive policy is *social* and up for debate while distribution is *inherent* and unchangeable. But the initial rules of the game of productive ownership and profit, industry operation and competition, and jobs are more accurately described as social and political. Both distribution and redistribution are policy in this sense, and Brady argues they should both be up for scrutiny.

2.   The idea that the United States is now "postrace" has been growing since the Civil Rights Act. Antiracist legislation has supposedly done its job, and affirmative action has now been deemed "reverse discrimination," so that race can no longer be an explicit factor in college admissions (Schmidt 2007). Barak Obama's election as U.S. president in 2008 solidified our belief that, in the terms of Stephen Colbert's satire, we "don't see race." A good place to start for analysis to the contrary is Katznelson (2005). See Tessler and Sears (2010) for consideration of the 2008 election season and the politics of race, and Bush (2010) for evidence of our contradictory experiences and constructions of race today, especially on college campuses.

3.   Wolff (Chapter 3, this volume; see Table 3.3) establishes the stability between 1983 and 2007 of wealth inequality by race and Hispanic origin. For example, the mean black-white ratio held at 0.19; the median ratio changed only from 0.07 to 0.06.

4.   For those Americans who own any wealth at all, home equity represents the bulk of their portfolio. The post-2008 recessionary period and accompanying housing crisis have resulted in what will hopefully be a temporary increase in the racial wealth gap. According to the Pew Research Center, "in 2009, the median net worth of white households—$113,149—was the highest of all groups. In sharp contrast, Hispanic and black households had median net worth of $6,325 and $5,677 respectively" (Kochhar, Fry, and Taylor, July 26, 2011).

5.   This average was over all states. AFDC real benefits varied widely between states, depending on eligibility standards.

BIBLIOGRAPHY

Adler, William M. 2001. *Mollie's Job: A Story of Life and Work on the Global Assembly Line*. New York: Simon and Schuster.

Anderson, Sarah, John Cavanagh, Chuck Collins, Sam Pizzigati and Mike Lapham. August 25, 2008. *How Average Taxpayers Subsidize Runaway Pay: 15th Annual Compensation Survey*. Washington, DC: Institute for Policy Studies and United for a Fair Economy. http://www.faireconomy.org/files/executive_excess_2008.pdf.

Anderson, Sarah, Chuck Collins, Sam Pizzigati and Kevin Shih. September 1, 2010. *CEO Pay and the Great Recession: 17th Annual Executive Compensation Survey*. Washington, DC: Institute for Policy Studies. http://www.ips-dc.org/reports/executive_excess_2010.

Aronowitz, Stanley. 2005. *Just Around the Corner: The Paradox of the Jobless Recovery.* Philadelphia: Temple University Press.

Banning, Kevin and Ted Chiles. 2007. "Trade-Offs in the Labor Union-CEO Compensation Relationship," *Journal of Labor Research*, Vol. 28, No. 2, pp. 347–57.

Blau, J. 1993. *Social Contract and Economic Markets.* New York: Plenum Press.

Bonacich, Edna, Lucie Cheng, Nomra Chinchilla, Nora Hamilton, and Paul Ong, eds., 1994. *Global Production: The Apparel Industry in the Pacific Rim.* Philadelphia: Temple University Press.

Brady, David. 2009. *Rich Democracies, Poor People: How Politics Explain Poverty.* New York: Oxford University Press.

Braun, Denny. 1991. *The Rich Get Richer: The Rise of Income Inequality in the United States and the World.* Chicago: Nelson-Hall Publishers.

Bush, Melanie E. L. 2010, 2nd ed. *Everyday Forms of Whiteness: Understanding Race in a "Post-racial" World.* Lanham, MD: Rowman and Littlefield.

Conley, Dalton. 1999. *Being Black, Living in the Red: Race, Wealth and Social Policy in America.* Berkeley: University of California Press.

Domhoff, G. William. 2006, 5th ed. *Who Rules America?: Power, Politics, and Social Change.* New York: McGraw-Hill.

Edsall, Thomas Byrne. 1984. *The New Politics of Inequality.* New York: W. W. Norton & Company.

Edwards, Richard. 1979. *Contested Terrain: The Transformation of the Workplace in the Twentieth Century.* New York: Basic Books.

England, Paula. 1992. *Comparable Worth: Theories and Evidence.* New York: Aldine de Gruyter.

Gans, Herbert J. 1995. *The War against the Poor: The Underclass and Antipoverty Policy.* New York: Basic Books.

Hacker, J. S. 2002. *The Divided Welfare State: The Battle over Public and Private Social Benefits in the United States.* New York: Cambridge University Press.

Handler, Joel F. and Yeheskel Hasenfeld. 2007. *Blame Welfare, Ignore Poverty and Inequality.* New York: Cambridge University Press.

Hays, Sharon. 2004. *Flat Broke with Children: Women in the Age of Welfare Reform.* New York: Oxford University Press.

Hirsch, Barry T. and David A. MacPherson. Last modified January 21, 2011. *Union Membership and Coverage Database from CPS.* http://www.unionstats.com, accessed June 12, 2011.

Jencks, Christopher and Paul E. Peterson.1991. *The Urban Underclass.* Washington, DC: The Brookings Institution Press.

Kalleberg, Arne L. 2007. *The Mismatched Worker.* New York: W. W. Norton & Company.

Katznelson, Ira. 2005. *When Affirmative Action Was White: An Untold History of Racial Inequality in Twentieth Century America.* New York: W. W. Norton & Company.

Kendall, Diana. 2011. *Framing Class: Media Representations of Wealth and Poverty in America.* Lanham, MD: Rowman and Littlefield.

Kochhar, Rakesh, Richard Fry and Paul Taylor. July 26, 2011. *Wealth Gaps Rise to Record Highs between Whites, Blacks, Hispanics.* Washington, DC: Pew

Research Center. http://www.pewsocialtrends.org/2011/07/26/wealth-gaps-rise-to-record-highs-between-whites-blacks-hispanics/.

Ladd, Everett Carll. 1994. *The American Ideology: An Exploration of the Origins, Meaning, and Role of American Political Ideas*. The Roper Center for Public Opinion Research.

MacLeod, Jay. 2009, 3rd ed. *Ain't No Makin' It: Aspirations and Attainment in a Low-Income Neighborhood*. Boulder, CO: Westview Press.

Marx, Karl. 1967. *Capital*. New York: International Publishers.

Marx, Karl. 1851–52/1978. The Eighteenth Brumaire of Louis Bonaparte. In Tucker, Robert C., *The Marx-Engels Reader*, 2nd edition. New York: W. W. Norton and Company.

Marx, Karl and Friedrich Engels. 1848/1967. *The Communist Manifesto*. New York: Pantheon Books.

Massey, Douglas and Nancy Denton. 1993. *American Apartheid: Segregation and the Making of the Underclass*. Cambridge: Harvard University Press.

McCartin, Joseph. 2011. *Collision Course: Ronald Reagan, the Air Traffic Controllers, and the Strike that Changed America*. New York: Oxford University Press.

McNamee, Stephen J. and Robert K. Miller Jr. 2009. *The Meritocracy Myth*. Lanham, MD: Rowman & Littlefield.

Milkman, Ruth. 1997. *Farewell to the Factory: Auto Workers in the Late Twentieth Century*. Berkeley: University of California Press.

Mills, C. Wright. 1959/2000. *The Sociological Imagination*. New York: Oxford University Press.

Oliver, Melvin and Thomas Shapiro. 1997. *Black Wealth/White Wealth: A New Perspective on Racial Inequality*. New York: Routledge.

Padavic, Irene and Barbara Reskin. 2002, 2nd ed. *Women and Men at Work*. Thousand Oaks, CA: Pine Forge Press.

Piven, Frances Fox and Richard Cloward. 1993/1971. *Regulating the Poor: The Functions of Public Welfare*. New York: Random House.

Przeworski, Adam. 1985. *Capitalism and Social Democracy*. New York: Cambridge University Press.

Quadagno, Jill. 1994. *The Color of Welfare: How Racism Undermined the War on Poverty*. New York: Oxford University Press.

Rubin, Beth. 1996. *Shifts in the Social Contract: Understanding Change in American Society*. Thousand Oaks, CA: Pine Forge Press.

Saez, Emmanuel. 2008. "Striking It Richer: The Evolution of Top Incomes in the United States." *Pathways Magazine*. Stanford Center for the Study of Poverty and Inequality.

Schmidt, Peter. 2007. *Color and Money: How Rich White Kids Are Winning the War over College Affirmative Action*. New York: Palgrave Macmillan.

Shapiro, Thomas. 2004. *The Hidden Cost of Being African American: How Wealth Perpetuates Inequality*. New York: Oxford University Press.

Skocpol, Theda. 1992. *Protecting Soldiers and Mothers: The Political Origins of Social Policy in the United States*. Cambridge: Harvard University Press.

Snyder, Rachel Louise. 2007. *Fugitive Denim: A Moving Story of People and Pants in the Borderless World of Global Trade*. New York: W. W. Norton & Company.

Tessler, Michael and David O. Sears. 2010. *Obama's Race: The 2008 Election and the Dream of a Post-racial America*. Chicago: The University of Chicago Press.

United States Census Bureau. 2010. *Income, Poverty, and Health Insurance Coverage in the United States: 2009*. Current Population Reports, Series P-60, No 238. http://www.census.gov/prod/2010pubs/p60-238.pdf.

Waldinger, Roger and Michael Lichter. 2003. *How the Other Half Works: Immigration and the Social Organization of Labor*. Berkeley: University of California Press.

Wilson, William Julius. 1987. *The Truly Disadvantaged: The Inner City, the Underclass, and Public Policy*. Chicago: University of Chicago Press.

Wilson, William Julius. 1997. *When Work Disappears: The World of the New Urban Poor*. New York: Vintage Books.

Winston, Pamela. 2002. *Welfare Policymaking in the States: The Devil in Devolution*. Washington, DC: Georgetown University Press.

Wolff, E. N. 2007. "Recent Trends in Household Wealth in the United States: Rising Debt and the Middle-Class Squeeze." Working Paper No. 502. Annandale-on-Hudson, NY: The Levy Economics Institute of Bard College. http://www.levyinstitute.org/pubs/wp_502.pdf.

Wolff, E. N. 2010. "Recent Trends in Household Wealth in the United States: Rising Debt and the Middle-Class Squeeze—an Update to 2007." Working Paper No. 589. Annandale-on-Hudson, NY: The Levy Economics Institute of Bard College. http://www.levyinstitute.org/pubs/wp_589.pdf.

Wright, Eric Olin. 1985. *Classes*. New York: Verso.

Chapter 8

Why Is So Much of the World Poor?

Shawn Humphrey and Christine Exley

INTRODUCTION

The first of the United Nations Millennium Development Goals is halving the proportion of individuals who live on less than $1.25 per day (2005 PPP) by 2015. Accomplishing this goal is more daunting for some regions of the world as opposed to others. For example, as of 2005, in sub-Saharan Africa and Southern Asia the share of the population living below $1.25 a day was 51 percent and 39 percent, respectively. In Latin America and the Caribbean and Western Asia, it was 8 percent and 6 percent, respectively (worldbank.org). There are three main explanations for this pattern of poverty: culture, geography, and institutions. While we will review all of these explanations separately, it is important to note that there exists much overlap between these explanations. Such a unifying and integral variable is productivity. For instance, consider a key driver of productivity—technology. One's culture may impact one's decision to use new technology or not, geography may prevent or encourage the use of certain technology, and institutions are undeniably important to the development of technology. Productivity also stands at the center of the analyses by both macroeconomists and microeconomists. While macroeconomists often point to productivity as the reason that rich countries produce so much more output than poor countries and hence experience higher levels of economic growth, microeconomists focus on an individual's level of productivity as a key determinant of her own wealth. Although the importance of productivity is undeniable, how to increase productivity is a complicated and not yet fully understood process. As such, the following sections of this chapter look to provide insight into these complexities in order to answer why some countries are poor and others are rich. The next section reviews the three main answers to this question: culture, geography, and institutions. The section that follows explains the macroeconomic approach to achieving economic growth, while the fourth section details the microeconomic approach to alleviating poverty. Lastly, the fifth section explores the institutions argument in more detail and the final section concludes.

OVERVIEW OF ANSWERS TO WHY SOME COUNTRIES ARE POOR

This section provides a brief overview of the three main answers to the question that is also the title of this chapter: why is so much of the world still poor?

Culture

If one mentions culture when explaining the determinants of poverty, some economists will quickly ask: what is culture? Since the answer to this question necessarily varies with the context and lacks easily quantifiable characteristics, many economists argue that no economic value can be gleaned by looking at culture, instead believing this is a question better left to sociologists and anthropologists. However, many economists have also developed appropriate approaches with which to learn how culture affects economic development.

Perhaps one of the first ways economists argued for the importance of culture arose from economists showing how analyses that include countless traditional economic variables (i.e., education, investment, and technology levels) still often fail to explain much of the observed outcomes. For instance, Gregory Clark (1987) examines the large differences in early 20th-century cotton production levels, where one New England worker operated more than six times the machines operated by a worker from Greece, Japan, India, or China. He determines that this difference cannot be explained by differences in technology, management skills, local capital, or input markets, which hence leads Clark to argue that cultural differences are a key driving force. While this process-of-elimination approach may never be entirely satisfying since it is unlikely that we will ever be able to rule out all possible explanations except culture, it has successfully pushed economists to consider factors outside of those traditionally examined.

In contrast to the process-of-elimination approach, some economists carefully define culture and then look to analyze the effect of culture on economic development directly. One approach using this framework is to define some variables as culture variables and show the importance of these variables. For example, Guiso, Sapienza, and Zingales (2006, 23) provide extensive evidence from a meta-analysis on the importance of cultural variables, which they define as "those customary beliefs and values that ethnic, religious, and social groups transmit fairly unchanged from generation to generation." Most recently, many studies now look to variables, such as trust and attitudes toward others, to explain economic development.

Another approach using this framework involves defining culture as a set of societal constraints and norms that dictate how and under what rules people interact in a society. Such a structured approach allows culture to be interpreted in a similar lens as institutions. For instance, Avner Grief (1994) explains that individuals in a society act in their best interest according to their culture, where culture encompasses a set of beliefs known to everyone and believed to guide everyone's decisions in a society. Grief examines the development of two premodern societies under this framework. First, he discusses the development in the 11th century of Genoa, a leading commercial Italian city-state. The Genoese traders operated under an individualist society where contracts were typically between individuals as opposed to families, and Genoese tended to adhere to Christian beliefs, such as their salvation being their own responsibility. Second, Grief examines the Maghribi traders, Jewish merchants that traded across the Muslim Mediterranean regions in the 11th century. The Maghribi operated in a collectivist society, for they shared the Muslim value that they were all part of one nation and operated as Jewish community with the foundation that all members are mutually responsible for each other. Grief then explains how these cultural practices led these societies to develop different institutions even though these societies coexisted in the same time and under similar constraints (i.e., available technology and environment). While the Maghribis' trading relied more on informal contracts based off of mutual trust (much like the collective nature of their society), the Genoese developed formal contracts, which are clearly needed in a society focused on individual as opposed to collective well-being. Extending past these two societies, Grief (1994, 943) notes that individualistic cultures are more conducive to the development of formal institutions that allow individuals to capture efficiency gains from individual specialization, and speculates that the medieval Latin societies, such as the Genoese, may have "cultivated the seeds of the 'Rise of the West.'" That is, to the extent that we agree with the father of modern economics, Adam Smith, that such specialization is essential to economic growth, it is clear that culture *can* significantly impact how supportive institutions are of economic growth.

Geography

There is no question that geographical location strongly correlates with the economic prosperity of countries today. In fact, as shown in Jeffery Sachs (2001), the level of poverty in countries seems to center at the equator and then diminish as one moves farther away from the equator.

While the correlation between the location of countries and poverty levels is clear, there exists a debate in economics about the causal relationship between geographical factors and poverty. Even though Sachs admits that his hypotheses about the impact of geography on economic growth are not yet fully proved, he argues that there exists strong evidence that technology has not been appropriately adapted to the constraints of tropical economies. The corresponding limited technology in the tropical areas prevents these societies from benefiting from scale economies and further inhibits their development. As such, Sachs argues that the international community should invest in and develop health and agricultural technologies that can help lift tropical economies out of poverty, and in fact, in his book *The End of Poverty*, Sachs (2005) boldly claims that doing so would allow poverty to be eliminated in our time.

Much like Sachs, Jared Diamond (1999) strongly relies on environmental differences to explain why some civilizations developed differently than others in his book *Guns, Germs and Steel*. By detailing the history of several civilizations across the world, Diamond explains economic development in a manner similar to evolution: societies develop as a function of their environment, where some environments are more favorable to economic development and hence are more likely to lead to prosperous societies. In particular, Diamond argues that there exist four main environmental factors that determine the development of a society. First, the wildlife and animals available for domestication determines if a society can accumulate a food surplus and hence if some people can afford to specialize in something other than food production, such as political or military technology. Second, ecological and geographical barriers impact the extent and speed of migration and diffusion with a region. Third, factors that affect diffusion across regions (in particular, continents) contribute to the level of domestication and available technology. Lastly, larger population sizes increase the pool of potential inventors and hence likelihood of success in innovation and technology. Diamond concludes by noting that while these easily quantifiable environmental factors do not explain all of the differences in development across countries, they do undeniably contribute to fostering more favorable or unfavorable conditions for development, which is, in essence, the central point of the geographical explanation.

Institutions

Much like culture, there does not exist one unique and precise definition of institutions in the economic literature. Many economists follow the New Institutional Economics' definition of institutions: institutions are "rules of the game in a society ... they structure incentives in human exchange, whether political, social, or economic" (North 1990, 3). That is, institutions encompass governments, economic policy, organizations, and other similar infrastructure with which society operates. Intuitively, it is not surprising that institutions have a strong impact on economic development. In fact, in economic development, the institutions explanation is the most studied and arguably most accepted explanation as to why some countries are poor.

Since institutions are inherently tied in with both culture and geography, it is often infeasible to reasonably identify and determine the extent of the effect of institutions on economic development. However, Acemoglu, Johnson, and Robinson (2002) present a convincing argument for the integral role of institutions in determining why some countries are rich and others are poor. They show a great "reversal of fortune" among countries colonized by the Europeans: countries that were relatively poor 500 years ago are now relatively rich, and vice versa. They explain this reversal by arguing that the Europeans imposed institutions favorable to economic growth in poor countries and unfavorable to economic growth in rich countries. In particular, Europeans tended to impose extractive institutions in rich countries in order to gain from the resources and services in these countries. On the other hand, Europeans were more likely to settle in and hence develop institutions more favorable toward investment and economic growth in less populated areas, which also tended to be poorer areas. In addition to highlighting the impact of institutions on economic development, this chapter suggests that geography may be less important; the reversal of fortune is strong evidence against any argument that relies on time invariant geographic factors, and the timing of the reversal is also inconsistent with other often argued time-varying geographic factors, as detailed in Acemoglu, Johnson, and Robinson (2002). Since this chapter represents only one of many strong cases for the institutions explanation, we will further detail the institutions explanation later.

THE MACROECONOMIC ANSWERS

Macroeconomics, which often focuses on society- or country-level measures, is one of the two main approaches with which to analyze economic development, and in particular economic growth. Robert Lucas (1988, 3) defines the problem of economic development as "simply the problem of accounting for the observed pattern, across countries and across time, in levels and rates of growth of per capita income." Lucas notes the well-known stylized fact that the poorest countries tend to have the lowest growth rates, while middle-income countries on the path to economic development tend to have the highest growth rates. An underappreciated fact of growth accounting is that apparent small differences in growth rates can have enormous consequences for income differences between countries over relatively short time spans. Consider two countries A and B with the same level of income at the same time in history. If country A grows 0 percent and country B grows 2 percent per year annually (only a 2 percentage point difference), then after 200 years country B will be 52 times richer than country A.

The three main explanations of economic development (geography, culture, and institutions) also appear in macroeconomics. Sachs's discussion of tropical versus nontropical economies represents a macroeconomic geography explanation and a broad classification of a society, by say the majority religion, representing a macroeconomic culture explanation. However, the study of growth and development from a macroeconomic perspective centers around institutions, which interact with ideas, inputs, and productivity.

In particular, these three factors influence the amount of output produced in a given society or country, which is a key measure of economic growth. First, we need ideas, whether existing or new, to create some output. Second, we must acquire the inputs, which include the physical capital (i.e., machines, materials), the human capital (i.e., knowledge, skills), and the labor used to create the output. Lastly, the productivity involved in the production process determines how much output is produced, given some level of inputs. That is, the amount of output produced is believed to be a function of inputs and productivity, where productivity measures how much output can be produced per unit of input. A higher productivity entails producing output more efficiently, whether that is in terms of a lower cost, shorter time, or ease of production. For instance, consider the production of a new irrigation system for farmers. First, the firm needs to create or to acquire a design plan for the construction of the irrigation system. Second, the firm must gather all of the materials, machines, and labor that will be used to create the system. Lastly, what determines the productivity of the firm, such as the management guidelines that they follow, impacts the number of irrigation systems that are created, given some level of inputs.

Charles I. Jones (2005) explains the importance of ideas, defined as instructions or recipes, in determining economic growth. First and foremost, ideas are nonrivalrous since one person using some ideas does not diminish another person's ability to use the same ideas. Let us return to the example of a firm creating an irrigation system. If another firm wishes to create this same system, they will not need to develop new ideas to do so since they can merely use the ideas of the initial firm. That is, the nonrivalrous and intangible nature of ideas allows us to avoid the problem of scarcity that is inherent in physical inputs. Therefore the creation of ideas is a powerful catalyst for development. As such, some countries may experience lower economic growth and hence are poorer since they lack institutions favorable to creating ideas, such as strong education systems and patenting laws.

Once ideas are created to produce an output, inputs are needed to actually produce the desired output. Macroeconomists often look to achieve growth and development by determining the optimal amount of inputs (human capital, physical capital, and labor) needed to create the output, where the optimal amount is normally defined as the amount that leads to the highest achievable profits. For instance, Hall and Jones (1999) note that the United States' output per worker is 35 times higher than Niger. Of this difference in the level of output per worker, they determine that physical and human capital differences in the United States and Niger can explain a 1.5- and a 3.1-fold difference, respectively.

In addition to inputs, macroeconomists study how productivity levels impacts growth and development. Hall and Jones (1999) note that productivity differences between the United States and Niger explain even more of the difference in the level of output per worker than the physical and human capital differences. Since the human and physical capital differences explain only a 4.65-fold difference (1.5 * 3.1) in the United States' output per worker relative to Niger, they note that this leaves a factor of over 7 (35/4.65) unexplained, which they attribute to productivity differences. They then argue that such large productivity differences across countries can largely be attributed to the differences in social infrastructure, where more productive countries possess a social infrastructure with less corruption, fewer impediments to trade, less government interference in production, and better enforcement of contracts.

THE MICROECONOMIC ANSWERS

In contrast to focusing on the economic growth of a society or country, microeconomists look at household or individual levels of poverty. Since data at this finer level are not as standardized or as common as country-level growth data often used by macroeconomists, a key step in microeconomists analyzing economic development involves data collection. One large source of data is household surveys, which often involve government or nonprofit organizations interviewing thousands of individuals using a door-to-door approach. Another popular and incredibly useful source of data arise from randomized experiments. In a randomized experiment, individuals are randomly assigned to a control or treatment group, where the treatment group receives some intervention of interest and the control group does not. That is, if a randomized experiment is both well designed and implemented, we can parse out the causal effect of the intervention by carefully comparing the control and treatment group before and after the intervention. This is an incredibly powerful tool, for micro-economists can use randomized experiments to determine the success or failure of various development interventions, ranging from malaria prevention to microfinance. Refer to Duflo, Glennerster, and Kremer (2006) as a great reference about the rationale for and how to implement randomized experiments.

Once microeconomists access appropriate data, their explanations for the differences in poverty levels also involve geography, culture, and institutions. For instance, microeconomists may point to an individual's beliefs and levels of trust as a cultural explanation for economic development, or they may point to the type of farmland that a household possesses as a geographical explanation. From an institution's perspective, economists often analyze how an individual behaves given the institutional rules she operates under. The following section sets up this individual-agent problem, which we then build upon to provide further insight into how institutions impact the individual's actions, outcomes, and ultimately wealth.

THE INSTITUTION'S ANSWER: POVERTY AND THE INDIVIDUAL

In order to examine poverty from an individual perspective, we will focus on the productivity of the individual. Quite simply, productivity refers to how much output an individual can produce with a unit of his time. When it comes to individual productivity, we know a few things. First, individual productivity is the key to material wealth. Second, the average resident of a rich country can produce more output with her time than her counterpart in a poor country. Third, the factors that influence an individual's level of productivity include the degree of specialization in his community and his access to capital (both physical and human) and technological innovations. Fourth, choosing to specialize, gaining access to capital, and taking advantage of technological innovations are all investment opportunities that are not guaranteed to be present in all communities. Fifth, investment opportunities entail a trade-off. An individual gives up current consumption and other alternative uses of her time in the pursuit of higher productivity and its attendant returns that lie in the future. Sixth, assuming they exist, not every individual will choose to pursue investment opportunities.

Let us take a closer look at an individual's investment decision. It is important to note that future returns are returns that can never be guaranteed. The favorable conditions under which an individual is considering her current investment decision may not hold in the future. Indeed, future returns are susceptible to a number of risks, such as macroeconomic shocks (i.e., hyperinflation, currency reevaluation) and environmental risks, both natural (i.e., floods, droughts) and human (i.e., pollution, overfishing). Consequently, before proceeding with an investment, a rational individual looks at the net private return that attends an investment. The net private return is calculated by weighing the expected marginal benefits (future productivity and future returns, which are discounted) against the expected marginal costs (current consumption and finance costs) that attend an investment. Of course, a higher net private return translates into a heightened incentive to take on the costly action of an investment. Conversely, a low net private return concludes in a diminished incentive to take on an investment. Our analysis, necessarily, will focus on the net private return that attends an investment and the multiplicity of factors that influence it. Hausmann, Rodrik, and Velasco (2006) provide a framework with which to analyze the net private return that attends an investment. It could be low for one of three reasons: the expected marginal benefits are low, the expected marginal costs are high, or a combination of the two.

Expected Marginal Benefits

There are two reasons that the expected marginal benefits could be low. First, the social returns that attend an investment, which is the summation of the private returns attained by all individuals impacted by the investment, could be low. For example, Yolanda is contemplating a 100 lempira investment in a freezer, with which to store and sell ice cream out of her home. However, she concludes that the social returns are only 90 lempiras—too low to make this investment worthwhile. The presence and size of social returns are positively associated with the existence and extent of markets. In Yolanda's case, the social returns are determined by the existence and extent of the ice cream market in her community. A market exists when at least one buyer and one seller conclude that an exchange of a particular good or service is mutually beneficial—that is, both consumer and producer surplus are positive. Taken together, consumer and producer surplus are known as the gains from trade. Pursuit of the gains from trade motivates buyers and seller to engage in a market transaction and thereby create markets. The number of these mutually beneficial exchanges between buyers and sellers determines the extent of a market. Consequently, any force that diminishes these mutual benefits threatens the existence and extent of markets and lowers the social returns.

For instance, the absence of an electrical grid, transportation network, and/or information network all could clearly limit the development of a market. Living, working, and investing in a malarial zone can circumscribe a market. More generally, whenever transaction costs, the cost of engaging in a market transaction, outweigh the gains from trade, a market either fails to materialize or falls in scope. Transaction costs include search (the time and resources spent looking for a market exchange partner), bargaining (the time and resources dedicated toward negotiating the terms of trade), and enforcement costs. Enforcement costs are critical. Before the conclusion of an exchange, the buyer may ask, "Will I get what I paid for?" Conversely, the seller may ask, "Will I get paid?" An exchange environment characterized by low enforcement costs allows both seller and buyer to answer affirmatively, realize gains from trade, and/or create or extend a preexisting market. Through its ability to minimize enforcement costs, trust is a fundamental market-making force. It is the role and responsibility of institutions through a combination of formal and informal rules and their enforcement characteristics, to engender trust among market exchange partners.

Poor institutions, which fail to overcome issues such as the high transaction costs discussed earlier, are a common and significant force that lowers social returns through their inability to get buyers and sellers to "yes." Without a large enough market, the social returns to some investments are low and hence an individual would not choose to invest. However, it is clear that this problem cycles, as a large market will not exist without individuals investing in it, but no individuals will invest without a large enough market. The extent to which institutions contribute to this cycle or could help break this cycle are discussed later.

The second reason that the expected marginal benefits could be low is due to low appropriability. For example, Yolanda's 100 lempira investment in a freezer could yield a 110 lempira social return. However, upon further reflection, she calculates that only 90 of the 110 lempira return will actually make it into her pocket. In this example, there is a discrepancy between Yolanda's private return and the social return. The other 20 lempiras could be captured by others.

Institutions, or the lack thereof, are key reasons as to why Yolanda may fail to capture the total return to her investment. Even potentially benevolent reasons, such as social norms of reciprocity that entitle a neighbor, friend, or family member to a portion of the returns or need-ing to pay taxes in order to fund local schools, may diminish her pri-vate returns. In a more unfortunate scenario, there may not exist sufficient security enforcement, from the police, military, or government, to prevent individuals from stealing her returns. Or, per-haps she must pay a large bribe in order to ensure such protection. Another possibility is that she lacks access to property rights, which could limit her returns in many ways. For instance, suppose Yolanda does not possess property rights to her home, which also doubles as her ice cream store. Then, at any time, the government could take ownership of her land and hence ice cream store, which would effec-tively eliminate any potential returns to her investment.

Hernando de Soto (2000) details the issue of lacking access to prop-erty rights in his book *The Mystery of Capital*. He argues that a lack of property rights decreases one's ability to turn assets into capital; that is, Yolanda cannot borrow against her home to fund her investment in buying a freezer since she does not own her house. This limits her ability to participate in the ice cream market and hence ability to make revenue. In return, this prevents her from further investments in other assets or human capital, and ultimately limits her productivity and hence ability to gain economically. While one seemingly obvious solu-tion is for Yolanda to acquire property rights to her home, de Soto notes that this is an immensely difficult, if not impossible, task in many devel-oping countries due to institutional constraints. In a case study where de Soto tasks his research team with acquiring the needed property rights to build a house on state-owned land in Peru, de Soto finds that doing so took six years and 11 months, and involved 52 government offices and 728 steps (de Soto 2000, 20). Such extreme institutional bar-riers to property rights are also found in other countries, such as the Philippines and Haiti. Since these barriers exist even for an experienced research team who can dedicate all of their time working to acquiring property rights (as opposed to also struggling to provide for their fam-ilies), it is clear that these institutional constraints to acquiring property rights may be too large of a hurdle for many to overcome.

EXPECTED MARGINAL COSTS

Even if the returns that attend an investment are high and a signifi-cant percentage is captured by our entrepreneur, her ability to act upon these plans may be fundamentally constrained by the high cost of investment and/or lack of access to finance. In particular, there exist three ways that entrepreneurs can finance the upfront costs of an investment: secure a loan, access their personal wealth or the wealth of friends and family members, and/or generate personal savings by cutting back on current consumption. The first two are valuable because they allow entrepreneurs to finance their investments through sources other than current consumption. In other words, they allow entrepreneurs to maintain a consistent standard of living while waiting on the delayed and uncertain delivery of benefits that attend an investment. In general, for the poor neither alternative is a real option. Their access to low-cost small-business loans is either limited due to the relatively high rates of interest they must pay or foreclosed because they lack the collateral with which to secure a loan, which recall is often the case due to the lack of property rights. Additionally, the poor, their friends, and their family, almost by definition, lack wealth. That leaves consumption. However, when one is engaged in a daily struggle of surviving on one or two dollars a day, there is not much room to cut back on consumption. Even if the poor can afford to cut back on consumption, there may not exist a safe, reliable, and worthwhile place in which to save, such as a trustworthy bank. This essentially brings us back to the need for institutions that can help overcome the poor's limited access to needed finance. Whether created by a small microfinance institution or formal government, institutions to provide the poor with a means to overcome high upfront costs may allow them to invest in opportunities where the net private return (expected marginal benefit–expected marginal cost) is positive. In return, the poor could increase their productivity and ultimately the community may achieve economic growth.

INDIVIDUALS TO MARKETS

To review, the costs of pursuing an investment opportunity are immediate and fully borne by the individual entrepreneur. On the other hand, the benefits of an investment are delayed, uncertain, and possibly up for capture by others. This combination of circumstances can conspire to convince the poor that they cannot afford to plan beyond the immediate future, erode the incentive to invest, limit the accumulation of productivity enhancing assets by the individual, and adversely impact their material welfare. Even more so, as fewer and fewer individuals choose to invest, markets become smaller and smaller, further eroding the incentive to invest. These self-reinforcing events could possibly conclude in the widespread collapse of markets in labor and other inputs, final goods and services, and finance. This is otherwise known as market failure—the inability of markets to allocate the economy's scarce resources and final goods and services to their highest valued use. In our example, Yolanda may not invest in the freezer due the high costs and lack of finance. Even though an ice cream business would have created a social surplus, she individually chooses to not invest in the freezer. If we assume other people in her community similarly find it to not be worthwhile to invest in an ice cream business, then a market for ice cream will not exist in her community at all despite the positive social returns. Another possible hindrance may be the lack of other markets, such as a market for milk needed to make the ice cream with. Yolanda's story is a story shared by billions of people around the globe.

If the size of the society's market is too small or limited, there is little incentive to specialize in an activity such as only selling ice cream as opposed to farming all your own food. A lack of specialization limits productivity and hence possible gains from trade in a market. To overcome this, the society needs to develop a great "variety and numbers of exchange," which North (1990, 34) notes require more complex agreements. In particular, as the size of the market increases, the exchanges become more impersonal and hence transaction costs (i.e., search, bargaining, and enforcement costs) increase. In order to diminish these transaction costs, a society needs to develop more complex institutions, such as formal contracts that enforce desirable trade rules. Hence, if a society can develop more complex institutions, then they can increase the size of their market, which creates an incentive to specialize. Specialization leads to an increase in productivity and hence gains from trade. That is, if more complex institutions exist, Yolanda may be able to specialize in selling ice cream, since she can securely trade among other people in her community. If other people in her community also then choose to specialize, the extent of the market will further increase, which, assuming appropriate institutions exist to deal with the larger market, leads to more gains from trade and eventually economic growth.

CONCLUSION

This chapter detailed many factors that hinder a society's ability to achieve economic prosperity. Frequently, adjusting institutions was presented as a way to overcome or mitigate these hindrances. That is, institutions should be made to complement a society's given geographical or cultural constraints in order to help the society achieve economic growth. Then, as economic growth accumulates over time, clearly a poor society can emerge as economically prosperous. While in theory such an institutional development should lead to economic prosperity, it is neither easy to nor clear how to implement such a process. Subsequently, as economists, we carefully test for what seems most likely to work and then carefully probe down that path.

While much success has been made in this regard, even the most successful paths fail sometimes. For instance, in their article "Miracle of Microfinance? Evidence from a Randomized Experiment," Banerjee et al. (2009) argue that microfinance is not necessarily a miracle in terms of development, despite the fact that it is one of the most popular and praised development approaches. They discover heterogeneous effects of microfinance, as it seems helpful only to certain types of people. Also, at least in the short run, they find no evidence that increasing microfinance opportunities impacts health, education, or women's role in decision making. Similarly, even with the strong theoretical and empirical evidence for the importance of formal property rights, Elinor Ostrom (1990) lays out how, under certain conditions, informal institutions can effectively govern common pooled resources, which often lack formal property rights that dictate to what extent and who can use them.

It is not surprising that there is no single answer or institution that will eliminate poverty, for every society inherently involves a different set of constraints, whether geographical, cultural, or otherwise. However, it is our hope that, as economists, we can help lead to the development of all the needed institutions to achieve global economic prosperity, a world where the question "why is so much of the world poor" is no longer relevant.

BIBLIOGRAPHY

Acemoglu, Daron, Simon Johnson and James A. Robinson. 2002. Reversal of Fortune: Geography and Institutions in the Making of the Modern World Income Institutions. *The Quarterly Journal of Economics* 117 (4): 1231–94.

Banerjee, Abhijit, Esther Duflo, Rachel Glennerster and Cynthia Kinnan. 2009. The Miracle of Microfinance? Evidence from a Randomized Evaluation. *J-PAL Working Paper.*

Clark, Gregory. 1987. Why Isn't the Whole World Developed? Lessons from Cotton Mills. *The Journal of Economic History* 47 (1): 141–73.

de Soto, Hernando. 2000. *The Mystery of Capital: Why Capitalism Triumphs in the West and Fails Everywhere Else.* New York: Basic Books.

Diamond, Jared. 1999. *Guns, Germs and Steel.* New York: W. W. Norton and Company.

Duflo, Esther, Rachel Glennerster and Michael Kremer. 2006. Using Randomization in Development Economics: A Toolkit. *MIT Department of Economics Working Paper No. 06-36.*

Grief, Avner. 1994. Cultural Beliefs and the Organization of Society: A Historical and Theoretical Reflection on Collectivist and Individualist Societies. *Journal of Political Economy* 102 (5): 912–50.

Guiso, Luigi, Paola Sapienza and Luigi Zingales. 2006. Does Culture Affect Economic Outcomes? *Journal of Economic Perspectives* 20 (2): 23–48.

Hall, Robert and Charles I. Jones. 1999. Why Do Some Countries Produce So Much More Output per Worker than Others? *The Quarterly Journal of Economics* 114 (1): 83–116.

Hausmann, Ricardo, Dani Rodrik and Andrés Velasco. 2006. Getting the Diagnosis Right: A New Approach to Economic Reform. *Finance and Development* 43 (1): 12–15.

Jones, Charles I. 2005. Growth and Ideas. *Handbook of Economic Growth* 1B: 1063–1111.

Lucas, Robert E. 1988. On the Mechanics of Economic Development. *Journal of Monetary Economics* 22: 3–42.

North, Douglass. 1990. *Institutions, Institutional Change and Economic Performance.* New York: Cambridge University Press.

Ostrom, Elinor. 1990. *Governing the Commons: The Evolution of Institutions for Collective Action.* New York: Cambridge University Press.

Sachs, Jeffrey. 2001. Tropical Development. *NBER Working Paper* No. 8119.

Sachs, Jeffrey. 2005. *The End of Poverty.* New York: Penguin.

World Bank. http://data.worldbank.org/indicator/SI.POV.DDAY.

Part IV

Demographic Groups and Discrimination

Chapter 9

What Explains Black-White Economic Inequality in the United States in the Early 21st Century?: The Effects of Skills, Discriminatory Legacies, and Ongoing Discrimination

Thomas N. Maloney and Ethan Doetsch

The place of African Americans in the United States was completely transformed over the course of the 20th century. This is true in a simple geographic sense, in that the mid-1900s were marked by waves of black migration out of the South and into other regions: in 1900, about 9 out of 10 blacks lived in the South, but by the end of the century only about half did (Maloney 2002). It is obviously also true in the arena of politics. The voting rights of blacks, especially those residing in the South, were very limited at the start of the century. By the end of the 1900s, blacks constituted an important voting bloc in many elections, and in the early 21st century Americans elected the first president of African descent. Blacks had also made great gains in the economic sphere, as there were substantial increases in their relative pay, wealth holding, and occupational status over the course of the century.

And yet full economic equality clearly had not been achieved by the start of the 21st century. The average weekly earnings of black men had risen to 75 percent of the average earnings of white men by the early 1980s. This ratio was still about 75 percent in 2009 (Ruggles et al. 2010; U.S. Bureau of Labor Statistics 2010a). Among women, black relative pay had actually fallen slightly from about 90 percent of the pay of whites to about 87 percent over these same years (U.S. Bureau of Labor Statistics 2010a). The black unemployment rate was about twice as high as the white unemployment rate throughout the 1970s, 1980s, and 1990s, and through the first decade of the 21st century (U.S. Bureau of Labor Statistics 2010b). There was more visible progress for blacks in terms of the poverty rate, as poverty among blacks fell from more than three times the white rate to just over two times the white rate during these same years. Still, a substantial racial gap remained in the incidence of poverty (U.S. Census Bureau 2010).

Why does such a large racial gap remain in terms of labor market outcomes and living standards? Some of this gap is explained by ongoing differences in skills, education, and training between black and white workers. Some of it reflects the persisting effects of patterns created by the pronounced, rigid, and often legal discrimination of the first half of the 20th century: profound residential segregation, wealth differences, and various "intergenerational factors" through which discrimination imposed on one cohort affects the life chances of their children. Finally, some of this gap reflects ongoing discrimination, not merely the legacy of past acts.

SKILL DIFFERENCES

According to mainstream economic theory, workers are generally paid in proportion to their productivity. Differences between black and white workers in characteristics that affect labor productivity will therefore contribute to the earnings gap. The share of the black-white pay gap that is explained by skill differences depends both on the size of the skill differences and on the "return" to skill—the dollar value of being a high-skilled worker rather than a mid- or low-skilled worker. Over the past 30 years, differences in skill accumulations and dramatic increases in the income gap between high-skilled workers and mid- and low-skilled workers have combined to worsen black-white earnings inequalities.

Skill is, of course, difficult to measure precisely or directly. The measure of job-related skills most commonly used by economists is educational attainment. Though it has narrowed in recent decades, there remains a significant racial gap in educational attainment, in terms of both quantity and quality, which subsequently affects earnings differentials. The latest available national estimates derived from the 2009 American Community Survey, which records the highest level of education attained for a nationally representative sample of U.S. residents, are informative as to quantity differences between races using a variety of different benchmarks (Ruggles et al. 2010). First, whites have higher levels of high school completion and, hence, are less likely to be low-skilled. Among white males aged 19 through 25 in 2009, 12.1 percent had not completed high school (or its equivalent). Over one-fifth of black males aged 19 through 25 had not completed high school. For females of the same age, the proportions without a completed high school education or equivalent are 8.7 percent and 12.8 percent for whites and blacks, respectively. Second, whites also have higher skill levels as measured by completion of a four-year college education. Among residents age 25 through 45, 20.7 percent of white males had completed a bachelor's degree as their highest level of education, whereas only 12.0 percent of black males had an equivalent level. Within the same age range, a completed bachelor's degree was the highest level of education for 24.0 percent of white females, compared with only 15.1 percent of black females. Furthermore, whites have higher skill levels as measured by postgraduate college education. Of white males age 25 through 45, 9.1 percent had attained a master's degree, doctoral degree, or professional degree beyond a bachelor's degree, in contrast to 4.1 percent of black males. For females, 11.6 percent of whites and 7.2 percent of blacks had attained an advanced, postgraduate degree. Across the board, whites have higher levels of education than black workers, although these differences are smaller among women (Ruggles et al. 2010).

These differences in the skill accumulations of black and white workers, as measured by education, have a significant impact on relative earnings, especially as pay differences across education categories have grown. Over the past 30 years, the earnings gap between college graduates and workers without a college education has increased markedly. This shift may be due to technological change that increases relative demand for workers with high skills, automation of tasks formerly performed by mid-skill or low-skill workers, and the movement of mid- and low-skill jobs to other nations with lower wage levels (Bound and Johnson 1992; Acemoglu 1999; Autor 2010). Due to these trends, greater education and skills have become increasingly demanded by U.S. labor markets and, absent increases in the number of highly educated, highly skilled workers, earnings for such workers have dramatically increased. By contrast, the same trends have decreased relative demand for and, hence, relative earnings of middle-skill, middle-income workers and low-skill, low-income workers. A simple comparison of the incomes of the average worker with a college degree and the average worker with only a regular high school diploma illustrates the earnings gap between highly skilled and medium-skilled workers. In 2009, employed males with a bachelor's degree age 25 to 45 earned on average 1.94 times the wage and salary income as equivalent workers with only a high school diploma. Among females, the college premium was of similar magnitude; female workers with a bachelor's degree earned 1.89 times the wage and salary income as females with only a high school diploma (Ruggles et al. 2010).

This growth in the returns to the upper end of the skills distribution relative to the middle and lower end since 1980 has exacerbated black-white earnings inequality. Black workers, as shown previously, are disproportionately concentrated in the middle and lower end of the education distribution, which has seen stagnant earnings growth. Conversely, whites are disproportionately concentrated at the upper end of the distribution, which has seen phenomenal growth in relative earnings over this period. Juhn, Murphy, and Pierce (1991) find that most of the slowdown in wage convergence between black and white male workers in the 1980s was the result of these two phenomena: the disproportionate concentration of black men toward the lower end of the skills distribution and the dramatic increase in the return to skill in recent years.

Differences in education quality, in addition to quantity, also have an important impact on the relative earnings of workers (Card and Krueger 1992). Many researchers suggest that black-white differences in scores on standardized tests like the Armed Forces Qualifying Test (AFQT) better reflect black-white skill differences than do simple measures of years of schooling, because differences in these scores are the result of differences in skill levels due to education quality as well as differences in quantity (Neal and Johnson 1996; O'Neill 1990). These researchers use data from the National Longitudinal Survey of Youth

1979, which follows the earnings of men and women aged 14 to 21 in 1978 through the 1990s and which collected information about the AFQT scores, family backgrounds, and schools of individuals surveyed. Some estimates suggest that differences in AFQT scores may explain around three-quarters of the black-white wage gap among young male workers and nearly all of the black-white wage gap among female workers (Neal and Johnson 1996, 874). Parental resources, as measured by workers' parental income, parental education, and family size, and school resources, as measured by the student-teacher ratio, proportion of disadvantaged students, dropout rate, and teacher turnover rate at a worker's high school, explain a sizable portion of the racial differences in AFQT scores, with the remainder likely explained by unobserved differences in elementary education quality (Neal and Johnson 1996, 887–90). Noting that education level and school quality, as measured by AFQT score, account for a large share of black-white income differences does not negate the importance of racial discrimination in explaining black-white earnings differentials. On the contrary, it highlights the importance of "premarket" racial discrimination in access to skills and quality education in explaining black-white income inequalities.

While racial differences in characteristics (like skill level) affect the black-white pay gap, racial differences in the impact of these characteristics on earnings may also have a hand in explaining the earnings gap; for example, an additional year of schooling might have very different payoffs for whites and blacks. New evidence, however, suggests that the return to education does not differ substantially between blacks and whites (Barrow and Rouse 2006). Both blacks and whites benefit equally from an additional year of education. Furthermore, civilian returns to education *quality*, as measured by AFQT scores, do not vary between blacks and whites (Neal and Johnson 1996, 879–80). Differences in skill levels, coupled with a large and growing impact of skill on pay, rather than differences in returns to skill by race, are important to explaining black-white earnings differences.

Beyond formal schooling, on-the-job training is an important method by which workers accumulate earnings-enhancing skills. Blacks were less likely than whites to receive on-the-job training in the 1970s and 1980s (Sexton and Olsen 1994). Naturally, such differences in training lead to differences in earnings. One estimate found that in the mid-1970s, differences in the amount of on-the-job training received accounted for nearly 20 percent of the wage gap between white and black males and about 10 percent of the wage gap between black and white females, all else equal (Duncan and Hoffman 1979). Recent research has been more encouraging, however. By the early 1990s, the training gap between whites and blacks substantially narrowed among younger workers (Veum 1996). However, an ambiguity in this result is that such studies cannot control for differences in the quality or type of on-the-job training. Black and white workers might receive the same number of training hours, but the training they receive may be of differing quality or in skills of different usefulness.

If differences in skill, as reflected in education and test scores, help explain black-white pay differences, then what in turn explains these skill differences? The legacy of past discrimination, in the form of residential segregation, wealth inequality, and related patterns of family structure, contributes substantially to these education and skill differences.

DISCRIMINATORY LEGACIES

Residential Segregation

Most large cities in the United States are marked by substantial segregation between black and white residents, with black neighborhoods often concentrated near the center of the city and white residents more typically found in urban fringes or in the suburbs. These residential patterns formed and were solidified during the era of the Great Migration, beginning in the late 1910s. The nature of this segregation has arguably changed over time, however. Initially, black neighborhoods were residentially segregated but "vertically integrated," with black business, political, and educational leaders found in the same neighborhoods as less-skilled and poorer blacks, as the residential choices of all African Americans were limited by various forms of discrimination in housing (Sugrue 1996). As housing discrimination became less prevalent, better-off blacks left the center city, leaving behind those with fewer resources. At the same time, the industries that had drawn black workers to these cities initially—autos, steel, and other heavy manufacturing—moved their production facilities to the suburbs or even overseas. Central cities became centers for jobs in finance and information processing, for which the remaining, less-mobile black population were poorly suited (Wilson 1987; Kasarda 1989; Collins and Margo 2001). These neighborhoods became characterized by very high rates of poverty and unemployment, and also by limited access to information about jobs and opportunities.

There is some debate as to whether the poor fortunes of the black population in these neighborhoods reflect effects of the neighborhoods themselves, or whether they simply reflect the lack of skill among the residents; that is, there is debate as to whether segregation itself is really harming the people who live in these densely poor neighborhoods, or whether they would do poorly wherever they lived. To know the answer to this question, we would have to be able to randomly relocate these families to different kinds of neighborhoods and look for changes in their labor market outcomes. While economic researchers cannot generally carry out experiments on this scale, something like this did occur in Chicago beginning in the late 1970s. Through the Gatreaux program, hundreds of black families were moved out of densely poor, inner-city neighborhoods and into less-poor neighborhoods, as part of the resolution of a housing discrimination case. The families who were moved did see some improvement in their employment levels, compared to those left behind. These individuals attributed their improved status to their closer proximity to suitable employers, and also to greater mobility arising from reduced concerns about safety (Rosenbaum and Popkin 1991). So, it appears that the neighborhood one lives in does directly affect one's job prospects, and that the legacy of residential segregation in U.S. cities therefore plays a role in ongoing economic inequality between blacks and whites.

In addition to these direct effects on employment, residential segregation also results in schooling segregation: in 1992, one-third of black students attended schools that were 90 percent black, and one-half of white students attended schools that were 90 percent white (Klinkner and Smith 1999, 323). Schooling segregation of this type may obviously result in differences in the school quality available to black and white students, producing the AFQT differences and pay differences described earlier. Evidence from the Census indicates that the extent of residential segregation between blacks and whites has declined since 1970. These changes have been most pronounced in growing cities in the West. However, large midwestern cities remain characterized by very high levels of segregation and the presence of quite isolated urban black communities (Glaeser and Vigdor 2001).

Wealth Differences

While income differences between blacks and whites remain substantial, especially among men, wealth differences are much larger. The ratio of the net worth of the average black household to the net worth of the average white household has been nearly constant at around 19 percent since 1983 (Masterson, Zacharias, and Wolff 2009, 17). Even when we adjust for the different education levels and income levels in the black and white communities, wealth differences remain very large. The ratio of black wealth to white wealth is between 20 percent and 30 percent even when we compare individuals with the same level of schooling or the same annual income. We should also note that these differences in wealth holding do not appear to be caused by differences in saving behavior: when we look at black and white individuals with the same income, we find they save similar shares of that income (Gittleman and Wolff 2004).

These large differences in wealth holding are, to a great extent, the accumulation of many generations of income differences. They also represent the long-term effects of discrimination in access to assets, such as home ownership. For instance, mortgage insurance and refinancing programs of the 1940s tended not to aid home buyers in black or mixed neighborhoods, rating these neighborhoods as "hazardous" based on their racial composition. This practice made it more difficult for blacks to get loans and purchase homes (Sugrue 1996, 59–72).

Differences in parental wealth have obvious effects on the economic opportunities available to children. Parental wealth may be transferred to children directly. In addition, parental wealth affects the likelihood that a child will complete high school and college. It also helps determine a family's neighborhood of residence, with implications for local job opportunities, access to information about employment, and school quality (Conley 1999). Thus, discriminatory income differences in the past, combined with past discrimination in access to mortgages and other forms of finance, have ongoing effects on racial inequality in the present.

Family Structure

Poverty is directly linked to family structure, specifically to single parenthood. The heads of such households must balance caregiving with working for a living. Because they have fewer resources and are more economically vulnerable, individuals residing in single-parent households are more likely to live below poverty levels. For example, in 2003 the poverty rate for individuals in households formed by a married couple with children was 8.1 percent, whereas the poverty rate was 37.3 percent for families headed by an unmarried female with children. Households with children headed by an unmarried man had a 22.0 percent poverty rate (Hoynes, Page, and Stevens 2006, 60).

Although persons living in single-parent families made up less than 15 percent of the population in 2003, about 40 percent of the nonelderly poor lived in single-parent households with children (Hoynes, Page, and Stevens 2006, 50).

Black households are more likely to be headed by a single parent. In 2009, 35 percent of blacks lived in families headed by a married couple and 38 percent of blacks lived in families headed by a single female. Family structure for whites was dramatically different—63.5 percent lived in married-couple families and 12.2 percent lived in single-female-headed families (Ruggles et al. 2010). Why are black and white family structures different? This is an enormously complex and very controversial question. Many scholars argue that high rates of single headship in the black community are caused, at least in part, by the poor job prospects and general economic instability faced by African American males, especially through the mid-20th century (Wilson 1987). Residential segregation, and the creation of densely poor black neighborhoods, worsened these problems. Single parenthood is clearly correlated with segregation as well as the poverty rate within one's neighborhood (Massey, Gross, and Eggers 1991). While housing segregation and labor market inequality probably do not account for all of the differences in family structure between the white and black communities in the United States, it seems clear that they have played a role in creating this differences. It also seems clear that these differences in family structure continue to contribute to black-white economic inequality.

Still, while differences in family structure are a source of black-white inequality, these differences cannot easily explain the slowdown in black economic progress in the past few decades. This is because the number of blacks living in female-headed families slightly declined during the 1990s (Massey, Gross, and Eggers 1991). Additionally, higher education levels, higher incomes, and higher labor force participation rates among females have increased the incomes of female-headed households, diminishing the strength of the relationship between family structure and poverty in recent years (Cancian and Reed 2001).

ONGOING DISCRIMINATION

Black-white pay differences are in part created by skill differences arising from gaps in schooling quantity and quality. These skill differences themselves can be seen as the legacy of past discrimination, including discrimination in housing markets that helped to create segregated neighborhoods, with harmful effects on black schooling, access to jobs, and family structure. They also reflect past discrimination in employment and earnings, which resulted in large black-white wealth gaps, with implications for subsequent generations. But racial inequality may not simply be the legacy of past discrimination. It may also arise from ongoing, active discrimination in the present.

A simple economic definition of labor market discrimination is "differential treatment (in employment, pay, promotion, or working conditions) of equally productive workers, due to differences in some nonproductive characteristic like race or skin color." Because productivity is hard to measure precisely and control for in the kinds of datasets that are usually available to economists, measuring the importance of discrimination in creating pay differentials between black and white workers is very challenging. In recent years, labor economists have turned to experimental methods in order to test for discrimination. They find substantial evidence that differences between black workers' and white workers' earnings are not just the result of differences in these workers' skills. Often, blacks and whites of apparently equal ability are paid unequally and receive different labor market opportunities (Altonji and Blank 1999, 3192).

These kinds of studies, typically called "audit studies," often involve sending out pairs of black and white research assistants, posing as job applicants, to apply for the same job using very similar resumés. Researchers then measure the differences in the probabilities of each member of each pair receiving a job. Because blacks and whites within pairs are chosen to be close matches in physical appearance and demeanor, are trained to interview similarly by the researcher, and have nearly identical resumés, differences in their job offers are thought to be a good indicator of racial discrimination. Turner, Fix, and Struyk (1991) had five pairs of applicants complete 191 audits in Chicago and five pairs complete 227 audits in Washington, DC. In 20 percent of the completed audits, white auditors advanced further than their black counterparts through the application, interview, and job offer stages of the hiring process, whereas only 7 percent of the time the black auditor advanced further than his or her white match (Turner, Fix, and Struyk 1991, 39). The authors find that this discriminatory treatment is more likely to occur at the interview or job offer stage, rather than the application stage. The hiring gap specifically was large and significant. In Chicago, the probability of the white applicant receiving an offer when the black applicant did not was

10 percent and the probability of the black applicant receiving an offer when the white applicant did not was only 5 percent. In Washington, DC, 19 percent of the time the white applicant received an offer and the black applicant did not, but only 6 percent of employers offered the black applicant the job instead of the white applicant (Turner, Fix, and Struyk 1991, 41). That the probability of the white auditor receiving better treatment than the black auditor was more than double that of the reverse provides strong evidence of racial discrimination in hiring practices.

A recent experiment that was undertaken by Bertrand and Mullainathan (2004) finds significant discrimination in the application process. These researchers sent artificial resumés to employers hiring in sales, administrative, and customer service jobs in Boston and Chicago. Using name frequency data from birth certificates and surveys, they gave some resumés distinctively black first names (e.g., Aisha, Latoya, Jamal, or Tremayne) and some distinctively white first names (e.g., Allison, Kristen, Brad, or Todd). The experimental design allowed the researchers to test whether resumés with black names get fewer callbacks for interviews than equivalent resumés with white names. They find that of two otherwise identical resumés, those with white names got 50 percent more callbacks than those with black names. The gap in callbacks was found across occupations and industries. That employers less frequently take a favorable view of resumés with black names suggests that employers are not racially blind when reviewing resumés (Bertrand and Mullainathan 2004).

Although audit studies indicate that racial differences in hiring exist, they cannot explain why. Several studies directly interview employers to attempt to determine employer motivations and attitudes with respect to race. These studies reveal differences in how employers perceive white and black workers specifically with regard to characteristics that the researchers call "soft skills," characteristics relating to personality, attitude, motivation, and behavior. In addition to "hard skills," those formal technical skills learned in school or training, soft skills are also rewarded in labor markets (Moss and Tilly 1996, 253).

Kirschenman and Neckerman (1991) interviewed a representative sample of 185 employers in Chicago and its suburbs, asking employer representatives questions about hiring practices, Chicago's labor force, and their thoughts about race in hiring and employment. They found that employers interpret race, socioeconomic status, and neighborhood in a nuanced manner. The employers they interviewed demanded soft skills, such as work ethic or communication ability, far more than formal skills gained in education, and they perceived persons hailing from lower classes or from the inner city as fundamentally lacking in these types of skills. Interviewees tended to associate black men with low-class or inner-city backgrounds and, consequently, had negative preconceptions of their soft skills. However, most employers believed that the black population included workers of various backgrounds and sought to sort out blacks having desirable backgrounds from those who did not with screening devices like skill testing, interviews, or reference networks. This extra scrutiny raises the difficulty of the job search process for black applicants. Not only must blacks show employers that they have the same characteristics as their white peers, they must also show employers that low-class, inner-city stereotypes are inapplicable to them. Equivalent white workers face no such hurdles (Kirschenman and Neckerman 1991).

Moss and Tilly (1996) interviewed representatives from 56 employers in various industries in Los Angeles and Detroit. Their results underscore the increasing demand of employers for soft skills due to competitive pressures and the disadvantage black workers have due to how employers perceive their levels of soft skills. When asked about the essential attributes sought in applicants, 86 percent of employers listed some component of soft skills among the most important criteria. Comparatively, 83 percent of employers listed basic math or literacy among the most important criteria. Forty-seven percent of employers listed a soft skill as the first in their list of most important criteria (Moss and Tilly 1996, 259). The soft skills most emphasized by employers were personal interaction, such as friendliness, teamwork, or fitting in, along with motivation, i.e., positive attitude, dependability, or commitment (Moss and Tilly 1996, 256–57). The authors argue that because of stereotypes, cultural differences, and actual skill differences, employers surveyed perceived black men as lacking in interaction ability and motivation. These perceptions subsequently penalize blacks in labor markets (Moss and Tilly 1996). Importantly, because individuals' soft skills are generally hard to identify and are revealed only over a long period of time, employers' perceptions of average differences between black and white workers in these characteristics may have a large impact on hiring, even if those perceptions are based on invalid and incorrect stereotypes.

Similar kinds of audit studies have been used to examine discrimination in other areas of the economy, including the housing market.

For instance, audit studies (using black and white potential home buyers with similar incomes, wealth holding, etc.) carried out by the Department of Housing and Urban Development found evidence of discriminatory "steering" of black home buyers into black neighborhoods and away from white neighborhoods by realtors as recently as 2000 (Dawkins 2004).

Of course, explicit discrimination in economic opportunities on the basis of race has been illegal since the passage of the Civil Rights Act in 1964. Enforcement of this law, along with similar "contract compliance" policies mandating fair treatment of black and white workers by all firms involved in government contract work, certainly contributed to the gains in relative pay achieved by black workers beginning in the 1960s (Butler, Heckman, and Payner 1989; Donohue and Heckman 1991; Leonard 1990). However, many researchers argue that enforcement of these policies was weakened beginning in the 1980s, as fewer resources were provided to the federal agencies responsible for their enforcement (Leonard 1990; Klinkner and Smith 1999, 300–303). At the state level, the use of "affirmative action" programs aimed at increasing the number of minority businesses receiving state contracts and at increasing the number of minority students at public universities has been curtailed through new laws (Klinkner and Smith 1999, 313–14). These policy changes may have contributed to the slowdown in black relative gains at the end of the 20th century.

UNDENIABLE, BUT INCOMPLETE, PROGRESS

It would be wildly inaccurate to suggest that African Americans had not made very large gains in their relative economic position over the course of the 20th century. It would also be wildly inaccurate to suggest that all evidence of discrimination, either past discrimination or ongoing discrimination, had disappeared by the end of the century. Difficult legacies remain in residential segregation, wealth accumulation, family structure, and skill acquisition that continue to create gaps in economic well-being between blacks and whites. In addition, ongoing discrimination persists, and the policy tools to combat it have arguably been weakened in recent years.

Fundamentally, the eradication of black-white inequality in the United States should not be seen as an "automatic" process that, once under way, will result in full equality if we simply wait long enough. The historical record shows that black relative gains have been rapid in some periods but negligible in others. Without ignoring the transformation of race relations in the United States in the past few generations, we must recognize that achieving the goal of full racial inequality will require ongoing effort and creative public policy.

BIBLIOGRAPHY

Acemoglu, Daron. 1999. "Changes in Unemployment and Wage Inequality: An Alternative Theory and Some Evidence." *American Economic Review* 89: 1259–78.

Altonji, Joseph G., and Rebecca M. Blank. 1999. "Race and Gender in the Labor Market." In *Handbook of Labor Economics*, Vol. 3c, edited by Orley Ashenfelter and David Card, 3143–3259. New York: Elsevier.

Autor, David. 2010. "The Polarization of Job Opportunities in the U.S. Labor Market: Implications for Employment and Earnings." *Center for American Progress Report.*

Barrow, Lisa, and Cecilia Elena Rouse. 2006. "The Economic Value of Education by Race and Ethnicity." *Economic Perspectives* 30: 14–27.

Bertrand, Marianne, and Sendhi Mullainathan. 2004. "Are Emily and Greg More Employable than Lakisha and Jamal? A Field Experiment on Labor Market Discrimination." *American Economic Review* 94: 991–1013.

Bound, John, and George Johnson. 1992. "Changes in the Structure of Wages in the 1980's: An Evaluation of Alternative Explanations." *American Economic Review* 82: 372–92.

Butler, Richard J., James J. Heckman, and Brook Payner. 1989. "The Impact of the Economy and the State on the Economic Status of Blacks: A Study of South Carolina." In *Markets in History: Economic Studies of the Past*, edited by David W. Galenson, 241–346. New York: Cambridge University Press.

Cancian, Maria, and Deborah Reed. 2001. "Changes in Family Structure." In *Understanding Poverty*, edited by Sheldon H. Danziger and Robert H. Haveman, 69–96. New York: Russell Sage Foundation.

Card, David, and Alan B. Krueger. 1992. "School Quality and Black-White Relative Earnings: A Direct Assessment." *Quarterly Journal of Economics* 107: 151–200.

Collins, William J., and Robert A. Margo. 2001. "Residential Segregation and Socioeconomic Outcomes: When Did Ghettos Go Bad?" *Economic Letters* 69: 239–43.

Conley, Dalton. 1999. *Being Black, Living in the Red: Race, Wealth, and Social Policy in America*. Berkeley: University of California Press.

Dawkins, Casey J. 2004. "Recent Evidence on the Continuing Causes of Black-White Residential Segregation." *Journal of Urban Affairs* 26: 379–400.

Donohue, John J., III, and James Heckman. 1991. "Continuous Versus Episodic Change: The Impact of Civil Rights Policy on the Economic Status of Blacks." *Journal of Economic Literature* 29: 1603–43.

Duncan, Greg J., and Saul Hoffman. 1979. "On-the-Job Training and Earnings Differences by Race and Sex." *Review of Economics and Statistics* 61: 594–603.

Gittleman, Maury, and Edward N. Wolff. 2004. "Racial Differences in Patterns of Wealth Accumulation." *Journal of Human Resources* 39: 193–227.

Glaeser, Edward L., and Jacob L. Vigdor. 2001. "Racial Segregation in the 2000 Census: Promising News." *Brookings Institution Center on Urban and Metropolitan Policy Survey Series.*

Hoynes, Hilary W., Marianne E. Page, and Ann Huff Stevens. 2006. "Poverty in America: Trends and Explanations." *Journal of Economic Perspectives* 20: 47–68.

Juhn, Chinhui, Kevin M. Murphy, and Brooks Pierce. 1991. "Accounting for the Slowdown in Black-White Wage Convergence." In *Workers and Their Wages: Changing Patterns in the United States,* edited by Marvin H. Kosters, 107–43. Washington: AEI Press.

Kasarda, John D. 1989. "Urban Industrial Transition and the Underclass." *The Annals of the American Academy of Political and Social Science* 501: 26–57.

Kirschenman, Joleen, and Kathryn M. Neckerman. 1991. " 'We'd Love to Hire Them, But . . .': The Meaning of Race for Employers." In *The Urban Underclass,* edited by Christopher Jencks and Paul E. Peterson, 203–32. Washington, DC: Brookings Institution Press.

Klinkner, Philip A., and Rogers M. Smith. 1999. *The Unsteady March: The Rise and Decline of Racial Equality in America.* Chicago: University of Chicago Press.

Leonard, Jonathan S. 1990. "The Impact of Affirmative Action Regulation and Equal Employment Law on Black Employment." *Journal of Economic Perspectives* 4: 47–63.

Maloney, Thomas N. 2002. "African Americans in the Twentieth Century." In *EH.Net Encyclopedia,* edited by Robert Whaples. http://eh.net/encyclopedia/article/maloney.african.american.

Massey, Douglas S., Andrew B. Gross, and Mitchell L. Eggers. 1991. "Segregation, the Concentration of Poverty, and the Life Chances of Individuals." *Social Science Research* 4: 397–420.

Masterson, Thomas, Ajit Zacharias, and Edward N. Wolff. 2009. "Has Progress Been Made in Alleviating Racial Economic Inequality?" *Levy Economics Institute LIMEW Report.*

Moss, Philip, and Chris Tilly. 1996. "'Soft' Skills and Race: An Investigation of Black Men's Employment Problems." *Work and Occupations* 23: 252–76.

Neal, Derek A., and William R. Johnson. 1996. "The Role of Premarket Factors in Black-White Wage Differences." *Journal of Political Economy* 104: 869–95.

O'Neill, June. 1990. "The Role of Human Capital in Earnings Differences between Black and White Men." *Journal of Economic Perspectives* 4: 25–45.

Rosenbaum, James E., and Susan J. Popkin. 1991. "Employment and Earnings of Low-Income Blacks Who Move to Middle Class Suburbs." In *The Urban Underclass,* edited by Christopher Jencks and Paul E. Peterson, 342–57. Washington, DC: Brookings Institution Press.

Ruggles, Steven, J. Trent Alexander, Katie Genadek, Ronald Goeken, Matthew B. Schroeder, and Matthew Sobek. 2010. *Integrated Public Use Microdata Series: Version 5.0* [Machine-Readable Database]. Minneapolis: University of Minnesota.

Sexton, Edwin A., and Reed Neil Olsen. 1994. "The Returns to On-the-Job Training: Are They the Same for Blacks and Whites?" *Southern Economic Journal* 61: 238–42.

Sugrue, Thomas J. 1996. *The Origins of the Urban Crisis: Race and Inequality in Postwar Detroit.* Princeton: Princeton University Press.

Turner, Margery A., Michael Fix, and Raymond J. Struyk. 1991. *Opportunities Denied, Opportunities Diminished: Racial Discrimination in Hiring.* Washington, DC: Urban Institute Press.

U.S. Bureau of Labor Statistics. 2010a. "Table 3. Median Usual Weekly Earnings of Full-Time Wage and Salary Workers by Age, Race, Hispanic or Latino Ethnicity, and Sex, Quarterly Averages, Not Seasonally Adjusted." Last modified July 20. http://www.bls.gov/webapps/legacy/cpswktab3.htm.

U.S. Bureau of Labor Statistics. 2010b. "Table A-2. Employment Status of the Civilian Population by Race, Sex, and Age." Last modified February 5. http://www.bls.gov/webapps/legacy/cpsatab2.htm.

U.S. Census Bureau. 2010. "Poverty Data—Historical Poverty Tables: People" Last modified September 16. http://www.census.gov/hhes/www/poverty/data/historical/people.html.

Veum, Jonathan R. 1996. "Gender and Race Differences in Company Training." *Industrial Relations* 35: 32–44.

Wilson, William J. 1987. *The Truly Disadvantaged: The Inner City, the Underclass, and Public Policy.* Chicago: University of Chicago Press.

Chapter 10

Closing the Gender Gap: What Would It Take?

Joyce P. Jacobsen

The economic turning point for humankind was the 19th century, marking the start of the Industrial Revolution, during which time growth rates in material well-being began rising steadily for the first time in human history thanks to a prolonged period (continuing through the present time) of technological change and increased productivity. But the economic turning point for women did not come until the last quarter of the 20th century, when they experienced greatly improved material well-being relative to men.

However, women continue to have less access to and less control of productive resources than do men. This fundamental inequality is true across time and place. Thus women make lower earnings on average than do men, are more likely to be poor than are men, and are less likely to be wealthy than are men. What would it take to change these patterns?

This chapter outlines the main dimensions of differences in women's and men's economic well-being and considers the potential causes of these differences. After delineating the causes, it will become clearer what would have to change in order for women to achieve significantly greater economic well-being relative to men. In conclusion, we will consider whether such changes are possible in the foreseeable future.

DIMENSIONS OF DIFFERENCE

Economic differences between individuals relate to differences in access to and control over productive factors, such as skills, machinery, land, and social networks. Even though individual access varies widely, in general men have more access to and control over productive factors than do women. These differences in access and control then manifest themselves in different outcomes on dimensions of well-being. Economic well-being is generally measured by the amount of earnings (income from labor) or total income (income from all productive sources, including returns from holdings of capital and land) that a person or household has in a year. There are also differences in wealth holdings, the monetary value of the stock of productive resources that a person or household controls, though these tend to be harder to measure on an individual basis.

While this chapter mainly focuses on contemporary U.S. data as examples of gender differences, the direction (though not the identical magnitude) of gender differences is the same for other societies, both contemporary and past. Women have always and everywhere been economically disadvantaged relative to men. However, men also have systematic disadvantages relative to women on many dimensions, as we shall see later.

DIFFERENCES IN INCOME, WEALTH, AND POVERTY

While women still earn less than men, the difference has shrunk considerably since the 1970s, both in the United States and abroad. Figure 10.1 shows for 1947–2010 the median annual income ratio (women to men) for workers in the United States. The median annual income is the amount of income that half those working make more than, and half make less than, and is a commonly used measure of group income. The figure shows this ratio for three groups: all workers, year-round full-time workers, and young year-round full-time workers (ages 25 through 34). The differences in these three ratios (with each group in turn showing a smaller earnings gap) demonstrate both that women tend to work fewer total hours than men (thus for all workers the gap is both in terms of different hours worked and less

Figure 10.1
Median Annual Income Ratios, Women to Men, 1947 to 2010.

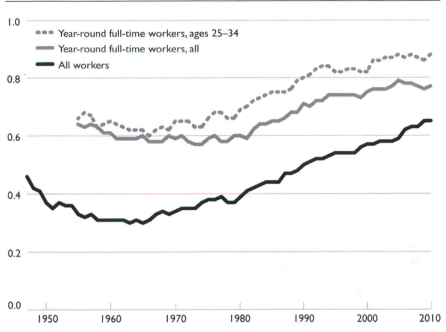

Source: US Bureau of the Census, Current Population Survey, as reported in the Current Population Reports Series P-60. Data are for persons with income, ages 14 and over in earlier years, ages 15 and over in later years.

earnings per hour) and that income gaps tend to widen for older workers (but are still occurring even among younger workers). While Figure 10.1 displays annual income rather than annual earnings, for most persons who are in the workforce earnings is the main source of income, and thus this measure can be taken as an indicator of differences in earnings as well. In all three series, the same pattern appears: a downturn in the years following World War II (indicating some backsliding in women's progress toward higher incomes during this period), followed by a long period of only incremental increase through the 1960s and 1970s, followed by a period of sustained rise from the 1980s. The series for all workers shows the most sustained continued increase as women have steadily increased their labor force participation relative to men, while the earnings for the higher-working groups show more flattening-out in the most recent years.

The most recent recession that began in 2008 found the group of all women earning their most ever relative to men by 2010, with 65 cents on the dollar, while the 25- to 34-year-old year-round full-time working women also reached their highest ever relative earnings with 88 cents on the dollar relative to their male peers (a peak they had previously attained in 2005 as well; all year-round full-time workers were at 77 cents on the dollar, down from a peak of 79 cents in 2005). This result came about in large part because men's incomes were flat or falling during this three-year period: while male workers' median earnings stood at $33,161 in 2008, they had dropped to $32,137 by 2010, while female workers' median earnings dropped by less (from $20,867 to $20,831). Thus one unfortunate perverse finding is that women may do better relative to men more because men are doing worse.

With regard to differences in wealth holdings by gender, while there has been much attention in recent years regarding the large and widening wealth inequality in the United States and many other countries (Russia and Brazil as two other examples), few commentators have focused on gender disparities in wealth. This is in large part because wealth is generally measured at the household level so that married couples generally have indistinguishable finances, at least in most available data sources. However, studies have found both that female-headed households have less wealth than married couple households and that single women have less wealth than single men (Schmidt and Sevak 2006; Neelakantan and Chang 2010). This is not surprising given that men earn more over their lifetimes than do women, thus implying that they will end up with significantly greater pension and retirement savings as well. There is also evidence that women are more risk averse than men and thus may end up compounding less wealth in part because they are less willing to bear the higher level of risk that higher returns require (Jianakoplos and Bernasek 1998).

Thus women are less represented among high-income households and also more represented among low-income households (Jacobsen 2007, Table 2.12). This latter fact shows up as well in their higher poverty rates at all points in the business cycle. Figure 10.2 shows the year-by-year trends in the U.S. poverty rates for males and females, from 1966 through 2010. While the poverty rates rise and fall in tandem with the business cycle, at all points in the business cycle the female poverty rate is higher than the male poverty rate. In the United States in 2010, a year in which poverty rates were rising, 16.2 percent of females and 14.0 percent of males were in poverty. The particularly hard-hit group is women (and children) in single-parent households,

Figure 10.2
Poverty Rates by Sex, 1966 to 2010.

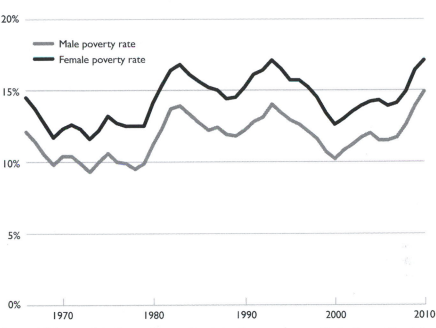

Source: US Bureau of the Census, Current Population Survey, as reported in the Current Population Reports Series P-60.

even when the mothers are working: in 2009, 28 percent of working unmarried mothers made incomes putting them below the poverty threshold (White House Council 2011, 24).

Thus it is clear from reviewing the data on earnings, income, and wealth that women have improved their position relative to men on average, but that an income gap persists. This statement holds for the world situation as well, though the exact income ratio varies from country to country.

DIFFERENCES IN OTHER INDICATORS OF WELL-BEING

So far we have defined economic well-being narrowly as access to income, whether through earnings or other sources. If we broaden our definition of economic well-being to include other aspects, do women improve their position relative to men?

One angle is to consider other aspects of well-being such as health and longevity. In other words, what if people who earn more (say, men) live fewer total years? Or if they spend more time in worse health? Then one might argue that their total well-being, measured on a life-time scale, is less than for lower-earning but longer- (and healthier) lived persons.

It is also interesting to consider how women and men spend their time during a given span of time. We have greatly expanded available time use data in the United States and many other countries over the past few years, making it much easier to see how people spend their time in a given day (or week). If women are working fewer hours of paid work than do men, how do they spend the time instead?

As a final measure of quality of time, what if one's ability to live life fully is constrained in various ways? For one thing, imprisonment would be a serious constraint, but so would be living in a society where one is not able to move about freely in public, because of either social constraints or fear of violence.

With regard to health and longevity, women compare favorably to men in the basic measure of longevity, as women in the vast majority of societies outlive men, with a median of about 4 years overall (Jacobsen 2006, Table 2.1) and by an average of 5 to 10 years in the industrialized countries. One of the major historical causes of female death, maternal mortality (death during or immediately following and related to childbirth), has dropped enormously over the course of the past century (World Bank 2011, Figure 3.12). While mortality rates have dropped for all persons (and life spans thus have increased greatly on average as well), there has been no comparable drop in a male-specific cause of death and males continue to die at higher rates from many causes. Men are also much more likely than women to suffer death or disability from a work-related injury. Thus even a measure of quality-adjusted life years (or disability-adjusted life expectancy) shows a significant gender gap of about the same size as for unadjusted life expectancy (Jacobsen 2006, Table 2.3).

However, one countervailing factor is that females are much less likely to be born than males in a number of countries. China and India, where over one-third of the world's population resides, have come under particular scrutiny for the much lower rates of female births, leading to the concept of "missing girls" (World Bank 2011, Table 3.2). While it is the case that the ratio at birth of boys to girls is generally higher than one (averaging around 105 boys to 100 girls at birth in the U.S. population, for example), in these countries the ratio is closer to 110 boys to 100 girls at birth. The net effect of differential birthrates is that, while women outnumber men among the elderly, men outnumber women among the young, meaning up through age 45 worldwide (U.S. Census Bureau, International Data Base, 2010 midyear data). This phenomenon appears to be caused in part by prenatal testing and sex-selective abortion, though it may also be due in part to undercounting of girls in the official data. At any rate, it is an interesting question as to how to value the trade-off between lower probability of being born and higher probability of a longer life span.

Turning to the question of different patterns of time use by gender, available time diary data for both industrialized and rural populations show much higher rates of nonmarket work activity by women than by men. While in the United States, men have increased their time spent in household work and child care and women have decreased their time spent in household work (but not so much in child care), women still spend more time in these forms of household production. Even women who have paid work spend more time than their spouses in household work (White House Council 2011, 35). However, for many other types of activities, including personal care and sleep, men and women have quite similar amounts of time spent. In less-industrialized countries, women spend significantly more time in household production activities, including often much time gathering fuel and water, and cooking. Thus they are productive members of society whether or not they perform paid work, but it is not clear that they are proportional beneficiaries of their unpaid labors, as much of its result goes to the children and other members of the household.

Finally, with regard to other quality-of-life issues, the evidence splits. Men both are responsible for, and suffer from, higher rates of violence. They are significantly more likely to be incarcerated (International Centre for Prison Studies 2011) as well as more likely to be the victim of a violent crime (Jacobsen 2006, 20). However, women are much more likely than men to suffer domestic violence as well as rape in both war and peacetime situations. Lifetime rates of domestic violence are quite high in some countries, with up to 50 percent of women in some societies reporting one or more incidents (World Bank 2011, 20). While estimating the costs of domestic violence in terms of lost productivity is difficult, it is nonetheless calculable in terms of both disrupted lives including lost days at work, and the costs of medical treatment (Jacobsen 2007, 78–79). Thus, this serves as an example of additional costs that women may incur as an effect of being women, costs that also come to bear in thinking about what it would take to close the gender gap between women and men.

CAUSES OF DIFFERENCE

Having now considered some of the dimensions of difference between women's and men's outcomes, we can now turn to considering why these dimensions arise. It is clear that different societies over time and space have placed different strictures on women's ability to participate fully in public life, including paid work. For example, U.S. women were not able to vote until 1920, Swiss women not until 1971, and women still cannot vote in Saudi Arabia. In some societies, women and men still lead highly segregated lives, including single-sex schooling, little participation by women in paid work, and significant gender segregation by type of work.

However, it is interesting to consider, for those societies where there are now few if any strictures against women's full participation in public life, why gender differences in well-being, particularly earnings differences, persist. We will consider what differences arise in work patterns, and tackle the difficult question of whether these differences come about through free choice on the part of women and men.

We will also consider how changing demographics and household structures over the course of the 20th century have interacted with women's participation in paid work, and how these changes have been both empowering for some women, but limiting for others, particularly in terms of access to income. Then we will undertake a final difficult task of considering what trends in these causes of difference are most likely in the next few decades of the 21st century.

Differences in Participation in Paid Work

One difference historically that explains why women have lower incomes than men is their lower earnings due to their lower participation in paid work. But while women still are less likely to participate in paid work than men, the difference has shrunk considerably in the post–World War II era, both in the United States and abroad. Figure 10.3 shows the year-by-year trends for the United States in labor force participation rates by sex and the percentage of the labor force that is female, from 1948 through 2010. Men have been steadily reducing their participation, particularly among the young (who tend to stay in school longer than in the past). Meanwhile women steadily

Figure 10.3

Labor Force Participation Rates by Sex and Percentage of Labor Force That Is Female, 1948 to 2010.

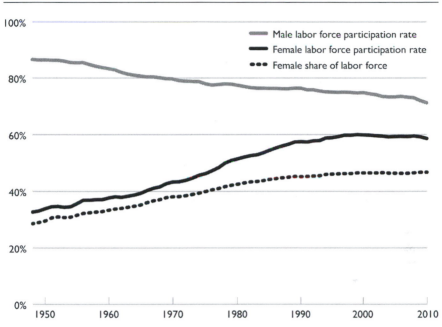

Source: Economic Report of the President. Data are for civilian persons ages 16 and over.

increased their work participation up through the early 1990s, at which point their participation rate leveled off at around 60 percent. Women now comprise between 46 to 47 percent of the labor force, a level they first achieved in 1993.

Thus the raw difference in labor force participation, while a clear explanation for past lower earnings for women, cannot be a large part of the explanation for lower earnings today. However, there are a number of other differences in the quantity and type of participation by gender. On average, men work more hours in a workweek and over the course of a year, are more likely to work overtime, and less likely to work part-time (interestingly, men and women are about equally likely to moonlight). Thus, as was seen in Figure 10.1, there are substantial differences in earnings between the average working woman and the average working man, and even part of the difference in earnings between more comparable workers (year-round full-time) is due to the larger total hours worked by men within this category.

However, it is also the case that men earn more on average per hour of work. Explanations for this difference fall into three categories: differences in human capital; differences in working conditions; and discrimination in pay, employment, and promotion. Let us consider the contribution of each of these explanatory categories in turn.

Differences in human capital refer to differences in productive capacity, which can be developed through formal education, work experience, and on-the job training. Differences in formal education in many developed countries, including the United States, now favor women. In the United States, women are now more likely to graduate from high school, more likely to get a college degree, more likely to get a graduate degree, and more likely to participate in adult education (White House Council 2011, 19–24). Ever since the late 1970s when graduate schools began welcoming women in larger numbers, women have increased their presence in the professions such as law and medicine enormously. This substantial increase in women's formal education, particularly in the higher-paid professions, has been a big factor in reducing the gender earnings gap. However, given the current educational disparity in favor of women, it also appears that education alone cannot reduce the remaining gap. Women still lag significantly in work experience, both because they are underrepresented still among older workers (particularly in the prime earning years of 35–54) and because they are still more likely to interrupt their work career (or cut back to part-time work) while their children are young. In many professions, interruptions in work can be costly, particularly if these interruptions happen in the early part of a person's career when it is most important that she works long hours. In those professions that grant tenure, including high school and college teaching, and law firms, interruptions can lead not only to lower earnings but also to premature exit from the profession. Finally, women are still less likely to receive on-the-job training.

Given that differences in human capital cannot explain all of the gender earnings gap, this leads us to consider additional differences in the types of jobs where women and men are found. What one studies in college and graduate school relates to both starting salaries and subsequent career paths, and women and men still display different patterns in field of study. For one thing, men are still much more likely than women to get a college or graduate degree in science and technology, including all engineering fields and computer science.

Men are also more likely to major in business, particularly in the more mathematical areas such as finance and operations management. Thus men received higher average starting salaries coming out of their formal education, in large part because of these differences in field of study. They may also end up on salary tracks that lead to higher salaries in midcareer, while women may end up on flatter salary tracks.

Gender segregation is still widespread in labor markets in all countries. Many occupations are predominantly occupied by one or the other gender (such as nursing by women, plumbing by men). Even within broad occupational categories such as doctor or lawyer, there are often significant differences in the subspecialties that women and men enter (such as pediatrics by women, surgery by men). It is very difficult to figure out why gender segregation is so prevalent and how it relates to differences in earnings by gender. There are numerous puzzling phenomena related to occupational gender segregation, such as why different occupations are dominated by different genders in different societies (for instance, clerical occupations are generally held by men in Pakistan, but by women in the United States), and why some occupations "tip" from being dominated by one gender to being dominated by the other (for example, bank tellers). However, it does appear that female-dominated occupations tend to pay less than comparable male-dominated occupations. If women "crowd" into some occupations that they find more desirable, this would tend to lower the earnings in these occupations compared to a situation in which women (and men) were distributed more evenly across occupations. For instance, if women systematically avoid the more technical occupations that require more math and science, then if these skills are both in general short supply and in demand within the economy, the entrants to those occupations (apparently more often men) will be more highly compensated.

One argument related to these observable differences in the jobs that women and men take has been that women's jobs are more desirable in other dimensions than pay. These can include fringe benefits, pleasant working conditions, a lower probability of on-the-job injury, and more interesting and meaningful work. Survey evidence does show that women are more interested than men in factors about work other than pay (Jacobsen 2007, Table 8.5). It also appears that women are in jobs that have different conditions, particularly in ones that are less risky (Filer 1985). Thus this is another possible explanation for part of the gender pay gap, though studies of this explanation have found that it cannot explain anywhere near as much as the human capital factors.

Even once all observable factors are controlled for between women and men, including the various factors listed previously, there still remains an unexplained difference in their earnings. The general explanation for this remaining difference is discrimination. When women and men do the same job but receive different pay, this would be considered discriminatory under the current labor law structure in most countries. However, while pay discrimination can happen and may not always go reported let alone punished, discrimination can also occur in many more subtle ways. "Glass ceilings" can mean that capable women are passed over for promotion to higher-paying jobs, while women may simply not be hired into other well-paying positions. There is also evidence that women are less likely than men to negotiate for higher salaries upon promotion (Babcock and Laschever 2003). Thus women may end up in lower-paying positions and/or in lower-paying firms because these more subtle barriers prevent them from achieving their full earnings capability.

DIFFERENCES IN DEMOGRAPHICS AND HOUSEHOLD STRUCTURE

A final issue is how changing life patterns interact with women's ability to participate fully in the labor market. While women may have much more freedom to make choices now than in the past, they still make constrained choices. Choice may be constrained by the need to coordinate child raising with career, by the need to balance a spouse's career aspirations with one's own (including the choice of where to live), and by the need to fulfill other family roles such as caretaker for an aging parent or a sick or disabled relative.

Family ties are becoming less numerous. Compared to 60 years ago, women and men now marry later in life (U.S. median age at first marriage is now 26 for women, 28 for men). They also are less likely to marry at all, less likely to have a child, more likely to have their first child later in life, and more likely to have fewer children in total (White House Council 2011, 8–12). Thus on the one hand, the constraints that come with having to balance concerns of spouse and children with one's career are less binding, particularly during one's 20s, leaving people relatively freer to pursue education and career. Indeed, it is likely in part that the reason these phenomena are occurring is because women are choosing to devote more energy to their careers relative to family life.

On the other hand, having less family, in particular being less likely to have a spouse, can also mean less financial support. In the United States, this is particularly problematic for black women, who are significantly more likely to be in female-headed households (43%, as compared to 14% of non-Hispanic white women). This is a big contributor to black women's high rates of poverty (28%, as compared to 11% of non-Hispanic white women) (White House Council 2011, 13–14). Thus becoming a single parent, whether through divorce or never having married, is a significant contributor to women's lower incomes and higher poverty rates relative to men.

In addition, as life spans increase and families shrink in size, the middle-aged increasingly find themselves more likely to be faced with how to deal with aging parents (and are less likely to have multiple siblings with which to share the responsibility). Thus caretaking can shift from taking care of children to taking care of one's parents, or even involve both types of caretaking at once (given the later age at which many women now have children). And even with a smaller number of children per family, as standards have been rising regarding appropriate child raising, the parental time and money devoted per child to raising those children to adulthood has been rising. Since women still tend to bear primary responsibility for caretaking (as witnessed by the higher number of hours spent in child care and other caretaking in time diary data), this phenomenon will tend to contribute to their lower incomes relative to men as well.

At this point, it appears unlikely that demographic changes will occur to reverse the direction of the changes that have already occurred. The drop in childbearing in particular is following a very long secular pattern of decline that dates back to before the 19th century (Jacobsen 2007, Figure 5.3). It also appears unlikely that marriage rates will rise, or that the age at first marriage will decrease significantly. What is more likely is that these trends will increasingly be found in the currently industrializing world. Indeed, other developed countries have even lower rates of marriage and childbearing than the United States at this point, and many areas in the developing world have experienced substantial drops in childbearing. Thus the conditions for increased female participation in the labor force appear to be in place, even as the possibility of high rates of female poverty for at least significant subsets of the population may also increase as family ties fray.

CONCLUSION: WHAT WOULD IT TAKE TO CLOSE THE GENDER GAP?

We have now reviewed the basic differences between women and men in terms of economic well-being, and have also reviewed the probable causes of these differences. We now turn to the final challenge of considering what it would take to close the gender gap. We have considered the gender gap in well-being (as an outcome measure) and also in access to and control of resources (as an input measure). We will consider in particular how the income gap in well-being might be narrowed, but broaden the discussion out to these other measures as well.

Logically speaking, it is not strictly necessary to know what causes difference in order to eradicate it. Society could, for instance, simply decree an equal income for all individuals regardless of gender (and other factors such as race). However, in considering policy alternatives it is useful to consider those that have a higher probability of being both undertaken and implemented effectively.

It is also the case that while doing nothing is of course a possibility, the costs of doing so are substantial. This is because the underutilization of women's productive capacity represents a loss in output, the additional goods and services that would be produced if women were able to utilize fully their productive capabilities. In a recent study I calculate the loss circa 2010 on a worldwide basis attributable to this underutilization at the equivalent of 7 percent of total output per year (Jacobsen 2012).

Thus what are some policy measures that could be taken to increase women's well-being relative to men? We may also want to add the constraint that any such policy should not come at the cost of making the worse-off men even worse off. For instance, policies that increase men's unemployment rate while reducing women's unemployment rate are clearly not preferred to policies that decrease both groups' unemployment rates. Similarly, raising everyone up to the poverty line (or over it) regardless of gender will be preferable, and nonetheless affect more women than men.

The current political climate in the United States and other developed nations is oddly gender blind. On the one hand, more and more women are active in politics, and powerful women, whether in corporations, politics, or the media, receive less and less notice as curiosities. On the other hand, many feminist issues are scarcely discussed anymore in the media and are not main topics on college campuses today (though topics such as date rape can still generate significant interest). This is both disturbing on the one hand, given that much progress remains to be made, but also reassuring on the other hand, in that a large degree of gender equality now appears, at least to the young, to be the status quo and thus no further discussion of it is required. However, it does mean that it is hard to get much traction for expanding policies to assist women at this point, and thus a broader discussion that focuses on equality in general and expanding capabilities and rights for all is more likely to be successful at this point.

With regard to increasing women's earnings relative to men, policies that take account of the work-family balancing act and attempt to make sure that some of the dual burden on women is eased are desirable. For example, family leave legislation in many countries allows women to take leave from work for childbearing without having to fear being fired from their company in the interim. This can make it more likely that women can continue in the career path that they trained for with minimal interruption. In addition, policies to increase subsidized, readily available, high-quality child care will quite likely increase female labor force participation as well as reduce breaks in their participation that can affect their earnings (Kimmel 1998).

It is less clear what other policies can increase women's earnings; much of the potential gain in this area may already have been made over the past few decades. If women continue to prefer certain occupations over others, and continue to have different lifetime work patterns than men, then it seems unlikely that full earnings parity can be achieved. Even in countries where boys and girls follow almost identical curricula up through high school, they exhibit different preferences for college majors and occupations. Thus it does not seem like the answer is to make additional changes to the education system.

This does not mean that more progress could not be made in increasing women's income other than through increasing their earnings. One big help to many low-income workers in the United States has been the Earned Income Tax Credit, the amount of which is in part dependent on how many children the worker has in her or his household. Another is the prevalence of child allowances in many developed countries so that additional income can be funneled to families with children.

It seems unlikely that policies can be passed that would affect demographic factors in a direction that would be unambiguously positive for women's well-being. For instance, while higher marriage rates would provide more household income, they might also constrain women's career choices. However, policies can be passed that are sensitive to the changing needs of women both over their individual life spans and over time for everyone. One such policy is to continue to increase enforcement of child support arrangements so that divorced women would not experience such a large drop in income. Another would be to consider how to deal with the increasing need for caretakers for the elderly. Right now family members who take care of relatives are not automatically compensated for such arrangements. Increased discussion in the developed countries' rapidly aging societies of how to support both the elderly and their family caretakers needs to take place.

Increasingly, discussion over well-being is turning away from a simplistic focus on earnings (or income, or per capita output) and toward a more holistic view of increasing capacity for life fulfillment. Such a discussion gives weight to closing gender gaps on other measures as well, such as literacy and political representation. These additional measures have been important in considering how standards can be applied across different countries and societies that have a range of social structures as well as different labor markets. For instance it is hard to argue against literacy as a universal goal that should be achieved regardless of gender. However, in practice there are still many countries where girls' education is considered as more optional than boys', and thus outside support is needed in order to assist poor families in educating their daughters as well as their sons.

This expanded discussion also considers whether there is a longer list of fundamental rights that should be guaranteed to all persons. These might include the right to potable water, the right to a clean and safe environment, and the right to access information. Again, it is hard to argue against achieving such goals equally for both genders, but it also may be necessary to support attainment of such goals more heavily for one gender than for the other. In the case of domestic violence for instance, women are disproportionately the victims and thus also require a larger share of resources in order to attack this problem.

Thus the answer to what it would take to close the gender gap is: a full commitment to gender equality on all dimensions of well-being, combined with a full commitment to equalizing access to and control of productive resources. While enormous progress has been made on both of these fronts, much remains to be done, particularly in the developing world. Still, as part of the ongoing expansion of human rights and respect for those rights, it is not inconceivable that by the end of the 21st century (and maybe even well before then), the remaining significant differences in well-being and capacity between the genders will be eradicated.

BIBLIOGRAPHY

Babcock, Linda and Sara Laschever. 2003. *Women Don't Ask: Negotiation and the Gender Divide*. Princeton, NJ: Princeton University Press.

Filer, Randall. 1985. "Male-Female Wage Differences: The Importance of Compensating Differentials." *Industrial and Labor Relations Review* 38: 426–37.

International Centre for Prison Studies. 2011. World Prison Brief.

Jacobsen, Joyce. 2006. "Men's Issues in Development." In *The Other Half of Gender: Men's Issues in Development*, edited by Ian Bannon and Maria C. Correia, 1–28. Washington, DC: World Bank.

Jacobsen, Joyce. 2007. *The Economics of Gender, Third Edition*. Malden, MA: Blackwell/Wiley.

Jacobsen, Joyce. 2012 (forthcoming). "Reducing Losses Due to Gender Inequality." In *The Way the World Is: Past, Present and Future Global Challenges*, edited by Kasper Anderskov and Bjorn Lomberg. Cambridge, UK: Cambridge University Press.

Jianakoplos, Nancy Ammon and Alexandra Bernasek. 1998. "Are Women More Risk Averse?" *Economic Inquiry* 36: 620–30.

Kimmel, Jean. 1998. "Child Care Costs as a Barrier to Employment for Single and Married Mothers." *Review of Economics and Statistics* 80: 287–99.

Neelakantan, Urvi and Yunhee Chang. 2010. "Gender Differences in Wealth at Retirement." *American Economic Review Papers & Proceedings* 100: 362–67.

Schmidt, Lucie and Purvi Sevak. 2006. "Gender, Marriage, and Asset Accumulation in the United States." *Feminist Economics* 12: 139–66.

U.S. Bureau of the Census. 2011. International Data Base. Accessed http://www.census.gov/idb/worldpopinfo.html.

White House Council on Women and Girls. 2011. Women in America: Indicators of Social and Economic Well-Being.

World Bank. 2011. World Development Report: Gender Equality and Development.

Chapter 11

From Dependency to Self-Determination: Native Americans and Economic Development in the 21st Century

Sarah Dewees and Raymond Foxworth

INTRODUCTION

Understanding the economic status of Native Americans at the beginning of the 21st century is a challenging task. There is tremendous diversity among Native American populations, Native nations, and their indicators of economic well-being. There are 565 distinct federally recognized tribal nations in the United States, each with a unique culture, history, and set of economic conditions, and several more state-recognized and -unrecognized tribes (Federal Register 2010a, 2010b). Each of these tribal nations faces a different set of economic challenges and opportunities, whether it be the size, location, and legal status of their land base, the number and quality of their tribal enterprises, or the size and characteristics of the natural resources they own and control. For example, some Native nations have reservations that measure in size at less than 100 acres, while the Navajo Nation has over 17 million acres within its boundaries. Some Native nations have a land base close to urban areas and operate successful gaming operations, such as the Mashantucket Pequot Tribal Nation. Other tribes have reservations that are located in remote rural areas far from vibrant urban markets. Tribes that possess land-based resources like natural gas, such as the Southern Ute Indian Tribe, have been able to generate significant revenue from tribal enterprises based on these natural resources. Yet many Native nations own land that has few natural resources, is of little agricultural value, and is remotely located, and these nations have not been as successful in developing profitable tribal enterprises.

Despite the diverse characteristics of Native nations, there are some common themes that help explain both the current economic status of tribal members living on and off reservations and their future potential economic trajectory. The most important common experience is the way federal policy has shaped and controlled the economic actions of American Indian nations and their citizens over the past 200 years. Only recently have American Indian leaders been able to decide for themselves their own economic development strategies, and the positive outcomes associated with this are already apparent. In this chapter, we will discuss how federal policy has contributed to the growth of inequalities between American Indian people and non-Native American populations over time, and how since the 1970s, it has created new opportunities for economic growth. It is important to understand that federal Indian policy has rarely been created in the best interest of Native Americans and instead has historically resulted in economic dependency on the federal government (Fixico 1998; Lui et al. 2005). Today, Native nations are working to overcome their historical patterns of dependency and take control of their own economies. As we begin to move into the 21st century and beyond, there is little doubt that Native nations will break from historical patterns of economic dependency and will begin to successfully control and guide their own economic futures.

WHO IS AN AMERICAN INDIAN?

There is great confusion about American Indian populations in North America, starting with the terminology used to describe people in this population. The terms "American Indian," "Native American," and "tribal citizen" will all be used in this chapter to describe individuals who are citizens of a tribal nation or have a heritage associated with the peoples who were indigenous to North American long before the explorer Christopher Columbus arrived in 1492.[1] It is important to understand that American Indians have a history and a legal status that is different from any other racial minority group in the United States. American Indians are members of independent, sovereign tribal nations, also referred to as Native nations. As sovereign nations, tribal nations have a unique relationship with the federal government, one that is rooted in American history and federal Indian case law. Tribal nations hold governing powers that allow them to form governments, make and enforce laws, prosecute violation of laws on their reservations, and direct economic activities on their reservation, and American Indian people hold a dual citizenship as citizens of their Native nation and as citizens of the United States. Each Native nation in the United States has a distinct legal, political, economic, and cultural system. These systems interact with federal and state governments in ways that are different from any other minority group in the United States.

Tribal Sovereignty

The sovereign status of Native nations is an outcome of treaties signed with foreign nations over 200 years ago during a period of time when European governments were starting colonies in the "New World" and negotiating with tribal leaders over control of land and natural resources. These treaties recognized Indian nations as sovereign political entities with powers of self-governance and independent control over internal and external legal affairs. Successive treaties and military conflicts limited the land holdings of many tribes but reaffirmed their independent sovereign powers. Different treaties signed with different Native nations, and subsequent federal legislation, have led to a complex and often confusing patchwork of federal Indian law that now guides the interaction between the federal government and tribal governments.

The governing powers of Native nations have been recognized by the U.S. federal government through countless treaty agreements, federal court cases, and acts of Congress. The legal and political relationship between the federal government and American Indian nations has been described in a number of ways; however, the legal definition that guides federal policy recognizes American Indian nations as *domestic dependent nations*. This legal definition, provided by U.S. Supreme Court Chief Justice John Marshall in 1831, suggests that the federal government acts as a trustee over the beneficiary that is Indian nations. The "trust" relationship between the federal government and Native nations states that the federal government, or its agents, are to act in the best interest of Native nations and "with the utmost integrity in its legal and political commitments to Indian peoples as outlined in treaties or governmental policies ... in its self-assumed role as the Indians' 'protectors' " (Wilkins 2002, 45). From this ruling comes the concept of the "trust responsibility," or the responsibility of the U.S. federal government to provide for the health and well-being of Indian nations and their citizens in exchange for treaties being signed or land exchanges. While it has not always turned out the way Chief Justice Marshal had envisioned, this trust responsibility has resulted in the U.S. government providing some health care, education, and other services to tribal nations to this day. It also guides and contributes to a legal, administrative, and bureaucratic framework that has shaped interactions between Indian nations and the U.S. government over the past 150 years (Pevar 2007). Formed in the early 1800s, the Bureau of Indian Affairs has administered a range of health, education, financial, and economic programs that were believed to be upholding the trust responsibility of the federal government in relation to Indian tribal governments. These programs included several economic development programs that were often administered in a top-down fashion with little input from tribal leaders. Unfortunately, many of these programs were marred by historical mismanagement and a paternalistic attitude toward Native nations and their citizens. By removing control and resources from tribal leaders, this system has created a condition of dependence on federal government programs. As will be described in this chapter, many of the programs designed to help Native nations and their citizens, most notably the management of land and trust funds for tribal citizens and nations, instead resulted in a siphoning of Indian-owned resources away from their Indian owners and therefore contributed to the underdevelopment we see on many Indian reservations today (Lui et al. 2005).

The legal and political status of American Indian nations plays an important role in helping us analyze and understand contemporary patterns of American Indian economic development and inequalities between citizens of Native nations and larger society. It is the legal and political status of Native nations that has allowed the federal government historically to pass policies that control and direct the affairs of Native nations. If American Indians were not recognized as citizens of sovereign nations, an analysis of American Indian economic inequality and marginalization would focus on similar factors that account for the marginalization or underdevelopment of other racial or minority groups in the United States. But the status of American Indians and their citizenship in relation to sovereign tribal governments requires us to understand how federal Indian policy has shaped historical patterns of economic inequality that still persist today.

TRENDS IN AMERICAN INDIAN POPULATION AND SOCIOECONOMIC INDICATORS

Starting in 2000, respondents to the U.S. Census could self-identify as one or more race. The U.S. Census Bureau states that in 2010 over 5.2 million people self-identified as having some American Indian or Alaska Native heritage, comprising 1.7 percent of the U.S. population (U.S. Census Bureau 2010). In 2000, 4.5 million people claimed to be American Indian or Alaska Native in combination with one or more other race, amounting to 1.5 percent of the U.S. population during that decade. Although Native Americans comprise a small percentage of the U.S. population, their population group is growing faster than the overall U.S. population—between 2000 and 2010 the population of this group increased by 26.7 percent compared to a growth rate of 9.7 percent in the overall U.S. population (U.S. Census Bureau 2010).

Contrary to popular belief, the majority of Native American people live in urban areas and not on remote, rural Indian reservations. In 2010, only 22 percent of Native Americans lived on reservation land and 78 percent lived in mostly urban areas. In 2007 Los Angeles County represented the largest concentrated population of American Indian or Alaska Native people, numbering around 146,500. Federal policies that encouraged tribal citizens to leave their reservations and seek wage labor in cities led to a massive out-migration of Native American populations over the past 150 years, and many people have left their reservations but kept up strong social ties with their home communities. Even today, many Native Americans live and work in urban areas but may move back and forth from reservation land, and therefore this population group remains very dynamic. Overall, American Indian people are more likely to live in the southwestern, northwestern, and Great Plains regions of the United States, although there are many tribes in the northeastern and southeastern regions as well. While California has the highest number of American Indian people living within its borders (it is also the most populous state in the nation), the states with the largest percentage of Native American people are Alaska, Oklahoma, New Mexico, Arizona, Montana, Oklahoma, North Dakota, and South Dakota (U.S. Census Bureau 2010).

The tribes with the most citizens, or the largest tribes, are the Navajo Nation and the Cherokee Nation.

Americans Indians have some of the highest rates of poverty among any racial or minority group in the United States, and they suffer from disproportionately low education levels and high levels of chronic diseases. Official unemployment on Indian reservations is close to 22 percent annually, and on some reservations, seasonal unemployment can be as high as 60 percent (Taylor and Kalt 2005, 28). Only 77 percent of Native Americans 25 and older have at least a high school diploma or GED, compared to 86 percent in the overall U.S. population. The number is even lower among Native Americans living on reservations where only 70 percent have a high school diploma or equivalent. While poverty levels for American Indians are high overall, they are often much higher for individuals residing on tribal reservation land. In 2004, over 30 percent of Native American families on reservations lived below the poverty level (U.S. Census Bureau 2004; National Center for Education Statistics 2008), and per capita income was $7,942 (see Table 11.1).[2] In 2006, 39 percent of American Indian or

Table 11.1
Socioeconomic Indicators, Reservation-Based American Indian Population versus U.S. Population (all races)

	2000–2004	
	Native Americans on Reservations	**Total U.S. Population**
Income and Employment		
Median household income†	$31,605	$44,684
Per capita income	$7,942	$21,587
Families below the poverty level†	30.70%	18.40%
Education		
High school graduates	70.90%	86.00%
College graduates	11.50%	28.00%

Notes: At the time of writing, the majority of data from the 2010 Census have not been released. Thus we tried to capture the more recent socioeconomic characteristics of Native peoples in the United States. Most data come from the U.S. Department of Commerce, Bureau of the Census, *We the People: American Indians and Alaska Native in the United States: Census 2000 Special Reports* (Washington, DC, 2006). The † indicates that data came from the 2004 American Community Survey, U.S. Department of Commerce, Bureau of the Census, *The American Community: American Indians and Alaska Natives* (Washington, DC, 2006). Some data are from the 2010 American Community Survey of the American Indian and Alaska Native population. These data are for American Indian reservations and for those identifying themselves only as Native American/Alaska Native on the U.S. Census.

Alaska Native children age five and under were living in poverty, a rate nearly twice that of children five and under in the total U.S. population, which was 21 percent (National Center for Education Statistics 2008). The American Indian population in the United States is comparatively very young, with a larger proportion of young people than most other population groups. About 30 percent of American Indians and Alaska Natives are children under 18 compared with about 22 percent of non-Hispanic whites (U.S. Census Bureau 2004).

It is noteworthy that the income gap between American Indians on reservations and the overall U.S. population is significant and has persisted over time. For example, according to the 1970 Census, the income gap between American Indians and the total U.S. population was $8,841 in inflation-adjusted dollars, with per capita income for American Indians living on a reservation averaging $4,347, compared to the national average per capita income of $13,188. According to the 2000 Census, this income gap remained about the same at around $13,000 with the per capita income of American Indians living on a reservation averaging $7,942 compared to the national average per capita income of $21,587 (see Figure 11.1). Similarly, poverty rates for the American Indian and Alaska Native population on reservations are

Figure 11.1
Real Per Capita Income, 1970–2000.

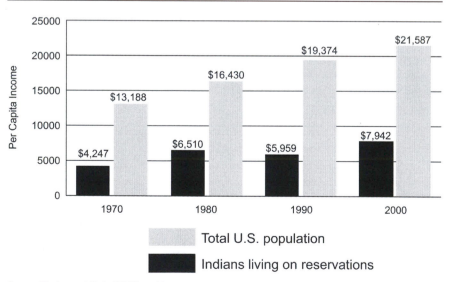

Source: Taylor and Kalt (2005), p. 7.

Figure 11.2
Poverty Rates, 1970–2000.

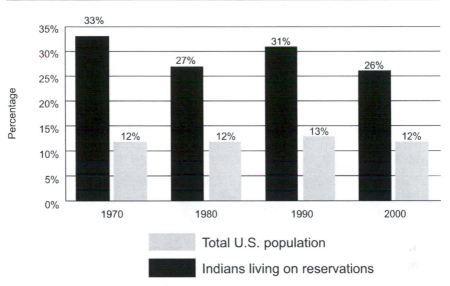

Source: Decennial censuses 1970, 1980, 1990, 2000.

much higher than that for the larger U.S. population, and the gap has been persistent over time. As these statistics demonstrate, while the income of many American Indians has grown over the last 30 years, these rates of growth have not allowed American Indians to catch up to the average income of larger society (see Figure 11.2).

HOW DID WE GET HERE? UNDERSTANDING FEDERAL INDIAN POLICY AND CURRENT ECONOMIC CONDITIONS

While the economic conditions of Native Americans may seem dire, especially for those individuals living on Indian reservations, there has been significant positive change over the last three decades and several examples of economic development success stories. But in order to understand the current economic challenges facing Native American people and tribal leaders, it is important to understand the conditions created by the last 200 years of federal Indian policy. History now widely recognizes that the economic and political structures of the federal government's policy toward American Indians extracted wealth from tribal territories and played a large role in impoverishing Native people (Lui et al. 2005). Reservations were viewed as sources of cheap raw materials, food, and labor, and as markets for the surrounding border towns' economy (Fixico 2005). This chapter will focus on the ways in which federal policies have systematically removed assets from Native populations and have contributed to the high poverty levels that exist for many Native American people. It is only by understanding these federal policy actions that we can begin to understand the conditions that exist in Native America in the current day, and the potential for positive change represented by the new millennium.

Early American Indian Economic Organization

In 1492, the year Columbus accidentally landed in what is now North America, indigenous Native American populations resided in and controlled the vast land areas of what is now the United States of America. Dynamic economies existed that were based on trading agricultural goods, cultural artifacts, and traditional forms of money and were inclusive of many different indigenous populations across North America as well as European fur traders and entrepreneurs. The first colonists benefited from the knowledge and technology of Native populations in many ways, and were dependent upon many of the goods and services provided in economic and cultural exchanges. The pilgrims at Plymouth survived the winter of 1620 with the assistance of the Wampanoag Tribe of Massachusetts, and many other residents of early settlements traded with the indigenous population for food and other goods (Weatherford 1991, 112). Such assistance in the form of food and agricultural help, coupled with a fear of Native populations' often superior military might, contributed to a relationship of respect between the early settlers and Native Americans.

Conflict and American Indian Removal—Reservations and Assimilation

As the number of settlers in the North America grew, conflicts intensified between the colonists and Indian nations. As the colonists' power increased, they battled Indian tribes over access to land and natural resources. Over time, the newly formed U.S. government was able to force Indian tribes to sign treaties that reduced their land holdings and regional power. In the late 1700s and early 1800s, the demand for Indian land increased even more as new populations arrived and agricultural technology improved. When Andrew Jackson was elected president in 1828, what had previously been an unofficial policy of increasing control of Indian lands for white settlement became official federal policy. Indian relocation and removal became "the dominant federal Indian policy of the nineteenth century" (Pevar 2002, 7). New federal policies emerged that led to the relocation of tribes to remote, underdeveloped rural areas where many Indian reservations are located today.

Simultaneously, policies of cultural indoctrination were initiated by the federal government. In an effort to encourage Native people to join Western economic activity and integrate into the growing U.S. society, the federal government enacted policies to "Kill the Indian and save the Man." In 1884 President Chester A. Arthur stated that in order to solve the United States' ever-present "Indian problem," the goal of federal policy should be to "introduce among the Indians the customs and pursuits of civilized life and gradually to absorb them into the mass of our citizens" (Cohen 2005, 129). In 1887 Congress passed the General Allotment Act to encourage Indian people to leave their tradi- tional land and adopt Western economic practices. The guiding belief behind the General Allotment Act of 1887 was that communal ownership of land by Native nations was uncivilized or "savage." The General Allotment Act allowed the federal government to take Indian land out of collective ownership by Native nations and grant it to individual Indians who would be conferred U.S. citizenship for abandoning their tribes and adopting the "habits of civilized life" (Getches et al. 1998). It was assumed that individual Indians would use their land to participate in the mainstream economy by success- fully managing agricultural operations and selling their products in the local economies, a strategy that largely failed due to low-quality land and poor training for Indian farmers. Land not allotted to individ- ual Indians was considered surplus and opened up for non-Indian ownership. This policy ended up removing vast amounts of land, an extremely valuable commodity, from Native nation control as individ- ual Indians lost their land when they could not pay taxes or debts, and as non-Indian farmers bought up excess land on Indian reservations. The General Allotment Act of 1887 resulted in the loss of an estimated 90 million acres of tribal land, and this land passed into the hands of both the federal government and new American immigrants for devel- opment and American expansion (Deloria and Lytle 1998). Perhaps even more damaging is the fact that much of the land on reservations today suffers from a "checkerboarded" pattern where different plots are owned by the tribal government, tribal members, or nontribal members, which has made it difficult to consolidate large areas of land for farming or other economic activity. This "checkerboarded" nature of the legal status and ownership of land is one of the most significant challenges facing tribal governments to this day.

Starting in the mid-1800s, the federal government developed federal employment and education programs to assimilate Indians, transforming former army barracks into educational institutions for Native peoples. As Ohio senator George Pendleton noted on the floor of Congress in 1880:

> Indians must either change their modes of life or they will be exterminated. ... We must stimulate within them to the very largest degree, the idea of home, of family, and of property. These are the very anchorages of civilization; the commencement of the dawning of these ideas in the mind is the commencement of the civilization of any race, and these Indians are no exception. (Gates 1979, 11)

The idea of cultural transformation as an effort to solve the United States' "Indian problem" was not only an effort to "civilize" Native people but also an effort to expose Native peoples to the ideas of private property of capitalism, and mainstream religious and cultural views. Educational programs were embedded with religious and cultural indoctrination and pushed Native people to leave their reservations for mostly urban areas. In large part, Native peoples today view this era of federal Indian policy as a period of land theft and cultural genocide.

American Indian Reorganization

In the 1930s, federal policy toward American Indians took a new direction. Not only did programs aimed at cultural transformation have a heavy federal price tag, but there was increasing criticism of these programs. Several studies including the Meriam Report of 1928 documented the dismal failure of assimilation policies that had resulted in growing poverty and deteriorating social conditions for Native peoples.[3] In an attempt to empower tribal nations in self-governance and stop the loss of land promoted by the General Allotment Act of 1887, the federal government passed the Indian Reorganization Act of 1934. Authors of this legislation hoped that it would restore collective ownership of land by Native nations and would provide tribal leaders with a legal governing structure to exercise control of internal governmental affairs related to natural resources, economic development, and land management. The Indian Reorganization Act did improve conditions in many ways, including stopping the loss of Indian land and converting it back to tribal ownership. However, many scholars have documented that the constitutions and legal structures that many tribes adopted were not a good cultural fit, and in many cases the act replaced more traditional forms of Native nation governance and democratic practices that had been in place prior to the arrival of Europeans (Cohen et al. 2006; Grinde and Johansen 1991).

American Indian Termination

In the 1940s, the pendulum of federal policy swung back in the other direction as war-related industrialization and economic growth created increased demands for Indian land and natural resources, and a model of cultural assimilation was once again in vogue with federal policy makers. Beginning in 1953, the U.S. Congress initiated a policy of tribal "termination" by which they ended the federal recognition of over 100 tribes and thereby cut these tribes off from several programs and services that had historically supported the well-being of tribal citizens. In 1953, with direct support from President Dwight D. Eisenhower, Congress passed House Concurrent Resolution No. 108, often called "the termination resolution." This legislation sought to remove governmental power from select tribal governments, discontinue the legal trust relationship between the federal government and those tribal nations, and discontinue federal benefits and support services that accompanied the trust responsibility. Many federal policy makers viewed this as progress for Indian nations and argued that it would "free" Indians from the oppressive, day-to-day control of the Bureau of Indian Affairs (Pevar 2002, 11, 68).

Regardless of the beliefs or intent of federal policy makers, the termination period had a devastating impact on terminated tribes and their citizens. Termination once again forced individual private property ownership upon individual tribal citizens, which once again resulted in significant land loss when many Indians either sold their land to whites or lost their land when they were not able to pay property tax on it. This further contributed to the erosion of the Native land base. Approximately 109 tribes and bands were "terminated" under the policy, and a minimum of 1,362,155 acres and 11,466 individuals were affected (Parker 1989, 53). While some of these tribes have since been reinstated, most are still struggling to this day to recover from such a devastating economic blow. By selling Indian land, Congress destroyed the economies of many tribes, reducing their members to poverty and dependence on public assistance.

Indian Political Activism and Increased Self-Determination

Partially in reaction to the severe policies of the 1950s, Indian political activism increased in the 1960s and 1970s. This activism dovetailed with the activism of the civil rights era and drew increased attention to Native American issues (Cornell 1990; Guilemin 1979, 287–306; Nagel 1997). In large part, this rise in American Indian political activism helped usher in a new era of federal Indian policies in the 1960s and 1970s. Largely under President Johnson's "War on Poverty," this period saw the creation of new federal policies aimed at increasing American Indian self-determination. This period was highlighted by the 1975 Indian Self-Determination and Education Assistance Act, which legislatively granted greater powers of tribal self-governance than under termination era policies.

The 1975 Indian Self-Determination and Education Assistance Act allowed Indian nations to take more ownership of Indian programs and directed the Bureau of Indian Affairs to collaborate with Native nations, rather than dictate programmatic efforts. The 1975 act created the legal framework for tribes to contract with the federal government to manage the budget, staffing, and operations of a range of health, education, economic, and social welfare programs, allowing tribes to build managerial capacity and design programs that were an appropriate cultural fit for their communities. This piece of legislation again swung the pendulum back from policies that diminished the power of tribal governments and moved toward a policy structure that promoted tribal self-determination.

During the 1980s and 1990s, a historical mismanagement of tribal financial and other resources by the Bureau of Indian Affairs began to finally be revealed. Due to a series of historical legislative, judicial, and administrative actions, most of Indian-owned land is held in trust by the U.S. government for tribal governments and their citizens. The Bureau of Indian Affairs also manages the leasing of this property as well as any natural resource exploration and extraction. Unfortunately, Bureau of Indian Affairs officials often failed to secure market rate for natural resource and land lease contracts and may have colluded with private business interests to reduce lease rates, resulting in a significant loss of revenue for many individuals and tribal governments (Wilkinson 1999). The 1970s and '80s represented a new era of litigation that brought to light much of the mismanagement as numerous tribes sued the federal government for compensation.

In 1999, federal judge Royce C. Lamberth ruled that the U.S. federal government was in breach of its fiduciary responsibility as a trustee for Indian financial accounts due to poor record keeping, lost accounts, lost money, and a lack of proper internal controls for financial management, among other issues confirmed in a 2003 report by the General Accounting Office. A class-action lawsuit filed in 1996 by Eloise Cobell, a banker and former treasurer for the Blackfeet tribe, had asked the federal government to provide a complete and accurate accounting of all the trust funds they had under management, something officials at the Department of the Interior have yet failed to do. In 2003, the lawyers for Eloise Cobell submitted a historical analysis of the trust funds that revealed that nearly $137.2 billion might have been lost, stolen, or misallocated from Indian tribes and their citizens. After years of litigation, this lawsuit was finally settled in 2011 for a fraction of the requested settlement amount.

CREATING NEW PATHS TOWARD AMERICAN INDIAN ECONOMIC DEVELOPMENT

As the previous section suggests, historical federal policy toward Indian nations created less than adequate conditions for economic development, and federal intervention and mismanagement hampered economic growth. Early federal Indian policies created a condition of economic dependency by removing tribal control of land and other natural resources and placing these resources into the hands of non-Indians, which often led to a loss of income by Indian nations and their citizens. Paternalistic policies of Indian reorganization and forced cultural assimilation imposed foreign, Western models of government on tribes and altered existing social, cultural, and political patterns of operation. The 1975 Indian Self-Determination and Education Assistance Act finally swung the pendulum of federal policy back toward greater self-determination and laid the groundwork for tribes to manage and operate more of their own programs. Today, Indian nations are moving away from a historical pattern of reliance on the federal government and taking a proactive stance to create conditions favorable to economic development and growth on Native homelands.

In the sections that follow, we discuss some of these new growth strategies and how these efforts are contributing to economic diversification and development for Native nations and their citizens.

Indian Gaming

Perhaps the most well-known (and most controversial) economic development strategy pursued by Indian nations in the past 30 years has been Indian gaming. Casino development has been a successful economic development strategy for many tribes. However, many misconceptions exist about this strategy and the impact it has had on the economic status of tribes and their citizens. What many people do not know is that Indian gaming was encouraged by federal officials in the 1980s as a way for tribes to generate a new income stream, reduce their economic dependency on the federal government, and move them toward economic self-sufficiency. Because tribes are sovereign nations and according to case law and federal legislation can operate gaming facilities even in states where state law restricts them, tribes were encouraged to pursue gaming as a way to bring outside revenue into tribally owned enterprises and promote economic development. Several tribes, especially those located near large urban markets, have opened successful gaming operations that generate significant revenue for tribal government operations.

However, the economic impact of Indian gaming has been uneven. While there are more than 200 Native nations in 28 states that have gaming operations, most of these gaming operations are small (in the form of small bingo parlors) and not very profitable for the tribe. A minority of operations account for a majority of the income—only 5 percent of all of Indian gaming operations generate 40 percent of the total Indian gaming revenue according to the Nation Indian Gaming Commission. Tribes with larger, well-run facilities that are located near large urban markets are more likely to generate significant income for their tribal enterprise. Most other tribes see only modest revenue from their tribal gaming operations. In many cases, state and local governments are also the benefactors of Indian gaming operations because these operations employ many local residents who in turn pay local and state income tax. In this way tribal gaming operations contribute significantly to the tax base and government revenue for local and state governments and promote economic development in their surrounding communities and region, a fact that is often overlooked in popular media coverage of Indian gaming.

Revenue from Indian gaming has helped many tribes build their physical and economic infrastructure and provide services to their citizens. Many tribes use gaming revenue to pay for facilities for their citizens such as community wellness centers, child care centers, and health clinics, and to pay for other tribal government operations such as the tribal police force or fire department. In addition, just like in any other business, gaming revenues are used to pay down debts associated with the enterprise and cover the operating expenses. A small number of tribes do pay out dividends to their members that assist in increasing the income level of tribal citizens, and research suggests that these payments improve the quality of life for Indian children and families (Costello et al. 2003). Unfortunately, there is a common misconception in the United States that Indian gaming operations, or Indian casinos, have solved the problem of Indian poverty. This is simply not the case. The gap between the income levels of Indians on reservations and the larger U.S. population still remains very large even for residents of reservations with casinos (Taylor and Kalt 2005).

Education and the Emergence of Tribally Controlled Schools and Colleges

In 1968, Navajo Community College (today known as Diné College) opened its doors as the first institution of higher education controlled and operated by a tribal government. Since that historical moment, over 30 tribally controlled colleges have opened their doors on tribal lands. These tribal colleges have emerged to serve the educational needs of tribal citizens, operating mostly in rural and isolated reservation areas where there are few other options for pursuing higher education. These institutions of higher education have gained national recognition for their ability to offer rigorous academic programs and integrate culturally relevant curriculum for Native student development (Benham and Stein 2003; Pavel et al. 2001). According to the American Indian Higher Education Consortium website, tribal colleges chartered by their affiliated tribal governments operate over 75 campuses in 15 states and one Canadian province and serve over 24,000 students.

Tribal governments created tribal colleges in part as a response to the low educational success rate for many Native students and the negative experiences many Native students had at mainstream institutions (Harvard Project on American Indian Economic Development

2008, 212). Higher educational attainment has long been a significant predictor of economic growth and development (Barro 1998; Brown 1999). Investments in education are said to be investments in the citizens of a nation to promote the growth of knowledge and other competencies necessary for citizens to participate effectively in the economy and government. Investments in education also have other economic benefits, including the creation of jobs on reservations and the development of a professional workforce. The growth of tribal colleges over the past 40 years represents a long-term investment in an economic development strategy that promotes educational attainment for tribal members, creates jobs for residents of reservations, and promotes an educated workforce for the tribal government.

Entrepreneurship

As tribal leaders enter into a new era of empowerment and self-determination, entrepreneurial activity on the part of tribal governments and tribal citizens has not been far behind. Much of the debate in the 1960s and 1970s about federal Indian policy centered around the need for tribally managed projects that reflected the interests, skills, and comparative legal, economic, and natural resource advantages of a tribal nation and its assets. Due to the sovereign status of tribal governments, a tribal enterprise can offer a comparative advantage over private enterprises that are regulated and taxed by state and federal governments, and many tribal leaders have been eager to start tribal enterprises that can compete in regional, national, and international markets.

In addition to gaming enterprises, tribal governments have created and successfully operated several different types of tribally owned businesses. For example, in 1994 the Winnebago Tribe of Nebraska launched the company Ho-Chunk Inc. to diversify the tribe's revenue streams and bring new revenue into the local community. Ho-Chunk Inc. is chartered under the laws of the Winnebago Tribe and operates several enterprises including local grocery stores, convenience stores, and hotels. It also operates a housing-manufacturing company that it uses to build tribal housing on the reservation. The Mississippi Band of Choctaw Indians has also created tribally owned businesses that create jobs, diversify the local economy, and build managerial capacity among their members. According to their website, they operate manufacturing, service, retail, and tourism businesses and provide almost 6,000 permanent, full-time jobs for tribal members and others in their region. The tribe is currently one of the 10 largest private employers in Mississippi, and has been able to raise the standard of living for its members and provide them with employment options in their local community.

In addition to business creation by tribal governments, many tribal leaders have recognized the importance of promoting small-business ownership and individual entrepreneurship on their reservations. On most reservations, the tribal government and other public sector entities (such as the school system, the federal Bureau of Indian Affairs, and the Indian Health Service) account for over 90 percent of all jobs. The private sector, or businesses owned by individuals, is underdeveloped due to a range of barriers unique to reservations. On many reservations, the physical infrastructure (roads, buildings), legal infrastructure (businesses codes, court systems, legal status, and checkerboarded nature of land), financial infrastructure (access to capital and financial services), and social infrastructure (local role models, effective leadership) are underdeveloped, and this has contributed to a low level of formal entrepreneurial activity by tribal citizens (Dewees and Sarkozy-Banoczy 2007). Tribes are working to overcome these barriers by funding organizations such as community development financial institutions (or CDFIs) to provide capital, financial services, and entrepreneurship training to tribal citizens. On the Cheyenne River Indian Reservation, Four Bands Community Fund was created in 2000 to provide financial education and entrepreneurship training and offer loans to tribal entrepreneurs wanting to start their own businesses. Four Bands Community Fund also works in partnership with the local tribal government to help create the appropriate legal and regulatory environment to support local business owners and promotes mentoring and leadership development. In the past 20 years, over 60 CDFIs have emerged to offer financing, training, and support to small-business owners on Indian reservations, and a small but vibrant private sector is slowly emerging on Indian reservations as a result.

Natural Resources on Indian Lands

The Southern Ute Indian Tribe is unique in that it is the only Native nation in the United States that has complete control of its energy resources (First Nations Development Institute 2009). The Southern Utes have not always exerted such control, however. Like many other Native nations, the Southern Utes used to have their energy resources

leased by outside corporations, mostly through lease negotiations conducted by the Bureau of Indian Affairs and many times without tribal
input. In many instances, the Southern Ute Indian Tribe found out that
they were not being paid market value for their resources (First
Nations Development Institute 2009). In 1992, the Southern Ute Indian
Tribe formed the Red Willow Production Company to buy back leases
and upgrade the performance of the wells on their reservation. Since
1992, the Southern Ute Indian Tribe has bought back 100 percent of
their leases and also has expanded their business of oil and gas production beyond their reservation borders. Their goal has been to create
a natural resource company that can yield maximum returns and dividends for tribal members.

In addition to oil, coal, and natural gas, Indian governments own
large quantities of land, some of which is valuable for agricultural
operations related to farming, ranching, and timber. In the lower 48
Indian nations in the lower 48 states hold approximately 30 percent
of the nation's coal resources, 10 percent of the natural gas resources,
and 5 percent of the oil resources. Some estimates suggest that cumula-
tively, a total of 10 percent of the nation's energy resources lie within
the boundaries of Native American reservations (Lui et al. 2005).
Though they own nearly 10 percent of the nation's energy natural
resources, tribes earn only marginal returns in comparison to the
returns produced by private industries. In reaction to evidence of
mismanagement by the Bureau of Indian Affairs, an increasing number of tribes have sought to take over the management of their natural
resource-based industries, a strategy that has resulted in increased economic growth on reservations. This has become even more common as
Native nations have developed their legal rights and internal capacity
to negotiate their own leases and not rely on the Bureau of Indian
Affairs to manage these economic activities.

In addition to oil, coal, and natural gas, Indian governments own
large quantities of land, some of which is valuable for agricultural
operations related to farming, ranching, and timber. In the lower 48
states, reservation lands account for over 56 million acres, and added
to the 44 million acres of Alaska Native lands, the total amount would
qualify as the fourth-largest land base in the United States after Alaska,
Texas, and California (Harvard Project on American Indian Economic
Development 2008, 161; Lui et al. 2005, 31). The majority of this
land—approximately 47 million acres—is used for ranching and
farmland (Harvard Project on American Indian Economic Development 2008, 161). Unfortunately, the majority of Indian agricultural land
is leased out to non-Native farmers and ranchers. However, several
Native nations, like the Oneida Tribe of Indians of Wisconsin, have

used their farmland to operate successful tribally owned farms that
create jobs and revenue for tribal citizens while at the same time producing healthy food for the local market. In addition to economic
activity related to farming and ranching, approximately 10 million
acres of Indian land is used for commercial forest operations (Harvard
Project on American Indian Economic Development 2008, 162). Many
tribes, including the Menominee Indian Tribes of Wisconsin, have
taken control of their forest operations and now use sustainable forest
management practices to harvest in a responsible manner and promote
economic revenue from their forests while protecting the natural resource for future generations.

As Native nations build their managerial capacity, they are increasingly taking control of the commercial operations related to tribally
owned natural resources. By exerting control over the leasing process
or initiating direct management of commercial operations related to
energy, agricultural, or forest resources, tribes are increasingly more
successful in capturing the economic benefits from these natural
resources and creating economic opportunities for tribal members.
This area of economic activity represents great potential for growth in
the new millennium.

CONCLUSION

The high poverty rates and extreme economic conditions on most
reservations are shocking and are a cause for great concern among
many tribal leaders. However, the economic strategies available to
tribal leaders in the new millennium represent a ray of hope as leaders
begin to exercise self-determination and self-governance in a way that
was impossible a mere 40 years ago. Despite such a short period in
which to implement new governance and economic development
strategies, there are many success stories that demonstrate the potential represented by the self-determination era.

It will take more than four decades to overcome over 200 years of
federal intervention and mismanagement of tribal affairs, however.
Many Native nations and their citizens are still struggling to recover
land on their reservation, design governance structures that reflect
their cultures, revitalize their languages and traditions, and provide
resources for a population that is recovering from the long-term effects
of colonialism and forced cultural assimilation. The large populations
of American Indian people who live in urban areas have met with

mixed economic success, and an increasing number of them are moving back to their traditional homelands to help revitalize the communities their families came from.

It is only by understanding the over 200 years of federal policy toward Native Nations and their citizens that we can understand some of the challenges they face today. The economic preconditions and legal structures that were created by paternalistic and colonial attitudes toward Native people 150 years ago still influence many of the interactions between federal policy makers and tribal leaders today and continue to present challenges to tribal leaders seeking their own path toward economic development. The passage of the 1975 Indian Self-Determination and Education Assistance Act represented the culmination of a new legal treatment of tribal governments and tribal leaders and has already begun to demonstrate the effectiveness of a new model of Indian self-governance. While there are still many challenges present for tribal leaders and their citizens, the next 200 years of economic development on Indian land hold great promise and potential.

NOTES

1.   We use these terms to describe individuals with American Indian and/or Alaska Native ancestry.

2.   While we rely on Census data for this chapter, we are aware that the low participation by Native Americans in the decennial Census and the American Community Survey may limit the accuracy of these data.

3.   The official name of the Meriam Report of 1928 was *The Problem of Indian Administration*. It was commissioned by the Institute of Government Research and was written by Lewis Meriam and published in 1928.

BIBLIOGRAPHY

Barro, Robert J. 1998. *Determinants of Economic Growth: A Cross-Country Empirical Study.* Cambridge: The MIT Press.

Benham, Maenette and Wayne Stein. 2003. *The Renaissance of American Indian Higher Education: Capturing the Dream.* Mahwah, NJ: Lawrence Erlbaum Associates, Inc.

Brown, David S. 1999. "Reading, Writing, and Regime Type: Democracy's Impact on Primary School Enrollment." *Political Research Quarterly* 52, no. 4: 681–707.

Cherokee Nation v. Georgia. 30 U.S. 1. (1831).

Cohen, Felix S. 2005. *Cohen's Handbook of Federal Indian Law*, 4th ed. Newark: LexisNexis.

Cohen, Felix S., David Eugene Wilkins, and Lindsay Gordon Robertson. 2006. *On the Drafting of Tribal Constitutions*. Norman: University of Oklahoma Press.

Cornell, Stephen. 1990. *The Return of the Native: American Indian Political Resurgence*. New York: Oxford University Press.

Costello, Jane, Scott N. Compton, Gordon Keeler, and Adrian Angold. October 15, 2003. "Relationships between Poverty and Psychopathology: A Natural Experiment." *JAMA*, 290, no. 15: 2023–29.

Deloria, Vine, and Clifford M. Lytle. 1998. *The Nations Within: The Past and Future of American Indian Sovereignty*. New York: Pantheon Books.

Dewees, Sarah and Stewart Sarcozy-Banoczy. 2007. "Transforming Economies: Entrepreneurship in Native Communities." In *Integrated Asset-Building Strategies for Reservation-Based Communities*. First Nations Development Institute, 155–88. Longmont: First Nations Development Institute.

Federal Register. 2010a. "Indian Entities Recognized and Eligible to Receive Services from the United States Bureau of Indian Affairs." *Federal Register* (October 1, 2010) 75: 90 p. 60810.

Federal Register. 2010b. "Indian Entities Recognized and Eligible To Receive Services From the United States Bureau of Indian Affairs." *Federal Register* (October 27, 2010) 75: 207 p. 66124.

First Nations Development Institute. 2009. "Native American Asset Watch: Rethinking Asset-Building in Indian Country." Longmont, CO: First Nations Development Institute.

Fixico, Donald L. 1998. *The Invasion of Indian Country in the Twentieth Century: American Capitalism and Tribal Natural Resources*. Niwot: University Press of Colorado.

Gates, Paul Wallace, ed. 1979. *The Rape of Indian Lands*. New York: Arno Press.

General Allotment Act of 1887. 24 Stat. 388, ch. 119, 25 USCA 331. (1887).

Getches, David H., Charles Wilkinson, and Robert Williams Jr. 1998. *Cases and Materials on Federal Indian Law*. 4th ed. St. Paul: West Publishers.

Grinde, Donald, and Bruce Johansen. 1991. *Exemplar of Liberty: Native America and the Evolution of Democracy*. Los Angeles: American Indian Studies Center, University of California.

Guilemin, Jeanne. 1979. "American Indian Resistance and Protest." In *Violence in America: Historical and Comparative Perspectives*, edited by Tedd Robert Gurr, 287–306. Beverly Hills: Sage Publications.

Harvard Project on American Indian Economic Development. 2008. "Education." In *The State of Native Nations: Conditions under U.S. Policies of Self-Determination*, 199–218. New York: Oxford University Press.

H.R. Con. Res. 108, 83d Cong. (1953).

Indian Citizenship Act of 1924, 43 Stat. 253, ante, 420. (1924).

The Indian Gaming Regulatory Act, P.L. 100-497, 102 Stat. 2475. (1988).

Indian Reorganization Act of 1934, P.L. 73-383. (1934).

Indian Self-Determination and Education Assistance Act, Pub. L. No. 93-638, § 1-209, 88 Stat. 2203, 2203–17 (1975).

Johansen, Bruce E. 1998. *Debating Democracy: Native American Legacy of Freedom*. Santa Fe: Clear Light Publishers.

Lui, Meizhu, Barbara Robles, Betsy Leondar-Wright, Rose Brewer, and Rebecca Adamson. 2005. *The Color of Wealth: The Story Behind the U.S. Racial Divide*. New York: The New Press.

Meriam, Lewis. 1928. *The Problem of Indian Administration*. Baltimore: Johns Hopkins Press.

Nagel, Joane. 1997. *American Indian Activism: Alcatraz to the Longest Walk*. Champaign: University of Illinois Press.

National Center for Education Statistics. 2008. *Statistical Trends in the Education of American Indians and Alaska Natives*. Washington, DC: U.S. Department of Education.

Parker, Linda. 1989. *Native American Estate: The Struggle over Indian and Hawaiian Lands*. Honolulu: University of Hawaii Press.

Pavel, D. Michael, Ella Inglebret, and Susan Rae Banks. 2001. "Tribal Colleges and Universities in an Era of Dynamic Development." *Peabody Journal of Education* 76, no. 1: 50–72.

Pevar, Stephen. 2002. *The Rights of Indian and Tribes*, 3rd ed. Carbondale: Southern Illinois University Press.

Taylor, Jonathan and Joseph Kalt. 2005. *American Indians on Reservations: A Databook of Socioeconomic Change between the 1990 and 2000 Censuses*. Cambridge: The Harvard Project on American Indian Economic Development.

U.S. Census Bureau. 2003. "The American Indian and Alaska Native Population, 2000." http://www.census.gov/prod/2002pubs/c2kbr01-15.pdf on October 26, 2011.

U.S. Census Bureau. 2004. "The American Community: American Indians and Alaska Natives." http://www.census.gov/prod/2007pubs/acs-07.pdf.

U.S. Census Bureau. 2010. "Census Brief: Overview of Race and Hispanic Origin." http://www.census.gov/prod/cen2010/briefs/c2010br-02.pdf.

Weatherford, Jack. 1991. *Native Roots: How the Indians Enriched America*. New York: Fawcett Columbine.

Wilkins, David Eugene. 2002. *American Indian Politics and the American Political System*. Lanham: Rowman & Littlefield.

Wilkinson, Charles. 1999. *Fire on the Plateau: Conflict and Endurance in the American Southwest*. Washington, DC: Island Press.

Chapter 12

Trends in Poverty and Inequality among Hispanics[1]

Pia Orrenius and Madeline Zavodny

Hispanics are a rapidly growing group in the United States and tend to be quite poor. In 2009, one in four Hispanics was poor. The proportion of black non-Hispanics who were poor was almost identical, but fewer than 1 in 10 white non-Hispanics were poor. Income inequality was higher among Hispanics than among non-Hispanic whites. Understanding why poverty and income inequality are so high among Hispanics is important since they are now the largest minority group in the United States.[2]

In 2010, 50.3 million people in the United States, or 16.3 percent of the population, considered themselves to be Hispanic. The Hispanic population grew 43 percent between 2000 and 2010, and it is projected to triple in size and account for almost 3 out of every 10 people in the country by 2050 (Passel and Cohn 2008). This population growth will come from future flows of Latin American immigrants, births to those immigrants once they reach the United States, and births to Hispanics already present in the country.

Immigrants currently play a leading role in the Hispanic population. Almost two-fifths of Hispanics are foreign-born, and another 36 percent were born in the United States but have at least one foreign-born parent.[3] Projections suggest that the native-born will comprise a growing share of the Hispanic population over time. In the United States, Hispanic births have outpaced immigration from Latin America since 2000, a trend that is expected to continue (Passel and Cohn 2008).

Who is considered Hispanic is an interesting question. Hispanic is considered an ethnicity in the United States, and Hispanics can be of any race (white, black, Asian, etc.). The United States has asked about Hispanic ethnicity in major surveys since the decennial Census in 1970. Most research on Hispanics uses survey data that include self-reported Hispanic ethnicity.[4]

Selectivity in who identifies themselves as Hispanic is problematic when examining poverty and inequality. If the likelihood that people identify themselves as Hispanic is related to their income, studies of Hispanics may misreport outcomes related to income. Indeed, research suggests that Hispanics with higher education and earnings are less likely to self-identify as Hispanic (Duncan and Trejo 2009, 2011). In addition, Hispanics with high earnings and more education are more likely to marry a non-Hispanic, which further reduces the likelihood their children will identify as Hispanic (Duncan and Trejo 2009, 2011). Such selectivity in self-identification causes average income to be understated and the poverty rate to be overstated among Hispanics. However, researchers have little choice except to use a self-reported measure of ethnicity when studying Hispanics, particularly the native-born. With this cautionary note in mind, we proceed to an examination of poverty and inequality among Hispanics. We first outline trends in poverty and income inequality among Hispanics and then turn to a discussion of the key factors underlying those trends.

TRENDS IN POVERTY

Table 12.1 reports poverty rates by race, ethnicity, and national origin using data from the 1970–2000 decennial Censuses and from the 2010 March Current Population Survey. The table gives poverty rates based on family pretax money income the previous calendar year. Money income includes wages and salaries, Social Security payments, cash welfare benefits, and other sources of cash income except for capital gains (or losses). It does not include the value of in-kind

Table 12.1

The Poverty Rate among Hispanics Has Changed Little since 1970

	Poverty Rate					Gini Index
	1970	1980	1990	2000	2010	2010
Non-Hispanic whites	10.0	8.5	8.7	7.9	9.5	0.456
Non-Hispanic blacks	34.7	28.6	27.9	23.7	25.7	0.496
Hispanics	25.2	22.8	24.4	22.1	25.4	0.481
Hispanic natives	25.2	20.1	21.6	18.3	20.6	0.481
Mexican ancestry	26.9	21.6	23.3	18.8	22.3	0.481
Puerto Rican ancestry	10.1	31.7	29.9	24.6	24.8	0.477
Cuban ancestry	4.0	14.7	15.2	12.1	15.6	0.467
Hispanic immigrants	25.8	26.6	27.6	24.8	29.0	0.470
Mexico	31.7	26.9	30.2	26.8	30.4	0.453
Puerto Rico	31.5	38.7	33.6	28.8	23.0	0.488
Cuba	13.1	12.9	14.6	15.2	19.1	0.490
Central America	14.4	21.8	25.9	22.1	23.5	0.462
Caribbean	16.0	32.4	32.7	28.5	27.6	0.431
South America	13.8	15.8	15.4	15.8	11.6	0.433
Recent immigrants (≤10 years)	20.2	28.9	34.5	32.1	32.9	0.469
Nonrecent immigrants	28.3	25.6	24.1	22.1	27.9	0.467

Source: Authors' calculations from data from the 1970–2000 Censuses from Ruggles et al. (2010) and the 2010 March Current Population Survey from King et al. (2010).

Note: Although people born in Puerto Rico are U.S. citizens by birth, this table lists them as immigrants for simplicity. Puerto Rican natives are people born in the 50 states and District of Columbia who report Puerto Rican as their Hispanic ethnicity, and similarly for Mexican and Cuban natives. Years shown are the survey year; the poverty rate and Gini index are based on family pretax money income the previous year.

benefits, such as food stamps. Official poverty status is determined by comparing family income with a poverty threshold based on family size and the age of family members.[5] Poverty status is the same for everyone in a family, and everyone in a household is assigned the head's immigrant status and ancestry.

The poverty rate among Hispanics has remained virtually unchanged since the 1970s. In 2009 (the 2010 data), the poverty rate was almost 16 percentage points higher among Hispanics than among non-Hispanic whites. That gap has fluctuated between 14 and 16 percentage points since 1970. There is little evidence that Hispanics are "catching up" with non-Hispanic whites, although the gap with non-Hispanic blacks has narrowed because poverty has declined considerably among blacks since 1970.

Native-born Hispanics have lower poverty rates than foreign-born Hispanics. Natives benefit from having more education, better English fluency, and being U.S. citizens by birth. However, the poverty rates would be considerably higher in Table 12.1 among native-born Hispanics, particularly in the 2010 data, if children were classified based on their own place of birth instead of the head's. Children are more likely than adults to be poor in the United States, and Hispanic children are particularly likely to be poor. Over one-third of all Hispanic children were living in poor families in 2009. The poverty rate is even higher—almost 40 percent—among foreign-born Hispanic children. Between 1969 and 1999, the poverty rate rose among children of immigrants, with the largest increase occurring among non-Mexican Hispanics (Van Hook et al. 2004).

Since 1970, the poverty rate has trended up among foreign-born Hispanics. This reflects a relative decline in education levels among inflows of Hispanic immigrants and a shift toward poorer immigrants, with both trends related to the rise in immigration from Mexico and Central America. Poverty rates differ by national origin and ancestry. Among Hispanic natives, those who report Mexican or Puerto Rican ancestry are considerably more likely to be poor than Cuban-Americans, although the poverty rate has risen among U.S.-born Cubans over time.[6] Looking at the foreign-born, poverty rates are highest among immigrants from Mexico and the Caribbean (not including Cuba) and lowest among immigrants from South America. Other research shows a similar pattern of considerable diversity across national-origin groups (e.g., Mogull 2005; Reimers 2006).

Poverty is particularly high among Hispanics who recently immigrated to the United States. Although poverty declines significantly with duration of U.S. residence, poverty rates among Hispanic immigrants do not catch up with those among either Hispanic natives or non-Hispanic whites over time. To illustrate this, Table 12.2 shows the evolution of the poverty rate over time in the United States for various cohorts of Hispanic immigrants.[7] The top panel includes all Hispanic immigrants, while the second panel includes those who were aged 18–34 in the first Census year following their arrival; the motivation for this subset is that most people are in that age range when they migrate. The bottom two panels follow Hispanic and non-Hispanic white natives, respectively, who are 18–34 in the Census year shown first.

Table 12.2
Poverty Rates Decline over Time for Immigrants But Remain Higher Than for Natives

	1970	1980	1990	2000	2010
Period of arrival for Hispanic immigrants:					
1965–70	24.7	17.5	17.5	15.8	13.7
1975–80		31.5	24.9	18.9	19.1
1985–90			35.4	23.3	19.7
1995–2000				31.4	27.1
2005–10					33.1
Period of arrival for Hispanic immigrants ages 18–34 in census year immediately following arrival:					
1965–70	22.4	16.7	16.4	15.2	16.2
1975–80		28.1	24.2	18.2	20.3
1985–90			32.6	22.9	19.4
1995–2000				30.3	29.0
2005–10					32.3
Hispanic natives ages 18–34 in year:					
1970	19.0	14.6	13.2	12.6	11.2
1980		16.8	15.1	12.1	12.2
1990			18.6	13.4	13.7
2000				17.5	14.8
2010					20.8
Non-Hispanic white natives ages 18–34 in year:					
1970	7.5	6.2	5.3	6.0	6.8
1980		8.5	6.4	5.6	7.3
1990			10.0	6.5	7.4
2000				10.7	8.7
2010					12.9

Source: Authors' calculations from data from the 1970–2000 Censuses from Ruggles et al. (2010) and the 2010 March Current Population Survey from King et al. (2010).
Note: Each row of the table shows how the poverty rate for a cohort has evolved over time. The columns show the period of arrival for immigrant cohorts or the year in which natives were ages 18–34.

TRENDS IN INCOME INEQUALITY

Incomes are less equal among Hispanics than among non-Hispanic whites but more equal than among non-Hispanic blacks. The last column of Table 12.1 presents the Gini index for various groups using data on 2009 family pretax money incomes from the 2010 March

Current Population Survey. The higher the Gini index (which must be between zero and one), the less equal the income distribution. The Gini index is higher among Hispanics than among non-Hispanic whites, indicating more inequality in family incomes. Among Hispanics, the top quintile of families takes home 51 percent of all Hispanic income, while the top quintile takes home 49 percent of total income among non-Hispanic whites. The opposite is true with respect to non-Hispanic blacks, where the top quintile gets 52 percent of total black income.

When comparing foreign- versus native-born Hispanics, incomes are more equal among Hispanic immigrants than among Hispanic natives and more equal among immigrants who have been in the United States longer than among recent immigrants. There are interesting differences by national origin as well.

Since about 1973, income inequality has risen considerably in the United States.[8] Real earnings have fallen at the bottom of the distribution while rising sharply at the top. Calculations of Gini indexes in the 1970 Census data analogous to those reported here for the 2010 data show an increase in inequality over that 40-year period for every race/ethnicity and nativity group we examine. As in the 2010 data, the pattern of Hispanics having more income inequality than non-Hispanic whites but less than non-Hispanic blacks holds in the 1970 data as well. However, incomes were more equal then among Hispanic natives than among Hispanic immigrants.

These stylized facts compare inequality across groups rather than looking at Hispanics' position in the overall income distribution. Consistent with their relatively high poverty rate, Hispanics are disproportionately at the bottom of the income distribution. In 2009, 15 percent of Hispanics were in the bottom decile of family incomes, and only 4 percent were in the top decile. Native-born Hispanics were even more overrepresented than foreign-born Hispanics at the very bottom of the income distribution, but they were also more likely to be at the top of the income distribution, although far less so than non-Hispanic whites.

There has been some improvement over time in Hispanics' position in the income distribution. During the period 1995 to 2005, the fraction of foreign-born Latinos in the bottom quintile of the hourly wage distribution fell. Nonetheless, 36 percent of foreign-born Latinos were in the bottom quintile (the bottom 20%) of wage earners in 2005, and only 6 percent were in the top quintile (Kochhar 2007).

KEY FACTORS IN HISPANIC POVERTY AND INEQUALITY

Explaining the Gap

Many factors contribute to the relatively high poverty and income inequality among Hispanics. The two are interrelated as well. The increase in income inequality since the 1970s has increased poverty among Hispanics relative to what it otherwise would have been (Iceland 2003). In addition, factors that increase poverty are likely to increase inequality, and vice versa.

We focus here on Hispanic poverty and the roles of immigrant status, education, ability to speak English, employment, and family composition in explaining the poverty gap vis-à-vis other groups. We use a Blinder-Oaxaca decomposition to estimate how much of the difference in the poverty rate between Hispanics and non-Hispanic whites is due to differences in those factors (Blinder 1973; Oaxaca 1973). To do so, we estimate a probit model of poverty status among household heads. The model includes variables measuring whether the household head is an immigrant, the head's education, English ability, and age (and age squared), the number of people (age 16 and older) working in the family, whether the head was employed all year, the number of people and number of children in the family, whether the head is a single female, and the family's metropolitan status and state of residence.[9] Using the estimated coefficients for non-Hispanic whites from that probit regression, we estimate how much of the difference in poverty rates can be attributed to differences in average characteristics between Hispanics and non-Hispanic whites. The portion that is not attributed to differences in average characteristics is attributed to differences in the estimated coefficients for Hispanics and non-Hispanic whites.[10] We perform the decomposition using data from the 2009 American Community Survey because it has data on self-reported English ability, which the Current Population Survey does not ask about. The data about economic variables therefore refer to the 2008 calendar year.

Differences in immigrant status partially explain why Hispanics are more likely to be poor than non-Hispanic whites. As the second row of Table 12.3 reports, 0.4 percentage points of the 12.1-percentage-point difference in the poverty rate between Hispanics and non-Hispanic whites is due to the greater fraction of Hispanics who are foreign-born. In other words, if the fraction of foreign-born was the same among Hispanics as among non-Hispanic whites, the poverty gap between the two groups would be 11.7 percentage points instead of

Table 12.3

English Ability, Education, and Employment Play Important Roles in Poverty among Hispanics

	All Hispanics	Hispanic Natives	Hispanic Immigrants
Difference between group poverty rate and poverty rate among non-Hispanic whites	12.1	8.1	15.0
Due to differences in:			
Immigrant status of head	0.4	0.0	0.7
Education of head	1.2	0.8	1.5
English ability of head	5.7	1.7	8.6
Age of head	1.4	1.8	1.1
Number of employed adults in family	0.0	0.1	0.3
Head employed all year	1.6	1.7	1.6
Number of children in family	0.8	0.1	1.4
Family size	−0.6	0.1	−1.0
Head is single female	0.0	0.3	−0.1
Metropolitan area	−0.3	−0.3	−0.4
State	−0.5	−0.4	−0.6
Difference not explained by differences in above characteristics	2.3	1.8	2.7

Source: Authors' calculations from data from the 2009 American Community Survey from Ruggles et al. (2010).
Note: Shown are results from a Blinder-Oaxaca decomposition of how much of the poverty gap between Hispanics and non-Hispanic whites can be attributed to average differences in the characteristics listed here. All rows are expressed in percentage points. The top row gives the total poverty gap and the bottom row gives the poverty gap after accounting for differences in sample means of the characteristics listed here.

12.1 points. This may seem small, but the model controls for other characteristics that tend to differ considerably between immigrants and natives, namely education and English ability.

Lower educational attainment among Hispanics contributes to the poverty gap. As the third row reports, differences in average education among household heads appear to boost the poverty rate by 1.2 percentage points among all Hispanics, 0.8 percentage points among Hispanic natives, and 1.5 percentage points among Hispanic immigrants relative to non-Hispanic whites. This method probably understates the role of education in poverty among Hispanic immigrants because it treats all education as the same regardless of where it was acquired. The return to education is typically lower for Hispanic immigrants because most of their education is acquired abroad (Duncan et al. 2006).

Limited ability to speak English is the most important factor in explaining why Hispanics are more likely to be poor than non-Hispanic whites. Differences in self-reported English ability among household heads explain 5.7 percentage points of the poverty gap for all Hispanics and 8.6 percentage points—over one-half the gap—for Hispanic immigrants. Interestingly, differences in English ability also matter, albeit less so, for native-born Hispanics.

The Hispanic population is relatively young, and this contributes to the poverty gap. As the decomposition shows, the average age of household heads among Hispanics, which is eight years lower than among non-Hispanic whites, is at least as important as education in explaining the poverty gap.

One common reason why families are poor is because of not enough work. The American Community Survey does not have the ideal variables to measure whether family members worked full-time year round, so we use two proxies: how many people currently in the family worked at all last year and whether the current head worked at least 50 weeks (year round) last year. The results in the table show that the number of employed adults in the family plays little role in the poverty gap. This is not a surprising result since Hispanic immigrant families are more likely to be multigenerational and have more workers than other families. Whether the head worked year round is more important. Differences between Hispanics and non-Hispanic whites in the proportion of heads employed all year boosted the relative poverty rate among Hispanics by about 1.6 percentage points.

The larger number of children in Hispanic families, particularly those headed by an immigrant, tends to boost poverty rates. The average Hispanic family has 0.6 more children than the average non-Hispanic white family. This tends to mechanically increase poverty since having more people in the family raises the income required to be above the poverty threshold and children are unlikely to contribute to family income. However, family size acts to reduce poverty among families headed by a Hispanic immigrant, even after controlling for the number of adult workers in the family.

Female-headed households account for over one-half of poor families in the United States. Families headed by a single female are disproportionately poor because they have only one potential earner, and that adult typically has relatively low educational attainment and does not work full-time. Female headship is less common among Hispanic immigrants than among Hispanic natives and therefore reduces the poverty rate among the former while raising it among the latter.

Place of residence appears to affect the poverty gap as well. Differences between Hispanics and non-Hispanics whites in urban status and state of residence actually lower the poverty gap. This may be surprising since many Latinos live in areas with poor housing, schools, and other amenities (Alba et al. 2010), but likely reflects Hispanics' increasing tendency to locate in regions of the country that experienced strong economic growth during the 2000s, such as the South, Southwest, and Mountain West. Another interesting factor we do not capture is whether families live in a predominantly Latino neighborhood, which might boost earnings by giving residents a bigger network or reduce earnings via more competition for jobs.

The Unexplained Poverty Gap

The decomposition results indicate that differences in characteristics, particularly in English ability and year-round employment, play important roles in explaining why Hispanics are more likely to be poor than non-Hispanic whites. Nonetheless, differences in average characteristics cannot fully explain the poverty gap. The bottom row of Table 12.3 shows how much of the gap is not explained by differences in means for the factors listed earlier in the table. Differences in those factors explain 81 percent of the poverty gap for all Hispanics, 78 percent for native-born Hispanics, and 82 percent for foreign-born Hispanics.

The unexplained portion of the gap is often attributed to discrimination because it is due to differences in the returns to characteristics. There are other reasons why returns to some characteristics might differ, most notably for education, as discussed previously. Other research, however, concludes that discrimination is an important factor in why Latinos earn less than non-Hispanic whites (Reimers 1983). That research indicates there are differences in the extent of discrimination across national origin groups, with discrimination appearing to be less important in explaining low wages for Mexicans and Cubans than for other groups of Hispanics (Reimers 1983; Trejo 1997). We do not look here at phenotype, or skin color, which may affect the extent of discrimination among Hispanics.

There are many other factors that are likely to contribute to poverty among Hispanics. One of these is lack of legal status. Nearly two-fifths of Hispanics are foreign-born, and almost one-fifth, or half of the foreign-born Hispanics, are likely to be undocumented immigrants. Unauthorized workers probably have lower earnings than comparable documented workers because they are willing to work for lower wages, in part because they have more difficulty finding an employer willing to hire them. They also change jobs more often, invest less in training, and tend not to take up fringe benefits.

In recent years, partly in response to government changes in the wake of September 11, 2001, employers have become more reluctant to hire unauthorized workers and more diligent in checking documentation, which is another factor that could be affecting the earnings of undocumented workers (Orrenius and Zavodny 2009). Family incomes also are lower because the undocumented are categorically ineligible for all government cash benefit programs. Any U.S.-citizen children in "mixed-status" families are eligible for benefits on the same basis as other U.S. citizens, but parents may be reluctant to file for benefits for fear of revealing their unauthorized status.

The period from late 2007 through mid-2009 marked a deep recession in the United States, which hurt all groups but particularly Hispanics. While the unemployment rate for Hispanics is always higher than for non-Hispanic whites, it is more volatile over the business cycle for Hispanics. In other words, unemployment rises more for Hispanics during recessions but falls more during expansions (DeFreitas 1986; Reimers 2000). Hispanics also become unemployed earlier in economic downturns and stay unemployed longer than non-Hispanics (Ewing et al. 2008). This greater volatility in unemployment is one reason why the business cycle has a bigger impact on incomes and poverty among Hispanics than among non-Hispanic whites (Cancian and Danziger 2009). Hispanics are more vulnerable to the business cycle because of their relatively low average level of education and concentration in cyclical sectors, such as construction (Orrenius and Zavodny 2010).

Relatively high unemployment takes a toll on Latinos in terms of accumulated work experience as well. A higher probability of not working at a given point in time turns into less accumulated work experience over time. Research shows that Mexican-American young adults earn less than non-Hispanics whites in part because they tend to have fewer years of actual work experience (Antecol and Bedard 2004). For the foreign-born, experience accumulated abroad also may matter relatively little to employers.

The low level of the minimum wage also likely plays a role in Hispanic poverty and inequality. Latino workers are disproportionately
likely to earn the minimum wage, particularly foreign-born Latinos.
While foreign-born Latinos made up only about 8 percent of hourly
workers during the period 1994–2007, for example, they accounted
for 18 percent of hourly workers paid exactly the minimum wage
(Orrenius and Zavodny 2011). Hispanics also are overrepresented
among workers who earn less or slightly more than the minimum
wage. The federal and state governments tend to raise the minimum
wage infrequently, and its real value erodes between increases as a
result of inflation. This may increase poverty at the bottom end of the
labor market, where many Hispanics are, and may increase income
inequality as well.

Other institutional features of the U.S. labor market, such as
low union coverage, may also affect poverty and inequality. About
11 percent of Latino workers are union members or represented by
a union, slightly below the overall unionization rate (Schmitt 2008).
Latino workers who are in a union earn almost 18 percent more than
comparable Latinos who are not represented by a union (Schmitt
2008).

In the United States, official poverty status is based on pretax cash
income. This measure does not include transfers via the tax system,
such as the child tax credit and the Earned Income Tax Credit (EITC),
or the value of in-kind benefits. It therefore misclassifies as poor some
families that receive large government transfers and in-kind benefits.
This misclassification is potentially large. For example, according to
the Census Bureau, including the EITC would lower the poverty rate
among Hispanics by about 4 percentage points.[11] In-kind benefits are
another important resource for Hispanics (Reimers 2006). Accounting
for these other sources of funds or resources would reduce poverty
and inequality among Hispanics.

The preceding analysis decomposes poverty status only during a
single year. Chronic poverty is of more policy concern than poverty
at a single point in time. Research indicates that Hispanics have
relatively high rates of chronic poverty as well as long spells of
poverty (Iceland 2003; Mauldin and Mimura 2001). However, there
is no difference between young adult Hispanics and non-Hispanic
whites in their exit rate out of poverty, controlling for observable
characteristics, which implies that the Hispanic poverty gap may
narrow in the future.

WHAT DOES THE FUTURE HOLD FOR HISPANICS?

Average statistics on poverty and inequality paint a bleak picture for Hispanics in the United States. The poverty rate among Hispanics overall has barely budged during the past 40 years, during which time the poverty rate among non-Hispanic blacks fell by over one-quarter. Inequality is rising among all groups, including Hispanics, and is higher among Hispanic natives than among Hispanic immigrants. The underlying causes for the poverty gap point out key challenges, such as low average levels of educational attainment and poor English ability, particularly among immigrants.

Hispanics have made little economic progress as a group because of the youthfulness of this population and the high rates of Hispanic immigration and its recency. But it is important to realize that the aggregate statistics mask considerable progress for many individuals. In addition, despite facing high poverty here, most immigrants are better off than they were in their home countries. Hispanic immigrants also tend to experience considerable income gains quickly after arrival in the United States, particularly when the macroeconomy is doing well, and their poverty rates fall significantly over time as a result. Hispanics, both immigrants and natives, have other important pluses as well, such as higher labor force participation rates than any other group considered here and lower unemployment rates than blacks. Hispanics also tend to live in thriving areas, which boosts their employment and earnings.

With native-born Hispanics growing quickly as a share of the Hispanic population, future progress likely depends on them. There are some bright spots. Poverty among Hispanic natives has fallen over time, albeit not as quickly as it has among blacks. When following an age cohort of Hispanic natives across decades, their poverty gap vis-à-vis similar cohorts of non-Hispanic whites shrinks by about 1.2 percentage points per decade. There has been considerable intergenerational progress in educational attainment and earnings among Latinos (Smith 2003, 2006). While 49 percent of Hispanic immigrants lack a high school degree, only 20 percent of second-generation Hispanics and 18 percent of third-generation and higher Hispanics lack a high school degree. Despite the improvement, this is still 10 percentage points above the share of non-Hispanic whites that lack a high school degree (8%).

Continued educational progress is crucial to narrowing the income and poverty gaps between Hispanics and non-Hispanic whites.

Current fiscal woes at the federal, state, and local levels appear likely to boost the cost of higher education and lower the quality of K–12 education for all groups, but the poor will be hardest hit by cuts in education budgets. This may bode ill for progress by native-born Hispanics and other minorities both in the short run and for years to come as these youths move into the labor force.

The widespread movement by Hispanics, particularly Hispanic immigrants, into new destinations across the United States that began in the 1990s is likely to affect income trends. This greater geographic dispersion seems likely to reduce poverty and inequality among Hispanics because the new destinations tend to be better along a variety of dimensions, including labor market opportunities, than traditional immigrant gateways (Alba et al. 2010; Capps et al. 2010). Whether the movement toward new destinations will continue and how growing Hispanic populations will change those communities are interesting questions that will affect poverty and inequality among Hispanics.

There are two troubling trends among native-born Hispanics that deserve attention: the rise in nonmarital births to Hispanic women and the growing elderly Hispanic population. Although nonmarital births are still relatively uncommon among Hispanic immigrants, they are common among Hispanic natives. Unmarried women account for over one-half of births among Hispanics (Hamilton et al. 2010). This is troubling given the high rate of poverty for female-headed households. It creates intergenerational concerns as well since children who grow up in poverty experience considerable disadvantages. More positively, however, the birthrate for Hispanic teens has been declining (Hamilton et al. 2010). Meanwhile, the elderly Hispanic population is growing. While the elderly tend to experience low poverty rates in the United States, elderly Hispanics are relatively unlikely to have a pension or receive Social Security benefits and therefore have high poverty rates (Reimers 2006). This population is likely to continue to grow, although the fraction that is poor may eventually decline as the Hispanic population becomes increasingly native-born and therefore more are eligible for Social Security and other government programs.

Future immigration patterns will affect Hispanics in the United States. Changes in U.S. immigration policy that reduce the number of low-skilled immigrants, who primarily enter under family preference categories or are undocumented, would improve the relative standing of the Hispanic population in the United States. The adverse wage effects of low-skilled immigration are the greatest among prior immigrants and low-skilled natives. Educational progress and economic development in sending countries also would benefit Hispanics in the United States by boosting the education levels of new immigrants. Such changes in underlying economic conditions typically occur only slowly, whereas policy can lead to an abrupt change in the characteristics of new immigrants.

Another policy change that would affect poverty and inequality among Hispanics is a legalization program in the United States. The U.S. experience with the Immigration Reform and Control Act in 1986 suggests that a large-scale legalization program would boost earnings and thereby reduce poverty among Hispanic immigrants.[12] There might be intergenerational effects as well, with U.S.-citizen children's life prospects improving as their parents benefit from legalization.

CONCLUSION

As the fastest-growing demographic group in the United States, what happens to Hispanic incomes and poverty matters for future U.S. economic prosperity. Hispanic immigrants have relatively high poverty rates, but they experience considerable progress soon after migration and have high labor force participation rates, high geographic mobility, high marriage rates, and low nonmarital birth rates. The future for Hispanics depends crucially on whether today's Hispanic youth can boost their educational attainment and English ability while retaining those positive attributes of Hispanic immigrants. Also important is the state of the macroeconomy. Hispanic economic outcomes are sensitive to the business cycle; poverty rates rose over 4 percentage points for Hispanic immigrants between 2000 and 2009 and jumped over 2 points among Hispanic natives. An improving macroeconomy in coming years will disproportionately help Hispanics. Lastly, government policies with regard to education and immigration also will play a key role in determining the future of Hispanic poverty and inequality.

NOTES

1. Jingsi Zu and Linda Bi provided excellent research assistance. The opinions expressed herein are those of the authors and do not necessarily reflect the views of the Federal Reserve Bank of Dallas or the Federal Reserve System.

2. For excellent broader discussions about Latinos, see, for example, Tienda and Mitchell (2006) and Suárez-Orozco and Páez (2009).

3. Authors' calculations based on March 2010 Current Population Survey data from King et al. (2010).

4. Most U.S. datasets (including the ones we use here) ask individuals whether they are Hispanic, not Latino. We therefore treat the two as equivalent here. We also use the terms "immigrant" and "foreign-born" interchangeably in this chapter. Immigrants are individuals born abroad who are not U.S. citizens at birth, although we categorize people born in outlying territories, including Puerto Rico, as immigrants here.

5. For a more detailed explanation of how poverty is determined in the United States, see http://www.census.gov/hhes/www/poverty/about/overview/measure.html.

6. People born in Puerto Rico are U.S. citizens by birth. We follow other researchers, such as Reimers (2006) and Sullivan and Ziegert (2008), and classify them (and other people born in U.S. territories) as immigrants here.

7. Raphael and Smolensky (2009) present a similar table for all immigrants relative to all natives (not just non-Hispanic whites). People are classified according to their own immigrant status, not the head's, in Table 12.2.

8. See Autor, Katz, and Kearney (2008) for a discussion of the extent and possible causes of the increase in income inequality in the United States.

9. Education is measured in four categories: no high school diploma or equivalent, high school diploma or equivalent, some college, and college graduate. English ability is measured using the five categories for self-reported English ability: only speak English, speak English very well, well, not well, and not at all.

10. For a more detailed discussion of the technique, see Sullivan and Ziegert (2008). Ideally we would have data on how many people in the family were employed full-time, year round (at least 35 hours per week for at least 50 weeks), but data on hours worked last year are not available in the 2009 American Community Survey.

11. See http://www.census.gov/hhes/www/cpstables/032010/rdcall/2_009.htm. Unauthorized immigrants are not eligible for the EITC.

12. Research indicates that Latin American immigrants who legalized their status under the 1986 Immigration Reform and Control Act (IRCA) experienced wage increases in the range of 6 to 13 percent (Kossoudji and Cobb-Clark 2002; Rivera-Batiz 1999).

BIBLIOGRAPHY

Alba, Richard, Nancy A. Denton, Donald J. Hernandez, Ilir Disha, Brian McKenzie, and Jeffrey Napierala (2010). "Nowhere Near the Same: The Neighborhoods of Latino Children." Pp. 3–48 in Nancy S. Landale, Susan McHale, and Alan Booth, eds., *Growing Up Hispanic: Health and Development of Children of Immigrants*. Washington, DC: The Urban Institute Press.

Antecol, Heather, and Kelly Bedard (2004). "The Racial Wage Gap: The Importance of Labor Force Attachment Differences across Black, Mexican, and White Men." *Journal of Human Resources* 39(2): 564–83.

Autor, David H., Lawrence F. Katz, and Melissa S. Kearney. (2008). "Trends in U.S. Wage Inequality: Revising the Revisionists." *Review of Economics and Statistics* 90(2): 300–23.

Blinder, Alan S. (1973). "Wage Discrimination: Reduced Form and Structural Variables." *Journal of Human Resources* 8(4): 436–55.

Cancian, Maria, and Sheldon Danziger (2009). "Changing Poverty and Changing Antipoverty Policies." Pp. 1–31 in Maria Cancian and Sheldon Danziger, eds., *Changing Poverty, Changing Lives*. New York: Russell Sage Foundation.

Capps, Randy, Heather Koball, and William Kandel (2010). "Economic Integration of Latino Immigrants in New and Traditional Rural Destinations in the United States." Pp. 49–72 in Nancy S. Landale, Susan McHale, and Alan Booth, eds., *Growing Up Hispanic: Health and Development of Children of Immigrants*. Washington, DC: The Urban Institute Press.

DeFreitas, Gregory (1986). "A Time-Series Analysis of Hispanic Unemployment." *Journal of Human Resources* 21(1): 24–43.

Duncan, Brian, V. Joseph Hotz, and Stephen J. Trejo (2006). "Hispanics in the U.S. Labor Market." Pp. 228–90 in Marta Tienda and Faith Mitchell, eds., *Hispanics and the Future of America*. Washington, DC: National Academies Press.

Duncan, Brian, and Stephen J. Trejo (2009). "Ancestry versus Ethnicity: The Complexity and Selectivity of Mexican Identification in the United States." Pp. 31–66 in Amelie F. Constant, Konstantinos Tatsiramos, and Klaus F. Zimmermann, eds., *Ethnicity and Labor Market Outcomes* (Research in Labor Economics, Volume 29). Bingley, United Kingdom: Emerald Group.

Duncan, Brian, and Stephen J. Trejo (2011). "Who Remains Mexican? Selective Ethnic Attrition and the Intergenerational Progress of Mexican Americans." Pp. 285–320 in David Leal and Stephen Trejo, eds., *Latinos and the Economy: Integration and Impact in Schools, Labor Markets, and Beyond*. New York: Springer.

Ewing, Bradley T., Angel L. Reyes III, Mark A. Thompson, and James C. Wetherbe (2008). "Examination and Comparison of Hispanic and White Unemployment Rates." *Journal of Business Valuation and Economic Loss Analysis* 3(1): 1–8.

Hamilton, Brady E., Joyce A. Martin, and Stephanie J. Ventura (2010). "Births: Preliminary Data for 2009." *National Vital Statistics Reports* 59(3): 1–29.

Iceland, John (2003). "Why Poverty Remains High: The Role of Income Growth, Economic Inequality, and Changes in Family Structure, 1949–1999." *Demography* 40(3): 499–519.

King, Miriam, Steven Ruggles, J. Trent Alexander, Sarah Flood, Katie Genadek, Matthew B. Schroeder, Brandon Trampe, and Rebecca Vick. Integrated Public Use Microdata Series, Current Population Survey: Version 3.0 [Machine-readable database]. Minneapolis: University of Minnesota, 2010.

Kochhar, Rakesh (2007). "1995–2005: Foreign-Born Latinos Make Progress on Wages." Report. Washington, DC: Pew Hispanic Center.

Kossoudji, Sherrie A., and Deborah A. Cobb-Clark (2002). "Coming out of the Shadows: Learning about Legal Status and Wages from the Legalized Population." *Journal of Labor Economics* 20(3): 598–628.

Mauldin, Teresa, and Yoko Mimura (2001). "Exits from Poverty among Rural and Urban Black, Hispanic, and White Young Adults." *Review of Black Political Economy* 29(1): 9–23.

Mogull, Robert G. (2005). "Hispanic-American Poverty." *Journal of Applied Business Research* 21(3): 91–101.

Oaxaca, Ronald. (1973). "Male-Female Wage Differentials in Urban Labor Markets." *International Economic Review* 14(3): 693–709.

Orrenius, Pia M., and Madeline Zavodny (2009). "The Effects of Tougher Enforcement on the Job Prospects of Recent Latin American Immigrants." *Journal of Policy Analysis and Management* 28(2): 239–57.

Orrenius, Pia M., and Madeline Zavodny (2010). "Mexican Immigrant Employment Outcomes over the Business Cycle." *American Economic Review Papers and Proceedings* 100(2): 1–8.

Orrenius, Pia M., and Madeline Zavodny (2011). "The Minimum Wage and Latino Workers." Pp. 169–91 in David Leal and Stephen Trejo, eds., *Latinos and the Economy: Integration and Impact in Schools, Labor Markets, and Beyond*. New York: Springer.

Passel, Jeffrey S., and D'Vera Cohn (2008). U.S. Population Projections: 2005–2050. Report. Washington, DC: Pew Hispanic Center.

Passel, Jeffrey S., and D'Vera Cohn (2011). Unauthorized Immigrant Population: National and State Trends, 2010. Report. Washington, DC: Pew Hispanic Center.

Raphael, Steven, and Eugene Smolensky (2009). "Immigration and Poverty in the United States." Pp. 122–50 in Maria Cancian and Sheldon Danziger, eds., *Changing Poverty, Changing Lives*. New York: Russell Sage Foundation.

Reimers, Cordelia W. (1983). "Labor Market Discrimination against Hispanic and Black Men." *Review of Economics and Statistics* 65(4): 570–579.

Reimers, Cordelia W. (2000). "The Effect of Tighter Labor Markets on Unemployment of Hispanics and African Americans: The 1990s Experience." Pp. 3–49 in Robert Cherry and William M. Rodgers III, eds., *Prosperity for All?: The Economic Boom and African Americans*. Washington, DC: Russell Sage Foundation.

Reimers, Cordelia W. (2006). "Economic Well-Being." Pp. 291–361 in Marta Tienda and Faith Mitchell, eds., *Hispanics and the Future of America*. Washington, DC: National Academies Press.

Rivera-Batiz, Francisco L. (1999). "Undocumented Workers in the Labor Market: An Analysis of the Earnings of Legal and Illegal Mexican Immigrants in the United States." *Journal of Population Economics* 12(1): 91–116.

Ruggles, Steven, J. Trent Alexander, Katie Genadek, Ronald Goeken, Matthew B. Schroeder, and Matthew Sobek. Integrated Public Use Microdata Series: Version 5.0 [Machine-readable database]. Minneapolis: University of Minnesota, 2010.

Schmitt, John (2008). "Unions and Upward Mobility for Latino Workers." Mimeo. Washington, DC: Center for Economic and Policy Research.

Smith, James P. (2003). "Assimilation across the Latino Generations." *American Economic Review Papers & Proceedings* 93(2): 315–19.

Smith, James P. (2006). "Immigrants and the Labor Market." *Journal of Labor Economics* 24(2): 203–33.

Suárez-Orozco, Marcelo M., and Mariela M. Páez, eds. (2009). *Latinos: Remaking America*. Berkeley: University of California Press.

Sullivan, Dennis H., and Andrea L. Ziegert (2008). "Hispanic Immigrant Poverty: Does Ethnic Origin Matter?" *Population Research and Policy Review* 27(6): 667–687.

Tienda, Marta, and Faith Mitchell, eds. (2006). *Hispanics and the Future of America.* Washington, DC: National Academies Press.

Trejo, Stephen J. (1997). "Why Do Mexican Americans Earn Low Wages?" *Journal of Political Economy* 105(6): 1235–68.

van Hook, Jennifer, Susan L. Brown, and Maxwell Ndigume Kwenda (2004). "A Decomposition of Trends in Poverty among Children of Immigrants." *Demography* 41(4): 649–70.

Chapter 13

The Economic Characteristics of Asian Americans in the 21st Century

Arthur Sakamoto and ChangHwan Kim

In contrast to most other nations around the world, the United States collects extensive economic statistics on racial and ethnic differentials. This heightened concern derives from a historical legacy of intense discrimination against racial and ethnic minorities including most notably the enslavement of African Americans and the subjugation of Native Americans. In addition, the growing demographic diversity of the contemporary American population due to high levels of immigration has further increased interest in economic differentials by race and ethnicity.

For a number of reasons including considerable anti-Asian prejudice, Asians were not very numerous in the United States prior to 1965. As late as 1960, Asian Americans constituted only about one-half of 1 percent of the total population (i.e., 1 out of 200 Americans). With the passage of the 1965 immigration legislation, however, the Asian population in the United States has increased dramatically. By the time of the 2010 U.S. Census, Asian Americans represented about 5 percent of the total population (i.e., 10 out of 200 Americans). With this 10-fold increase in their proportionate representation during the last half century, Asian Americans have gone from being a tiny, obscure group on the fringes of American society to being highly visible, widely recognized, and broadly accepted participants in the social fabric of the contemporary United States. Given this general incorporation into mainstream American life, an evaluation of the current economic circumstances of Asian Americans is timely in order to provide a broader portrayal of the significance of race and ethnicity in the 21st century.

Nonetheless, it should be first noted that determining the racial and ethnic makeup of the U.S. population is a somewhat complicated task. These terms cannot be precisely defined, and people are allowed to self-report in variable ways that increase the complexity of the responses for most sorts of classification schemes. We simply use the categories and definitions that are utilized by the U.S. Census Bureau, which created the data that we investigate.[1]

When considering statistics on foreign-born Asian Americans, however, we do make finer distinctions than what the U.S. Census Bureau reports because previous research has shown that labor market success varies depending upon the timing of immigration. In particular, following Kim and Sakamoto (2010), we break down the foreign-born into three separate groups. The first is the 1.0 generation, which refers to persons who immigrated as adults and did not receive any education in United States; their schooling was entirely obtained overseas. Next is the 1.25 generation, which refers to persons who received their primary and secondary schooling overseas but completed their highest level of schooling—either a bachelor's (BA) or a graduate degree—in the United States. The 1.5 generation then refers to persons who immigrated to the United States at a young age and attended high school (and possibly primary schooling as well) in the United States. The findings of Kim and Sakamoto (2010) suggest that the most favorable labor market outcomes are evident for the 1.5 generation while the worst are for the 1.0 generation with the 1.25 generation being intermediate.

We investigate data from the American Community Survey (ACS), which is conducted annually in recent years by the U.S. Census Bureau. The ACS is a household survey that is large and nationally representative of the American population. By using the ACS data combined for the years 2007, 2008, and 2009, an adequate sample size for small minority groups is obtained. Our statistical results thus provide a descriptive snapshot of the nation for the period 2007 to 2009.

EDUCATIONAL ATTAINMENT

Asian Americans as a minority group are distinctive for their generally high levels of educational attainment. As an overall racial category, the average level of educational attainment among Asian
Americans exceeds that of whites (Sakamoto, Goyette, and Kim
2009). This pattern contrasts significantly with African Americans,
Hispanics, Native Americans, and Pacific Islanders whose average levels of educational attainment are lower than among whites.

As shown in Table 13.1, 48.8 percent of the total Asian American
population (or the "Asian AOIC" population, which refers to "Asian
Alone or in Combination," meaning that biracial Asians are also
included) has a BA degree in comparison to 30.8 percent of the white
population.

Nonetheless, some ethnic variability is evident among Asian
Americans. First of all, several groups have lower proportions of having
a BA degree than whites including Vietnamese (26.2%), Cambodians
(13.3%), Hmong (12.0%), and Laotians (11.9%). These are the groups that
are most often noted as being "disadvantaged" Asians. Although
researchers sometimes refer to "Southeast Asian Americans" in general
as having lower educational attainments than whites, this designation
is not quite accurate. Thai, Indonesians, and Malaysians also have Southeast Asian origins, but Table 13.1 shows that these latter groups have
higher proportions of having a BA degree than do whites.

Educational statistics about ethnic groups are informative in general,
but they must be interpreted with caution when making claims about
educational opportunity in the United States. Many Asian Americans
are 1.0-generation immigrants who completed their schooling in Asia
many years ago. Their educational attainments are not representative of
Asian Americans who were reared in the United States and educated
in American schools. For example, among 1.5- and second-generation
Vietnamese, educational attainments exceed those of whites (Sakamoto
and Woo 2007). Vietnamese Americans are a case of notable upward
social mobility, because most of the first-generation immigrants were
not highly educated yet their second-generation offspring surpass whites
in terms of average educational attainment completed in the United
States (Sakamoto and Woo 2007).

Studies of the educational attainments of 1.5- and second-generation
Cambodians, Hmong, and Laotians are unfortunately rare and limited
by smaller sample sizes. Based on the currently available evidence, the
most likely pattern seems to be that these groups continue to lag

Table 13.1

Descriptive Statistics for Asian Americans in the United States, 2007–2009[a]

	Population Size (n)	(%)	Foreign Born (%)	Speak English Very Well [age 16+][b] (%)	Age (Years)	Living in Pacific Region (%)	BA Degree or Higher [age 25+] (%)	Poverty Status (%)	Annual Family Income ($)	Annual Personal Income[c] ($)	Manager, Profession & Related[d] Occupation (%)
Asian American—Single Race											
Chinese	3,070,268	(23.1)	71.0	49.4	37.6	43.3	52.0	14.3	87,802	55,976	52.2
Japanese	740,183	(5.6)	44.4	74.5	46.2	64.9	46.6	10.5	81,677	60,075	52.1
Filipino	2,389,574	(18.0)	70.8	75.8	38.2	59.7	48.0	6.7	85,626	46,044	41.4
Asian Indian	2,550,225	(19.2)	73.5	75.3	32.4	20.9	69.6	9.4	108,313	68,036	63.3
Korean	1,349,613	(10.1)	76.1	48.9	36.2	39.7	51.7	16.5	73,508	52,424	44.9
Vietnamese	1,452,456	(10.9)	69.7	41.3	34.8	43.2	26.2	14.8	67,534	39,584	29.9
Cambodian	213,248	(1.6)	61.7	47.5	31.5	46.5	13.3	20.1	53,994	30,621	18.9
Hmong	197,166	(1.5)	46.0	53.3	24.1	40.8	12.0	28.2	49,839	26,962	19.9
Laotian	181,298	(1.4)	62.2	50.5	32.1	42.1	11.9	14.4	56,666	30,955	17.1
Thai	152,022	(1.1)	78.7	53.9	37.2	36.1	43.2	15.4	62,699	37,412	33.8
Bangladeshi	80,031	(0.6)	74.0	49.4	29.2	5.8	48.7	24.5	55,042	35,352	33.5
Indonesian	55,840	(0.4)	78.5	62.9	35.8	48.3	47.7	12.9	71,412	45,109	41.6
Malaysian	14,104	(0.1)	85.0	75.0	34.2	24.5	60.8	15.2	83,463	58,940	55.1
Pakistan	265,849	(2.0)	69.9	67.5	30.0	13.6	54.2	16.8	87,306	57,775	43.6
Sri Lankan	31,901	(0.2)	83.0	75.1	35.6	32.4	55.5	14.3	87,678	60,526	59.3
Other Asian	227,264	(1.7)	65.8	57.7	31.7	29.5	44.5	20.2	74,115	44,006	38.3
Multiethnic Asian	339,894	(2.6)	47.4	68.8	28.6	50.4	43.7	11.9	82,865	48,493	40.7
(Subtotal)	13,310,935	(100.0)	69.2	60.8	35.9	41.8	49.9	12.5	85,654	52,858	47.0
Asian American—Bi/Multiracial											
White Asian (non-Hispanic biracial)	1,108,858	(58.5)	14.5	95.3	20.0	40.0	42.6	10.0	77,385	51,362	43.2

(continued)

Table 13.1 (Continued)

	Population Size (n)	(%)	Foreign Born (%)	Speak English Very Well [age 16+][b] (%)	Age (Years)	Living in Pacific Region (%)	BA Degree or Higher [age 25+] (%)	Poverty Status (%)	Annual Family Income ($)	Annual Personal Income[c] ($)	Manager, Profession & Related[d] Occupation (%)
Black Asian (non-Hispanic biracial)	126,726	(6.7)	24.0	95.1	21.8	30.6	31.3	16.9	57,816	41,325	35.7
Other biracial and multiracial Asian	661,501	(34.9)	16.2	89.1	25.0	60.2	26.5	14.4	66,900	41,506	31.5
(Subtotal)	1,897,085	(100.0)	15.7	92.9	21.9	46.4	35.1	12.0	71,855	46,683	38.1
Asian American total (Asian AOIC)	15,208,020		62.5	63.6	34.1	42.4	48.8	12.4	84,501	52,365	46.3
Non-Hispanic Whites	198,961,810		4.6	98.2	39.9	12.1	30.8	11.6	71,900	49,865	38.2

[a]Statistics refer to means for continuous variables and percentages for dichotomous variables, and are based on the data obtained by pooling together the 2007, 2008, and 2009 American Community Surveys.

[b]Speak English includes both "Speak English Only" and "Speak English Very Well."

[c]Age 25–64 with positive total annual income only.

[d]Age 20–64 in management, professional, and related occupations including ACS occupation codes 1 to 364.

behind whites in terms of educational attainment among those who were reared in the United States (Sakamoto and Woo 2007). Further research on Cambodians, Hmong, and Laotians is clearly needed.

Many other Asian groups, however, have high proportions of college-educated persons including Asian Indians (69.6%), Malaysians (60.8%), Sri Lankans (55.5%), Pakistanis (54.2%), Chinese (52.0%), Koreans (51.7%), Bangladeshis (48.7%), Filipinos (48.0%), Indonesians (47.7%), Japanese (46.6), Other Asians (44.5%), Multiethnic Asians (43.7%), and Thai (43.2%). For single-race Asian Americans overall, the proportion with a BA degree is 49.9 percent, although it is considerably lower at 35.1 percent (only somewhat above whites) for biracial Asian Americans.

Regarding the educational attainment of the 1.5 and second generations for these groups, strong conclusions about smaller subpopulations are difficult to reach due to the limited sample sizes that are available for researchers to study at this time. For the larger groups, however, higher levels of educational attainment is evident for 1.5- and second-generation Asian Indians, Chinese, Filipinos, Japanese, Koreans, Vietnamese, Other Asians, and Multiethnic Asians (Sakamoto and Xie 2006; Sakamoto and Woo 2007; Sakamoto, Takei, and Woo 2011; Xie and Goyette 2004). As these groups constitute the vast majority of the Asian American population, Asians as an overall category generally surpass the educational attainments of whites (Sakamoto, Goyette, and Kim 2009) as was noted earlier.

Further evidence regarding the high educational attainment of Asian Americans as an overall category is evident in Table 13.2. This table uses data from the 2003 National Survey of College Graduates and is thus limited to the population that has at least a BA degree. Table 13.2 shows that, among college graduates, 14.4 percent of Asian American men have a professional degree (such as a medical degree or a law degree) compared to 8.7 percent of white men. For Asian American women, 11.5 percent have a professional degree compared to 4.5 percent of white women. The high educational attainment of Asian Americans is not limited to the level of education. Asian Americans are more likely to major in science, technology, engineering, and mathematics (STEM) fields of study, and these degrees are typically more financially lucrative in the labor market, at least on average. Table 13.2 further shows that Asian Americans are more likely to have graduated from a university that is classified as being at the "Research I" level, which is generally considered to be more prestigious and higher quality. Several major factors

Table 13.2

Descriptive Statistics for Highly Educated Asian Americans, Aged 25 to 64, 2003[a]

	Whites	AA-NB	AA-1.5	AA-1.25	AA-1.0
I. Male Workers					
Annual Earnings (dollars)[b]	94,831	86,264	96,558	97,400	81,728
Level of Highest Education Completed (%)					
BA	63.9	59.8	62.7	21.3	66.1
MA	23.6	22.2	23.7	54.0	18.3
PhD	3.9	3.6	4.0	21.8	5.8
Professional Degree	8.7	14.4	9.7	2.9	9.9
(Total)	(100.0)	(100.0)	(100.0)	(100.0)	(100.0)
Highest Degree from Research I University (%)	30.1	51.0	39.1	41.8	—
Major for Highest Degree (%)					
Computer, Math, Engineering, Tech	15.8	21.7	33.7	53.6	36.7
Natural Science	7.3	9.8	7.8	11.0	12.3
Health/Medical	6.4	13.7	11.0	5.7	13.5
Social Science	9.7	9.1	8.9	2.2	6.7
Management and Business	28.7	25.3	24.9	19.2	19.2
Education, Art, Humanities, and Social Service	18.3	10.6	7.0	4.2	7.0
Other majors	13.8	9.8	6.8	4.1	4.6
(Total)	(100.0)	(100.0)	(100.0)	(100.0)	(100.0)
II. Female Workers					
Annual Earnings (dollars)[b]	56,350	64,415	68,960	75,093	54,226
Level of Highest Education Completed (%)					
BA	63.7	60.5	63.9	27.9	77.9
MA	29.5	25.4	21.5	55.8	13.7
PhD	2.3	2.6	2.2	11.3	2.0
Professional Degree	4.5	11.5	12.4	5.1	6.5
(Total)	(100.0)	(100.0)	(100.0)	(100.0)	(100.0)
Highest Degree from Research I University (%)	25.1	50.7	39.6	36.3	—
Major for Highest Degree (%)					
Computer, Math, Engineering, Tech	3.8	7.3	12.8	30.4	10.9
Natural Science	4.6	6.2	9.0	10.4	10.7
Health/Medical	13.4	16.9	20.9	13.7	25.8
Social Science	10.7	11.5	15.1	4.6	9.2
Management and Business	16.1	20.6	25.1	25.0	18.3
Education, Art, Humanities, and Social Service	38.6	24.3	10.7	10.6	18.3
Other majors	12.8	13.1	6.4	5.4	6.8
(Total)	(100.0)	(100.0)	(100.0)	(100.0)	(100.0)

[a]Statistics are based on data obtained from the 2003 National Survey of College Graduates. Workers aged 25 to 64 with positive earnings only. AA-NB refers to those who are born and educated entirely in the United States. AA-1.5 refers to those who immigrated and had both high school and tertiary education in the United States. AA-1.25 refers to those who immigrated and earned their highest degree in the United States but completed high school overseas. AA-1.0 refers to those who immigrated as adults and received their entire education in foreign countries.

[b]Dollar figures are inflation adjusted to 2008 dollars.

account for the higher educational attainments of Asian Americans including simply the general tendency for highly educated parents to be more likely to have (in comparison to less educated parents) children who are successful in school (Sakamoto, Goyette, and Kim 2009). That is, across all racial groups, the educational attainments between parents and offspring are positively correlated. Because Asian immigrants to the United States tend to be more likely to be college educated, their children are in general more likely to achieve a BA degree. Given this socioeconomic tendency, the educational advantages of the smaller groups (Bangladeshis, Indonesians, Malaysians, Pakistanis, Sri Lankans, and Thai) are likely to carry over to their 1.5 and second generations to some extent. In the case of Cambodians, Hmong, and Laotians, these 1.0-generation immigrants had, on average, only a junior high school education (or even less), so the fact that their 1.5 and second generations lag behind whites in terms of schooling is not surprising (Sakamoto and Woo 2007).

The higher educational attainments of Asian American parents interact with another important factor affecting the schooling of their offspring, namely, immigration status. That is, another basic socioeconomic tendency across all racial groups is that the children of immigrants tend to have higher educational attainments (Sakamoto, Goyette, and Kim 2009). This is especially true to the extent that immigrants are particularly "selective" in the sense that fewer members of their original home populations are able to come to the United States (Feliciano 2005). Although whites are much less likely than Asian Americans to have immigrant parents, those whites who are second generation have rates of college completion that are higher than third-and-higher-generation whites and are somewhat closer to those of Asian Americans (Takei and Sakamoto 2009).

The "selective" nature of immigrants seems to be associated with higher levels of ambition, motivation, or discipline at least among those who voluntarily choose to come to the United States for the purpose of improving their standard of living. These "selective" characteristics tend to influence their second-generation offspring, who are frequently reminded of the sacrifices that their parents made in order to come to the United States to take advantage of enhanced opportunities. Immigrant parents may sometimes find that their own labor market prospects are rather constrained (due to inferior English-language skills or the lack of U.S. educational credentials), and may psychologically compensate for this limitation by motivating their children into becoming high academic achievers in a way that maximizes their chances for career success (Goyette and Xie 1999).

While the Asian 1.0-generation immigrants tend to have high levels of schooling, and while the immigrant effect on their offspring's educational attainment is significant, controlling for these two factors does not fully explain the advantage of Asian Americans over whites (Goyette and Xie 1999; Sakamoto, Goyette, and Kim 2009). An additional factor is likely cultural. It relates to the more collectivist orientation of Asian families, which was the normative experience into which 1.0-generation Asian immigrants were socialized. Thus the educational attainments of white second-generation children with highly educated parents from Western countries still seem to be slightly lower than the educational attainments of Asian American second-generation children with highly educated parents (Sakamoto, Goyette, and Kim 2009).

EARNINGS, PERSONAL INCOMES, AND OCCUPATIONAL ATTAINMENTS

Table 13.1 shows the mean personal annual income for persons aged 25 to 64 who have some income. In most cases, most of this income derives from labor market earnings obtained through employment (or possibly self-employment). Groups with a greater proportion of BA graduates tend to have a higher mean personal income (e.g., Asian Indians, Pakistanis, Sri Lankans, and Chinese) while it is lower among groups with a smaller proportion of BA graduates (e.g., Vietnamese, Cambodian, Hmong, and Laotians). For the Asian AOIC population overall, mean personal income ($52,365) exceeds that for whites ($49,865).

Mean earnings from labor market participation by generation are shown in Table 13.2 for persons who are highly educated (i.e., have at least a BA degree). For white men, mean earnings is $94,831 while it is $86,264 for native-born Asian American men, $96,558 for 1.5-generation Asian American men, $97,400 for 1.25-generation Asian American men, and $81,728 for 1.0-generation Asian American men. For white women, Table 13.2 shows that mean earnings is $56,350 while it is $64,415 for native-born Asian American women, $68,960 for 1.5-generation Asian American women, $75,093 for 1.25-generation Asian American women, and $54,226 for 1.0-generation Asian American women.

In general, women have lower earnings than men, and 1.0-generation immigrants have lower earnings than whites and Asians who obtained their highest level of schooling in the United States. Asian Americans of the 1.25 generation tend to have high earnings because of their relatively large proportion of persons who have completed a PhD degree (i.e., which was often their main reason for coming to the United States). Native-born Asian American women have higher earnings than white women partly because of the much larger proportion of professional degrees among the former group.

Although educational level is certainly an important determinant of earnings in today's highly competitive labor market, many other factors are also relevant. Asian Americans' concentration in STEM fields of study, and completion of their degrees from more prestigious academic institutions have additional positive effects on their earnings.

Years of accumulated work experience is another factor associated with higher earnings as it leads to more developed work skills and the competitiveness of one's resumé. In practice, accumulated work experience is correlated with age, especially for men and for women who do not reduce their labor force participation due to family responsibilities (notably child rearing). Having excellent English-language skills is certainly an asset in today's labor market, but recent immigrants from Asian countries often lack complete fluency in either speaking or writing. On the other hand, Asians Americans are more likely to reside in the Pacific region of the United States where wages tend to be slightly higher in part due to the higher cost of living (especially housing) in that region.

Detailed studies of the earnings of Asian Americans have tried to take into account all of these factors simultaneously (using multivariate statistical methods) in order to assess whether Asian Americans receive, on average, the same earnings as do whites with similar measured characteristics. The broader objective of these studies is to provide information about the probability that Asian Americans face some sort of systematic racial discrimination in the way that they are rewarded in the labor market. The general idea of the methodology is to control for productivity-related characteristics of workers and then assess whether, net of these measured factors, the earnings of Asian Americans are similar to those for whites. Such analyses can never be 100 percent certain in their conclusions due to various limitations that are common in the social sciences (including the lack of a complete set of relevant control variables such as IQ or workers' preferences regarding types of employment and regional location). Nonetheless, to the extent that informative data are used and appropriate statistical methods are applied, these studies provide useful evidence about the likelihood of systematic racial bias against minorities.

Results for Native-Born Asian Americans

For example, some studies of native-born Asian Americans have investigated U.S. Census data from the earlier part of the 20th century before the passage of civil rights legislation during the 1960s prohibiting racial and ethnic discrimination in the labor market. These studies using data from the 1940s and 1950s find substantial wage, earnings, and occupational disadvantages that are pervasive for native-born Asian American men in the pre–civil rights era (Sakamoto, Wu, and Tzeng 2000; Sakamoto, Goyette, and Kim 2009). Despite often having college degrees in an era when such credentials were relatively rare, many native-born Asian American men would be unlikely to be hired by white-owned companies that paid high wages. Significant proportions of native-born Asian American with college degrees thus ended up working as gardeners, grocers, and other workers in related lower-status occupations in Asian American economic enclaves (Sakamoto, Goyette, and Kim 2009). Systematic racial discrimination against Asian Americans seems to be the most likely conclusion to be reached from these studies because they are based on native-born men who were not lacking in either English-language skills or American educational credentials.

Research using more recent data for the post–civil rights era finds notable declines in the negative effects of being Asian American for native-born men. The passage of the civil rights legislation during the 1960s has certainly helped to promote a more equitable labor market that does not openly discriminate against racial minorities at least in the case of Asian Americans. Current studies of the wages and earnings of native-born Asian American men find that their racial disadvantage in the contemporary labor market is probably small (and perhaps negligible), especially as compared to other factors that affect earnings, and is almost certainly smaller than in the pre–civil rights era.

College-educated Asian Americans are more highly concentrated in STEM fields of study (as we have seen), and because those majors tend to be more lucrative in the labor market, Asian Americans who do indeed possess those degrees should have higher earnings as a result (to the extent that Asian Americans choose to enter into those types of jobs in the labor market). For the most part the empirical evidence indicates that, at least for native-born Asian American men, the payoff for investing in these fields of study is similar to that of whites. Although the mean earnings of native-born Asian American as shown in Table 13.2 are lower than whites, part of this differential reflects the fact that native-born Asian American men tend to be younger than white men.

One factor that may continue to disproportionately affect the earnings of native-born Asian American men is their high concentration in the Pacific region of the United States. Other studies have shown that almost two out of three native-born Asian American men reside in that region, which is characterized by a high cost of living (Kim and Sakamoto 2010). To the extent that native-born Asian Americans freely choose to live in the Pacific region as a preference despite having job opportunities in other regions, then this choice is unproblematic and does not reflect racial discrimination (Sakamoto, Goyette, and Kim 2009). However, if native-born Asian Americans tend to face discrimination in other regions and therefore are more likely to live in the Pacific region because it is more accepting of Asian Americans, then this situation would indicate a continuing source of labor market inequity. While regional earnings differentials are not dramatic, and while we suspect that native-born Asian Americans tend to reside in the Pacific region mainly as a matter of voluntary preference for its amenities, further research on this topic is needed.

Studies of the earnings of native-born Asian American women are unfortunately scarce. Those that are available do not find that native-born Asian American women are systematically earning less than comparable white women. Women in general earn less than men, but a racial disadvantage does not appear to be significant for native-born Asian American women. Even after controlling for having more STEM degrees, native-born Asian American women seem to sometimes be earning more than comparable white women (Greenman 2011).

One additional topic that is sometimes raised is whether Asian Americans are underrepresented in higher management positions due to a discriminatory preference for white managers in the upper reaches of the corporate hierarchy. Even after controlling for having earned a business degree, Takei and Sakamoto (2008) find that native-born Asian American male managers supervise about 14 percent fewer employees than do comparable white managers. This differential may well derive from racial discrimination, and this issue merits further research. Nonetheless, we would also mention an alternative possible explanation, which is that Asian Americans may simply be more "risk adverse" about embarking on careers where one's productivity may be more subjectively assessed and thus more influenced by luck, personalities, and social connections. The latter may perhaps play a somewhat more significant role in climbing the corporate ladder than in scientific careers where knowledge is more objectively defined (Kim and Tamborini 2006). In the case of native-born Asian American women, Takei and Sakamoto (2008) do not find that they differ from white women in terms of managerial authority.

Results for Foreign-Born Asian Americans

Foreign-born Asian Americans are often quite heterogeneous in terms of the labor market experiences, skills, abilities, and credentials. Generally speaking, the 1.5 generation seems to be fairly successful in terms of labor market outcomes. Being raised and schooled primarily in the United States, the 1.5 generation is fully native in English-language skills, is completely familiar with American culture, and is not handicapped by having foreign educational credentials. They also have the added push of having Asian immigrant parents who frequently have extremely high expectations for the achievements of their children. We are not aware of any systematic study that finds that 1.5-generation Asian Americans earn less than comparable whites. In many cases to the contrary, 1.5-generation Asian Americans have a slight earnings advantage over whites for both men and women.

At the other end of the spectrum is the 1.0 generation. These are Asian Americans who were born overseas, completed all of their schooling outside of the United States, and came to the United States as adults. They often have college degrees obtained in Asia, but foreign educational credentials rarely carry over to the U.S. labor market (Sakamoto, Goyette, and Kim 2009). In addition, many Asians coming to the United States as adults may have substantial English-language deficiencies in the first few years in the United States. Research shows that college-educated, 1.0-generation Asian American men typically earn about 20 percent less than white men with similar ages and educational levels, but this differential is likely to be intrinsically associated with being an immigrant (for the reasons stated previously) rather than being pure racial discrimination (since native-born Asian American men lack such a large disadvantage).

The 1.25 generation is intermediate in a couple of respects. Because their highest level of schooling is by definition obtained in the United States, their educational attainment is not discounted in the United States (i.e., their degree is from an American university). Accordingly, among college-educated Asian American men, the earnings disadvantage of the 1.25 generation is not as severe as for the 1.0 generation.

However, because the 1.25 generation did not come to the United States at an early age, they still typically face some English-language difficulties that may limit their career development especially in its early stages. Thus the earnings of 1.25-generation men are still penalized to some extent (perhaps about half of the disadvantage faced by the 1.0 generation) in comparison to white men with the same levels of schooling, fields of study, and demographic characteristics.

In regard to occupational attainment, the 1.0 generation typically has the most disadvantaged outcomes relative to their educational level. Because their foreign university credentials usually are not considered in the U.S. labor market, the 1.0 generation may often end up in jobs that do not require a college degree such as self-employment in small businesses or lower-level service occupations. The 1.0 generation is more likely than other Asian Americans to be employed in ethnic-related jobs (e.g., in a Chinese travel agency) where their native Asian-language skills may be useful for their work. With greater experience in the U.S. labor market and improved English-language skills, the 1.0 generation may often take up other service work outside of ethnic enclave employment.

Beyond the 1.0 generation, the other groups of Asian Americans are usually at least as likely as whites to be employed in higher-level occupations. As shown in Table 13.1, 46.3 percent of Asian AOIC population is employed in managerial, professional, and related occupations compared to just 38.2 percent for whites. As noted earlier, native-born Asian Americans have a much higher propensity to obtain professional degrees, and Xie and Goyette (2004, 18) report that almost one out of seven physicians and dentists in the United States is Asian American. The particular ethnic groups that notably lag behind whites are those with lower average levels of educational attainment including Vietnamese (29.9%), Cambodians (18.9%), Hmong (19.9%), and Laotians (17.1%).

POVERTY STATUS AND FAMILY INCOMES

While labor market earnings are the primary source of income for most persons as individuals, in practice most people also reside in households that include other family members. Incomes are to some extent pooled across family members (especially among the adults such as husband and wife), and the consumption of goods and services takes place within a family context. This is especially true of Asian Americans because they are more likely than whites to be living within a family rather than residing alone. Indeed, Asian Americans are three times more likely than whites to be living in a three-generation household (i.e., consisting of an elderly parent, adult parents, and young children), which is still considered normative in many Asian countries (Xie and Goyette 2004, 21). On average, family size is slightly larger among Asian Americans than among whites.

Table 13.1 shows the statistics for mean annual family income (which here also includes households consisting of individuals living alone). For the Asian AOIC population, mean family income is $84,501 compared to $71,900 for whites. Groups that stand out as having the highest family incomes include Asian Indians ($108,313), Chinese ($87,802), Sri Lankans ($87,678), and Pakistanis ($87,306). Groups that stand out as having the lowest family incomes include Hmong ($49,839), Cambodians ($53,994), Bangladeshi ($55,042), and Laotians ($56,666). Mean family income for biracial and multiracial Asian Americans ($71,855) is essentially the same as for whites.

Table 13.1 also shows that the poverty rate for whites is 11.6 percent while for the Asian AOIC population it is slightly higher at 12.4 percent. Several Asian American groups have lower poverty rates than whites including Filipinos (6.7 percent), Asian Indians (9.4 percent), biracial white Asians (10.0 percent), and Japanese (10.5 percent). On the other hand, Table 13.1 also shows that several Asian American groups have notably high poverty rates including Cambodians (20.1%), Other Asians (20.2%), Bangladeshi (24.5%), and Hmong (28.2%). Although not shown in Table 13.1, the poverty rate for African Americans was 28.2 percent for this time period (i.e., 2007 to 2009), which is the same as for the Hmong who are the poorest group among Asian Americans.

More detailed statistics on poverty among Asian Americans are provided by Takei and Sakamoto (2011). Their analysis seems generally consistent with our earlier discussion regarding the substantial role of immigration in affecting aggregate patterns of socioeconomic differentials relating to Asian Americans. In the case of poverty, Takei and Sakamoto (2011) find that the slightly higher poverty rate among Asian Americans compared to whites is largely due to immigration. Asian Americans are more likely to be immigrants, and immigrants usually have higher poverty rates. Among adult native-born Asian Americans (i.e., excluding native-born Asian American children whose family incomes depend upon the earnings of their immigrant parents), poverty rates are actually lower than among whites. Due to their higher educational levels, adult native-born Asian Americans have a lower poverty rate than adult whites.

Among foreign-born Asian Americans, poverty is highest among the most recent immigrants; poverty rates decline significantly among foreign-born Asian Americans after residing in the United States for five years. Poverty among foreign-born Asian Americans is slightly higher than poverty among foreign-born whites, but this is largely because the former group is more likely to be a recent immigrant. Among foreign-born persons who have lived in the United States for at least five years, poverty among Asian Americans is very similar to that of whites (Takei and Sakamoto 2011, 264).

CONCLUSION

Asian Americans have gone from being a tiny and obscure group as recently as 1960 to becoming a broadly recognized racial category that has been widely accepted into most walks of American life in the 21st century. Asian Americans appear to be routinely represented in the national media, in marketing and advertisements, in the professions, in science and industry, in educational institutions, in the military, in some sports, and in many of the fine arts. If anything, their visibility in American society may even exceed their proportionate representation of the U.S. population, probably because of their higher levels of education and income. We furthermore predict that, as the adult population of native-born Asian Americans continues to increase, more Asian Americans will become increasingly visible in the upper echelons of business, politics, and entertainment.

Some authors have selectively emphasized unfortunate incidents in Asian American history and have overgeneralized individualistic experiences in order to portray Asian Americans as being constantly persecuted by extreme and omnipresent racial discrimination (Chou and Feagin 2008). While we agree that some degree of racism (as well as other forms of deviance) persists and will likely always remain problematic at least to some extent, the economic statistics on the typically favorable characteristics of this minority group suggest that relatively successful racial integration into mainstream society may be a more accurate description of contemporary Asian Americans in general (Sakamoto, Goyette, and Kim 2009). To be sure, disadvantages relative to whites are systematically evident for foreign-born and foreign-educated Asian Americans, but their 1.5-generation and native-born offspring are often excelling in American schools and are frequently earning good salaries in desirable jobs at non-Asian-American companies in an era when inequality is rising, unemployment is becoming more widespread, and poverty remains unabated.

These latter unfortunate trends do of course affect Asian Americans as well, including especially the Hmong, Laotians, and Cambodians who remain the most disadvantaged ethnic groups among Asian Americans. Their disadvantages appear to stem, however, primarily from their social class characteristics rather than their racial minority status per se. On average, most Hmong, Laotians, and Cambodians lack competitive levels of educational attainment, and this increasingly important characteristic is what seems to set them apart from most of the other ethnic groups of Asian Americans in term of socioeconomic characteristics. At least when considered as an overall group, Asian Americans seem to be generally well served by the U.S. educational system. Even if there may perhaps be a small disadvantage relative to whites with the same educational level and field of study (Kim and Sakamoto 2010), the propitious fact remains that most 1.5-generation and native-born Asian Americans have significantly higher educational credentials that do provide greater lifetime socioeconomic rewards, which many whites in the United States lack but wish they had.

In closing, we reiterate that the contemporary American labor market is increasingly becoming unequal, and that Asian Americans are generally affected by this trend as well. Having higher educational attainments is helpful in avoiding the worst consequences of rising inequality, but not all Asian Americans are above the national average in terms of schooling. In general, Asian Americans are an important example of a minority group that has been fairly successful (at least on average) in integrating into mainstream society, but this case of multicultural acceptance does not negate the continuing problems of poverty and inequality that affect the members of all racial groups in the United States in the 21st century.

NOTE

1. For a detailed discussion of the concepts and measures upon which these data are based, the reader may refer to http://www.census.gov/acs/www/data _documentation/documentation_main/.

BIBLIOGRAPHY

Chou, Rosalind S. and Joe R. Feagin. 2008. *The Myth of the Model Minority: Asian Americans Facing Racism*. Boulder, CO: Paradigm Publishers.

Feliciano, Cynthia. 2005. "Educational Selectivity in U.S. Immigration: How Do Immigrants Compare to Those Left Behind?" *Demography* 42: 131–52.

Goyette, Kimberly and Yu Xie. 1999. "Educational Expectations of Asian American Youths: Determinants and Ethnic Differences." *Sociology of Education* 72: 22–36.

Greenman, Emily. 2011. "Asian American-White Differences in the Effect of Motherhood on Career Outcomes." *Work and Occupations* 38: 37–67.

Kim, ChangHwan and Arthur Sakamoto. 2010. "Have Asian American Men Achieved Labor Market Parity with White Men?" *American Sociological Review* 75: 934–57.

Kim, ChangHwan and Christopher R. Tamborini. 2006. "The Continuing Significance of Race in the Occupational Attainment of Whites and Blacks: A Segmented Labor Market Analysis." *Sociological Inquiry* 76: 23–51.

Sakamoto, Arthur, Kimberly A. Goyette and ChangHwan Kim. 2009. "Socioeconomic Attainments of Asian Americans." *Annual Review of Sociology* 35: 255–76.

Sakamoto, Arthur, Isao Takei and Hyeyoung Woo. 2011. "Socioeconomic Differentials among Single-Race and Multi-Race Japanese Americans." *Ethnic and Racial Studies* 34: 1445–65.

Sakamoto, Arthur and Hyeyoung Woo. 2007. "The Socioeconomic Attainments of Second-Generation Cambodian, Hmong, Laotian and Vietnamese Americans." *Sociological Inquiry* 77: 46–77.

Sakamoto, Arthur, Hyeyoung Woo and ChangHwan Kim. 2010. "Does an Immigrant Background Ameliorate Racial Disadvantage? The Socioeconomic Attainments of Second-Generation African Americans." *Sociological Forum* 25: 123–46.

Sakamoto, Arthur, Huei-Hsia Wu and Jessie M. Tzeng. 2000. "The Declining Significance of Race among American Men During the Latter Half of the Twentieth Century." *Demography* 37: 41–51.

Sakamoto, Arthur and Yu Xie. 2006. "The Socioeconomic Attainments of Asian Americans." Pp. 54–77 in *Asian Americans: Contemporary Trends and Issues* edited by Pyong Gap Min. Thousand Oaks, CA: Sage Publications.

Takei, Isao and Arthur Sakamoto. 2008. "Do College-Educated, Native-Born Asian Americans Face a Glass Ceiling in Obtaining Managerial Authority?" *Asian American Policy Review* 17: 73–85.

Takei, Isao and Arthur Sakamoto. 2009. "Demographic Characteristics of Third-Generation Asian Americans: Socioeconomic Attainments and Assimilation." Presented at the 2009 Population Association of America annual meeting, Detroit, MI.

Takei, Isao and Arthur Sakamoto. 2011. "Poverty among Asian Americans in the 21st Century." *Sociological Perspectives* 54: 251–76.

Xie, Yu and Kimberly Goyette. 2003. "Social Mobility and the Educational Choices of Asian Americans." *Social Science Research* 32: 467–98.

Xie, Yu and Kimberly A. Goyette. 2004. *A Demographic Portrait of Asian Americans.* New York: Russell Sage Foundation.

Chapter 14

Are Gays and Lesbians "Mainstream" with Respect to Economic Success?

Michael E. Martell

Gays and lesbians are often portrayed as members of an elite economic class in political rhetoric (Rubinstein 2002) and in popular culture (for example, in television shows such as *Will and Grace, Queer as Folk,* and *Noah's Arc*). These portrayals are not supported by sound research addressing the economic success of lesbians and gays. This chapter discusses the origins of the notion of homosexual affluence and summarizes recent advances in our knowledge of the economic reality facing gays and lesbians today.

Conclusions from a growing body of research paint a nuanced picture of the economic status of gays and lesbians. While lesbian households are more likely to be in poverty than heterosexual households, individual lesbians appear to enjoy an earnings premium compared to heterosexual women. Gay households are no more likely to be in poverty than heterosexual households. However, gay households are more likely to be "low-income" households than heterosexual households, and individual gay men experience a large earnings penalty compared to heterosexual men.

PERCEPTIONS OF GAY AND LESBIAN ECONOMIC SUCCESS ORIGINATED IN THE 1980s

Stereotypes of economic affluence that contribute to the confusion over the economic reality of gays and lesbians stem from early investigations into the economic characteristics of gays and lesbians by marketing firms in the 1980s. This marketing research yielded misleading results regarding homosexual affluence because the investigation technique was flawed.

Flawed investigations from marketing firms in the 1980s suggested that the general population had lower average incomes than gays and lesbians. Despite being inaccurate, these findings gave rise to the myth of homosexual affluence that still pervades popular belief (Badgett 2001). The myth of homosexual affluence gave rise to characterizations of gays and lesbians as being "DINKs" (Double Income No Kids) with high levels of conspicuous consumption and as having high levels of discretionary expenditures (Badgett 2001).

Investigating earnings, or any individual characteristic, of any population usually involves sampling. Proper sampling occurs when researchers isolate a sample of people who are representative of a larger population. In this case, researchers want to find a sample of gays and lesbians that is representative of the entire gay and lesbian population. By comparing the income of gays and lesbians in a representative sample to the income of heterosexuals, researchers can note if there is any difference between the average income of gays and lesbians and the average income of heterosexuals.

Improper sampling yielded misleading estimates of average incomes for gays and lesbians. The average income of gays and lesbians was higher than the average income of heterosexuals in early surveys because this comparison was done incorrectly. The comparison was done incorrectly because the sample of gays and lesbians surveyed was more affluent than most gays and lesbians. The sample of gays and lesbians was selected using lists of those who subscribe to magazines, who tend to have higher incomes than those who do not subscribe to magazines. Comparing the general population to gay and lesbian magazine subscribers was tantamount to comparing a middle-class heterosexual to an upper-class gay or lesbian. It should have come as no surprise that rich gays and lesbians earned more than typical heterosexuals (Badgett 2001).

INVESTIGATING GAY AND LESBIAN ECONOMIC SUCCESS INVOLVES UNIQUE DIFFICULTIES

Income and economic achievement of gays and lesbians is difficult to investigate properly because data are scarce. Samples of the gay and lesbian population that are representative of the entire gay and lesbian population are rare. The most accessible data cover the United States, which most research addresses.[1] There are two main representative datasets covering the gay and lesbian population that contain useful income information: U.S. Census data and the General Social Survey (GSS). Census and GSS data have been heavily utilized to generate knowledge regarding inequalities for gays and lesbians in the labor market. The knowledge generated has been corroborated by a small amount of research using alternative data samples, which are highlighted in Table 14.1, that verify the robust findings based on Census and GSS data.

The existing data samples are not perfect. Imperfections start with methods of classifying survey respondents as homosexual. GSS data require that we infer that those who engage in sex with the same sex are homosexual. The sample of gays and lesbians in the GSS data is small, which introduces some statistical difficulty when attempting to draw conclusions from a small sample to a larger population, but representative of both single and cohabiting gays and lesbians. Census data require that we infer that those who cohabitate with a member of the same sex are homosexual. While Census data contain a large sample of those who are identified as homosexual, the data do not represent homosexuals who are not cohabiting or are single. Despite the drawbacks of data, using samples of homosexuals with incomes that are representative of the overall population has provided the necessary information to estimate more accurately measures of the economic success of gays and lesbians than early marketing surveys provided.

Imperfections from classifying individuals based on cohabitation status or sexual behavior create some uncertainty in understanding the economic status of gays and lesbians. Gays and lesbians who are cohabiting are not necessarily representative of all homosexuals just as those who are married are not necessarily representative of all heterosexuals. Single men earn less than married men (Loh 1996), which is a pattern that could extend to homosexual populations making the use of Census data less appropriate than GSS data. Indeed Jepsen (2007) finds evidence of such a pattern among lesbians even though research is yet to find support for the same pattern among gay men (Zavodny 2008). Thus data analysis using Census data provides results that are representative only of cohabiting homosexuals. On the other hand, classifying respondents as homosexual based on sexual behavior can capture single and cohabiting gays and lesbians. It should be noted that those who engage in same-sex sex are not necessarily gay or lesbian (Laumann et al. 1994). Both homosexual and heterosexual individuals may engage in sex with members of the same sex or a different sex, or not engage in sex at all. However, it is a relatively trivial extrapolation that those who are behaviorally homosexual have characteristics and achieve economic statuses that make these individuals representative of the overall homosexual population.

Uncertainty in understanding results based upon assumptions required by data has motivated much research to understand the empirical findings regarding the economic success of gays and lesbians. Given uncertainty, researchers have undertaken many varying approaches, which are summarized in Table 14.1, to measure the economic success of gays and lesbians. These varying approaches have for the most part yielded consistent results. The consistency of results in varying research approaches validates the insights that this body of research has generated.

GAYS AND LESBIANS ARE NOT EQUAL

Understanding the economic success of gays and lesbians requires an analysis of the standing of gays and lesbians across the entire income distribution. Investigating the entire income distribution provides an assessment of the likelihood of gays and lesbians to be poor or rich as well as the relative status of more typical gays and lesbians, or those in the middle of the income distribution. Gays and lesbians are more likely to be in poverty and earn less on average than heterosexuals. This suggests, even though research has not explicitly measured it, that gays and lesbians are also less likely to be rich than heterosexuals.

Table 14.1
Summary of Research on Gay and Lesbian Earnings Differentials

Authors	Data	Identification	Estimation Technique	Findings
Badget (1995)	GSS 1989–91	Sexual behavior	Imputed median of income categories from CPS, OLS	Gay penalty, insignificant lesbian premium
Blandford (2003)	GSS 1989–96	Sexual behavior	Selection for full-time work status, OLS on imputed median categories from CPS	Gay penalty, lesbian premium
Berg & Lien (2002)	GSS 1991–96	Sexual behavior	Maximum likelihood on income categories	Gay penalty, insignificant lesbian premium
Comolli (2005)	GSS 1994–2002	Sexual behavior	Maximum likelihood on income categories	Gay penalty, lesbian premium
Black et al. (2003)	GSS 1989–96	Sexual behavior	Maximum likelihood on income categories	Gay penalty, lesbian premium
Cushing-Daniels & Yeung (2009)	GSS 1988–2006	Sexual behavior	Selection for full-time workers, midpoint of income categories	Gay penalty, insignificant lesbian premium
Martell (2010)	GSS 1994–2008	Sexual behavior	Imputed median of income categories from CPS, OLS	Gay penalty, lesbian premium
Klawitter & Flatt (1998)	1990 U.S. Census	Cohabitation status	OLS on annual income	Gay penalty, lesbian premium
Allegretto & Arthur (2001)	1990 U.S. Census	Cohabitation status	OLS on hourly earnings	Gay penalty

(continued)

Table 14.1 (Continued)

Authors	Data	Identification	Estimation Technique	Findings
Albelda et al. (2005)	2000 U.S. Census	Cohabitation status	OLS on annual earnings	Gay penalty, lesbian premium in Massachusetts
Clain & Leppel	1990 U.S. Census	Cohabitation status	Selection on full-time work status, OLS on earnings	Gay penalty, lesbian premium
Gates (2009)	2000 U.S. Census	Cohabitation status	OLS on hourly wages	Gay penalty, lesbian premium
Antecol et al. (2007)	2000 U.S. Census	Cohabitation status	OLS and decomposition	Gay penalty, lesbian premium
Elmslie & Tebaldi (2007)	2004 CPS	Cohabitation status	OLS on hourly wages and annual earnings	Gay penalty, insignificant lesbian premium
Carpenter (2004)	BRFSS 1996–2000	Self-reported	OLS on categorical income midpoint	Penalty for all same-sex couples
Carpenter (2005)	CHIS 2001[**]	Self-reported	OLS on last month's earnings	Insignificant effect for gay and lesbian, penalty for bisexuals
Carpenter (2007)	NHANES III[***] 1988–96	Sexual behavior	Maximum likelihood on categorical income	Gay penalty, no penalty or premium for lesbian

[*]Behavioral Risk Factor Surveillance Survey.
[**]California Health Interview Survey.
[***]National Health and Nutrition Examination Survey.

259

While those who are rich are at the very top of the income distribution, those who are in poverty are near the very bottom of the income distribution. Households earning income that is less than twice as high as the poverty line are typically considered to be low income (Albelda et al. 2009). Albelda et al. (2009) are the only scholars to look at those near the poverty line in the homosexual community. They address the likelihood of cohabiting homosexuals to be in poverty or to have low incomes.

Households of cohabiting gay men are equally likely to be in poverty and more likely to be low income than heterosexual households. Overall percentages of the population of homosexual and heterosexual households in poverty are misleading. While 5.4 percent of heterosexual households are in poverty, only 4 percent of gay households are in poverty. Similarly, a higher percentage of heterosexual households have low income (17.7%) than gay households (11.0%) (Albelda et al. 2009).[2] These percentages do not take into consideration that gay and heterosexual households may have different characteristics unrelated to sexual orientation that impact their economic status. To correct for these possibly different characteristics and more accurately ascertain the likelihood of gay households to be in poverty all else equal, researchers can predict the likelihood of being low income or in poverty using several household characteristics including sexual orientation and isolate the relationship between sexual orientation and being low income or in poverty. Albelda et al. (2009) show that gay households are 1 percent more likely to be low income than heterosexual households. The increased likelihood of being low income persists when researchers isolate the effect of sexual orientation from the possibility of gay households having fewer children and more education than heterosexual households.

Households of cohabiting lesbians are more likely to be in poverty and earn low incomes than heterosexual households. A higher percentage of lesbian households (6.9%) are in poverty than different-sex households (5.4%). Households that are low income comprise 17.4 percent of all lesbian households, and low-income households comprise 17.7 percent of all heterosexual households (Albelda et al. 2009). Once again, considering the role of other characteristics in predicting the likelihood of being in poverty or a low-income household better targets the relationship between sexual orientation and being in poverty or a low-income household for cohabiting lesbians. Cohabiting lesbians are 2.9 percent more likely to be low income than heterosexual households all else equal (Albelda et al. 2009).

An assessment of the likelihood of being poor complements the larger and more robust literature investigating inequality for more typical workers with earnings in the middle of the income distribution. To assess the economic success of more typical gay or lesbian workers, research has investigated the equality of average earnings of gays and lesbians relative to heterosexual workers. Investigating the equality of average earnings provides insights to the experiences of those in the middle of the income distribution, instead of those at the bottom (the poor) or the top (the rich) of the income distribution. All the research addressing average earnings controls for other relevant factors to isolate the impact of sexual orientation on wages.

Gay and lesbian households have lower annual earnings than heterosexual households. Carpenter (2004) uses unique data on same-sex households to show that all households with same-sex cohabitants, gay or lesbian, have lower annual earnings than heterosexual households. Annual earnings are approximately 10 percent lower for gay households and 24 percent lower for lesbian households compared to heterosexual households.

Differences in household earnings provide insights to the economic success of gays and lesbians but cannot isolate the impact of sexual orientation on individual economic success very well. Homosexual households are different from heterosexual households in two ways: sexual orientation and the sex composition of households. Economic inquiry has long established that women earn significantly less than men (Altonji and Blank 1999), and discrimination based on sex may disproportionately affect lesbian households in addition to any differential treatment related to sexual orientation. To more accurately identify the impact of sexual orientation on earnings and understand the economic status of gays and lesbians, most researchers have investigated the individual earnings of lesbians and gays.

Research at the individual level has provided more insight into the status of gays and lesbians. At the individual level researchers have investigated differences in annual earnings and hourly wages, as Table 14.1 shows. Wages more accurately reflect the compensation of workers for the value of their labor. Since we expect those who work more to earn more, differences in annual earnings may stem from workers supplying different amounts of labor. To estimate an inequality in compensation that more accurately reflects labor supply choices of gays and lesbians than annual earnings, many researchers measure differences in hourly wages.

Gay men have lower annual earnings and wages than heterosexual men. Researchers have found convincing and robust evidence of an earnings penalty for gay men using GSS data (Badgett 1995; Blandford 2003; Berg and Lien 2002; Black et al. 2003; Cushing-Daniels and Yeung 2009) and Census data (Albelda et al. 2005; Klawitter and Flatt 1998; Clain and Leppel 2001). Carpenter (2007) uses an additional sexual behavior data source to find a significant penalty for gay men. These earnings penalties range from 14 percent (Black et al. 2003) to nearly 33 percent (Blandford 2003).[3] Similarly, researchers have found a negative wage penalty for gay men using GSS data (Comolli 2005; Martell 2010) and Census data (Gates 2009; Elmslie and Tebaldi 2007; Antecol et al. 2009, Allegretto and Arthur 2001). Estimates of the gay wage penalty range from 4.5 percent to 23 percent, which is generally a smaller penalty than those experienced by women and workers of color (Altonji and Blank 1999).

Research has yielded mixed evidence suggesting that lesbians have higher annual earnings and wages than heterosexual women. Using GSS data, researchers have documented an annual earnings premium for lesbians (Blandford 2003; Comolli 2005; Black et al. 2003; Elmslie and Tebaldi 2007) and an insignificant difference between earnings of lesbians and heterosexual women (Badgett 1995; Berg & Lien 2002; Cushing-Daniels and Yeung 2009). Using Census data, researchers have more robustly found evidence of a lesbian premium (Klawitter and Flatt 1998; Albelda et al. 2005; Clain and Leppel 2001), with one exception, which finds an insignificant difference in earnings for lesbians (Elsmlie and Tebaldi 2007). Carpenter (2007) uses an additional sexual behavior data source to find an insignificant difference in earnings for lesbians. Estimates of the size of the lesbian premium range from zero (when the difference in earnings is insignificant) to 38 percent. Researchers have more consistently found a significant wage premium for lesbians using GSS data (Martell 2010; Comolli 2005) and Census data (Gates 2009; Antecol et al. 2007), although Elmslie and Tebaldi (2007) are an exception and find an insignificant difference in wages using Census data. The size of the wage premium for lesbians ranges from zero to 31.6 percent (Antecol et al. 2007). These diverging results cause researchers to be less confident in our knowledge of the impact of sexual orientation on wages for women. The less consistent results regarding the economic status of lesbians offer a less concrete understanding of the lesbian experience than the gay experience. The current literature strongly suggests that lesbians enjoy an earnings premium, even if it may be shrinking (Cushing-Daniels and Yeung 2009).

EXPLAINING INEQUALITIES FOR GAYS AND LESBIANS

The existence of wage and earnings inequalities suggests that a discriminatory process afflicts gay and lesbian workers. Attributing differentials to a discriminatory process requires an investigation into the role of other factors in the determination of earnings. Other factors or choices affecting gay and lesbian workers may explain some of the inequalities that we see. For instance, earnings increase as workers increase their labor supply. Our labor supply decisions depend on our attachment to the labor force. Those without children may devote more time to the labor force, since they have fewer household obligations. Our labor supply is also hallmarked by our occupational attainment. Lower levels of skilled occupational attainment may also contribute to lower earnings. Lower earnings will also result from any differences that exist in education or work experience between gay and lesbian workers and heterosexual workers. Ruling out these factors to determine the role of discriminatory preferences has been the direction of recent research addressing gays and lesbians.

Labor supply choices do not entirely explain earnings differentials. Estimates of earnings differentials exist even when researchers compare wages or compare the likelihood that individuals will engage in the labor market. Additionally, while the presence of children (a proxy for labor market attachment) decreases earnings for all women, it has little impact on all men (Martell 2010). Gays and lesbians are less likely to have children than heterosexual households (Black et al. 2007), but this cannot explain the gay penalty and can possibly explain only some of the lesbian premium (Antecol et al. 2007; Martell 2010). Some research has shown that gay men work less than heterosexual men and that lesbians work more than heterosexual women (Elmslie and Tebaldi 2006; Antecol and Steinberger 2012). This pattern could help explain the gay penalty and lesbian premium. However, cohabiting gays and lesbians are more likely to be unemployed than those in heterosexual marriages (Leppel 2008), which causes us to expect lower earnings for both gay men and lesbians. That gay men may work less when employed is consistent with working less in the presence of prejudice or discrimination (Goldschmidt et al. 2004). Discriminatory treatment is also supported by the persistence of an economic inequality when research incorporates labor supply by predicting wages instead of household income or annual earnings. The persistence of inequalities suggests that labor supply choices alone do not explain wage differentials.

Occupational attainment does not explain wage differentials. Wage differentials could result from gay and lesbian workers being clustered into particular jobs. Indeed, Badgett and Folbre (2003) argue that occupational choices are determined by expected payoffs in the labor market and the marriage market. Marriage market returns may cause heterosexual women to select into more feminine and less remunerative jobs than lesbians. Badgett and King (2001) find limited evidence that gays and lesbians are more likely to work in occupations that have a higher percentage of workers who are more tolerant of homosexuality. Despite Badgett and King's evidence of occupational clustering, Antecol et al. (2007) finds that earnings differentials for gays and lesbians do not vary substantially across occupational groups.

Differences in worker characteristics such as human capital attainment, marital status, and presence of children between homosexual and heterosexual workers do not explain negative wage differentials. Gay men have more education and fewer children than heterosexual men, which should cause them to have higher earnings than heterosexual men. Similarly, lesbians have fewer children than heterosexual women, which could explain part of their wage premium (Black et al. 2007). However, dissecting the wage differentials experienced by gay men and lesbians into a portion that can be explained by differences in worker characteristics, Martell (2010) and Antecol et al. (2007) show that the differential is entirely unrelated to worker characteristics for both gay men. The lesbian premium can be explained by differences in worker characteristics either in part (Antecol et al. 2007) for cohabiting lesbians or not at all (Martell 2010).

The existence of wage differentials that are unrelated to differences in worker characteristics or labor supplies suggests that wage differentials are the result of a prejudicial process. Generally, wage differentials unattributed to differences in worker characteristics are assumed to arise from discrimination. Traditional notions of discrimination, however, do not apply to gays and lesbians given their invisible minority trait. An invisible minority trait presents gays and lesbians the opportunity to try to avoid discrimination by passing as heterosexual. Passing, though, may not be a desirable choice.

A prejudicial process among firms may result in gay men accepting compensating differentials (Martell 2010). Compensating differentials can exist if gay workers prefer to reveal their orientation. Gay workers have pressure to avoid passing because passing as heterosexual entails costs due to anxiety and dishonesty with oneself and others (Woods 1993). To avoid these costs, gay workers may be willing to accept lower wages. Lower wages may be compensated by a tolerant work environment that provides a psychic income for gay workers who do not have to pass as heterosexual to avoid discrimination.

Compensating differentials do not explain the wage premium for lesbians. We have fewer explanations for the lesbian wage premium. Possible explanations can be that the premium stems from preferential treatment from employers or systematic differences between the labor market choices of workers. From the employer side, the existence of a lesbian premium that may exist simultaneously with a gay penalty could be that the labor market rewards perceived masculinity. If lesbians are perceived, accurately or not, as more masculine than heterosexual women and gay men less masculine than heterosexual men, than lesbians would be expected to earn more and gay men less. A more plausible explanation of the lesbian premium would stem from choices or abilities of workers. Badgett and Folbre's (2003) suggestion that lesbians select into higher-paying and less feminine jobs and gay men into more feminine, less remunerative jobs has been supported with limited analysis by Black et. al. (2007) but is inconsistent with the persistence of wage differentials across occupational groups (Antecol et al. 2007). It is posited that heterosexual women expect higher wages from their husbands and therefore specialize in household production or devote less time to wage earning in the labor market than their lesbian counterparts (Berg and Lien 2002; Orrefice 2011). Indeed, lesbians and gay men are less likely to have a stay-at-home partner who specializes in housework (Black et al. 2007), but as discussed earlier, choices that affect labor supply do not explain wage differences. The most consistent estimates of the lesbian premium are from Census data that capture only cohabiting lesbians. It is quite possible that these lesbians enjoy a "marriage" premium (Jepsen 2007). Cohabiting lesbians seem to be able to dedicate more of their time to the labor market than married heterosexual women and less time doing household labor, allowing them more time to advance their professional career (Orrefice 2011). It seems as if the lesbian earnings premium stems from the characteristics and choices lesbians make in the labor market. Future research should investigate the characteristics of lesbians that may provide them with a heightened ability to succeed professionally.

INEQUALITIES FOR GAYS AND LESBIANS ARE ALLEVIATED BY PUBLIC POLICY

To alleviate wage differentials, public policy has been implemented on the local, city and state level. On the state level, 22 states (including the District of Columbia) have implemented laws making sexual orientation discrimination illegal. Additionally, there are many more city and county ordinances making sexual orientation discrimination illegal (Klawitter and Flatt 1998; Human Rights Campaign 2009; Klawitter 2011). Bills introducing federal laws have been introduced repeatedly in Congress but have never passed.

State-level laws decrease wage differentials for gay workers. Testing the impact of any city, county, or state law making sexual orientation discrimination illegal on homosexual wage differentials, Klawitter and Flatt (1998) do not find evidence of public policy impacting wage differentials for cohabiting gays or lesbians. However, it is likely that state laws have more of an impact on labor markets since state governments have larger budgets and more institutionalized enforcement mechanisms than city governments (Jasinnas 2000). Isolating the impact of state laws on wage differentials for gays and lesbians provides a clearer assessment of the role of public policy. Gates (2009), Martell (2010), and Klawitter (2011) show that gay men in states with employment nondiscrimination acts making sexual orientation discrimination illegal have smaller wage differentials than gay men in states without such laws using both Census and GSS data.

ADDITIONAL PUBLIC POLICY WILL PROMOTE ECONOMIC EQUALITY FOR GAYS AND LESBIANS

Adequately addressing inequality for gay and lesbian workers will require additional public policy. Existing public policy has improved the economic status of gays and lesbians, but gays and lesbians still have not achieved mainstream economic status. Mainstream economic status requires further public policy because it is unlikely that mainstream status will evolve simply with the passing of time and corresponding increasing levels of tolerance. Increasing tolerance and equality are not necessarily the product of historical trajectories. Indeed, historical research (Chauncey 1994) suggests that history has not shown decreasing levels of oppression and discrimination against gays and lesbians, but substantial variation in the extent of oppression over time. This variation in oppression could cause inequalities to rise if gay and lesbian rights advocates do not enact important public policy to achieve more mainstream economic status. Fortunately, there are many policy proposals can serve as the means to this goal.

Public policy aimed to alleviate poverty promotes economic equality for gays and lesbians. Since gays and lesbians are more likely to be in poverty than heterosexuals, policies to help those in poverty are likely to increase economic equality for gays and lesbians. Gays and lesbians will benefit from increased minimum wage laws, a larger Earned Income Tax Credit, and other social assistance programs for the poor (Albelda et al. 2009). Poverty can also result from employment termination. Current federal law does not make employment termination based on sexual orientation illegal. Making sexual orientation discrimination illegal on the federal level will help protect gays and lesbians from poverty as a result of discrimination in hiring, firing, and compensation.

Policies aimed at alleviating gender inequality may help lesbian households. While individual lesbians do not suffer from negative wage differentials on average, lesbian households are more likely to be low income or in poverty. Decreasing the overall gender wage gap may increase earnings for lesbians as well as heterosexual women and thereby decrease the propensity of lesbian households to live in poverty.

Allowing same-sex marriage is also likely to increase economic equality for gays and lesbians. Marriage is a profound social institution that provides a framework for relationship stability. Relationship stability facilitates long-term financial planning and saving that helps individuals and households maintain living standards in times of economic distress. Marriage facilitates the sharing of partner benefits such as retirement and Social Security benefits, which are important to older gays and lesbians who may face disadvantage related to age and sexual orientation. Marriage also facilitates the sharing of health care, which is quite important to those who live in poverty (Albelda et al. 2009). In the absence of marriage, same-sex partners face very high tax rates on the inheritance of retirement benefits or jointly owned property upon death (Gates and Bennett 2004) thereby limiting the ability of gays and lesbians to accumulate shared wealth. Supporting wealth accumulation through marriage will foster mainstream economic status for gays and lesbians.

Existing public policy and policy proposals treat only the symptoms of an underlying societal process that gives way to economic inequality. Economic inequality is the result of a culture of prejudice and intolerance toward gays and lesbians that restricts the choices of and opportunities facing gays and lesbians. Intolerance results in the termination of gay and lesbian employees, but it can also motivate gay and lesbian workers to choose occupations or employers that they expect to be more tolerant resulting in employment segregation. While employment segregation may be partially the result of a choice of gays and lesbians, it is the result of a choice that heterosexual workers never have to consider. Heterosexual workers do not have to make choices that may decrease their economic livelihood because of cultural intolerance. Increasing tolerance should be a primary goal of public policy as the erasure of inequality requires the promotion of a culture of tolerance and acceptance. A culture of tolerance and acceptance can promote the necessary equality of opportunities that gays and lesbians need to freely function in the economy and achieve mainstream economic success.

NOTES

1. A smaller literature has investigated the economic success of gays and lesbians in the Netherlands (Plug and Berkhout 2004), Canada (Carpenter 2008), Greece (Drydakis 2009), and Australia (Weichselbaumer 2003).

2. Albelda et al. (2009) compare only homosexual households to same-sex married households.

3. Additionally, Carpenter (2005) utilizes a unique data source to replicate the impact of sexual orientation on individual income with workers who self-identify their sexual orientation and finds that bisexuals face an income penalty but that there is no penalty or premium for gays and lesbians. Distinguishing bisexuals from gays and lesbians is not possible in GSS or Census data.

BIBLIOGRAPHY

Albelda, Randy, Ash, Michael, and Badgett, M. V. Lee. 2005. "Now That We Do: Same-Sex Couples and Marriage in Massachusetts." *Massachusetts Benchmarks*, 7(2): 16–24.

Albelda, Randy, Badgett, M. V. Lee, Schneebaum, Alyssa, and Gates, Gary. 2009. *Poverty in the Lesbian, Gay and Bisexual Community*. Los Angeles: The Williams Institute, March. http://escholarship.org/uc/item/2509p8r5 (accessed January 19, 2011).

Allegretto, Sylvia and Arthur, Michelle. 2001. "An Empirical Analysis of Homosexual/Heterosexual Male Earnings Differentials: Unmarried and Unequal?" *Industrial and Labor Relations Review*, 54(3): 631–46.

Altonji, Joseph G. and Blank, Rebecca M. 1999. "Race and Gender in the Labor Market." In *Handbook of Labor Economics*, edited by O. Ashenfelter and D. Card, Chapter 48, pages 3143–325.

Antecol, Heather, Jong, Anneke, and Steinberger, Michael. 2007. "The Sexual Orientation Wage Gap: The Role of Occupational Sorting, Human Capital and Discrimination." *Institute for the Study of Labor (IZA): Discussion Paper No. 2945*.

Antecol, Heather and Steinberger, Michael D. 2009. Labor Supply Differences between Married Heterosexual Women and Partnered Lesbians: A

Semi-parametric Decomposition Approach. Working Paper accessed: http://economics-files.pomona.edu/steinberger/research/Antecol_Steinberger_Labor_Supply_Differences_March2010.pdf

Antecol, Heather and Steinberger, Michael D. Steinberger 2012. Labor Supply Differences between Married Heterosexual Women and Partnered Lesbians: A Semi-parametric Decomposition Approach," *Economic Inquiry*, forthcoming.

Badgett, M. V. Lee. 1995. "The Wage Effects of Sexual Orientation Discrimination." *Industrial and Labor Relations Review*, 54(3): 726–39.

Badgett, M. V. Lee. 2001. *Money, Myths and Change: The Economic Lives of Lesbians and Gay Men*. Chicago: The University of Chicago Press.

Badgett, M. V. Lee and Folbre, Nancy. 2003. "Job Gendering: Occupational Choice and the Marriage Market." *Industrial Relations*, 42(2): 270–98.

Badgett, M. V. Lee and King, Mary. 2001. "Lesbian and Gay Occupational Strategies." In *Homo-Economics: Capitalism, Community and Lesbian and Gay Life*, edited by Amy Gluckman and Betsy Reed, pages 73–85.

Bennett, Lisa, and Gates, Gary J. 2004. "The Cost of Marriage Inequality to Gay, Lesbian, and Bisexual Seniors." A Human Rights Campaign Foundation Report. Washington, DC: Human Rights Campaign.

Berg, Nathan and Lien, Donald. 2002. "Measuring the Effect of Sexual Orientation on Income: Evidence of Discrimination?" *Contemporary Economic Policy*, 4: 394–414.

Black, Dan A., Makar, Hoda R., Snaders, Seth G., and Taylor, Lowell J. 2003. "The Earnings Effects of Sexual Orientation." *Industrial and Labor Relations Review*, 56(3): 449–69.

Black, Dan A., Sanders, Seth G., and Taylor, Lowell J. 2007. "The Economics of Lesbian and Gay Families." *Journal of Economic Perspectives*, 21(2): 53–70.

Blandford, John M. 2003. "The Nexus of Sexual Orientation and Gender in the Determination of Earnings." *Industrial and Labor Relations Review*, 56(4): 622–42.

Carpenter, Christopher S. 2004. "New Evidence on Gay and Lesbian Household Incomes." *Contemporary Economic Policy*, 1: 78–94.

Carpenter, Christopher S. 2005. "Self-Reported Sexual Orientation and Earnings: Evidence from California." *Industrial and Labor Relations Review*, 58(2): 258–73.

Carpenter, Christopher S. 2007. "Revisiting the Income Penalty for Behaviorally Gay Men: Evidence from NHANES III." *Labour Economics*, 14: 25–34.

Carpenter, Christopher S. 2008. "Sexual Orientation, Work and Income in Canada." *Canadian Journal of Economics*, 41(4): 1239–61.

Chauncey, George. 1994. *Gay New York: Gender, Urban Culture, and the Making of the Gay Male World, 1890–1940*. New York: Basic Books.

Clain, Suzanne H. and Leppel, Karen. 2001. "An Investigation into Sexual Orientation Discrimination as an Explanation for Wage Differences." *Applied Economics*, 33(1): 37–47.

Comolli, Renzo. 2005. The Economics of Sexual Orientation and Racial Perception. PhD Diss., Yale University.

Cushing-Daniels, Brendan and Yeung, Tsz-Ying. 2009. "Wage Penalties and Sexual Orientation: An Update Using the General Social Survey." *Contemporary Economic Policy*, 27(2): 164–75.

Daneshvary, Nasser, Waddoups, C. Jeffrey, and Wimmer, Bradley. 2008. "Educational Attainment and the Lesbian Wage Premium." *Journal of Labor Research*, 29: 365–79.

Drydakis, Nick. 2009. "Sexual Orientation Discrimination in the Labour Market." *Labour Economics*, 16(4): 364–72.

Edinaldo, Tebaldi and Elmslie, Bruce. 2006. "Sexual Orientation and Labor Supply." *Applied Economics*, 38(5): 549–562

Elmslie, Bruce and Tebaldi, Edinaldo. 2006. "Sexual Orientation and Labor Supply." *Applied Economics*, 38(5): 549–62.

Elmslie, Bruce and Tebaldi, Edinaldo. 2007. "Sexual Orientation and Labor Market Discrimination." *Journal of Labor Research*, (28)3: 436–53.

Human Rights Campaign. 2009. The State of the Workplace. Washington, DC: Human Rights Campaign. Retrieved: January 11, 2011 http://www.hrc.org/documents/HRC_Foundation_State_of_the_Workplace_2007-2008.pdf.

Gates, Gary. 2009. The Impact of Sexual Orientation Anti-discrimination Policies on the Wages of Lesbians and Gay Men. *California Center for Population Research Working Paper Series*.

Goldschmidt, Art, Sedo, Stanley, Darity, William, and Hamilton, Darrick. 2004. "The Labor Supply Consequences of Perceptions of Employer Discrimination during Search and On-the-Job Training: Integrating Neoclassical Theory and Cognitive Dissonance." *The Journal of Economic Psychology*, 25: 15–39.

Jepsen, Lisa. 2007. "Comparing the Earnings of Cohabiting Lesbians, Cohabiting Heterosexual Women, and Married Women: Evidence from the 2000 Census." *Industrial Relations*, 46(4): 699–727.

Klawitter, Marieka. 2011. "Multilevel Analysis of the Effects of Antidiscrimination Policies on Earnings by Sexual Orientation." *Journal of Policy Analysis and Management*, 30(2): 334–58.

Klawitter, Marieka and Flatt, Victor. 1998. "The Effects of State and Local Antidiscrimination Policies on Earnings for Gays and Lesbians." *Journal of Policy Analysis and Management*, 4: 658–86.

Laumann, Edward O., Gagnon, John H., Michael, Robert T., and Michaels, Stuart. 1994. *The Social Organization of Sexuality: Sexual Practices in the United States.* Chicago: The University of Chicago Press.

Leppel, Karen. 2008. "Labour Force Status and Sexual Orientation." *Economica*, 1–11.

Loh, Eng S. 1996. "Productivity Differences and the Marriage Wage Premium for White Males." *The Journal of Human Resources*, 31(3): 566–89.

Martell, Michael E. 2010. *Sexual Orientation Disclosure and the Process of Discrimination* PhD Diss., The American University.

Orrefice, Sonia. 2011. "Sexual Orientation and Household Decision Making: Same-Sex Couples Balance of Power and Labor Supply Choices." *Labour Economics*, 18(2): 145–58.

Plug, Erik and Berkhout, Peter. 2004. "Effects of Sexual Preferences on Earnings in the Netherlands." *Journal of Population Economics*, 17: 117–31.

Rubinstein, William B. 2002. "Do Gay Rights Laws Matter?: An Empirical Assessment." *Southern California Law Review*, 75(65): 65–118.

Weichselbaumer, Doris. 2003. "Sexual Orientation Discrimination in Hiring." *Labour Economics*, 10(6): 629–42.

Woods, James D. 1993. *The Corporate Closet: The Professional Lives of Gay Men in America*. New York: The Free Press.

Zavodny, Madeline. 2008. "Is There a 'Marriage Premium' for Gay Men?" *Review of Economics of the Household*, 6: 369–89.

Chapter 15

Pension Policy and Income Inequality in the 21st Century

Mary Ellen Benedict[1] and John Hoag

INTRODUCTION

During the last half of the 20th century, the U.S. government made sweeping policy changes to ensure that elderly citizens increased their standard of living. During the 1960s the government instituted changes to the Social Security program to address the problem of rising poverty rates for the elderly population; these changes resulted in a decline in poverty for the age group. In 1959, the poverty rate for those over 65 was 35 percent; by 1974, the rate had declined to 15 percent (Cawthorne 2008). Additional changes in the following decades guaranteed that employees actually received promised pension plans and lowered the restrictions placed on pension vesting (Turner and Beller 1989). Further developments provided individual incentives for tax-deferred pension savings. Other policy changes increased the portability of private pensions, but at increased risk to individuals. In all, the policy changes related to pensions, both public and private, have permitted our elderly to enjoy a better standard of living than their counterparts who lived in the first half of the century.

In this chapter, we ask whether these long-standing pension policies are helpful to the well-being of our senior citizens today, and, more generally, important in reducing overall U.S. income inequality. This analysis seems especially important given the recent debates on changing Social Security and Medicare. The chapter begins with a discussion of pension policy in the United States. We then estimate the income distribution based on a money income variable that includes values for private pensions and Social Security. The analysis includes the decomposition of a measure of income inequality by age groups and by income component. Concluding remarks discuss pension policy in light of the findings.

U.S. PENSION POLICY

Social Security

At the turn of the 20th century, there were some private pensions in the United States, primarily offered by railroads and a few large companies (Williamson 1992). However, the majority of the population was not covered by either private or public pensions. With the exception of providing a pension for Civil War veterans in the late 1800s, the United States lagged behind European counterparts in the development of a public support system for the elderly. Germany, for example, had instituted such a system in the late 1880s ("Historical Background and Development of Social Security").

Although there was political interest in such a plan, it was never pushed through Congress. When the Great Depression hit, it became clear that something needed to be done about the poverty of the elderly. In 1934, President Roosevelt appointed a committee to look into the possibility of a social program aimed at alleviating the poverty of the elderly, who were particularly hard hit by the Depression. Fourteen months after the committee was appointed, legislation was passed instituting Social Security. Government began to collect taxes for the program by 1937, and payouts were to begin in 1942. The legislation was quickly amended so payouts could begin in 1940. Included in the amendment were provisions to extend benefits to the spouse and minor children of the recipient ("Historical Background and Development of Social Security").

Benefits were increased in the 1950s and a cost-of-living adjustment (COLA) was added in 1972. However, the formula for the COLA increased benefits at an unsustainable rate. In 1977, amendments to the law attacked this problem, but created a new problem as a result, commonly known as the "notch" generation. Because of the funding changes, those born between 1916 and 1927 had smaller benefits than those born before 1916 or after 1927 ("Historical Background and Development of Social Security"). Added changes have been made since that time in an effort to keep Social Security solvent, including tax increases and benefit cuts in 1983 (Munnell 1985). Long-run solvency is an issue that continues to be of interest, although it appears that the program can be maintained by either slightly higher taxes or slightly lower benefits (Bower 2011; Goss 2011).

Given the size of the benefits offered by Social Security, it seems unlikely that the benefits were intended as the only source of retirement income. More likely, income from family, private pensions, savings, and possible employment were considered the primary sources of old-age income. The size of the benefits under Social Security, which have increased over time, have improved the economic well-being of the elderly, though those relying primarily on Social Security will not have a satisfactory retirement. The average monthly Social Security benefit for a retired worker is $1,177 in 2011 (Social Security Online 2011). Individuals and families relying solely on this benefit will live at or near the poverty line.[2]

Private Pensions

Only 12 private pensions existed at the beginning of the 20th century. The growth of employer-based pensions was slow until the 1940s, when tax law, collective bargaining, and wage and price controls during World War II provided incentives to employers and employees to move some compensation to pension plans (Clark, Craig, and Wilson 2003). Most early pensions were *defined benefit* plans, which provide a formula for calculating benefit amounts. The formula is usually based on years of service and salary and results in a monthly or annual benefit payout from the day of retirement until the retiree's death. Most defined benefit plans require that a worker meet some minimum tenure with the firm to receive the full benefits of the retirement package. Workers who leave the employer prior to vesting receive their contributions back, but fail to receive the accrued pension benefit at retirement. Because employers enjoyed cost savings if workers left prior to vesting, early plans often had long vesting periods, sometimes as much as 25 years (Kotlikoff and Wise 1989). Workers also found themselves terminated just months before vesting occurred.

In addition, the defined benefit plans were backloaded, so the benefit accrual was faster in later years of service compared to earlier years. Further, employers had incentives to underfund plans since the funds were not necessary until many years later when workers had accrued enough years to be vested (Warshawsky 1989).

Because too many employers failed to live up to their pension promises, Congress enacted the Employee Retirement Income and Security Act (ERISA) in 1974 (Employee Retirement Income Security Act 1974). This landmark legislation established standards for plan funding, participation, and vesting. After its enactment, the number of private pension plans grew 156 percent by 1987, and the number of participants grew 76 percent (Turner and Beller 1989). Vested employees grew from 32 percent to 45 percent (Turner and Beller 1989). ERISA also established the Pension Benefit Guarantee Corporation (PBGC) to ensure payment of legal benefits for vested participants in the event that an underfunded plan was terminated (Turner and Beller 1989).

Although ERISA provided important protections to employees with private pension plans, the law ignored some problems and created new ones. The risk of underfunding shifted to the PBGC, resulting in the default of some underfunded plans and shifting the burden of payments to taxpayers. The payouts to retirees from the PBGC were substantially lower as well, as the guarantee covered the benefit only up until the date of plan termination. ERISA also permitted firms to obtain excess assets in overfunded defined benefit plans, when plans grew substantially due to the high interest rates in the 1980s. Overfunding provided incentives for firms to terminate the plans, keep the excess value for the firm, and revert to *defined contribution* plans, which were less costly to the firm. Defined contribution plans require a certain level of contribution made by the employer and the individual; the retirement benefit depends on the final account balance at retirement, and workers typically receive a lump sum benefit. Defined contribution plans tend to require short vesting periods and are more likely to be portable if workers switch employers. However, because of the pension plan reversions, retirees often received much lower benefits than if the defined benefit plan had remained intact until the workers' retirement (Benedict 1991).

Since 1974, the federal government has tried to reduce these problems through the enactment of a variety of laws. Some laws changed the tax code to provide incentives to individuals to contribute to individual retirement accounts (IRAs) or to employer-sponsored plans and to reduce vesting requirements to five years (Tax Reform Act of

1976; Revenue Act of 1978; Tax Reform Act of 1986). The Omnibus Reconciliation Act of 1990 placed an excise tax on pension plan reversions and reduced the amount of backloading. These laws increased protection for workers and have been the impetus for movement to private retirement savings and to defined contribution plans.

The most recent law, the Pension Protection Act of 2006, sets standards for minimum plan funding and prohibits underfunding in order to protect retiree benefits and to reduce the insurance risk of the PBGC. However, the restrictions of the act have also increased the number of defined benefit plan "freezes," where the employer terminates the plan at a certain date and bases final retirement benefit payouts on that date, thus reducing overall employer costs and lowering individual retirement payouts.

Like Social Security benefits, employer-based retirement benefits helped to raise the standard of living for our elderly, especially after the enactment of ERISA. However, as we move toward defined contribution plans, which require less in contributions from employers and place more financial risk on the worker, the equalizing effect of private pensions may disappear.

MEASURES OF INEQUALITY: THE GINI COEFFICIENT AND THE LORENZ CURVE

Before proceeding further, a brief discussion of two measures of income inequality is necessary because we use the measures later in the chapter. The first, the Gini coefficient, takes on values between zero and one. If every individual in a society had the same income, the Gini coefficient would be zero (society is in perfect equality). If only one person in the society had all of society's income and all others had none, the Gini would be equal to one (perfect inequality). Thus higher levels of the Gini are associated with more unequal distributions.

Associated with the Gini coefficient is the Lorenz curve. To find the Lorenz curve, one first sorts each individual in society by lowest to highest income. The population is then divided into equal parts (usually 10, which are called *deciles*). For each decile, the researcher finds the associated percent of total income. A graph with the cumulative population on the horizontal axis and the corresponding cumulative income on the vertical axis yields the Lorenz curve. If each individual or household had the same income, the bottom 10 percent would have 10 percent of the income and subsequent deciles of the population would have 10 percent of the income. In this case, the Lorenz curve would be the straight line from the origin with slope of one and is often called the *line of equality*. All societies have some curve that lies below the line of equality, because all societies have some income inequality.

The link between the Gini and the Lorenz curve is that the Gini represents the area above the Lorenz curve and below the line of equality. Note that researchers employ the Gini and the Lorenz curve for individuals, families, and households; the choice depends on the research question. Using these tools, researchers have found that the following results generally hold:[3]

1. The elderly are generally not as well off as the rest of the population.
2. The elderly have become relatively better off since about 1970 and, when assets are included, may have caught up to the rest of the population.
3. Social Security is likely an important part of the reason why the elderly have improved economic well-being.
4. Using measures of wealth and assets improves the absolute and relative standing of the elderly in the study of income distribution.
5. Income among the elderly is more unequally distributed than for other segments of the population.

INCOME MEASUREMENT AND THE 2007 PSID

Income Measurement

We employ the 2007 Panel Study of Income Dynamics (PSID) to investigate how the income of the elderly affects the overall income distribution for the United States. The 2007 PSID provides household and individual data on 8,829 households for 2006. We use household-level data for our analysis and the head of household information for age and gender comparisons.

Total household income is the sum of annual labor, private pension, public pension (Social Security), transfer income, and income from stocks, dividends, interest, business income, and other income not counted within the first four income components:[4]

- Labor income includes all job-related income from wages and salaries, overtime, tips, bonuses, commissions, income from private practice, and labor income associated with a self-owned business.
- Private pension income includes the current value all pension and annuity income. For retirees, it is the total dollar value received

through private pension sources in 2006. For nonretirees, pension income uses self-reported estimates of the current value of pensions and annuities if they were converted to cash.

- Social Security income includes all Social Security income for the year. Note that a household headed by someone younger than 65 can include Social Security income if the household includes any person receiving money from the program.
- Transfer income is comprised of any cash transferred to the household, including TANF (Temporary Assistance for Needy Families), food stamps (money value), Social Security disability (DI), child support and alimony, and financial aid from family members and others outside of the household unit.
- Other income includes income from stocks, bonds, dividends, interest, business income, less the associated labor income from the business and any other income not listed above.

Table 15.1 presents average total income and the average for each income component. The table also presents income by five age categories, beginning with the youngest to the oldest age group of 65 years of age or older.[5] The summary statistics indicate that average total income grows larger as household heads age, until age 65, where the average total income is less than that for all other age groups, except for those headed by individuals less than 25 years of age. A second feature of income is that labor income is a large share of total income for all age groups, except for the households headed by senior citizens. In that case, household income tends to be more evenly divided among the different income components. Note that the average value of private pensions is quite small (under $500) until the age group 45–54, indicating several possible scenarios since income can include retirement earnings at any age: either younger heads and their families fail to save for retirement in their early years, they work for firms where pensions are backloaded (i.e., defined benefit plans), or an elderly individual in the household provides some retirement income. In any case, the amount is small relative to other forms of household income.

The Measurement of Income Inequality

As noted earlier, one typical measure of income inequality is the Gini coefficient. This measurement permits us to investigate how each income component and population subgroup contributes to overall

Table 15.1
Average Total Household Income and Income Factors for All Households and by Age Groups

	All Households N = 8,289	Age <25 N = 623	Ages 25–34 N = 1,978	Ages 35–44 N = 1,646	Ages 45–54 N = 1,819	Ages 55–64 N = 1,117	Age 65+ N = 1,056
Total Income	$65,262.22	$25,910.84	$54,213.83	$74,206.67	$83,132.29	$84,356.36	$46,115.23
	(83705.39)	(21,308.50)	(48,571.02)	(77,869.46)	(122,196.40)	(94,878.72)	(54,587.91)
Labor	54,106.47	23,415.24	50,168.51	67,325.57	73,889.91	66,921.10	12,805.18
	(77,817.61)	(20,725.98)	(44,628.98)	(72,177.48)	(115,563.60)	(86,567.81)	(32,305.27)
	[82.91%]	[90.37%]	[92.54%]	[90.73%]	[88.88%]	[79.33%]	[27.77%]
Private Pensions	2,698.73	97.33	206.66	488.31	1,030.937	6,450.03	11,374.76
	(12,308.24)	(866.33)	(1,551.76)	(3,880.43)	(6,612.76)	(15,453.42)	(26,740.47)
	[4.14%]	[0.38%]	[0.38%]	[0.66%]	[1.24%]	[7.65%]	[24.67%]
Social Security	2,455.11	147.33	317.61	705.49	1,025.80	2,073.54	12,855.79
	(6,112.36)	(1,278.11)	(1,837.54)	(3,402.99)	(3589.78)	(6,162.90)	(8,780.30)
	[3.76%]	[0.57%]	[0.59%]	[0.95%]	[1.23%]	[3.2%]	[27.88%]
Transfer Income	4,506.04	1,933.91	2,179.66	2,545.53	3,007.75	8,084.35	12,354.57
	(13,187.00)	(4,208.34)	(5,593.58)	(6,340.75)	(8,626.89)	(16,511.07)	(26,751.66)
	[6.90%]	[7.46%]	[4.02%]	[3.43%]	[3.62%]	[9.58%]	[26.79%]
All Other Income	3,742.25	409.33	1,553.18	3,677.04	5,229.409	5,652.30	5,486.33
	(20,874.56)	(3,124.11)	(11,397.60)	(22,810.40)	(28,495.94)	(22,118.13)	(20,461.30)
	[5.73%]	[1.58%]	[2.86%]	[4.96%]	[6.29%]	[6.70%]	[11.9%]

Data Source: 2006 Panel Study of Income Dynamics. Standard deviations are in parentheses; share of total income is in brackets. Due to rounding, the shares may not total to 100 percent of income.

income inequality. We begin with an estimate of the overall income inequality and decompose the measurement by age categories.

To investigate the impact of groups on the overall income distribution, the usual decomposition is:

$$G = G_b + \sum a_k G_k + R \tag{1}$$

where G is the overall Gini coefficient. G_b is a measurement of between group inequality, defined as the inequality that would exist "if every income in every subgroup were to be replaced by the relevant subgroup means" (Lambert and Aronson 1993). The second term is a measure of how much within-group inequality affects the overall income distribution, where a_k is the product of population share and income share of subgroup k and G_k is subgroup k's estimated Gini coefficient. R represents correlation among income groups in relation to the total distribution; Lambert and Aronson (1993) call R an overlapping effect, where some members of group i have higher incomes than group j, but on the whole group i's average income is lower than that of group j.

Table 15.2, column 1 presents the results of this estimation. For all households, the Gini coefficient is 0.473, an estimate in line with other studies using data for the same period.[6] Inequality is lower for the households headed by those aged 25–34 (0.404) or less than 25 years (0.410). Inequality is substantially higher for households headed by the elderly (0.487) and by those aged 45–54 (0.473). The results indicate that the relatively large within-group inequality for these latter two age groups is a contributing factor to overall income inequality in the United States.

Estimated Lorenz curves for each of the age categories are presented in Figure 15.1. The curves demonstrate that the large inequality of households headed by the elderly (the solid black line) compared to other age groups is due to relatively smaller shares of cumulative income going to those in the 30th to 90th percentile, with a relatively high level of income going to the households in the richest decile (the sharp increase in the slope at the 90th decile).

Why the larger within-group inequality for the elderly? It is likely those over the age of 65 have more income inequality because those who have substantial wealth are few, and the many have relatively low income because as they retire, they lose the primary component of household income, that is, labor income.

Table 15.2
Decomposition of Household Income Impact of Factor Shares by Age Group

	Gini Coefficient (1)	Labor Income (2)	Pension Income (3)	Social Security Income (4)	Transfer Income (5)	All Other Income (6)
All Households	**0.4733** (0.462, 0.485)	**0.050** (0.041, 0.061)	**-0.011** (-0.014, -0.007)	**-0.043** (-0.045, -0.040)	**-0.040** (-0.042, -0.036)	**0.030** (0.462, 0.486)
Age <25	**0.410** (0.393, 0.437)	**0.051** (0.022, 0.056)	-0.0001 (-0.002, 0.002)	**-0.005** (-0.009, -0.001)	**-0.049** (-0.060, -0.027)	**0.013** (0.001, 0.025)
Age 25–34	**0.404** (0.390, 0.417)	**0.024** (0.008, 0.039)	-0.0005 (-0.002, 0.008)	**-0.010** (-0.012, -0.007)	**-0.038** (-0.0459, -0.034)	**0.024** (0.015, 0.037)
Age 35–44	**0.432** (0.406, 0.446)	0.015 (-0.013, 0.030)	-0.003 (-0.005, 0.0002)	**-0.015** (-0.018, -0.012)	**-0.038** (-0.045, -0.032)	**0.035** (0.021, 0.059)
Age 45–54	**0.473** (0.432, 0.504)	**0.020** (0.0004, 0.035)	**-0.006** (-0.009, -0.003)	**-0.019** (-0.021, -0.014)	**-0.034** (-0.038, -0.029)	**0.031** (0.014, 0.052)
Age 55–64	**0.467** (0.438, 0.500)	**0.062** (0.046, 0.084)	**-0.032** (-0.042, -0.022)	**-0.044** (-0.053, -0.038)	**-0.049** (-0.061, -0.040)	**0.029** (0.019, 0.046)
Age 65+	**0.487** (0.468, 0.506)	**0.101** (0.066, 0.117)	0.009 (-0.014, 0.035)	**-0.170** (-0.086, -0.159)	-0.014 (-0.039, 0.014)	**0.058** (.039, 0.086)

Data Source: 2007 Panel Study of Income Dynamics. Standard errors from a bootstrap estimation process are used to create the 95 percent confidence internal estimates from this process are in parentheses. Statistically significant estimates are in bold.

Figure 15.1
Income Distribution by Age Category.

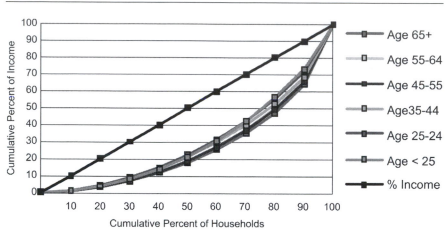

We next investigate the impact of income component shares for the entire sample and then by age categories. Because this decomposition considers different shares of income and not subpopulations, the method requires a different model. López-Feldman (2006) provides a decomposition model by income factor:[7]

$$G = \sum_{k=1}^{k} S_k G_k R_k$$

where the overall Gini coefficient is an additive function of the income share of component k (S_k), the estimated inequality of component k (G_k), and the Gini correlation of component k with the distribution of total income. The advantage of this estimation method is that one can estimate the effect on total income inequality of a 1 percent change in income component k.[8]

The impact of income component shares is presented in Table 15.2. Statistically significant estimates are in bold; 95 percent confidence intervals are in parentheses. Confidence intervals indicate to the reader how important the impact from a component is from a statistical point of view. If the estimated impact is positive and the confidence interval contains upper and lower values that are both positive, then the impact is statistically important. Likewise, if the estimated impact is negative and the confidence interval contains upper and lower values that are both negative, the impact is again statistically important.

In other words, "good" confidence intervals in the table do not contain zero as a possible value.

The results indicate that labor income, which represents the largest source of income for all groups (noted in Table 15.1), typically has a positive effect on income inequality. For example, a 1 percent increase in labor income increases the Gini coefficient by 5 percent. The labor income effect is negligible for the 35–44 age group and is highest for the households headed by a senior citizen (10.1%), suggesting that the relatively large income inequality for the elderly arises from differences between those who work and those who do not.

The other income component that increases income inequality is the Other Income category. Recall, this category includes income primarily from investment and business and comprises a relatively small percentage of total income for households, although its share grows with age (see Table 15.1). For the elderly-headed households, a 1 percent increase in this factor increases total income inequality by 5.8 percent.

The other income components are equalizing, although private pension income does little to affect income inequality. Only those households headed by individuals in the 45–54 or 55–64 age groups have a statistically significant effect in relation to private pensions; interestingly, private pensions have no impact on income inequality for households headed by those aged 65 or older. On the other hand, Social Security and transfer income have statistically significant effects for all age groups in the dataset. For the younger age groups, it appears that Social Security income has a small equalizing impact from household members who do not head the household but who receive Social Security payments. For the elderly, a 1 percent increase in Social Security income lowers total income inequality by 17 percent, clearly the largest effect in Table 15.2 for any income factor. A 1 percent increase in transfer income also reduces total income inequality for the elderly by 1.4 percent. Transfer income has a larger effect on the other age groups, lowering total income inequality from 3.4 to 4.9 percent.

Social Security and transfer income could be especially important for elderly women. Even though the labor force participation rate for women has grown substantially over the past 50 years, many of the women over the age of 65 spent their working years during a time when societal expectations required women in this age group to leave the labor force when children arrived in the home. This group of women has been shown to depend on Social Security and transfer income in other studies (Root and Tropman 1984), most likely due to lower lifetime earnings, shorter lifetime work experience, and longer lives compared to males.

Table 15.3 presents the average total income and decomposition by income factor for the oldest age category and by gender. The results indicate that within-group inequality is lower for both males and females compared to the overall inequality for the group, suggesting that the between-group inequality between households headed by elderly men and those headed by women is a factor in raising the overall inequality for this age category. In other words, the fact that households headed by elderly males have higher incomes than those headed by elderly females explains in part the greater income inequality for the elderly compared to other groups. This result is due to two factors. First, male-headed households often include spouses; in our sample, 79.5 percent of the male heads of household are married and married male heads have more than double the income of single female heads. Second, single male-headed households also have larger total income than those households headed by females.

Additionally, Social Security income lowers within group inequality for both males and females at about the same level (19.3% for males, 20.1% for females). What is new is that income inequality for females is positively affected by private pension income. A 1 percent increase in private pension income increases the total income inequality for elderly women by 5 percent, suggesting that those women who either had a job with retirement income or had a husband with survival spouse benefits tend to do better than those households headed by elderly women without private pensions. This is in line with what we would expect in terms of annual total income because private pensions are most likely to be earned by those in the upper half of the income distribution (Benedict and Shaw 1995). Another interesting effect for each subgroup is that transfer income does not have an impact on within group income inequality, although it does reduce overall income inequality for the elderly. In summary, it appears as though Social Security income is especially important in reducing income inequality for both elderly males and females, while labor income and the income category that captures investment raise income inequality.

CONCLUSION

In this chapter, we have examined the effect of pensions on income inequality generally, and for the elderly specifically, by using data from the 2007 Panel Study of Income Dynamics. We find that the elderly are

Table 15.3
Decomposition of Household Income Impact of Factor Shares for the Elderly by Gender

	Age 65+ N = 1,056	Males N = 610	Married N = 485	Single N = 125	Female N = 446
Total Income	$46,115.23 (54,587.91)	$60,968.54 (63,111.45)	$68,269.08 (66,887.76)	$32,642.47 (32889.41)	$25,800.17 (29,959.01)
Gini Coefficient	**0.487** (0.468, 0.506)	**0.437** (0.352, 0.459)			**0.449** (0.406, 0.491)
Labor Income	**0.101** (0.066, 0.117)	**0.114** (0.074, 0.144)			**0.087** (0.054, 0.129)
Pension Income	0.009 (−0.014, 0.035)	−0.010 (−0.052, 0.21)			**0.050** (0.0004, 0.113)
Social Security Income	**−0.170** (−0.086, −0.159)	**−0.193** (−0.214, −0.174)			**−0.201** (−0.226, −0.172)
Transfer Income	**−0.014** (−0.039, 0.014)	−0.022 (−0.064, 0.012)			0.001 (−0.058, 0.056)
All Other Income	**0.058** (.039, 0.086)	**0.075** (0.049, 0.113)			**0.086** (0.027, 0.135)

Data Source: 2007 Panel Study of Income Dynamics. Standard errors from a bootstrap estimation process are used to create the 95 percent confidence internal estimates from this process are in parentheses. Statistically significant estimates are in bold.

less well-off than the nonelderly. Further, there is greater income inequality among the elderly than for any other age group. Despite the relatively large income inequality for this age group, Social Security and transfer income act to make the income of the elderly more equal. Additional decomposition on the elderly income indicates that elderly women have a less equal distribution of income than elderly males, and that for both, only Social Security income acts to reduce the inequality.

What do the results imply about pension policy in the United States? Today there is a growing debate about the future of the Social Security program, with some congressional representatives and senators asking for increased retirement eligibility ages and reduced benefits. In response to a Senate request on the subject, the Government Accountability Office (GAO) recently provided a report on the topic. The GAO estimates that by 2050, the percentage of persons over the age of 65 will grow to 20 percent of the population, up from 13 percent in 2000, and thus the concern for solvency is legitimate (GAO 2010). However, in the same report, the agency argues that raising the retirement age or reducing benefits will improve the solvency of the program by delaying retirement for seniors, but such changes will also have serious negative consequences on that same population and may not reduce overall federal aid to the elderly. Elderly workers with disabilities may increase demand for other programs if too young to retire and collect traditional Social Security benefits. Thus higher demand for Social Security Disability (DI) or Supplemental Security Income (SSI) may erode any financial gains from changes to the Social Security program. Further, those who retire early are typically individuals with health problems. They already receive a reduced benefit from early retirement, lost wage income due to the inability to work, and higher medical costs. In sum, changing the public pension system so that older workers have smaller benefits will ultimately create larger income inequality for the elderly. The GAO suggests alternative policies to keep the program solvent, such as using tax policy to encourage employers to retain older workers or to provide older workers with incentives to stay working.

The Social Security Administration provides estimates of some possible changes that are needed to make the program sustainable. It seems likely that with some combination of lifting the limit on taxable income, raising the tax rate, reducing the cost-of-living adjustments, and increasing the retirement age, the system can be made sustainable (Social Security Administration 2011). Each of these has costs for the individuals, but to do nothing and fund the program solely by contributions once the trust fund is exhausted would reduce projected benefits to 75 percent of the current estimates (Proposals Addressing Trust Fund Solvency). In any case, the equity issues of any change are a substantial part of the decision process.

Our results also indicate that private pension income has a small equalizing effect for the sample data, but no effect on income inequality for elderly men and a positive effect on inequality for elderly women. As noted earlier, previous research indicates that annual pension benefits increase income inequality (Benedict and Shaw 1995). Further, defined contribution plans in particular may have a small positive effect on income inequality if those with wealth find the tax deferment advantages of such programs beneficial (those with wealth tend to use such plans to reduce lifetime income taxes), while those with small incomes find it difficult to add to such savings. In our sample, about 58 percent of the heads of household who were elderly had a pension, and those who did tended to have higher income in the other categories. In the end, it may be that private pensions contribute little or nothing to the overall income equality of the elderly in the United States, thus placing more pressure on government public pension and transfer programs to ensure that our elderly at least retain their relative standing in the income distribution.

NOTES

1.   Both authors are professors in the Economics Department of Bowling Green State University (BGSU). Mary Ellen Benedict has won awards for her teaching, research, and service, most recently being named Distinguished Teaching Professor at BGSU in 2010. John Hoag has also garnered numerous awards for his work as department chair and university professor, being awarded the Faculty Senate Distinguished Service Award in 2003 and the BGSU Chair/Leadership Award in 2009. Dr. Hoag recently retired from his position as chair of the Economics Department; Dr. Benedict has taken over the position.

2.   The Department of Health and Human Services reports that the poverty guideline for a one-person family is $10,890 and for a two-person family is $14,710 (Department of Health and Human Services, 2011). The average retiree Social Security annual benefit would be $14,124.

3.   See Wolff and Zacharias (2009a) and Duncan and Smith (1989) for a review of the literature.

4.   Other researchers have used alternative income measures, particularly net wealth, where the present value of housing and other assets are included. Given today's general decline of housing values and volatility of the value of other assets, we avoid making incorrect assumptions about asset growth and focus on money income in 2006.

5. Note that the PSID provides sample weights for each annual wave of data. Although we first employed the weights, we found that our estimates for income inequality were higher than the usual values reported by others (e.g., using the 2006 Current Population Survey data). Unweighted data provided estimates in line with other studies using 2006 income values and so we present all statistics without making use of the sample weights. We use bootstrapped standard errors to provide an asymptotically efficient measure of variability. Results with weighted data are available from the authors.

6. For example, using the 2006 American Community Survey data, Webster and Bishaw (2007) estimate the 2006 U.S. Gini coefficient to be 0.464.

7. López-Feldman follows earlier work by Lerman and Yitzhaki (1985) to develop his estimator.

8. The marginal effect is estimated as: $\dfrac{S_k G_k R_k}{G} - S_k$.

BIBLIOGRAPHY

Benedict, Mary Ellen. "Pensions and the Implicit Contract Theory." PhD dissertation, School of Urban and Public Affairs, Carnegie Mellon University, 1991.

Benedict, Mary Ellen and Kathryn Shaw. "The Impact of Pension Benefits on the Distribution of Earned Income." *Industrial and Labor Relations Review* 48 (1995): 740–57.

Butrica, Barbara A., Howard M. Iams, Karen E. Smith, and Eric J. Toder. "The Disappearing Defined Benefit Pension and Its Potential Impact on the Retirement Incomes of Boomers." Discussion Paper 09-01, The Urban Institute, Washington, DC, 2009.

Cawthorne, Alexander. "Elderly Poverty: The Challenge Before Us," Center for American Progress, July 2008, accessed June 27, 2011, http//www.americanprogress.org/issues/2008/07/elderly_poverty.html.

Clark, Robert, Lee A. Craig, and Jack W. Wilson. *A History of Public Sector Pensions in the United States*. Philadelphia, University of Pennsylvania Press, 2003.

Department of Health and Human Services, Poverty Guidelines, accessed June 30, 2011, http://aspe.hhs.gov/poverty/11fedreg.shtml.

Duncan, Greg J. and Ken R. Smith. "The Rising Affluence of the Elderly: How Far, How Fair, and How Frail?" *Annual Review of Sociology* 15 (1989): 261–89.

Employee Retirement Income Security Act. 1974. P.L. 93-406, 88 Stat. 829.

Gleckman, Howard, "Social Security: Fixing It Isn't That Hard," *Christian Science Monitor Online*, June 11, 2011, accessed June 27, 2011, http://www.csmonitor.com/Business/TaxVOX/2011/0621/Social Security fixing it isn't hard.

Goss, Stephen C. 2011. "Estimated Financial Effects of a Proposal to Restore 75-Year Solvency for the Social Security Program Requested by Senator Kay Bailey Hutchison," Social Security Administration, accessed June 27, 2011, http://www.ssa.gov/OACT/solvency/index.html.

Government Accountability Office. "Social Security Reform: Raising the Retirement Ages Would Have Implications for Older Workers and SSA Disability Rolls." GAO-11-125, 2010.

"Historical Background and Development of Social Security," accessed June 27, 2011, http://www.ssa.gov/history/briefhistory.3html.

Kotlikoff, Laurence J. and David A. Wise. *The Wage Carrot and the Pension Stick: Retirement Benefits and Labor Force Participation*. Kalamazoo: W. E. Upjohn Institute for Employment Research, 1989.

Lambert, Peter J. and J. Richard Aronson. "Inequality Decomposition Analysis and the Gini Coefficient Revisited." *The Economic Journal* 103 (1993): 1221–27.

Lerman, Robert I. and Shlomo Yitzhaki. "Income Inequality Effects by Income Source: A New Approach and Applications to the United States." *Review of Economics and Statistics* 67 (1985): 151–56.

López-Feldman, Alejandro. "Decomposing Inequality and Obtaining Marginal Effects." *The Stata Journal* 6 (2006): 106–11.

Munnell, Alicia. "The Outlook for Social Security in the Wake of the 1983 Amendments," in *The Economics of Aging*, ed. Myron H. Ross. Kalamazoo: W. E. Upjohn Institute for Employment Research, 1985.

Omnibus Reconciliation Act of 1990. H.R. 5835, 101st Congress, Public Law 101-508.

Pension Protection Act of 2006. H.R. 4, 109th Congress, Public Law 109-280.

Proposals Addressing Trust Fund Solvency, Social Security Administration, http://www.ssa.gov/OACT/solvency/index.html.

Revenue Act of 1978. 1979. H.R. 13511, 95th Congress, Public Law 95-600.

Root, Lawrence and John E. Tropman. "Income Sources of the Elderly." *The Social Service Review* 58 (1984): 384–403.

Social Security Online. 2010. Estimated Financial Effects of a Proposal to Restore 75-Year Solvency for the Social Security Program Requested by Senator Kay Bailey Hutchinson, accessed June 9, 2011, http://www.socialsecurity.gov/OACT/solvency/index.html

Social Security Online. 2011. Frequently Asked Questions, accessed June 30, 2011, http://ssa-custhelp.ssa.gov/app/answers/detail/a_id/13/~/average-monthly-social-security-benefit-for-a-retired-worker,

Tax Reform Act of 1976. 1976. H.R. 10612, 94th Congress, Public Law 94-455.

Tax Reform Act of 1986. 1987. H.W. 3838, 99th Congress, Public Law 99-514.

Turner, John A. and Daniel J. Beller, eds. *Trends in Pensions*. U.S. Department of Labor, Pension and Welfare Benefits Administration, 1989.

Warshawsky, Mark J. "The Institutional and Regulatory Environment of Private Defined Benefit Pension Plans" in *Trends in Pensions* (U.S. Department of Labor, Pension and Welfare Benefits Administration, 1989): 187–210.

Webster, Bruce H., Jr. and Alemayehu Bishaw. "Income, Earnings, and Poverty Data from the 2006 American Community Survey." U.S. Census Bureau, American Community Survey Reports, ACS-08, U.S. Government Printing Office, Washington, DC, 2007.

Williamson, Samuel. "U.S. and Canadian Pensions before 1930: A Historical Perspective," in *Trends in Pensions 1992*, eds. John Turner and Daniel Beller (U.S. Government Printing Office, Washington DC, 1992): 34–45.

Wolff, Edward and Ajit Zacharias. "Household Wealth and the Measurement of Economic Well-Being in the United States." *Journal of Economic Inequality*, 7 (2009a): 83–115.

Wolff, Edward and Ajit Zacharias. "A New Look at the Economic Well-Being of the Elderly in the United States, 1989–2001." *Journal of Income Distribution*, 18 (2009b): 146–79.

Chapter 16

What We Know about Discriminatory Differentials in Labor Market Outcomes

Matt Parrett

This chapter reviews the current learning with respect to discriminatory differentials in labor market outcomes, with a primary focus on earnings. Discriminatory differentials by race,[1] gender, and physical appearance are covered.

INTRODUCTION

The existence of raw earnings differences between different demographic groups in the United States is well established.[2] For example, in 2009, blacks who were full-time wage and salary workers had median weekly earnings of approximately 80 percent of the median weekly earnings of white full-time wage and salary workers (U.S. Department of Labor 2010). Looking across gender reveals a similar finding—women who were full-time wage and salary workers had median weekly earnings in 2009 of roughly 80 percent of the median weekly earnings of male full-time wage and salary workers (U.S. Department of Labor 2010).

On one hand, these earnings differences might reflect what are referred to as premarket differences. For example, it could be that they are the result of differences in productivity, which is typically proxied using a variety of human capital measures (e.g., years of schooling, job experience). That is to say, whites and males might earn more than blacks and females, respectively, because they have more years of schooling and more job experience. Such earnings differences could also reflect differences in occupational choice. For example, it might be that whites and males choose to enter into higher-paying occupations than blacks and females, respectively.[3]

Alternatively, these earnings differences could be the result of discrimination. Discrimination is said to exist if there are unexplained differences in earnings between people with the same premarket characteristics. For example, Hannah, a white female, and Jack, a white male, work as medical doctors in the same family medicine practice in Chicago. Hannah and Jack have equal levels of human capital (same medical school, same internship and residency, same number of years of experience, same number of years on the current job) and are equally productive in that they see the same number of patients per week. However, Jack is paid a higher salary than Hannah, which suggests discrimination.

SOURCES OF DISCRIMINATION

There are three principal sources of discrimination in the labor market—employers, customers, and coworkers (Becker 1971). Employer discrimination occurs when *employers* are prejudiced against certain groups and act on these prejudices. Such preferences might result solely from the employer's own tastes and preferences or, referring to the identity economics literature, might instead reflect social codes that tell people how they are supposed to think of themselves and how they are supposed to interact with others (Akerlof and Kranton 2010). For example, Auto Shop Owner X, who is white, pays his white mechanics more than his equally productive black mechanics. Customer discrimination occurs when *customers* are prejudiced against certain groups and act on these prejudices. For example, most of the customers of Retail Store X, which is located in a predominantly white suburb, prefer to interact with white salespeople, thus rendering white salespeople more productive in a sense than black salespeople. Based on this productivity difference, Retail Store X will pay its white salespeople more than its black salespeople, even though Retail Store X per se may not hold any prejudices. Finally, coworker discrimination occurs when *coworkers* are prejudiced against certain groups and act on these prejudices. For example, Large Factory X, which is located in a mostly white area, employs a large number of white workers who are uncomfortable working alongside their equally productive black colleagues. Thus Large Factory X, which has to employ at least some white workers due to the limited supply of nonwhite labor, pays its white workers a wage premium to keep them, even though Large Factory X per se may not hold any prejudices. The result is that Large Factory X's white workers earn more than the factory's equally productive black workers. Economic theory suggests that only employer and coworker discrimination can be eliminated by market forces (Kahn 1991), and even then, some type of government intervention would probably be necessary.

Another common source of labor market discrimination is statistical discrimination. Statistical discrimination occurs when employers judge members of a particular group based on the characteristics of the group itself. For example, Billing Department X pays college graduates more than high school graduates because college graduates are more productive, on average, than high school graduates. However, according to Darity and Mason (1998), statistical discrimination cannot persist because if average group differences are merely perceived and not real, then employers should over time learn that their beliefs are in error. On the other hand, the authors say that if average group differences are indeed real, then in a world with antidiscrimination laws employers are likely to find ways to predict the future performance of potential employees with sufficient accuracy without having to rely on group membership.

MEASURING LABOR MARKET DISCRIMINATION: THE REGRESSION APPROACH

As stated earlier, discrimination is said to exist if there are unexplained differences in earnings between people with the same premarket characteristics. To make such comparisons using real-world data, researchers often rely on a statistical procedure known as regression analysis. Regression analysis allows the researcher to test for a statistical relationship between an outcome measure (e.g., earnings) and a group membership indicator (e.g., white, black) while holding constant variables that measure various premarket attributes.[4] A statistically significant group membership indicator suggests discrimination, as it indicates black-white earnings differences due solely to race.[5]

A potential issue with the regression approach is that unobserved, and therefore not controlled for, differences between demographic groups might be driving observed earnings differences between the groups. For example, if the quality of schooling received by whites systematically exceeds the quality of schooling received by blacks, then a study using the regression approach that does not control for school quality will overstate the presence of discrimination.[6] As another example, consider a researcher using the regression approach to study beauty discrimination. The researcher finds a statistically significant, positive coefficient on the beauty variable, implying that more attractive people earn more than less attractive people; however, the interpretation is not as straightforward as one might think. The result might reflect discrimination on one hand, but on the other hand it might be that beauty is a proxy for other productive factors that are not easily measured and therefore not captured by the data, such as self-motivation and discipline.[7] Even if the latter can be ruled out, the researcher may have a difficult time identifying the type of discrimination.

These kinds of ambiguities are ubiquitous throughout the regression literature on discrimination. Looking first at the regression literature on racial discrimination, the extent to which the black-white raw earnings differential is attributable to discrimination versus premarket differences between blacks and whites has been widely studied. Regarding the former camp, Darity and Mason (1998), in a fairly extensive review of this literature, conclude that a standard result is that a significant portion of the earnings gap between black and white males in the United States cannot be explained by variables included to control for premarket differences between members of the two racial groups.[8] This result, which suggests discrimination, is corroborated, they say, by studies that examine the effect of within-race skin shade on earnings. The benefit of such an approach is that it minimizes the effect that unobserved differences can have on the findings. According to Darity and Mason (1998), such studies provide evidence that lighter-complexioned blacks tend to have superior incomes than darker-skinned blacks in the United States. A recent study by Goldsmith et al. (2007) further confirms this, finding that the wage difference between white workers and medium or dark-skinned blacks are considerably larger than in comparison to their lighter-skinned counterparts and that, among blacks, lightness is rewarded in the labor market. Anchoring the other camp, Neal and Johnson (1996) argue that controlling for a single measure of skill (Armed Forces Qualification Test), something that is not observable in most datasets, explains all of the black-white wage gap for young women and much of the gap for young men. The authors conclude that the black-white wage gap primarily reflects a skill gap, which in turn can be partly attributed to observable differences in family backgrounds between whites and blacks. This sentiment, which is vigorously refuted by Darity and Mason (1998), is strongly echoed by Heckman (1998) and reinforced by more recent studies by Carneiro et al. (2005), O'Neill and O'Neill (2005), and O'Neill et al. (2006).[9]

Looking next at the regression literature on gender discrimination, Blau and Kahn (2007), using two, nationally representative datasets, the Current Population Survey (CPS) and the Panel Study of Income Dynamics (PSID), find that after controlling in regression analyses for human capital, race, industry, and occupation, an unexplained gender wage gap of 9 to 17 percent remains.[10] The authors say that this unexplained gap might overstate discrimination if omitted factors such as working conditions or motivation are at play, but could understate discrimination in the presence of occupational segregation. Regarding the latter, Blau and Kahn (2007), because they include controls for occupation and industry, are essentially examining gender differences in earnings across males and females in the same occupation and industry. However, it might be that women are steered, because of discrimination, into lower-paying occupations and industries, so that looking at male-female earnings differences within occupation and industry understates the degree to which women are being discriminated against. Evidence of occupational segregation comes from looking at the Index of Dissimilarity, which is defined mathematically as follows:

$$\text{Index of Dissimilarity} = \frac{1}{2}\sum_{j=1}^{j}\left|P_j^M - P_j^W\right|$$

where P_j^M and P_j^W measure, respectively, the percentage of men and women in occupational category j. The Index value indicates the percentage of men, women, or a combination of the two that needs to shift occupations in order for the two genders to have equal occupational distributions and ranges from 0 to 100. A value of 0 means equal occupational representation by gender, whereas a value of 100 implies complete occupational segregation by gender. For example, computing the Index for two occupations, Occupation 1, in which 80 percent of males and 40 percent of females work, and Occupation 2, in which 20 percent of males and 60 percent of females work, yields the following value:

$$\text{Index of Dissimilarity} = \frac{1}{2}[|80 - 40| + |20 - 60|] = 40$$

This means that 40 percent of men, women, or a combination of percentages that adds up to 40 must shift occupations for males and females to have equal occupational distributions in this case. For example, if 20 percent of men switch from Occupation 1 to Occupation 2 and 20 percent of women switch from Occupation 2 to Occupation 1, then the Index value becomes 0:

$$\text{Index of Dissimilarity} = \frac{1}{2}[|60 - 60| + |40 - 40|] = 0$$

According to Blau and Kahn (2000), after remaining at roughly two-thirds for each Census year since 1900, the Index of Dissimilarity fell from 67.7 in 1970 to 59.3 in 1980 and 52.0 in 1990. Recent estimates by Gabriel and Schmitz (2007) indicate a 2001 index value of 31.1. The main cause of these reductions is the movement of women into predominately male jobs (Blau and Kahn 2000). The extent to which occupational segregation is due to gender differences in preferences versus discrimination remains largely unanswered (Blau and Kahn 2000).

Consider, lastly, the regression literature on physical appearance discrimination. Anchoring this literature is the seminal piece by Hamermesh and Biddle (1994), which uses data from two broad household surveys for the United States and Canada. In all three surveys, the interviewer was asked to rate or categorize the survey respondent's physical appearance on a five-point scale (1 = Strikingly Beautiful or Handsome, 2 = Above Average for Age [Good Looking], 3 = Average for Age, 4 = Below Average for Age [Quite Plain], 5 = Homely). The authors combine categories "1" and "2" and call it "Above-Average" and combine categories "4" and "5" and call it "Below-Average," with category "3" remaining "Average." Hamermesh and Biddle (1994) find that there is a 7 to 9 percent earnings penalty for being below-average looking and a 5 percent earnings premium for being above-average looking. Looking across gender, the 9 percent penalty and 5 percent premium for men are at least as great as the 5 percent penalty and 4 percent premium for women. The likely culprit, according to the authors, is either employer or coworker discrimination. However, the authors also find evidence, albeit weak, that the labor market sorts the best-looking people into occupations where their looks are productive, suggesting that customer discrimination might also play a role.

In sum, the consensus from the regression literature on racial discrimination seems to be that black males earn between 5 and 19 percent less than white males and that black females earn anywhere from 9 percent less to 7 percent more than white females, while the consensus from the regression literature on gender discrimination appears to be that females earn between 7 and 17 percent less than males.[11] Given the much smaller size of the physical-appearance discrimination regression literature, the Hamermesh and Biddle (1994) finding of a 7 to 9 percent earnings penalty for being below-average looking and a 5 percent earnings premium for being above-average looking acts as an appropriate consensus finding for beauty discrimination. Regarding height- and weight-based discrimination, Mitra (2001) finds no effect of height and weight on male earnings and no effect of weight on female earnings. Mitra (2001) does, however, find that an additional inch of height increases the earnings of female professionals and managers by roughly 2.5 percent.

MEASURING LABOR MARKET DISCRIMINATION USING OCCUPATION-SPECIFIC DATA

To deal with the ambiguities of the regression approach, researchers sometimes look at narrowly defined occupations, the benefits of which are threefold. First, controlling for productivity is often easier because either such data are readily available for the occupation in question or because focusing on a specific occupation makes it easier to identify an appropriate set of productivity proxies. Second, while for many occupations there are many actors (employers, customers, coworkers), for some occupations there is but a sole actor. For occupations that fall into the latter category, the matter of identifying the source of discrimination is straightforward. Finally, because members of a particular occupation are more similar than members of different occupations, focusing on a particular occupation should lessen (but will not completely eliminate) the effect of differences in unobserved or omitted factors across members.

One oft-studied occupation, for which detailed productivity data are available, is professional sports. For example, Kahn and Sherer

(1988) examine racial differences in 1985–86 salaries of individual professional basketball players and find that although white and black players earn similar mean compensation, white players have a higher conditional mean compensation. That is, the authors find that after controlling for productivity and other differences between players in a regression analysis, white players earn 20 percent more than black players, which suggests discrimination.[12] Kanazawa and Funk (2001) examine Nielsen ratings data for locally televised NBA games and find that even after controlling for a variety of factors that might impact ratings, viewership increases when there is greater participation by white players. Combining this with another finding by the authors that higher ratings generate more advertising revenue suggests that white players have a higher marginal revenue product than that of comparable black players. This, the authors say, can explain much of the race-based earnings gap that exists in professional basketball, such as the 20 percent differential found in Kahn and Sherer (1988).

Using unique survey data collected outside of five Virginia restaurants, and controlling for (subjective) server productivity, as well as a variety of other factors, Parrett (2011) compares the tip earnings of male and female servers and finds evidence of customer discrimination, but only among those customers who frequent the restaurant the least.[13] More specifically, Parrett (2011) finds that female servers earn comparable tips to male servers when the service quality they produce is exceptional (high quality), but for any lower service quality their tips are smaller, suggesting that female servers are being held to a very high standard and that if this standard is not met, they are treated unfavorably in comparison to male servers who produce the same level of service quality. Additionally, Parrett (2011) finds that it is male customers driving these results.

Finally, Biddle and Hamermesh (1998) study the effect of beauty on earnings using longitudinal data on a large sample of graduates from a highly selective law school they denote Law School X. Beauty for each graduate in the sample is measured by a panel of four persons, each of whom independently provides a rating of the graduate's matriculation photograph on a five-point scale similar to that used in Hamermesh and Biddle (1994). Because each entering law school class was rated by a different panel of four observers, each graduate's average beauty rating was standardized within the graduate's entering class.[14] Biddle and Hamermesh (1998) find that better-looking attorneys who graduated in the 1970s earned more than others after five years of practice, an effect that grew with experience. The authors rule out employer discrimination as a culprit based on an absence of larger returns to beauty among employed versus self-employed lawyers. That attorneys in the private sector are better looking than public sector attorneys, that attorneys switch between the public and private sectors based partly on looks, that the monetary return to beauty rises rapidly in the private versus public sector, and that men who are more attractive have a greater chance of making partner early all suggest, according to Biddle and Hamermesh (1998), that the likelier culprit is customer (client) discrimination.

THE AUDIT STUDY APPROACH TO MEASURING LABOR MARKET DISCRIMINATION

Another way of dealing with the ambiguities of the regression approach is to rely on audit studies. Audit studies typically focus not on discriminatory differentials in earnings but instead in hiring. In an audit study, employers with advertised job openings are approached by people from two different groups (e.g., male and female) posing as applicants. The applicants' work histories and resumés are constructed by the researcher so as to make it that the only difference between the applicants is their group affiliation. If members of one group are treated differently than members of the other group, like if female applicants receive fewer callbacks than male applicants, then discrimination is said to exist. Despite offering greater control over differences in premarket attributes between the groups being studied, audit study results, just like regression study results, can also be driven by unobserved differences between the groups, making drawing conclusions more difficult.

A survey of audit studies of racial discrimination by Darity and Mason (1998) reveals that relative to whites, blacks (1) are less likely to receive an interview, (2) are less likely to receive a job offer, conditional on receiving an interview, and (3) are offered less pay and are steered toward lower-level positions, conditional on receiving an offer. However, as alluded to previously, and as pointed out by Heckman (1998) and acknowledged by Darity and Mason (1998), audit study results could be getting driven by unobserved differences between the groups being studied, such as the ability to make a first impression. Hence the use of correspondence tests in which researchers send fictitious letters of inquiry or resumés from prospective "applicants" to employers whereby the letter or resumé signals the applicant's membership to a particular group. The letters and resumés are designed so as to demonstrate comparable credentials and skills across the members of the groups being studied. Like with the audit study approach, if members of one group are treated differently than members of the other group, for example if black applicants receive fewer callbacks than white applicants, then discrimination is said to exist. In a recent correspondence test study, Bertrand and Mullainathan (2004) send fictitious resumés to help-wanted ads in Boston and Chicago newspapers, whereby resumés are randomly assigned African American- or white-sounding names in order to manipulate perceived race. The authors find that relative to African American-sounding names, white-sounding names receive 50 percent more callbacks for interviews.

Neumark (1996) reports the results of an audit study of gender discrimination in which comparably matched pairs of males and females apply for jobs as waiters and waitresses at various Philadelphia restaurants. Neumark finds that for female applicants to high-priced restaurants, their probabilities of receiving an interview and an offer are approximately 35 and 40 percentage points lower than the probability of a male applicant receiving an interview and an offer, respectively.

THE EXPERIMENTAL APPROACH TO MEASURING LABOR MARKET DISCRIMINATION

A final way that the ambiguities of the regression approach have been addressed is through the use of the experimental approach. Roughly speaking, an experiment works as follows. There are two groups, the treatment and the control, the latter of which does not receive the treatment. Subjects are randomly assigned to one of the two groups, which ensures that differences in the outcome measure between the two groups are due solely to the treatment. For example, Mobius and Rosenblat (2006) examine the beauty wage gap using laboratory experiments in which "employers" determine wages of "workers" who perform a maze-solving task that is independent of beauty.[15] The authors find a sizable beauty premium, which they attribute to three things—more attractive workers are more confident, more attractive workers are considered more able by employers (controlling for confidence), and more attractive workers have better oral skills (controlling for confidence).

On the plus side, experiments provide the researcher with almost complete control over potential confounds. However, there are downsides to the experimental approach. One such downside is that due to their controlled nature, experiments often lack proper context. Another drawback to the experimental approach is that the subject pool almost always consists entirely of undergraduate students whose behavior may or may not generalize to the greater population. Such downsides, though, typically apply more to laboratory settings and less so to field settings, like the one examined by Goldin and Rouse (2000), who look at the impact of the adoption of blind auditions by symphony orchestras in which a screen is used to conceal the candidate's identity from those evaluating the candidate. Using data from actual auditions, the authors find that the screen increases the probability that a female will be advanced and hired.

CONCLUSION

Taken together, the findings from the discrimination literature strongly suggest the presence of discriminatory differentials in hiring and earnings based on race, gender, and physical appearance. This begs the question of what explains their existence. Standard economic theory suggests that because of market forces, employer, coworker, and statistical discrimination cannot persist. The implication, then, is either that the main culprit is customer discrimination or that market forces are somehow being impeded. Regarding the latter, it might be that employers do not profit maximize, which, according to Heckman (1998, 112), is sustainable, saying that "if a bigoted employer prefers whites, the employer can indulge that taste as long as income is received from entrepreneurial activity, just as a person who favors an exotic ice cream can indulge that preference by being willing to pay the price." However, regardless of source, the persistence of such differentials indicates a continued need for government involvement.

NOTES

1.   The focus here will be on black-white discriminatory differentials, as these are by far the most widely studied racial groups in the literature.
2.   Unfortunately, raw earnings data by physical appearance are not readily available.
3.   Of course, differences in productivity or occupational choice across demographic groups could reflect discrimination.

4. For example, running a regression analysis of earnings (dependent variable) on the independent variables race (black/white) and years of schooling allows the researcher to examine black-white differences in earnings holding constant years of schooling. That is, it allows the researcher to examine black-white differences in earnings across blacks and whites with the same number of years of schooling. Regression analyses are typically run via computer using statistical software such as STATA or Eviews. Microsoft Excel also has regression capabilities.

5. Sometimes researchers who use the regression approach apply what is known as the Blinder-Oaxaca decomposition procedure. This procedure, which involves running additional regression analyses, allows the researcher to sort out the extent to which earnings differences between two groups are due to (1) differences in premarket attributes between the two groups and (2) discrimination, and generally leads to the same conclusion originally reached using the regression approach (Darity and Mason 1998).

6. Continuing with the example in the fourth endnote, if school quality is unobserved in the dataset (and thus not included as an independent variable), positively related to earnings, and systematically differs between blacks and whites as described here, then school quality will not get held constant in examining black-white differences in earnings. Thus some of the observed difference in black-white earnings, even after holding years of schooling constant, will reflect black-white differences in school quality. This will result in an overestimate of the impact of race on earnings and thus an overestimate of discrimination.

7. Being beautiful takes work—exercise, diet, learning the various beauty tips, etc.

8. According to Neal (2004), much of the existing literature reveals that black-white wage gaps among working women remain quite small compared to the corresponding gaps among men and that black-white gaps in potential wages are much larger among men than women—hence the heavier focus in the black-white labor market discrimination literature on black and white males.

9. It should be noted that the black-white skill gap could itself be the result of discrimination.

10. O'Neill and O'Neill (2005) obtain similar results using nationally representative data.

11. These figures come from the studies cited here in this chapter.

12. Thus looking across equally productive white and black players (holding productivity constant), black players earn less than white players. Combining this with the fact that white and black players earn similar amounts in the raw data suggests that black players are more productive than white players. Thus, in the raw data, the increase in earnings blacks receive for being more productive is essentially offset by a decrease in black earnings due to discrimination.

13. Detecting discrimination is difficult. Even more difficult is detecting the source of discrimination. In this setting, it is easy to infer customer discrimination because the customer (other than the server) is the sole actor.

14. Each graduate i in entering class j receives four beauty ratings—B_{ij1}, B_{ij2}, B_{ij3}, B_{ij4}. To create a single beauty measure for each graduate i in entering class j: (1) for each entering class j, the mean (μ_j) and standard deviation (σ_j) across all beauty ratings for all graduates of entering class j was computed; (2) graduate i's beauty

ratings were standardized as follows: $b_{ij1} = [B_{ij1} - \mu_j] / \sigma_j$, $b_{ij2} = [B_{ij2} - \mu_j] / \sigma_j$, $b_{ij3} = [B_{ij3} - \mu_j] / \sigma_j$, $b_{ij4} = [B_{ij4} - \mu_j] / \sigma_j$; and (3) finally, graduate i's single beauty measure was computed as the average of b_{ij1}, b_{ij2}, b_{ij3}, and b_{ij4}.

15. Note that the experiments were conducted in Argentina.

BIBLIOGRAPHY

Akerlof, George, and Rachel Kranton. "Identity Economics." *The Economists' Voice* (June 2010): 1–3.

Becker, Gary. *The Economics of Discrimination*. Chicago: University of Chicago Press, 1971.

Bertrand, Marianne, and Sendhil Mullainathan. "Are Emily and Greg More Employable Than Lakisha and Jamal? A Field Experiment on Labor Market Discrimination." *American Economic Review* 94 (2004): 991–1013.

Biddle, Jeff, and Daniel Hamermesh. "Beauty, Productivity, and Discrimination: Lawyers' Looks and Lucre." *Journal of Labor Economics* 16 (1998): 172–201.

Blau, Francine, and Lawrence Kahn. "Gender Differences in Pay." *Journal of Economic Perspectives* 14 (2000): 75–99.

Blau, Francine, and Lawrence Kahn. "The Gender Pay Gap." *Economists' Voice* (June 2007): 1–6.

Carneiro, Pedro, James Heckman, and Dimitriy Masterov. "Labor Market Discrimination and Racial Differences in Premarket Factors." *Journal of Law and Economics* 48 (2005): 1–39.

Darity, William, Jr., and Patrick Mason. "Evidence on Discrimination in Employment: Codes of Color, Codes of Gender." *Journal of Economic Perspectives* 12 (1998): 63–90.

Gabriel, Paul, and Susanne Schmitz. "Gender Differences in Occupational Distributions among Workers." *Monthly Labor Review* (June 2007): 19–24.

Goldin, Claudia, and Cecilia Rouse. "Orchestrating Impartiality: The Impact of 'Blind' Auditions on Female Musicians." *American Economic Review* 90 (2000): 715–41.

Goldsmith, Arthur, Darrick Hamilton, and William Darity Jr. "From Dark to Light: Skin Color and Wages Among African-Americans." *Journal of Human Resources* 42 (2007): 701–38.

Hamermesh, Daniel, and Jeff Biddle. "Beauty and the Labor Market." *American Economic Review* 84 (1994): 1174–94.

Heckman, James. "Detecting Discrimination." *Journal of Economic Perspectives* 12 (1998): 101–16.

Kahn, Lawrence. "Customer Discrimination and Affirmative Action." *Economic Inquiry* 29 (1991): 555–71.

Kahn, Lawrence, and Peter Sherer. "Racial Differences in Professional Basketball Players' Compensation." *Journal of Labor Economics* 6 (1988): 40–61.

Kanazawa, Mark, and Jonas Funk. "Racial Discrimination in Professional Basketball: Evidence from Nielsen Ratings." *Economic Inquiry* 39 (2001): 599–608.

Mitra, Aparna. "Effects of Physical Attributes on the Wages of Males and Females." *Applied Economics Letters* 8 (2001): 731–35.

Mobius, Markus, and Tanya Rosenblat. "Why Beauty Matters." *American Economic Review* 96 (2006): 222–35.

Neal, Derek. "The Measured Black-White Wage Gap among Women Is Too Small." *Journal of Political Economy* 112 (2004): S1–S28.

Neal, Derek, and William Johnson. "The Role of Premarket Factors in Black-White Wage Differences." *Journal of Political Economy* 104 (1996): 869–95.

Neumark, David. "Sex Discrimination in Restaurant Hiring: An Audit Study." *Quarterly Journal of Economics* 111 (1996): 915–41.

O'Neill, Donal, Olive Sweetman, and Dirk van de Gaer. "The Impact of Cognitive Skills on the Distribution of the Black-White Wage Gap." *Labour Economics* 13 (2006): 343–56.

O'Neill, June, and Dave O'Neill. *What Do Wage Differentials Tell Us about Labor Market Discrimination?* National Bureau of Economic Research Working Paper 11240, Cambridge: National Bureau of Economic Research, 2005.

Parrett, Matthew. "Customer Discrimination in Restaurants: Dining Frequency Matters." *Journal of Labor Research* 32 (2011): 87–112.

U.S. Department of Labor. *Highlights of Women's Earnings in 2009*. Report Number 1025, Washington, DC: GPO, 2010.

Chapter 17

Housing Discrimination and Residential Segregation

Haydar Kurban

INTRODUCTION

Residential separation by race, ethnicity, and income is a persistent and prevalent fact of urban life in the United States (Massey and Denton 1993). Residential segregation imposes enormous costs on African American and Hispanic[1] communities by limiting their housing choices and increasing housing prices in the inner cities. The costs of renting and owning in the inner cities have become less affordable for lower-income inner-city residents (Quigley and Raphael 2004). When jobs started to move to the suburbs in the 1950s, white residents followed but African Americans were left in the inner cities. Exclusion from the white suburbs disconnected inner-city African Americans from the employment opportunities in the suburbs (Kain 1968).

Residential segregation is caused by many factors, including income and wealth differentials, historical and current government policies, active discrimination in the real estate market, and prejudice against African Americans and Hispanics (Schwab 1992). The range of residential choices available to African Americans and Hispanics continues to be constrained not only by the lower levels of income and wealth but also by a variety of discriminatory practices by real estate agents, landlords, and lenders (Yinger 1998).

Housing discrimination is defined as the differential treatment of housing market participants on the basis of their race and ethnicity (Yinger 1998). The differential treatment occurs in terms of difference in housing choices, prices, and contract terms offered to a minority individual and a white individual of similar income and family characteristics. Discrimination by location of housing, loan terms, and housing types offered affects the cost of housing. Differential treatment in mortgage markets increases the price of housing through higher interest rates. Similarly, inferior loan terms also increase housing prices because disproportionately more African American and Hispanic home owners receive subprime mortgage loans. Discrimination in housing markets has negative effects on housing market outcomes and labor market outcomes. It forces African American and, to a lesser degree, Hispanic households to settle for less desirable housing choices, away from their jobs, compared to the range of housing opportunities available to the white households of similar income and family characteristics.

The home ownership gap between whites, African Americans, and Hispanics had narrowed during the last economic expansion but widened again after the 2008 recession. From 2005 to 2010 white, African American, and Hispanic home ownership rates decreased from 72.7 percent to 71 percent, 48.2 percent to 45.4 percent, and 49.5 percent to 45.4 percent, respectively (U.S. Census Bureau 2010). The improvement in minority home ownership rate in the 1990s was temporary as it was mainly driven by the expansion of subprime loans (Gramlich 2007). African American and Hispanic home owners disproportionately received more subprime loans because either they did not qualify for 30-year-fixed-rate prime loans or they were steered toward the riskier subprime loans by lending institutions (Gramlich 2007).

While the incidence of discrimination against African American and Hispanic home buyers declined between 1989 and 2000, the incidence of discrimination for Hispanic renters increased. During the recent housing boom, despite its illegality, African American and Hispanic home seekers were still steered away from white neighborhoods (Turner, Freiberg et al. 2002). Housing discrimination studies document that African American and Hispanic home seekers face discrimination at various stages of the housing transaction. Consequently,

African Americans and Hispanics are more likely than whites with similar borrower characteristics to receive higher-cost mortgage loans, to lose their homes to foreclosure (Yinger 1995), and to be denied home mortgage loans (Munnel et al. 1996). Discriminatory barriers such as withholding information on available units impose considerable costs on African American and Hispanic home seekers (Yinger 1995). African Americans are far less likely than whites to become home owners and far more likely to live in the neighborhoods identified with inferior housing (Yinger 1998; Massey and Denton 1993). Since home equity is the largest source of wealth for most American families, these disparities in home ownership rates are the main cause of persistent racial wealth inequality (Shapiro and Oliver 1995; Quigley and Rafael 2004). Ultimately, this discrimination in the housing market has perpetuated black-white disparities in educational attainment, income, and even health.

A brief review of the government programs, laws, and regulations related to housing discrimination and residential segregation is presented in this chapter. The impacts of government programs, fair housing laws, and regulations are evaluated, based on whether they expand or limit housing choices. A government program that spatially expands housing choices reduces housing segregation. Similarly, any government program that limits housing choices increases housing segregation.

This chapter is organized as follows. The following section reviews concepts and terms and causes of housing discrimination. The third section covers discrimination in private housing markets. The fourth section covers the costs of housing discrimination on the victims as well as the overall economy. The fifth section reviews the past and present government programs and their impact on housing discrimination and residential segregation. The final section summarizes the conclusions of this chapter.

HOUSING DISCRIMINATION: CONCEPTS, TERMS, AND CAUSES

Housing discrimination comprises a wide array of discriminatory practices in housing markets. A brief discussion of the concepts and terms related to housing discrimination is presented in this section. Prejudice refers to aversion toward an individual member of a racial group regardless of the individual's attributes. Economic models describe prejudice as negative preference of an individual toward a certain group of people (Yinger 1976). Discrimination, by contrast, is a behavior that denies a particular group of people rights or opportunities given to others. Segregation is the physical separation of racial and ethnic groups.

Fair housing laws and regulations ban housing discrimination based on prohibited characteristics, including race, gender, religion, familial status, sexual orientation, and ethnicity (see http://www .hud.gov/fairhousing). With the amendment of fair housing laws, new prohibited characteristics have been added to expand legal protection against uncovered housing discrimination practices. Fair housing laws prohibit two forms of discrimination: disparate treatment and disparate impact (Yinger 1999). Disparate-treatment discrimination takes place when housing market agents use different standards to treat the home seekers of different racial or ethnic backgrounds. Disparate-treatment discrimination measures whether two individuals with similar financial abilities are offered similar housing choices by housing market agents. Disparate-impact discrimination arises when housing market agents apply the same rules for every market participant, but the rules may adversely impact households in certain racial or ethnic groups. Even if the actions of housing agents are not discriminatory in intent, they are discriminatory in outcome. Making housing unavailable to persons on the basis of income or poor credit history is not considered discriminatory. However, if the denial decision is based on the characteristics that are correlated with race, then disparate-impact discrimination occurs (Yinger 1998). For instance, if a lending institution did not finance older homes, the basis for denial would not be one of the classes protected by fair housing laws. Yet if in proportion more African Americans live in older houses, as a group they will be more negatively affected than white residents. Even if this action does not have discriminatory intent, the impact is discriminatory.

Housing discrimination has multiple causes (Yinger 1998). Discrimination in the housing market is in some cases driven by the housing market agent's prejudice and in other cases by the search for more profit through serving the prejudiced white customers. Empirical studies on the role of market agents' prejudice in housing discrimination have reached different conclusions. Yinger (1986) and Ondrich, Ross, and Yinger (1997) find no evidence to support the hypothesis that African American and Hispanic housing agents discriminate less than their white counterparts. On the other hand, Yinger (1995) concludes that African American and Hispanic customers experience less discrimination when they deal with African American and Hispanic housing agents. According to Yinger (1995), the likelihood of a particular housing unit to be reserved for white customers decreases by 25 percent if the housing agent is not white.

As summarized by Yinger (1998), housing discrimination studies point out that the incidence of discrimination is less prevalent in the neighborhoods that have a smaller share of African Americans and Hispanics. Since housing agents respond to the prejudices or preferences of white home owners, they tend to discriminate more in integrated neighborhoods when the African American or Hispanic population share gets closer to the tipping point[2] than in overwhelmingly white neighborhoods. The incidence of discrimination increases with the rise in African American or Hispanic population share in the white neighborhoods. However, once the tipping point is reached, white home owners start to move out and the housing agents have less incentive to discriminate.

Another type of housing discrimination arises when housing market agents give higher priorities to the transactions that are more likely to be completed (Yinger 1998). Housing audit studies find that housing agents perceive that housing transactions involving white customers are more likely to be completed and thus more profitable (Yinger 1995). When housing agents use race or ethnicity to predict the odds of a housing transaction being successfully finalized, their decisions are based on the characteristics of the group, not those of the applicant. The use of average group characteristics rather than personal characteristics in evaluation of individual applications is considered as statistical discrimination (Arrow 1972; Phelps 1972).

PRIVATE DISCRIMINATION AND RESIDENTIAL SEGREGATION

Housing discrimination practiced by white residents, real estate agents, and lending institutions constitutes the most important cause of persistent residential segregation in the U.S. urban areas (Yinger 1995; Massey and Denton 1993). Schwab (1992) identifies four causes of residential segregation: social and economic status, ethnicity, active discrimination against certain racial groups, and avoiding particular racial groups due to prejudice. Segregation by social and economic class and segregation by ethnicity and race are considered voluntary when residents avoid the neighborhoods in which their ethnic or racial group loses the majority status. A careful review of the literature by Massey and Denton (1993) indicates that active discrimination against African Americans and Hispanics is the main cause of residential segregation.

Earlier discrimination models had divergent predictions for racial residential segregation. Some models (Schelling 1972; Courant 1978) showed that household preferences for neighborhood racial/ethnic composition or proximity to other races/ethnic groups (Yinger 1976) may give rise to complete segregation. If whites have a stronger preference than African Americans or Hispanics to reside among white residents, complete segregation may emerge as the only long-run equilibrium (Courant 1978). Some economic models viewed residential segregation as a temporary disequilibrium in housing markets (Muth 1969; Becker 1957). These models predicted that as long as all whites do not have prejudice, racial segregation breaks down. Discrimination driven primarily by prejudice is viewed as unprofitable. The willingness of some whites to live in the integrated neighborhoods creates profit opportunities for unprejudiced housing agents. Through competition, unprejudiced housing agents are expected to drive the discriminating ones out of business. However, the persistent pattern of residential segregation in U.S. urban areas indicates that racial segregation is anything but an unsustainable short-term disequilibrium phenomenon of urban housing market. The implicit collusion between white buyers and housing markets agents erects discriminatory barriers to exclude African Americans and Hispanics from white neighborhoods. For instance, withholding information (an important discriminatory barrier) about available housing units in white neighborhoods severely restricts the housing choices of African American and Hispanic households (Yinger 1999).

The stereotypes, prejudices, and disparities rooted in past discrimination may give housing agents incentives to continue to discriminate (Yinger 1998). When housing discrimination is consistent with profit maximization, competition in housing markets will not eliminate it. Many studies, including Courant (1978), Yinger (1976), and Bayer and McMillan (2008), investigate the relationship between housing discrimination and residential segregation within a competitive equilibrium framework. Courant (1978) explicitly incorporates racial preferences where segregation emerges as spatial equilibrium provided that at least some whites have racial prejudice against African Americans. Housing market agents respond to these preferences by making fewer housing choices available to African Americans in white neighborhoods.

Theoretical models give rise to different outcomes depending on whether white prejudices are incorporated as centralized discrimination or decentralized discrimination (Cutler, Glaeser, and Vigdor 1999; Bayer and McMillan 2008). In the case of centralized discrimination, white prejudices limit housing opportunities in white neighborhoods, and searching for housing in only nonwhite neighborhoods may emerge as an optimum behavior for minorities. If white prejudices are incorporated as decentralized discrimination, they manifest themselves as negative externalities in white utility functions (Yinger 1976). The prejudiced white households sort themselves into the overwhelmingly white neighborhoods. The price of housing will be higher in these neighborhoods compared to the price of equivalent houses in the integrated neighborhoods. In the case of centralized discrimination, nonwhites will carry the burden of discrimination by paying higher prices for inferior housing choices.

Various methods including regression analysis and audits are employed to detect housing discrimination. The U.S. Department of Housing and Urban Development has developed an audit method called matched paired-testing to more directly and conclusively test for discrimination. This audit method allows researchers to observe how economic agents treat two applicants with similar qualifications but different racial or ethnic background. In paired-testing, testers from a protected class[3] and a majority group are selected. The testers are trained to ask similar questions when they seek for housing. The application packages are designed so that in two-group pairs all pairs have the same qualifications. The only difference is that one tester of the pair belongs to a protected group and the other belongs to the majority group. Then all equally qualified paired testers are sent to look for a housing unit to purchase or rent. Paired testers visit every housing agent in the study and ask similar questions about advertised housing unit. Testers independently keep records of their visits with the housing agent. If the protected-class testers are consistently treated worse than their teammates, it shows that the housing agents in the study are systematically engaged in housing discrimination (Yinger 1998). An important advantage of paired-testing is that it directly tests for housing discrimination, and nonwhite testers are treated as control groups.

Housing discrimination is also indirectly tested by regression analysis. House values or housing rents are regressed against the variables related to housing characteristics, neighborhood characteristics, and race and ethnic compositions of the neighborhoods. The estimated regression coefficients measure the equilibrium prices of housing and neighborhood characteristics as well as the price differential due to racial or ethnic discrimination in housing markets. An important shortcoming of the regression approach is that it is subject to omitted variable bias (Kiel and Zabel 1996; Bayer and McMillan 2008). Omitted variable bias arises when the relevant control variables correlated with group membership are not included in the regression. The bias can either underestimate or overestimate discrimination. When the race variable of interest is correlated with omitted neighborhood variables, the coefficient of the race variable is biased toward zero (Kiel and Zabel 1996). Regression analysis has limited use in identifying the channels through which housing discrimination causes residential segregation because empirically it is not possible to separate the impact of centralized discrimination from that of decentralized discrimination. When white households sort themselves out to avoid African Americans, the regression coefficient of the race variable does not reflect the preferences of the average housing consumer, but rather measures the preferences of the marginal housing consumer residing in the integrated neighborhoods (Bayer and McMillan 2008). Housing prices are expected to sharply decline after the population share of African Americans and Hispanics exceed the tipping points. The sudden change in racial composition affects house prices in a nonlinear fashion when neighborhoods experience sudden population shifts.

The regression approach is indirect as it attempts to isolate the impacts of discrimination on prices or other outcomes without directly observing discriminatory behavior. In contrast, the audit approach allows researchers to observe housing agents in "the act of discrimination" (Yinger 1986). Paired-testing results from audits are more robust as they directly control for omitted variable bias. Unlike regression analysis, paired-testing measures discrimination directly by documenting both the differential treatment in prices and housing choices offered to the testers. Regression analysis measures only the price differentials, and the difference in the quantity and quality of housing choices offered to the paired testers are not observed. In a reliable audit procedure, paired testers do not differ on any characteristic relevant to their treatment in housing market other than race, ethnicity, sex, or religion. Even a carefully designed and implemented audit has its limitations. Audit method can control for the omitted variable bias arising from the differences in personal characteristics, but it cannot guarantee that the testers from the same protected group will react similarly to discriminatory treatments (Yinger 1995). Thus audits cannot completely eliminate omitted variable bias, but they can minimize it (Yinger 1998).

THE COST OF RESIDENTIAL SEGREGATION

Residential segregation has imposed enormous costs on African Americans and Hispanics. Historically, the lower minority home ownership rate is partly attributed to discrimination in mortgage lending (Yezer 2008). African Americans and Hispanics are more likely to receive higher-cost subprime loans, be targeted for predatory lending, and to be in danger of losing their homes to foreclosure than are white households with similar borrowing characteristics (Yinger 1995; Turner 2002). Since home equity is the largest source of wealth for most American families, disparities in home ownership are seen as a major determinant of persistent racial inequality (Shapiro and Oliver, 1995; Quigley and Rafael 2004). The early empirical models (Kain and Quigley 1970; King and Mieszkowski 1973; Muth 1969) have documented that African Americans received inferior housing services compared to the white population of similar socioeconomic status. Similarly, recent studies (Yinger 1995; Yinger 2001; Turner et al. 2002) conclude that African Americans and Hispanics are interested in residing in integrated neighborhoods but are still excluded from the white neighborhoods.

The concentration of poverty in the inner cities is a direct consequence of residential racial segregation. Problems associated with urban poverty become exacerbated by the isolating effect of residential segregation. Poor neighborhoods in the inner cities are associated with housing dilapidation, lack of business services, crime, and other social and economic problems (Turner, Ross et al. 2002).

The costs of renting and owning in the inner cities have become less affordable (Quigley and Raphael 2004). Affordability is defined as the percentage of income spent on housing. If the share on housing cost exceeds 30 percent of income, housing is considered less affordable. Housing discrimination negatively affects affordability through three channels. First, the inner-city residents are disconnected from the suburban employment opportunities and they have to settle for lower-paying and temporary jobs. Second, they pay a higher price per unit of housing because the more affordable suburban housing choices are not available and more buyers and renters bid for the limited housing supply in the inner cities. Third, the probability of being unemployed or finding only part-time jobs is higher. Lower wages and higher housing prices together make housing more unaffordable in the inner city.

By using the data generated by the Department of Housing and Urban Development's Housing Discrimination Study, Yinger (1997) quantified the value of lost opportunities that resulted from discrimination. He estimated that when a minority household searches for a house, they must pay, on average, a discrimination tax of about $3,700. This is the cost of not receiving a lower rate mortgage loan or a better house in terms of location or any other attribute. The estimated cost of discrimination for all African American owners and renters combined is about $3 billion per year. For Hispanics it is estimated about $2 billion per year.

GOVERNMENT'S ROLE IN HOUSING DISCRIMINATION AND RESIDENTIAL SEGREGATION

Historically, government policies and practices have helped to create and perpetuate the highly segregated residential patterns that still persist in the metropolitan areas (Massey and Denton 1993). The federal government through discriminatory housing policies also contributed to housing discrimination and residential segregation. The New Deal policies established the Federal Housing Administration in 1934 and made the housing market accessible to the lower-income white population through a series of new measures and regulations, such as long-term, amortized mortgages, and insurance against private lenders' loss. Moreover, the federal government created a secondary mortgage market to diversify risks in the primary mortgage market. Yet, through race-based discriminatory rules, these measures denied benefits to African Americans (Massey and Denton 1993). The Veterans Administration administered GI Bill loan programs with subsidized mortgages for veterans. These programs also systemically excluded African Americans. The Federal Housing Administration and Veterans Administration endorsed the use of race-restrictive covenants[4] until the 1950s. In fact about 50 percent of all suburban houses in the 1950s and 1960s were financed by the racially discriminatory programs of the Federal Housing Administration and Veterans Administration. Similarly, "redlining," a discriminatory rating system adopted by the Federal Housing Administration, was used to deny or limit financial services to the inner-city neighborhoods based on racial composition not the residents' creditworthiness (Massey and Denton 1993).

After the 1968 Fair Housing Act and Equal Credit Opportunity Act were enacted, most of the housing discrimination practices, including race-restrictive covenants, racial steering, and redlining, became illegal. The United States Department of Housing and Urban Development and the U.S. Department of Justice have enforced the terms of the act to prevent discrimination in private housing transactions. The act also directs the federal government to take affirmative steps to remedy private discrimination, to avoid governmental policies that perpetuate segregation, and to further fair housing in order to reverse the historical patterns of racial segregation and discrimination. Since 1968, the federal government has made several extensions to the original Fair Housing Act. Among the most important are the 1984 Fair Housing Assistance Program, the 1986 Fair Housing Initiatives Program, and the 1988 amendments to the Fair Housing Act. In addition the Home Mortgage Disclosure Act, enacted in 1973 and amended in 1989, and the 1977 Community Reinvestment Act have had positive impacts in alleviating the cost of housing discrimination and increasing the rate of homeownership among African American households (Galster 1999; Yinger 1999).

Some government programs that were designed to alleviate poverty have also increased residential segregation. Historically, the construction of public housing has spatially limited the number of housing choices for African Americans and increased the concentration of poverty in the inner city (Massey and Denton 1993). The Low Income Housing Tax Credit program is another important government program that perpetuates existing patterns of residential segregation. The Low Income Housing Tax Credit encouraged the construction of low-income housing in a few lower-income neighborhoods in order to increase the supply of affordable housing.

The Section 8 Housing Choice Voucher Program, on the other hand, can ameliorate residential segregation. It provides a greater number of location choices for residents but cannot necessarily put a dent in residential segregation. This is a relatively small program and is unlikely to have a significant impact. The Section 8 Housing Choice Voucher Program is a tenant-based rental voucher program administered by the Department of Housing and Urban Development. Through local public housing authorities, housing vouchers are issued to qualified lower-income households to seek privately owned rental housing. Section 8 vouchers dispersed the lower-income minority population to the neighborhoods that have better access to jobs and education. Thus they are intended to increase the number of housing choices for the lower-income residents and decrease the degree of housing segregation.

Many suburban communities enacted local ordinances, often in zoning codes, to preserve racial, ethnic, and income compositions of their neighborhoods. Minimum lot zoning is the requirement that lots must be of a certain minimum size and houses must be set back from the street a certain minimum distance. This is one of the most cited exclusionary zoning practices blamed for increasing urban sprawl and decreasing the supply of affordable housing. Large plots of land are required to build within the zoning code restrictions, which practically made the construction of modestly priced housing very costly. Communities have remained accessible to wealthier citizens because of these ordinances, effectively excluding the low-income families from better communities. Such zoning ordinances have not always been enacted with conscious intent to exclude lower-income households, but it has been the unintended consequence of such policies (Massey and Denton 1993). State and local governments implement mandatory school attendance zoning and minimum lot zoning. They basically keep lower-income minority population in and around the inner city and away from the suburbs.

Both public housing and LIHTC programs increase the supply of housing in the existing segregated neighborhoods. In fact they perpetuate race-based housing segregation, and spatially do not expand the housing choices for African Americans. Fair housing laws, if enforced, can reduce active discrimination practiced by housing agents and white residents. However, voluntary segregation driven by consumer preferences is outside the purview of fair housing law and remedies (Clark and Fossett 2008). White residents prefer to live in neighborhoods where whites account for more than 50 percent of the population (Clark and Fossett 2008). Similarly, most African Americans prefer to reside in the neighborhoods where their own race accounts for about half the population (Krysan and Farley 2002). Given that African Americans nationally account for about 12 percent of population, the preferences of whites and African Americans about their neighborhoods' racial composition are important factors in promoting racial segregation.

Housing policies that reduce the costs of segregation rather than directly target racial segregation have received more attention. Section 8 programs are designed to relocate public housing residents to improve their access to suburban jobs. Evidence from empirical studies indicates that an effective mix of government policies against housing discrimination and residential segregation should include enforcement against active discrimination, education and outreach to promote ethnic diversity, as well as incentives to increase the supply of mixed-income housing (Turner, Freiberg et al. 2002). To strengthen enforcement, federal government should provide more funding for paired-testing of real estate agents, rental-housing providers, lending institutions, mortgage brokers, and insurance companies (Turner, Freiberg et al. 2002).

CONCLUSION

African American and Hispanic residents have been discriminated against at various stages of the housing transaction. Housing discrimination drastically limits the housing choices of African American and Hispanic households and perpetuates residential segregation. The black-white disparities in educational attainment, incomes, wealth, and health are attributed to residential segregation caused by discrimination in housing markets. As a result, African Americans are far less likely than whites to become home owners, and far more likely to live in inferior housing in the neighborhoods identified with higher incidence of poverty, and poor access to schools and jobs (Massey and Benton 1993).

Various federal housing programs initiated after the enactment of the Fair Housing Act have made housing consumption more affordable for African Americans and Hispanics. Some of these programs, such as public housing, increased residential segregation. Others, those designed to help poor residents to seek for housing outside the inner city, have reduced the cost of residential segregation. The methods, paired-testing and regression analysis, employed to measure and detect active discrimination have produced mixed results. Recent studies indicate that audits are more useful in detecting housing discrimination (Yinger 1998; Turner, Freiberg et al. 2002). Fair housing laws, if enforced, can reduce active discrimination practiced by housing agents and white residents. However, voluntary segregation caused by consumer preferences is outside the purview of fair housing law and remedies (Clark and Fossett 2008). To complement the existing fair housing laws and remedies, there are needs for different types of government programs to promote diversity by race, ethnicity, and income in urban areas.

NOTES

1.   Hispanic refers to households from Mexico, Central America, and South America.

2.   Tipping point is the maximum African American population share tolerated by whites. When the African American population share reaches tipping point, there will be a rapid transition from largely white neighborhood to largely African American neighborhood.

3.   Discrimination is defined as unfavorable treatment of a person solely on the basis of that person's membership in a "protected class." Fair housing laws in the United States require that people in a "protected class" and people in the "majority" should be treated equally in housing market. Those discriminated against based on race, disability, gender, age, familial status, and religion are considered as a "protected group" by fair housing laws. For example, racial and ethnic minorities and disabled individuals are classified as protected groups, but white individuals are classified as majority.

4.   A race-restrictive covenant was a legal restriction registered against title. It banned the sale of the property to a person from a specific race.

BIBLIOGRAPHY

Arrow, Kenneth J., and L. Hurwicz. 1972. "Decision Making under Ignorance." In C. F. Carter and J. L. Ford (eds.), *Uncertainty and Expectations in Economics: Essays in Honour of G. L. S. Shackle*. Oxford: Basil Blackwell.

Bayer, Patrick, and Robert McMillan. 2008. "Distinguishing Racial Preference in the Housing Market: Theory and Evidence." In *Hedonic Methods in Housing Markets: Pricing Environmental Amenities and Segregation*, edited by Andrea Baranzini, José Ramirez, Caroline Schaerer, and Philippe Thalman. 225–44. New York: Springer.

Becker, Gary S. 1957. *The Economics of Discrimination*. Chicago: University of Chicago Press.

Clark, William A. V., and Mark Fossett. 2008. "Understanding the Social Context of the Schelling Segregation Model." *Proceedings of National Academy of Sciences USA* 105: 4109–114.

Collins, William J. 2004. "The Political Economy of Fair Housing Laws Prior to 1968." Working Paper. 10610. National Bureau of Economic Research.

Courant, Paul N. 1978. "Racial Prejudice in a Search Model of the Urban Housing Market." *Journal of Urban Economics*. 5: 329–345.

Cutler, David M., Edward L. Glaeser, and Jacob L. Vigdor. 1999. "The Rise and Decline of the American Ghetto." *Journal of Political Economy* 107: 455–506.

Galster, George C. 1999. "The Evolving Challenges of Fair Housing since 1968: Open Housing, Integration, and the Reduction of Ghettoization." *Cityscape* 4: 123–38.

Glaeser, Edward, and Jacob L. Vigdor. 2001. "Racial Segregation in the 2000 Census: Promising News." The Brookings Institution.

Gramlich, Edward M. 2007. *Subprime Mortgages: America's Latest Boom and Bust.* Washington, DC: Urban Institute.

Kain, John F. "Housing Segregation, Negro Employment, and Metropolitan Decentralization." 1968. *Quarterly Journal of Economics* 82: 175–97.

Kain, John F., and John M. Quigley. 1975. *Housing Markets and Racial Discrimination: A Microeconomic Analysis.* New York: Columbia University Press.

Kiel, Katherine A., and Jeffrey E. Zabel. 1996. "House Price Differentials in U.S. Cities: Housing and Neighborhood Racial Effects." *Journal of Housing Economics* 5: 143–65.

King, Thomas A. and Peter Mieszkowski. 1973. "Racial Discrimination, Segregation, and the Price of Housing." *Journal of Political Economy* 81: 590–606.

Krysan, Marian, and Reynolds Farley. 2002. "The Residential Preferences of Blacks: Do They Explain Persistent Segregation?" *Social Forces* 80: 937–69.

Massey, Douglas S., and Nancy A. Denton. 1993. *American Apartheid: Segregation and the Making of the Underclass.* Cambridge, MA: Harvard University Press.

Munnel, Alicia, Lynn Browne, James McEneaney, and Geoffrey Tootell. 1996. "Mortgage Lending in Boston: Interpreting the HMDA Data." *American Economic Review* 86: 25–53.

Muth, Richard. 1969. *Cities and Housing.* Chicago: University of Chicago Press.

Ondrich, Jan, Stephen Ross, and John Yinger. 1997. "Measuring the Incidence of Discrimination Using Fair Housing Audits." Metropolitan Studies Occasional Paper No. 167, Center for Policy Research, Syracuse University.

Phelps, Edmund S. 1972. "The Statistical Theory of Racism and Sexism." *American Economic Review* 62: 659–661.

Quigley, John M., and Steven Raphael. 2004. "Is Housing Unaffordable? Why Isn't It More Affordable?" *Journal of Economic Perspective* 18 (1): 191–214.

Ross, Stephen L., and John Yinger. 2002. *The Color of Credit: Mortgage Lending Discrimination, Research Methodology, and Fair-Lending Enforcement.* Cambridge, MA: MIT Press.

Schelling, Thomas C. 1972. "A Process of Residential Segregation: Neighborhood Tipping." In Pascal, Anthony (ed.), 157–84. *Racial Discrimination in Economic Life.* Lexington, MA: D. C. Heath.

Schwab, William. (1992). *The Sociology of Cities.* Englewood Cliffs, NJ: Prentice-Hall.

Shapiro, Thomas, and Melvin L. Oliver. 1995. *Black Wealth/White Wealth: A New Perspective on Racial Inequality.* New York: Routledge.

Turner, Margery Austin, Fred Freiberg, Erin Godfrey, Carla Herbig, Diane K. Levy, and Robin R. Smith. 2002. "All Other Things Being Equal: A Paired Testing Study of Mortgage Lending Institutions." U.S. Department of Housing and Urban Development Office of Policy Development and Research. http://www.huduser.org/publications/pdf/aotbe.pdf.

Turner, Margery, Stephen Ross, George Galster, and John Yinger. 2002. *Discrimination in Metropolitan Housing Markets: National Results from Phase 1 HDS 2000.* Washington, DC: U.S. Department of Housing and Urban Development.

U.S. Census Bureau 2010. *American Community Survey.* http://www.census.gov/acs/www/.

Yezer, Anthony M. 2008. "Discrimination in Mortgage Lending." In *A Companion to Urban Economics*, edited by Richard J. Arnott and Daniel P. McMillen, 197–210. Malden, MA: Blackwell Publishing.

Yinger, John. 1976. "Racial Prejudice and Racial Residential Segregation in an Urban Model." *Journal of Urban Economics* 3: 383–96.

Yinger, John. 1986. "Measuring Discrimination with Fair Housing Audits: Caught in the Act." *American Economics Review* 76: 881–93.

Yinger, John. 1995. *Closed Doors, Opportunities Lost: The Continuing Cost of Housing Discrimination.* New York: Russell Sage Foundation.

Yinger, John. 1997. "Cash in Your Face: The Cost of Racial and Ethnic Discrimination in Housing." *Journal of Urban Economics* 42: 339–65.

Yinger, John. 1998. "Evidence on Discrimination in Consumer Markets." *Journal of Economic Perspectives* 12: 23–40.

Yinger, John. 1999. "Sustaining the Fair Housing Act." *Cityscape* 4: 93–105.

Yinger, John. 2001. "Housing Discrimination and Residential Segregation as Causes of Poverty." In *Understanding Poverty*, edited by S. H. Danziger and R. H. Haveman, 359–91. Cambridge, MA: Harvard University Press.

DATE DUE

			PRINTED IN U.S.A.